THE MIRROR MAKERS

THE
MIRROR
MAKERS

A HISTORY OF AMERICAN ADVERTISING AND ITS CREATORS

STEPHEN FOX

WILLIAM MORROW AND COMPANY, INC.
NEW YORK | 1984

Copyright © 1984 by Stephen R. Fox

Grateful acknowledgment is made for permission to reprint the following:

From the Fairfax M. Cone Papers: Box 73, Folder 7; Box 111, Folder 10; Box 140, Folder 14; Box 140, Folder 15. Reprinted with the permission of The Department of Special Collections, University of Chicago Library, Chicago, Illinois.

Verses by Draper Daniels originally published in 1960 in *Advertising Age.* Reprinted with the permission of Myra Daniels.

From the Margaret Divver Papers: Margot Sherman to Divver, November 10, 1948. Reprinted with the permission of Schlesinger Library, Radcliffe College, Cambridge, Massachusetts.

Material gathered from the papers of David Ogilvy. Reprinted with the permission of David Ogilvy.

From the Lydia Pinkham Papers: Dan to Will Pinkham, file 3118; Warren (Ohio) *Tribune* to Lydia Pinkham, October 5, 1882, file 757; H. P. Hubbard to Charles Pinkham, April 24, 1885; Hubbard to Will Pinkham, October 21, 1880; Hubbard to Charles Pinkham, August 15, 1885; Chicago *Mirror* to Lydia Pinkham, August 1882; J. Walter Thompson to Pinkhams, September 13, 1883; Lord & Thomas to Lydia Pinkham, September 5, 1882. Reprinted with the permission of Schlesinger Library, Radcliffe College, Cambridge, Massachusetts.

Further acknowledgment is extended to the State Historical Society of Wisconsin for use of material from NBC, Randall Barton, Richard Meyer, and Jessie M. Brophy.

Library of Congress Cataloging in Publication Data

Fox, Stephen R.
    The mirror makers.

    Includes bibliographical references and index.
    1. Advertising—United States—History. I. Title.
HF5813.U6F66 1984   659.1'0973   83-19326

ISBN 0-688-02256-1

Printed in the United States of America

First Edition

1 2 3 4 5 6 7 8 9 10

BOOK DESIGN BY ANN GOLD

For Karen, Linda, and Janet

PREFACE

Practically everyone dislikes it. Advertising interrupts radio and television programs, crowds editorial matter off the pages of newspapers and magazines, disfigures city streets, defaces the countryside, and even lurks at eye level for tired, vulnerable standees on the subway. Nobody believes it, or at least admits to believing it. It usually appeals to the less agreeable aspects of human nature: greed, vanity, insecurity, competitiveness, materialism. At cocktail parties, people in the advertising business wince when asked what they do for a living.

But there it is, one of the dominant forces in twentieth-century America. Among the pillars of our popular culture, advertising stands with TV, sports, movies, pop music, and the print media as unavoidable features of modern life. With this striking difference, however: the names of TV personalities, athletes, movie stars, musicians, and writers come readily to mind. Yet who can name the major figures of American advertising? Even Raymond Rubicam and William Bernbach, the two men who have done the most to raise advertising's esthetic and ethical standards, are barely recognized outside the trade.

This book, then, focuses especially on the people—copywriters, artists, executives, and others—who have produced twentieth-century American advertising. The story unfolds in a series of cycles, with superficial adjustments to certain basic continuities. Advertising remains a personal business. Ads and commercials reflect, to a greater extent than most business products, the quirks and personalities of the people behind them. I have therefore aimed to write a group biography of the men and women who have worked in advertising.

More broadly, I have tried to understand the relationship between advertising and American culture. I started this book, as an observer of contemporary America, with the impression that advertising wields substantial independent power to create and shape mass tastes and behavior. Now, after changing my mind a couple of times while writing this book, I have concluded that advertising gathered power early in this century, reached a peak of influence in the 1920s, and since then—despite consistent gains in volume and omnipresence—has steadily lost influence over American life. Some reasons for this apparent paradox are explored in my last chapters. Here I would merely suggest that advertising has become a prime scapegoat for our times: a convenient, obvious target for critics who should be looking at the deeper cultural tendencies that only find reflection in the advertising mirror.

—STEPHEN RUSSELL FOX

Cambridge, Massachusetts
June 23, 1983

CONTENTS

ONE

ADVERTISING PREHISTORY: THE NINETEENTH CENTURY

The advertising agency of the 1870s conducted its affairs from a one-room office. A prospective "customer" (who would not be called a "client" until several decades of professional aspiration later) climbed a flight of stairs, opened the office door, and found himself in the agency—right in the middle of it, with no railing or counter to detain him. In one corner of the room sat the boss, whose name the firm generally bore. In another corner the estimate man, who quoted rates and expenses, sat with his heavy scrapbooks at a slanted-top desk. A bookkeeper stood by his upright station, with the copying press and office safe close at hand. Finally, a checking clerk and office boy tended to their miscellaneous tasks. No telephones or typewriters intruded on the sounds of scratching pens and riffling papers. At the rear of the office, separated by a low partition, were rows and rows of cubbyholes filled with periodicals, like the reading room of a large public library. This collection, smelling agreeably of newsprint and printer's ink, let the agent claim that he kept regularly on file all the leading newspapers and magazines, so that an advertiser might check on the appearance and placement of his notices. The office staff of five was considered adequate for all but the largest agencies.

There were no copywriters, art directors, account executives, or marketing experts. None of these mainstays of twentieth-century advertising had yet been invented. On one occasion Daniel M. Lord, starting out as an agent in Chicago in the 1870s, presumed to offer

13

an advertiser unsolicited advice about how to improve his ad. "Young man," he was told, "you may know a lot about advertising, but you know very little about the furniture business." To work in advertising demanded no particular knowledge of copy or design or the product being celebrated. Instead it required an acquaintance with the periodicals in any given territory, some sense of the going advertising rates, and—in particular—a rare gift for haggling.

The business was young and formless, with the same lack of ethical norms and restraints that in general characterized the Gilded Age. When the very first advertising agent, Volney Palmer, opened his shop in Philadelphia in 1843, he in effect worked for the newspapers he represented: soliciting orders for advertising, sending along (but not preparing) the copy thus obtained, and collecting payment from the advertisers. He acted as agent for the media, not the advertisers. His successors—notably Samuel Pettengill, who started in Palmer's Boston office and then launched his own firm in New York, the largest agency of the 1860s—did act as independent space brokers, retaining the title of agent but taking their pay in a commission from the fees paid to publishers. This system acquired endless variations and secret arrangements, corrupted by an inherent conflict of interest: the agent was selling space for the publisher while supposedly giving expert and impartial advice to the advertiser on how best to spend his advertising budget. Actually the agent wanted only to buy space from the publisher as cheaply as possible and then sell it to the advertiser as profitably as possible, without telling either what rate the other was getting. Caught in the middle, the agent was trusted by neither. Thus these early agents, according to Daniel Lord's pardonably exaggerated recollection, owed their lives "to the fact that there was a law against killing them."

For most publishers, advertising agents were a tolerated nuisance. Daily newspapers derived only about a third of their income from advertising; national magazines took even less. Robert Bonner's *New York Ledger,* the first weekly publication to hit a national circulation of 400,000, carried no advertising at all. Not that Bonner underestimated the power of advertising: the *Ledger* reached its heights on the power of the first great ad campaign. Bonner, born an Irish Presbyterian in 1823, had come to the United States as a teenager and entered the printer's trade. When he took over the *Ledger,* newspaper advertising columns were limited to small agate type, single columns, and severe restrictions on displays and illustrations. By a perhaps accidental inspiration, Bonner got around these limits. He filled an entire page of the *New York Herald* with a single agate-type admonition to read the *Ledger,* repeated over and over, column after column. (Leading to a joke told by the Christy's Minstrel troupe: "Why, I can repeat a whole page of the *Herald* after just glancing at it.") Bonner then advertised in major newspapers across the country, making the *Ledger* a national success. Yet the *Ledger*'s own pages remained undefiled by the very device that it rode to fortune.

Advertising was considered an embarrassment—the retarded child, the wastrel relative, the unruly servant kept backstairs and never allowed into the front parlor. A firm risked its credit rating by advertising; banks might take it as a confession of financial weakness. Everyone deplored advertising. Nobody—advertiser, agent, or medium—took responsibility for it. The advertiser only prepared the ad, but did not place it; the agent only served as an errand boy, passing the advertiser's message along to the publisher; the medium printed it, but surely would not question the right of free speech by making a judgment on the veracity of the advertiser.

In the absence of any government regulation, the entire business was conducted in a half-light of bunkum and veiled appearances. Publishers routinely lied about the circulations of their journals, since a higher circulation meant a better rate per line for the ads they carried. Agents were given rate cards explaining in minute detail the cost of advertising in a given medium. Actually the rate cards meant only the start of negotiations. One publisher of a prominent weekly would make the rounds of New York advertising agents, offering a firm rate of twenty-five cents a line. "Everybody liked him," one of the agents later recalled, "but few had confidence in his circulation. When he made his rounds in the morning he stood out for his rates less twenty-five per cent. After a tolerably agreeable luncheon and strictly between friends he would occasionally agree to a thirty-three per cent commission. After dinner it was mutually agreed that a rate card didn't amount to much between friends and fifty per cent to a good fellow was agreed upon. At one o'clock in the morning he sold a thousand lines for fifty dollars cash money."

The ads themselves, restricted only by the imaginations and pliable consciences of the writers, offered endless enticements in the general spirit of P. T. Barnum ("I thoroughly understood the art of advertising," he said with satisfaction). Gold mines and oil wells. Free offers and cash prizes. A steel engraving, approved by the U.S.

government, of George Washington (which turned out to be a post-age stamp). A foolproof opportunity never to be repeated. A chance to make a great fortune with no risk.

And, especially, "patent medicines," which in most cases were neither patented nor medicinal. In the decades after the Civil War, these nostrums became the first products to be advertised on a large national scale, the first to aim directly at the consumer with vivid, psychologically clever sales pitches, the first to show—for better or worse—the latent power of advertising. To the public, advertising and patent medicines were linked in an association that only harmed the reputations of both. These dubious remedies offered manufacturers cheap production, easy distribution, and profit margins so high that companies could risk large chunks of their gross sales on a device, advertising, that was as yet generally mistrusted. "I can advertise *dish water,* and sell it, just as well as an article of merit," bragged one owner of a patent remedy. "It is all in the advertising."

At a time of endemic medical quackery, patent medicines were not necessarily more harmful than other, more expensive treatments. Some were only versions of old folk concoctions that, even if ineffective, might deliver a harmless placebo effect. But the most successful ones held out more: addictive doses of opium or morphine or (most typically) a medicinal dollop of alcohol. Justified by the manufacturer as a "preservative," this alcohol content—as high as 44 percent—made the medicines especially popular in temperance regions and among the pious. Before the Civil War, patent medicines had a total annual sale of about $3.5 million. During the war many soldiers tried the concoctions in the field and then went home with a habit. Manufacturers started sending printed inserts to country newspapers with space to fill. These "patent insides" offered a sprinkling of reading matter in a sea of lurid ads, set in a format to resemble news stories, presenting lovingly detailed descriptions of the excruciating fate awaiting anyone who failed to use the product: rheumatism, eczema, arthritis, obliquely described sexual matters, consumption, liver problems, and a versatile respiratory affliction called catarrh. By the turn of the century the total patent medicine business had climbed to $75 million.

Ethical questions aside, the pioneers in this field displayed undeniable entrepreneurial gifts. Anyone riding a train between New York and Philadelphia could not miss learning the virtues of Drake's Plantation Bitters, as proclaimed by the passing signs on barns, houses, and even rocks. J. H. Drake himself would travel from city to city. Taking a good hotel room, he would advertise for the sick to drop in for a free medical consultation. The diagnosis invariably included a pressing need for one of "Dr." Drake's products. His Plantation Bitters bore the cryptic slogan "S.T. 1860 X." Nobody knew what it meant. Perhaps, according to one theory, it translated as "Started Trade in 1860 with Ten Dollars Capital." Or (a more cynical guess) since the product's active ingredient was Santa Cruz rum, perhaps it referred to Saint Croix. Dr. Drake insisted the slogan was meaningless, only a device to make people curious—at which it well succeeded.

St. Jacob's Oil, the most heavily advertised product of the 1880s, was a liniment marketed for all purposes by a Baltimore wholesale druggist, Charles A. Voegeler. At first it was promoted as Keller's Roman Liniment, with a picture of Caesar on the label and the assertion that his legions had used it to conquer the world. This approach did not sell. So the name was changed, with the further explanation that it was made by monks in the Black Forest of Germany. The public, no fool, found this pitch more agreeable. The product sold well until the manufacturer, in a burst of confidence, stopped advertising. St. Jacob's Oil soon disappeared from the shelves. Once an advertiser mounted this young, unruly beast, it seemed, he could not get off.

Lydia Pinkham's Vegetable Compound almost made the same mistake. A Quaker from a temperance family in Lynn, Massachusetts, Lydia Pinkham would occasionally cook up batches of a folk remedy for "female complaints" and give it to friends. Her sons persuaded her to go into business. So on her kitchen stove, one day in 1875, she brewed a mixture of four kinds of roots, fenugreek seed, and 19 percent alcohol, and bottled it for sale. Dan and Will Pinkham at first promoted it through a four-page pamphlet; then Will took a chance and, risking sixty dollars, printed the pamphlet as a full-page ad in the *Boston Herald*. Three wholesalers rushed in with orders. A second ad a few days later produced even more business. Sensing the possibilities, the Pinkhams drew only modest living expenses and poured their earnings into newspaper advertising.

"Encouraging Reports From All Sections," proclaimed a headline that read like a news item. "The Positive Cure for All Female Complaints." The middle-class Victorian woman was a delicate creature, and Lydia Pinkham had the cure for everything from menstrual problems to difficult pregnancies to a prolapsed uterus. Yet more: the compound was found to comfort diseases of the kidney too ("I really believe," Dan Pinkham confided to brother Will, "we can sell as much for that complaint as the other"). When some druggists balked at the sexual aspects of the campaign, Dan established its harmlessness by putting ads in a Protestant journal to give "a kind of religious tone to our Compound and get the good will of a few Methodists." Many newspapers took cases of the product instead of cash payment and then sold the goods to local wholesalers and druggists, who then passed the product along to consumers on the basis of the advertising: a triangular trade beneficial to all parties save perhaps the consumer. Newspapers might print editorials or news stories about the remarkable Mrs. Pinkham in the hope she would renew their ad contracts. "We have published free notices during the year concerning yourself," the *Warren* (Ohio) *Tribune* advised her, "which of course you have not overlooked nor failed to appreciate."

The campaign's most effective device turned out to be Lydia Pinkham's own placid, trustworthy face. After first intimating that she was a doctor, the family in 1879 shifted to a down-home appeal stressing the compound's natural ingredients and the good name of the founder, "an untitled woman," pictured in demure Quaker dress. Even after her death in 1883, her likeness remained as the ubiquitous trademark, and customers were urged to write to "Mrs. Pinkham" for answers to their most intimate health problems. From newspapers, magazines, billboards, and streetcar signs, Lydia Pinkham stared forth, the most universally recognized female face of the day. College boys gathered around their pianos and chorused:

> So we sing, we sing, we sing to Lydia Pinkham
> And her love for the human race.
> She makes her Vegetable Compound
> And the papers publish her face.

For a decade the Pinkham advertising was masterminded by Harlan Page Hubbard, an agent based in New Haven, Connecticut. While conceding that graphic testimonials from satisfied customers were "a little rank," Hubbard had no objections to pressuring publishers to accept the ads: "As long as they will take them . . . and they will sell the medicine, we will put them out." "They seem to think," he remarked of an Iowa newspaper, "that to publish the word *uterus* would be the cause of bringing all the old maids of the place down on them." Himself devoid of scruples, by buying space at low rates and selling it to the Pinkhams at high ones Hubbard made commissions of up to 50 percent, while assuring the Pinkhams he was making no more than 15 percent. When the family learned of this deception it retaliated, not by firing Hubbard but by slashing the advertising budget. Annual sales fell from $260,000 to under $58,000. Finally, in 1890, the Pinkhams hired a new agent, limited his commission to 10 percent, and resumed advertising. Over the next ten years, with advertising costs averaging 44 percent of revenues and the founder's face once again omnipresent, annual sales went up by 2500 percent.

For the nascent advertising business, the success with patent medicines cut two ways. In at least some cases, sales grew when advertising was applied and withered when it was withdrawn. Thus, it seemed, advertising could work. But the product itself was disreputable, promoted by such extravagant claims that people—even in the act of plunking down their money—could hardly believe them. "It seems as if no acuter instance could be found," declared the psychologist William James, "of the way in which, in our country, private greed is suffered to override the public good." Perhaps, the public could plausibly surmise, legitimate products of real quality did not need to advertise—in fact, by advertising might risk being tarred by an association with patent medicines.

The climate of trust in the 1880s:

H. P. Hubbard, agent, referring to a publisher: "I stand ready to meet them and show my hand clear and clean. They are a gang of thieves, and will do anything to get rid of paying what they justly owe."

A Chicago newspaper, referring to H. P. Hubbard: "This man Hubbard is a *thief* and we are going to advertise him well. He beats us down to one-half of our prices and at the end of three months refuses to pay our bill—crawls out of it by *lying* and stating that we had not put our ads in as agreed."

By slow degrees the advertising business reformed itself. The steps toward respectability included the extraction of honest circulation statements from publishers, the writing of contracts for truthful relations between agents and advertisers, the launching of successful major campaigns by national advertisers other than patent medicines, and the spreading popularity of an advertising style associated with a copywriter of undoubted integrity. Taken together, these developments allowed advertising people—not for the last time—to congratulate themselves on putting to rest the bad old days and ascending to a higher moral plane.

George P. Rowell began this reform process. A farm boy from New Hampshire, at seventeen he made his way to Boston and started working as a canvasser and bill collector for a newspaper. During the holiday season of 1864, on his own time, he sold ads for a theater program and netted $600 for a few weeks' work. The following year he opened his own agency in Boston. A Hartford publisher asked him about the cost of advertising in newspapers in New Brunswick and Nova Scotia; Rowell knew nothing about that territory, but went around to print shops in Boston, collecting scattered information from anyone who had worked in the maritime provinces. He managed to compile a list of publications and rates that, however fragmentary and outdated, satisfied the Hartford publisher.

Rowell began to see the potential profit for anyone who could make an accurate survey of the chaotic world of newspapers. He organized a system of special contracts by which he offered advertisers an inch of space in one hundred New England weeklies for $100 a month, buying space in bulk and retailing it in little bits, guaranteeing to pay publishers regardless of whether he sold the ads. He next placed the contracts on an annual basis, expanded outside New England, and prospered beyond his hopes. In 1867 he moved his office to the lusher fields of New York and soon displaced Pettengill as the largest agency. "Among publishers," he claimed, "we are noted for paying our bills more promptly than any other agency."

In 1869 Rowell brought out the first annual edition of *Rowell's American Newspaper Directory,* on the model of a similar guide published in England, but with the addition of circulation figures as the prime feature. For the first time agents and advertisers had a tolerably complete guide to over 5,000 American and Canadian newspapers. Rowell asked publishers for their circulations; if no satisfactory answer came forth he made his own estimate. By an arcane system of codes and symbols Rowell conveyed other vital data for a given entry: a circulation figure printed in plain Arabic numerals was deemed trustworthy; "Z" meant the paper gave a statement considered dubious; "Y" meant the paper gave no statement at all; "!!" implied something suspicious about the paper; a white pyramid meant the paper might have expired; and so on. The *Directory* made Rowell well esteemed by agents and advertisers, not so well by publishers, who charged that a paper had to place an ad in the annual volume to get a good circulation rating. "The book created for its originator so many enemies," Rowell recalled, "that for many years it seemed wise for him to steer clear of newspaper offices when on traveling expeditions, for profit or pleasure, unless some representative of the office looked him up at the hotel and exhibited signs of amity."

The next step in reforming the business was undertaken by Francis Wayland Ayer. Like Rowell, he came from New England forebears but left the region to make his fortune elsewhere. In 1868, age twenty, he arrived in Philadelphia and took a temporary job selling ad space for a religious weekly. Thus exposed, a year later with $250 in capital he started N. W. Ayer & Son, naming it after his father out of filial loyalty (and to give the firm an aura of longevity and permanence). He soon was conducting business on the basis of his "open contract." It bound the agent and advertiser together with both parties knowing the exact financial terms, and with the agent—instead of simply buying space low and selling it high—taking his pay as a set commission, at first 12.5 percent, later 15 percent, of the publisher's fees. The agent therefore worked for the advertiser, not for himself or for the publisher, though he still in effect drew his pay from the publisher. As promoted by Ayer's associate H. N. McKinney, the open contract eventually became the norm for the advertising business and thereby removed a prime source of corruption.

Ayer was himself a powerful symbol of rectitude. A Sunday school superintendent and prominent Baptist layman, he was a paragon of sobriety, without humor or small talk, who liked to spend his time purposefully. He bought a farm outside Philadelphia as an escape from business worries, but despite himself turned it into a profitable dairy operation. For advertising, which needed models of good conduct, Ayer represented a useful change from the adman as bunco artist. George Rowell, who took long vacations and enjoyed convivial spirits, hardly knew what to make of Wayland Ayer: he "thinks of work all the time, eats little, drinks nothing but water," Rowell noted wonderingly; "has no vices, small or large, unless overwork is a vice; is the picture of health; and I sometimes think a good deal such a man as Oliver Cromwell would have been had Oliver been permitted to become an advertising agent." Ayer never accepted ads that he thought might offend "a woman of refinement," and would not touch products relating to "vile diseases, disreputable business or intoxicating drinks."

While Rowell and Ayer were improving agency ethics, new products were changing the nature of retailing. Previously, the local jobber had stood between the manufacturer and the consumer, interpreting each to the other, controlling distribution and even affecting the specifications and quantities of the goods produced. In the absence of national networks of railroads and telegraphs (and of Rowell's *Directory*), markets were local and idiosyncratic. The jobber knew his territory and told the manufacturer what he could sell. After the Civil War, improved transit and communication systems and—especially—an explosion in manufacturing capacity brought new possibilities: an equality between supply and demand and the novel problem of competitive selling in an economy of abundance. The first products to exploit this new situation were small household goods, cheap to buy and quickly used up, that housewives formerly had made themselves from the raw ingredients or bought from a local manufacturer. If these goods did not always measure up to every advertising claim, they at least—unlike patent medicines—did perform useful, harmless functions, and so improved the general credibility of advertising.

One day in 1865, a druggist in Fort Wayne, Indiana, named Joseph C. Hoagland mixed a batch of five pounds of baking powder in his drugstore. The recipe was no secret: anyone could combine sodium bicarbonate with an acid substance to produce this substitute for yeast. Yet the premixed version found a quick market in Fort Wayne. Hoagland had an entrepreneurial vision. He called it Royal Baking Powder and put ads in religious and women's periodicals, serving as his own agent, only patronizing papers that would give him the agent's commission. In the 1870s he was one of the first big advertisers to feature a picture of the product in his ads. When he prospered he moved the operation to New York. He commanded the upper left quarter of a magazine's back cover, a favored position, with the inevitable picture of a can and the motto "Absolutely Pure." By the early 1890s Royal was spending $600,000 a year on newspaper ads, the largest budget in the business.

In the mid-1870s a New York soapmaking firm, Enoch Morgan's Sons, produced a small gray cake of scouring soap to be used for floors and other heavy purposes. The Morgans went to their family physician and asked for an impressively Latin-sounding name for the new product. "Sapolio," said the doctor. Like the Pinkhams, the Morgans at first tried to sell their invention by distributing pamphlets to retailers. One pamphlet in verse form was written by Bret Harte, then a failing writer with his best stories behind him, scratching out a precarious living in New York:

> The shades of night were falling fast
> As through an Eastern village passed
> A youth who bore, through dust and heat,
> A stencil-plate, that read complete
> > "Sapolio."
> On household fences, gleaming bright,
> Shone "Gargling Oil" in black and white;
> Where "Bixby's Blacking" stood alone,
> He straight beside it clapped his own—
> > "Sapolio."

Harte soon departed for Europe, his advertising career over, and Sapolio shifted its promotions to other media.

In 1884 the firm hired an advertising manager, Artemas Ward, who over the next two decades, by various inventive devices, made Sapolio the most generally recognized trade name of the day. Ward was the great grandson of his namesake, George Washington's predecessor as commander in chief during the Revolutionary War (and no relation to the humorist Artemus Ward). He had grown up in New York, the son of an Episcopal minister, and worked at printing and editing until the Morgans offered him a job. At the time Sapolio was only a seasonal product, sold most heavily for spring and fall cleanings. With his initial budget of $30,000, Ward put brief notices featuring proverbs ("Be Clean!" "Sapolio Scours the World") in country weeklies and streetcars. He circulated a legend that the slogan "Oilopas Esu" had been found in an Egyptian tomb; it seemed mysterious until spelled backward. Ward underwrote an intrepid mariner who sailed a fourteen-foot sloop (with Sapolio prominently featured on the sail) from Atlantic City to Spain. Other ocean travelers arriving in New York harbor were greeted by a thousand-foot sign urging the use of Sapolio. As his advertising costs mounted to a thousand dollars a day, Ward made Sapolio unavoidable without making it obnoxious. "Through steady and persistent advertising," he said later, "the sales in the slow months were so increased that all months came to look alike to Sapolio."

A hand and bath soap of comparable ubiquity was impossible as long as the article was made from animal fats rendered from garbage and slaughterhouse wastes: such soap was too perishable for national marketing. But when made from vegetable fats and perfume, the product might outgrow a regional market. At the Cincinnati soap and candle works of the Procter family, according to company lore, a certain batch of this new compound was mixed too long, so that it filled with air. The resulting soap had a novel property: it floated in water. The company decided to make this accidental innovation a selling point. Harley T. Procter found a name for the new product in church one day, when he heard a passage from Psalms: "All thy garments smell of myrrh, and aloes, and cassia, out of the ivory palaces whereby they have made thee glad." Ivory soap was launched in 1882, and "It floats" and "99⁴⁴/₁₀₀ pure" became two of the most durable slogans in the history of American advertising.

The only advertiser's face of the late 1800s as familiar as Lydia Pinkham's belonged to William L. Douglas, a shoemaker from Brockton, Massachusetts. True to the pattern of most advertising pioneers, he rose from humble beginnings, had little formal education, and found success through an Algeresque blend of grit and luck. As a boy of seven he was apprenticed to an uncle to peg shoes. Later he toiled in a cotton mill and then returned to his first craft, climbing quickly from journeyman to foreman and, in 1876, starting his own shop. In a small way he began advertising a line of mass-produced, modestly priced men's shoes. After seeing a poster bearing the unmistakable likeness of P. T. Barnum he decided to feature himself, and a facsimile signature, in his ads. His bald pate, droopy mustache, and earnestly fretful look became so well known that a letter with only his picture pasted on the envelope would routinely find its way to Brockton.

"The three-dollar-shoe man" gave his ad account briefly to the S. R. Niles agency of Boston, but soon hired away A. Q. Miller of that firm to be his own advertising manager. At first Douglas concentrated on rural weeklies, seeking customers beyond the easy reach of mass production and retail stores who would order his shoes through the mail. As he prospered he sold through shoestores and finally started his own chain of retail outlets, his advertising costs growing from an initial $10,000 annually to $175,000. By 1894 his factory, the biggest employer in Brockton, was producing 3,600 pairs a day. Douglas bought the local paper and entered Democratic politics, applying his acumen as an advertiser to a new field. He served as mayor of Brockton; representative to both houses of the state legislature; and finally as governor of Massachusetts, winning election in the midst of the Republican landslide of 1904.

Royal Baking Powder, Sapolio and Ivory soap, and the Douglas shoe—among the most heavily advertised products of the day—by their success marked the first turning of a cycle, a phenomenon that would always remain the most consistent aspect of American advertising. Robert Bonner, P. T. Barnum, and the patent medicines had prospered by blaring overstatement. The newer advertising successes sold through pitches that were quieter, more believable, even charming: "Oilopas Esu" as a transparent contrivance made people smile. Not necessarily *better* advertising, the new style sold more goods because it was *different.* As later history would repeatedly show, the public grew used to a certain style of advertising, stopped responding to it, but perked up when shown a new fashion. In most important respects advertising has proceeded not down a line but around a circle.

In the 1880s the most influential exponent of credible understatement was a Philadelphia department store. John Wanamaker looked like a preincarnation of W. C. Fields but in fact was a temperate Presbyterian who had worked briefly as a YMCA secretary and, after starting his dry goods store, never sold playing cards and refused to advertise in Sunday papers. Having considered the ministry, he went into business with, among other motives, an evangelical purpose ("the idea clung to my mind that I could accomplish more in the same domain if I became a merchant and acquired means and influence with fellow merchants"). He made quick profits by selling Civil War uniforms and put every spare cent into advertising in handbills, billboards, and especially newspapers. With most retail stores offering prices open to argument and a general air of *caveat emptor,* Wanamaker in 1874 announced a policy of fixed prices and money-back guarantees. The public responded so gratefully at Wanamaker's two clothing outlets and his huge Grand Depot department store that in 1880 he hired, for the first time in American retailing, an employee to spend all his time writing ad copy.

John E. Powers is one of the grand enigmas in the annals of advertising. The first great copywriter, the most influential adman of his time, he walled himself behind a barricade of caustic cynicism and cold incisiveness. Greatly admired but neither well known nor well liked, he avoided interviews with inquiring journalists (as he now deflects the curiosity of historians). He was a trim, laconic man who held the world at bay with suspicious eyes behind impenetrable steel-rimmed glasses. Apparently he was born on a farm in central New York in 1837. As to his family background, education, and early years the record is mute. He pursued a varied business career—working for a life-insurance company, traveling to England to sell a sewing machine, serving as a subscription agent for the *Nation*—until he surfaced in New York in the late 1870s, writing ads part-time for the Lord & Taylor department store. As he later recalled it, his copy did not bring many customers into the store, but it struck some spark in John Wanamaker, who brought him to Philadelphia in 1880.

The first day on the job, Powers set the tone of his new working relationship by advising his employer to change the name of his department store to Wanamaker's: "Grand Depot is mispronounced French. Nice people don't like it." "I've spent thousands of dollars to fasten that name on it," Wanamaker replied. "You've lost that money," Powers insisted; "better not lose any more." The name was changed. For about nine months Powers wrote one newspaper ad per day, six days a week, but felt that only one of the six really connected with the public. Toying with different styles, he ultimately decided that hard-selling, detailed copy did not work because it overloaded the public's attention span and taxed its credulity. So he tried writing diffident little essays that mentioned only a few items. "That was the discovery," as he explained it. "Print the news of the store. No 'catchy headings,' no catches, no headings, no smartness, no brag, no 'fine writing,' no fooling, no foolery, no attempt at advertising, no anxiety to sell, no mercenary admiration; hang up the goods in the papers, one at a time, a few today, tomorrow the same or others." He used familiar, colloquial language, spoken rather than written English, short sentences and simple constructions— "my talking style of writing," he called it, accessible to a child. He avoided italics, letting the words themselves carry the argument, and set it all in plain Roman type instead of more hyperbolic display styles.

Most strikingly, he was candid to a fault. He disarmed the public's sales resistance by understating his case and qualifying his claims. "Liked to tell the off story of any particular goods I mentioned," as he put it. "Plainly sought the public's advantage against us. It was their store." He described Wanamaker's as "a great, rough, unhandsome store" dealing in "everything, almost" with prices "pretty apt to be below the market." Given articles of merchandise "look better than they are, but worth a quarter (25 cents), we guess." As to another item, "the price is monstrous, but that's none of our business." Once the manager of the shoe department gave him false information for an ad; Powers retaliated by not running anything about shoes for a year. However strange this kind of advertising may have seemed, people bought it: sales volume doubled from $4 million to $8 million in a few years.

Powers still proved himself incapable of getting along with anyone. He took no orders, even from the boss. "You are the most impudent man I ever saw," Wanamaker told him one day. "I am sure you didn't hire me for my manners," Powers shot back, confident of no argument on *that* point, at least. He wrote to a formula, novel at first, that later acquired a certain rigidity. He allowed no eye-attracting headlines or ornaments or display lines. Pictures were banned as a waste of space. His essays sold so softly they might neglect to make any pitch at all beyond a promise that if you don't like it, you can get your money back. One advertisement dealt only with the new stairways at City Hall. Eventually Wanamaker ran out of patience—"We didn't always agree," Powers conceded—and fired his copywriter in 1883, hired him back in 1884, and fired him for good in 1886. Powers went on to a lucrative career in free-lance copywriting, commanding total autonomy and the unheard-of fee of one hundred dollars a day, but he kept ripping the scabs off his old wounds. "He is the biggest coward I know," he said of Wanamaker in 1892.

For the advertising business, Powers was an astonishing revelation: an adman with pride and independence, who told only the truth and talked back to his employers. Not richly supplied with self-esteem, the business embraced him as its first lodestar, pointing the way to a more respectable future. His successor at Wanamaker's, Manly Gillam, tinkered with the format and graphics of the Powers formula but retained its essential aspects. Powers himself, in his later work for such products as Macbeth's Lamp Chimneys and Murphy Varnishes, showed how simple truth telling could sell more than dry goods ("What is it for? That is the first question to settle. A varnish that is perfectly adapted to one use, may be utterly worthless for some other use"). Away from New York and Philadelphia, out in the hinterlands, aspiring admen like Charles Austin Bates, Earnest Elmo Calkins, and Claude Hopkins found him an inspiration—"the model and ideal of all men who had advertising ambitions," as Hopkins remembered it. The "Powers style" of common sense, direct and factual copy, and the importance of content instead of manner became the new fashion in advertising circles.

In 1895 a reporter from the new advertising journal *Printers' Ink,* another brainchild of George Rowell's, called on the legend at his office in New York. "I don't care to be interviewed," Powers said curtly. Had he been reading *Printers' Ink?* "Never read any of these advertising publications. They ain't worth reading." Well, how did he go about writing his copy? "The first thing one must do to succeed in advertising is to have the attention of the reader. That means to be interesting. The next thing is to stick to the truth, and that means rectifying whatever's wrong in the merchant's business. If the truth isn't tellable, fix it so it is. That is about all there is to it."

For centuries, ever since its most rudimentary beginnings, advertising had appeared in three basic formats: handbills and circulars, outdoor signs like those posted by Bret Harte's Sapolio man, and (especially) newspapers. Now, in the late 1800s, with the business sitting up and stretching itself, advertising took on another major format. For the first of three times in its history, American advertising helped create a powerful new medium of information, entertainment, and—not coincidentally—selling.

The first entrepreneur to sense the potential of magazines as a vehicle for advertising was a *wunderkind* from Augusta, Maine, named E. C. Allen. He grew up on a farm five miles from Augusta and started his business career at seventeen by peddling books. Two years later Allen launched a pulp magazine, the *People's Literary Companion,* as a device to advertise his formula for a soap powder. Sixteen pages of stories, fashions, and household hints scattered among the advertisements, the *Companion* cost subscribers only fifty cents a year, with many copies distributed for less. Unlike other magazines of the day, it lived by advertising and so attracted readers with its bargain price. Circulation leaped quickly over 500,000 and its young publisher, not yet twenty-one, had to build a six-story publishing house to handle the volume. Eventually Allen's empire included 500 employees and a dozen magazines for home and farm readerships. Imitators repeated his success in Augusta, making that small city of less than 10,000 inhabitants the national capital of the "mail-order journals," as they were called. Allen became a millionaire and might eventually have left Augusta and made his name in a larger pond. But he died young, at forty-two, and his name soon disappeared along with his mail-order empire.

The polite magazines of the era took pride in *not* imitating Allen's methods. He not only littered his pages with ads; he also spent up to $150,000 a year promoting his magazines in newspaper advertising. Polite editors would not soil themselves in these ways. The two leading women's magazines, *Godey's* and *Peterson's,* did surrender their back covers to the Great American Tea Company, but inside restricted advertising to less than a page per issue. The genteel literary monthlies—the *Atlantic, Harper's, Scribner's*—were underwritten by publishing houses that filled back pages with ads for their own books. *Scribner's* and the *Atlantic* allowed a few pages of advertising by outsiders, *Harper's* none at all. George Rowell once offered *Harper's* $18,000 for a back-cover ad promoting the Howe Sewing Machine but was turned down. All these magazines aimed their substantial reading matter at a more affluent, literate readership than E. C. Allen's subscribers. This "better" class of readers might be offended by more ads—but also offered advertisers a more lucrative potential market than the mail-order journals. The problem, then, was to combine Allen's use of advertising with the audience and literary tastes of the polite magazines. This task was accomplished principally by three men who, like Allen, came from New England but who, like George Rowell and Wayland Ayer, left the region for the opportunities of New York and Philadelphia.

J. Walter Thompson promoted magazine advertising from the agency side of the business. Born in Pittsfield, Massachusetts, in 1847, he grew up in Ohio, where his building-contractor father had gone to build a bridge across the Sandusky River. Toward the end of the Civil War the boy left home to serve in the Navy. After completing his service, following a long shipboard duty marked by a monotony of pork and beans, Thompson landed in New York, a green country boy looking forward to a fancy restaurant meal. He went straight to a place on Fulton Street. With the waiter drumming his fingers behind him, Thompson helplessly surveyed the complicated bill of fare. "Pork and beans," he said in defeat.

A fast study, the rube soon learned how to operate in New York. He applied to George Rowell for a job as a clerk. Rowell chatted with him, decided he would be "too easily discouraged for an advertising man," and hired someone else. Thompson then entered the one-man agency of William J. Carlton as bookkeeper and assistant and quickly asserted himself. The firm did a modest business, mainly with Methodist magazines. Thompson persuaded Carlton that he should leave his desk and venture outside, soliciting new accounts. Looking around, Thompson was struck that the polite magazines ran only a page or two of ads in each issue. "This advertising came unsolicited and almost undesired," he recalled. "The publishers received it and printed it almost under protest and with a sublime indifference to results. Did it pay the advertiser? Would he increase the amount of space he used? Would he renew his advertisement? Such questions did not trouble the minds of the magazine publishers." Yet these magazines, instead of being ignored like outdoor signs or thrown away like handbills or read daily and discarded like newspapers, were prestige items that entered people's homes and then adorned reading tables for a month, being picked up and read repeatedly, often by the lady of the house who made the household purchases. Thompson "was amazed," he said later, "that the business and publishing world hitherto had failed to grasp the possibilities of such a medium in the advertising business."

Thompson submitted a case in point by placing an ad for asbestos roofing in *Godey's* and *Peterson's*. These women's journals seemed an unlikely medium for a product bought, presumably, by men. Yet the ads sold more roofing than any promotion in the company's history. Thompson then repeated the demonstration with an ad for jackstraws in *Peterson's;* within twenty days the merchant received over three thousand dollars' worth of orders in sums no larger than thirty-five cents. On the crest of these successes, Thompson approached the literary monthlies and found his warmest reception at *Scribner's.* By 1876 it was carrying twenty pages of ads per issue, with no loss of its literary integrity, and with the competition rethinking its advertising policies. By specializing in magazines Thompson acquired a monopoly over the field. In 1878 he bought out Carlton, paying $500 for the business and $800 for the office furniture, and renamed the agency after himself.

He attracted advertisers by flourishing a "Standard List" of twenty-five, later thirty, magazines under his exclusive contract, including the *Atlantic, Century* (successor to *Scribner's*), *Harper's, Lippin-*

cott's, Godey's, Peterson's, and the North American Review: virtually all the "best" American magazines. His power gained entry for even the more dubious advertisers, including patent medicines, thus improving their image by association. "I have succeeded in getting Lydia Pinkham into or rather on Century," he proudly informed the Pinkhams in 1883. "They may not like it, but that is immaterial to me. I was bound she should occupy a position on the highest notch, and there she is, engaged in her legitimate occupation." In 1889 he branched out by undertaking a $200,000 newspaper contract for Bonner's New York Ledger (at which point Wayland Ayer, previously a specialist in newspapers, took on some magazine contracts as well).

Thompson had prospered not by cutting down competitors but by inventing his own domain. For that reason, perhaps, he acquired no real enemies. "No man is more sympathetic or accessible," Printers' Ink commented, "and for years he has been friend and adviser to both great and small, and sometimes peacemaker." He was a handsome man of medium height, brown hair and beard, with (according to an associate) "the most wonderful blue-gray eyes I have ever seen, kindly, and humorous or serious, as his mood chanced to be." In his youth he had a fine tenor voice and sang in Brooklyn churches. All his life he loved water sports and was often pictured in yachting attire. Slightly deaf, he avoided large social affairs and preferred to dine with one or two friends, where he could follow the conversation. At the office he maintained a room, called the "Pickwick Club," where salesmen could wait and work in comfort.

His prosperous agency amassed a cash cushion large enough to absorb occasional losing accounts, further cementing it to customers. "The prime business quality that endears J. Walter to all of us is that he does business with real money," one publisher noted. "I guess J. Walter has made mistakes in extending credits along with the rest of them. But when that has happened, he never came round to see us. We got our pay in real money, even when he didn't get his." As clients kept appearing—Pabst beer, Mennen talcum powder, Kodak, Prudential Insurance, Durkee's Salad Dressing—the agency created the position of account executive, one man who spent all his time superintending only a given number of accounts. From his start in the untested magazine field, Thompson eventually turned his business into one of the first and most influential prototypes of a modern advertising agency.

As Thompson was an adman with an appreciation for magazines,

Cyrus H. K. Curtis was a magazine publisher with an appreciation for advertising. Late in life, a multimillionaire and the most honored man in his field, Curtis was asked what had made him successful. "Advertising," he said. "That's what made me whatever I am. . . . I use up my days trying to find men who can write an effective advertisement." Not a gifted writer or editor, Curtis excelled at promotion and picked good talent to run his publications. He invented the modern American magazine: his own advertising brought large circulations, which attracted other advertisers to his pages, which allowed him to pay top prices for the most expensive writing talents, which further fattened his circulations and brought him even more money with which to advertise. "It is not expense," he would say of his ad budgets, "it is investment. We are investing in a trademark. It will all come back in time."

A native of Portland, Maine, Curtis arrived in Boston in 1868, eighteen years old, to clerk in a dry goods store. On his lunch hour he sold newspaper ad space to merchants; after a year he quit the store to sell ads full-time. In 1872 he started his first magazine, the *People's Ledger*. On a business trip to Philadelphia he found a printer willing to print the magazine for $1,500 less than he was paying in Boston. "I figured that I could live on this saving," he recalled, so he moved the operation to Philadelphia. The *Ledger* failed, but Curtis borrowed $2,000 from his brother-in-law and, in 1879, launched a farmers' weekly, *The Tribune and Farmer*. His wife, Louisa Knapp Curtis, laughingly told him that its women's section reflected a man's obtuseness about what really interested women. He challenged her to do better. Under her direction the women's section drew so much mail that in 1883 Curtis spun off a separate eight-page supplement, the *Ladies' Home Journal,* with his wife remaining as editor. After one year circulation stood at 50,000. It doubled after an advertising campaign placed by Wayland Ayer's agency; after more advertising it doubled again, then again, to 400,000, an unprecedented figure for a polite magazine of some literary ambition.

In 1889 Curtis retired his wife and brought in a new editor, Edward W. Bok. From a background in New York publishing, Bok had a particular interest in advertising and what he called "the psychology of publicity." Curtis doubled the subscription cost, to a dollar a year, and launched a fearless expansion campaign, with Ayer advancing $200,000 in credit and guaranteeing notes for another $100,000. The *Journal*'s ad columns were also liberally filled with

Ayer clients. Curtis spent $150,000 on advertising in 1890, $200,000 a few years later, and soon hired a sales force just for the *Journal*. "I want business men to advertise in the *Journal*," he explained, "and to show them that I believe in the principles which I advance, I advertise largely myself. . . . A man can never advertise too much." The *Journal* reached 750,000 readers in 1895, almost double the circulation of any other adult magazine. Always charging forward, Curtis then launched a man's counterpart to the *Journal* by buying the *Saturday Evening Post*, a moribund weekly with a tenuous lineage allegedly tracing back to Benjamin Franklin. Under George Horace Lorimer the *Post* in five years went from a circulation of 2,200 to 325,000, and then to 2 million ten years later.

None of this astonishing success much affected Curtis himself. A small, silent man, he never asked anyone for advice and sat in meetings without speaking. When pressed, he gave one-word answers. He bought an opulent estate and sat in his sumptuous dining room eating a supper of milk and gruel. His favorite recreation was playing his enormous pipe organ. His favorite card game was solitaire, his favorite companion a dog. He had no confidants or close friends, no ego or bombast or presence. "One might almost say he is silent," remarked Bok, picking his words carefully, but with the assurance of a man who had married the boss's daughter. "He has a way of living to himself and within himself that, unless one understands him well, is easily misunderstood." He gave his editors their heads, concentrated on advertising and promotion, and let his fortune pile up.

The booming Curtis publications reflected a revolution that was overtaking the entire magazine field. The old polite magazines were sober and ponderous, making no concessions to general popularity. Illustrations consisted of a few woodcuts at most; light or humorous articles were rare; formats and typefaces were monotonously booklike. "The magazine was taken seriously, as it deserved to be," Thompson recalled. "It occupied a place in the public's esteem somewhere between the catechism and a government report." Circulations by later standards were modest: in 1887 the *Century* led with 222,000, followed by *Harper's* at 185,000 and the *Atlantic* far behind at 12,500. They carried, at most, about $30,000 worth of advertising per issue. Selling for twenty-five or thirty-five cents a copy, they still derived most of their income from subscriptions and newsstand sales.

Thompson helped make serious magazines more commercial;

Curtis made popular magazines more serious. From opposite directions they converged on a single point. Frank Munsey, lacking their ethical restraints, took their innovations and in his own abrasive way pushed the magazine revolution further along. One of the most disliked men in the history of American publishing, Munsey—according to the normally affable William Allen White—"contributed to the journalism of his day the talent of a meat packer, the morals of a money changer, and the manners of an undertaker. He and his kind have about succeeded in transforming a once-noble profession into an eight per cent security."

Munsey grew up on a farm thirty miles north of Augusta, Maine, a solitary boy especially close to his mother. (As an adult he never married, had no close attachments to women or men either, and left most of his fortune to the Metropolitan Museum of Art, which he had never visited.) Starting to work at fifteen, he arrived in Augusta in 1877, age twenty-three, to manage the local office of Western Union. He worked half a block from E. C. Allen's publishing house and lived in Allen's rooming house, and could not miss the example of Allen's success. "The publishing germ gradually got into my blood," Munsey recalled. One month after his mother's death in 1882, he left for New York and started his first magazine.

At this point a cluster of inventions opened new technical possibilities for a monthly publication. The halftone replaced the slower, more expensive woodcut and gave printers a quick, simple way to reproduce photographs. The linotype typesetting machine made hand-printing methods obsolete. Better presses and binding machines made feasible larger, quicker press runs. The net effect meant a monthly could be produced faster, with more and better illustrations, at greater volume and less cost. The shorter lead time between the writing of an article and its appearance in the magazine allowed a monthly to become more topical, with more articles dealing controversially with politics and current events and fewer taking timeless, unhurried looks at art and *belles lettres*.

Whatever his other limits, Munsey saw the implications of these changes more quickly than his competitors did. In 1891 he launched *Munsey's Magazine* with a newsstand price of a quarter an issue. He ran light, topical pieces and many pictures of women in discreet stages of undress. After two years of moderate success he startled the publishing world by cutting the price to a dime, with subscriptions reduced from three dollars to one. Obviously he intended to live by advertising revenue, not sales to readers. The American News Company, which monopolized magazine distribution, refused to handle the new *Munsey's,* claiming it could not make a profit if such a magazine cost only ten cents. Munsey sidestepped the problem with a campaign of direct-mail and newspaper ads, and then organized his own Red Star News Company. "We deal direct with news dealers," he assured the public, "and save two profits you pay on other magazines. *No middlemen; no monopoly.*" The public, growing concerned about the effects of trusts and monopolies, bought the pitch. In 1895 two other general monthlies, *McClure's* and *Cosmopolitan,* also dropped their prices to a dime. *McClure's* quickly doubled its circulation and started growing so fast that it lost money: advertising rates contracted according to an earlier, smaller circulation did not pay the bills for a much larger press run.

Now the genteel homes that had once admitted the *Century* and *Harper's,* with their few ads tucked in the back of the issue, let in *McClure's* and the *Ladies' Home Journal,* with up to one hundred pages of ads scattered all through the magazine, catching and holding one's eye. A much larger number of homes that once read no magazine at all now scanned, or at least looked at, *Munsey's* and the *Saturday Evening Post.* In 1885 only four general magazines had claimed 100,000 or more readers, with an aggregate total of 600,000. Two decades later there were twenty such magazines, with a combined circulation of 5.5 million. The magazine world had been transformed: a revolution prodded, celebrated, and paid for by advertising.

❧❧

As the business climbed slowly toward respectability, it became more specialized, the inevitable sign of any occupation starting to entertain a higher opinion of itself. As late as 1892, no general agency had a regular employee spending all his time writing copy. "We had one copywriter," Albert Lasker recalled of his early days at Lord & Thomas, "who gave us half his time and got thirty-five dollars a week, and we did Hannah & Hogg whiskey, and he got his pay mostly in sampling the whiskey." But John E. Powers had already shown that one could make a living writing copy without working for an agency. On his model, then, copywriting was first recognized as a gainful occupation on a free-lance basis. Many old-line agencies resisted hiring anyone who would only sit around and write, and do no soliciting or clerical work. "Writers of advertisements amuse me a good deal," Artemas Ward said scornfully in 1890. "They have all the conscious pride of a hen; they cackle whenever they lay an egg. Their idea is that on the future of that egg depends the future of the world. . . . The talent for writing advertising, when separated from other business qualities, is not rare."

One of the first to follow Powers' lead was Nathaniel C. Fowler, Jr. From a background of writing for various New England newspapers, he started his own advertising agency in Boston and prospered with the Columbia bicycle account. In 1891 he sold the agency to write copy full-time, declaring that one man should prepare the ad and another—the agent—should place it. He started a school of advertising; published how-to-do-it manuals; compiled a thousand-page tome, *Fowler's Publicity,* summing up the field; and even wrote an autobiographical novel, *Gumption.* Along with Mortimer Remington of J. Walter Thompson, he devised the Gibraltar trademark and slogan ("The Strength of Gibraltar") for the Prudential Insurance Company. Withal, he insisted that advertising was young, and nobody was an expert. "The man who knows how to advertise has not been born," he declared. "The man who thinks he knows how to advertise is born at the rate of one hundred a minute."

No such doubts clouded the brow of Charles Austin Bates. "I will agree to get better results with the same amount of money for any advertiser in America," he announced. "That sounds like a great big chunk of pure egotism. Maybe it is, but it is true." A serious poker player, Bates ran his advertising career like a poker game. He came from nowhere, all bluff and charming smile, blazed into New York, made a fortune, lost it, and disappeared: all within ten years. By his cometlike trajectory Bates demonstrated both the glory and the danger of the young advertising business.

Born in Indianapolis, his mother a writer of popular fiction, Bates was always oriented toward the printed word. After high school he started working as a printer and opened his own shop at the age of twenty ("There is nothing about printing that I do not know," he said later in his self-effacing way). In 1890 he bought the *Indianapolis Leader,* a populist weekly; it had a subscription to *Printers' Ink,* so Bates found out about John E. Powers and the $10,000 salary Wanamaker had paid him. A new world opened before his wondering eyes: "My God! *Ten thousand dollars a year!* Why, our postmaster received only $3,500 and drove to his job every morning in a two-horse surrey!" Bates started modestly by writing copy for a local laun-dryman, charging twenty-five cents an ad, and late in 1892 per-suaded an Indianapolis department store to hire him as advertising manager. He sent his work to *Printers' Ink,* which reprinted some of it with measured praise. For two dollars he placed five ads in *PI,* ad-vising the world of his talents, and drew enough response to be con-vinced that New York was ready for him. So he arrived in Manhattan in September 1893, twenty-seven years old, with ample self-confidence and a little more than a year of advertising experi-ence.

He was a tall, thin, boyish-looking man with a disarming smile and dark, curly hair and beard. "I worked for that smile for five years," Earnest Elmo Calkins said later. To another observer he looked "so much like a Hindu juggler that she was afraid he would take a snake out of his pocket." Bluffing with his slender hand, he declared himself a professional, an "ad-smith," who practiced ad-vertising in the same sense a doctor practiced medicine. He talked his way into a weekly column for *Printers' Ink,* in which he reviewed current campaigns and offered critiques drawn from his purportedly extensive knowledge of the field. He was, he said, a disciple of "the Wanamaker-Powers-Gillam style" that treated advertising as "sim-ply business news." It was not literature, so grammar and fine writ-ing sold no goods. Instead, he urged, feature the price and describe the product in simple, plain English, without assuming too much intelligence in the audience. "Advertisers should never forget that they are addressing stupid people," he announced. "It is really as-tonishing how little a man may know, and yet keep out of the way of the trolley cars."

Within two years he was, he allowed, the best-known advertising writer in the country, making, he claimed, over $20,000 a year and spending, he said, $10,000 a year advertising himself. He hardly needed to: *PI* gave him a regular pulpit for free. With few others holding themselves out as advertising experts, Bates happily leaped into the breach, dispensing advice both sensible and contradictory (advertising was variously "the most complex business in the world" and "as simple and certain as daylight"). He ran his own copy-writing business and a separate agency to place the copy, charging ten dollars for a quarter-page magazine ad, twenty-five dollars for a full page, and ten dollars for a medical notice, "my particular spe-cialty." That last enthusiasm undid him. In 1899 he invested heavily in a patent medicine, Laxacola, but could not sell it despite his best ad-smithing. "What we could do for other people," he recalled sadly, "we could not do for ourselves." He went broke, faded out of the pages of *Printers' Ink,* and forsook advertising for other fields, leaving a decidedly ambiguous legacy for other aspiring copywriters.

Nonetheless, writers of advertisements were starting to regard themselves as engaged in a separate and legitimate trade. Powers, Fowler, and a few others—notably Wolstan Dixey in New York and E. A. Wheatley in Chicago—continued in free-lance work. More typically, copywriters joined the staffs of agencies as they took over from advertisers the task of preparing the ads. The agency thus assumed more responsibility for the content and truthfulness of the ad, improving somewhat the ethical level of the trade. Along the same lines, admen in the 1890s founded clubs and associations that implied a growing self-consciousness and modest gestures toward self-policing. In New York this group was called the Sphinx Club because nothing discussed internally was to be repeated to outsiders. "The men in the business did not know one another," one early member recalled. "It was thought that if they were to sit around the same table once a month there would be a little less throat-cutting and general misbehavior. It worked out just that way."

Advertising seemed headed, if not for maturity, then at least a robust adolescence. Familiar as a promoter of small household goods, it had wielded small influence in the heavy industries that really powered American business. Railroads, for example, had typically limited advertising to running timetables in local newspapers, usually in exchange for free transportation on the railroad. Now the larger lines, seeking interstate passengers, went heavily into magazines and other high-toned media. The Pennsylvania and Union Pacific each budgeted over $200,000 a year for advertising, with four other lines spending $100,000 or more. "Every enterprise, every business," said Chauncey Depew of the New York Central, "and I might add every institution, must be advertised in order to be a success."

It was now routine for any new product to be introduced by a wave of advertising. The list for the 1890s included bicycles, Kodak cameras ("You press the button; we do the rest"), Coca-Cola, Van Camp pork and beans, Postum, Cream of Wheat, Campbell's Soup, and the Ingersoll watch. When the newly formed National Biscuit Company decided to launch a prepackaged biscuit in 1898, it went to N. W. Ayer & Son for advice. The concept was novel: biscuits were normally sold in bulk, from barrels, with the grocer dispensing given quantities as needed and making no claims for the product's freshness and cleanliness. National Biscuit wanted to try marketing biscuits in airtight packages. H. N. McKinney of Ayer suggested a name, Uneeda. An initial outlay of $100,000 for advertising brought so many orders that the manufacturer, unable to buy enough tin, had to abandon tin for cardboard boxes. Lavishly promoted with a trademark (a profiled boy in storm slickers) and a slogan ("Lest you forget, we say it yet, Uneeda Biscuit"), the product acquired the first million-dollar advertising campaign and some less successful imitators: Uwanta beer, Itsagood soup, and *Ureada Magazine*.

As the century ended, the advertising business could look back on the period since the Civil War with satisfaction. The total volume of advertising had gone from $50 million to $500 million; ad expenditures as a percentage of the gross national product had increased from .7 to 3.2 percent. People in the business, if not yet universally esteemed, no longer had to skulk in doorways. Ayer, the biggest agency, had 160 employees and anually placed over $2 million worth of advertising. "It appears to me," William Dean Howells had said in 1893, "that our enterprising American advertising has about reached the limit." But obviously the limit was nowhere in sight. Russell Conwell, the popular success preacher, even approved the advertising of religion—for Christ had said, "Let your light so shine before men, that they may see your good works, and glorify your Father which is in heaven."

TWO

THE AGE OF LASKER

In the first decade of the twentieth century, the advertising agency evolved into something close to its present form. The innovations of the late 1800s pointed the business toward an emphasis on the ad itself instead of the selection of media or the size of the advertiser's budget. Though the larger agencies were now hiring copywriters, an advertisement typically was still sent in rough form to the printer. There the foreman of the composing room would devise his own layout and typography, based not on a particular marketing strategy but rather on whatever pleased his eye, or whatever typefaces he had available. This haphazard arrangement changed when artists and designers joined copywriters on agency staffs and started asserting that the "look" of an ad meant as much as its message. With writers and artists grasping for more responsibility in the ad-making process—and launching their own permanent quarrel about the relative importance of words and art—the role of the account executive expanded, as agencies needed a mediator between the business realism of the client and the touchy egos of the creative staff. Pioneered at J. Walter Thompson, the account executive position was expanded, refined, and stamped by the emphatic personality of Albert D. Lasker. With his contributions, the dynamics of agency work took on permanent form—client on one side, creatives on the other, with the account executive shuttling between them. If the early twentieth century in advertising history can be described in a phrase, it would be: The Age of Lasker.

❦❦

This period was marked by three turns in the ongoing cycles of fashions in advertising style and copy. The first turn had begun in the 1890s, when the business circled away from the plain language and unornamented severity of the Powers style. "The desirability of the 'commonplace' style decreases," *Printers' Ink* noted, "as the number using it increases." So headlines, illustrations, and diverse typefaces became more popular. At the same time, prodded by the self-proclaimed success of Charles Austin Bates, advertising began to seem a fit occupation—or at least a safe haven—for a writer. Advertising took on more literary qualities in the hands of people with literary ambitions. "They came from newspaper offices, studios, the bar, and the pulpit," observed Nathaniel Fowler, who was not impressed; "and they literally poured into the advertising arena a stream of delicious nonsense which, if it could have been hardened, might have served for the decoration of afternoon tea cups."

The most influential exponent of this new style was Earnest Elmo Calkins, a skilled copywriter whose greatest impact lay, ironically, in the art and design of advertising. Like most of his peers in this second generation of admen, he was not an old Yankee from New England. He was born in 1868 in Galesburg, Illinois, where his father drove a grocery wagon, studied law at night, and later was elected city attorney. Deafened by measles at the age of six, Earnest retreated into a world of books and imagination; from Milton, the precocious boy later recalled, he learned "vocabulary and images, a feeling for words, for their deeper meanings, their power of suggestion." At twelve he acquired by accident a small handpress. Playing with it, he issued broadsides and fearless first issues of stillborn periodicals. In high school he worked in the local weekly's print shop, setting in type the patent-medicine ads disdained by everyone else in the shop, feeling the symptoms of the grisly diseases so lovingly described in the ads. At his hometown Knox College he helped edit the literary monthly and, in return for an editorial notice, received a free subscription to *Printers' Ink*. His deafness, bookish habits, and early experience all reinforced a lifelong affinity for words in print. "I was born," he said, "with printer's blood in my veins."

Since newspaper work seemed to require sound hearing, Calkins turned to advertising. *Printers' Ink* lured him to New York: he stayed briefly with a miserable job, went back home, wrote copy for a Peo-

ria department store, and won an ad-writing contest for which
Charles Austin Bates served as a judge. Bates then offered him a
copywriting job at fifteen dollars a week. Braving New York again,
Calkins arrived in 1897 to work for the disarming Bates smile. "Mr.
Bates beamed on me," he recalled, "and I expanded in the warmth
of his smile like a morning glory in the sun." Bates taught him to
prune his writing—"let's cut out the genuflections"—and defended
it when clients turned it down.

The Bates agency had an art department, one of the first in the
business, presided over by George Ethridge, who had studied at art
schools in New York, London, and Paris. In quarreling with
Ethridge over the makeup of an ad, Calkins was pushed into a new
field, also not barred by his deafness. After seeing an art exhibit at
the Pratt Institute, which he remembered as one of the most stirring
experiences of his life, he took a Pratt night class in industrial design.
A new idea: the craftsmanlike application of art to practical things.
What advertising needed, Calkins decided, was more eye appeal, a
more practiced attention to form, color, and visualization. At the
Bates agency, Calkins began to give Ethridge elaborate, hang-the-
expense instructions on how an ad should *look;* Ethridge would then
try to execute the design more cheaply. "Ethridge knew," as Bates
recalled it, "that an art department not only must produce an acceptable product, but one in which there might be a possibility of
profit. Earnest Elmo was never by any chance troubled by such sordid considerations."

These arguments—worsened, perhaps, by Bates' misfortunes with
Laxacola—made Calkins receptive when Ralph Holden suggested
they start their own agency. Three years younger than Calkins, originally from Philadelphia, Holden was in charge of new business at
the Bates agency. One of his new accounts had pointed out that
Calkins and Holden were his only contacts at the agency: why then
did they not simply go into business for themselves? Holden then
quit and challenged Calkins to go with him. They started in a one-
room office split into three cubicles, with two thousand dollars in
borrowed money and a staff of a stenographer and an office boy.
Setting a pattern to be replayed many times in advertising history,
the agency was powered by the volatile chemistry between a creative
man and an account man. Practical and gregarious, Holden went
outside and brought in the business; walled inside by his deafness
and its attendant shyness, Calkins did the ads. "He was a business

man," Calkins said of his partner, "with a business mind, accurate, exact, definite, qualified to talk terms, make arrangements, and report clearly and conscientiously, while I, concerned with the creative, imaginative, artistic side of the work, was apt to be vague and impatient of details. To put it briefly, Ralph contributed the brass tacks and I the red fire."

The firm started by advertising itself. Calkins wrote a series of house ads addressed to manufacturers. He presented advertising as the key to changed business conditions: the consumer, not the jobber or dealer, now had to be sold; high-quality staple items, not just novelties, were now routinely advertised; in this difficult milieu Calkins & Holden could act as more than "mere agents" for the advertiser. Cyrus Curtis—always looking for someone to write better copy for his magazines—saw one of these ads and, unannounced and with none of the panoply befitting his power, came by the office one day. "I place all my advertising through Ayer," he explained, "and will continue to do so—but they can't write the sort of stuff I want." He hired Calkins & Holden to prepare a campaign—to be placed by Ayer—on the advantages of advertising in *Ladies' Home Journal* and the *Saturday Evening Post*. With that heady start, the agency was established. The older shops might claim they could buy space cheaply through large volume and inside deals; C & H redirected attention to what filled the space, not what the advertiser paid for it. "They have produced copy of so original a character," *Printers' Ink* noted, "that the placing end of their agency is entirely secondary."

To Calkins, copy meant not just the words but "that combination of text with design which produces a complete advertisement," as he defined it. The first duty of an ad, according to Calkins, was to get the reader's attention: to stop and hold the eye of someone turning the pages of a magazine or newspaper. That required more attention in designing an ad to display and atmosphere, the "look" of the ad. Sure of his own esthetic tastes, Calkins sought the best artists he could find to execute his visions. The real talents, he found, disdained advertising work as commercial prostitution. For a time he resorted to the camera, spending long hours in photographers' studios looking for the right models. Eventually he hired artists who satisfied him. Earl Horter, who previously had lettered price tags for Wanamaker's, drew in a broad and simple style; Walter Fawcett complemented him with his delicately etched silhouettes. These and others—including, early in their careers, the industrial designer

Walter Dorwin Teague and the wood engraver Rudolph Ruzicka—worked in an art department that quickly became a model for the advertising trade. Under art director Tom Hall and his successor René Clarke, C & H produced "the finest art work of any agency in New York at the time," one veteran of advertising art recalled fifty years later. "We all looked up to the pictorial leadership of the agency." Calkins found himself considered an expert on the touchy chore of "handling" artists, of reconciling their "unrestrained imaginative temperament" with "a hard-headed, bookkeeping, business instinct."

This delicate oil-and-water mix found its ultimate expression in the agency's ads. They were restrained and tasteful, what later would be called soft sell. For Arrow collars, Tom Hall created a campaign stressing the accessories and backgrounds of the man who wore the product. Instead of picturing the collar by itself, Hall put it around the neck of a stylish young man, impossibly clear of eye, clean of jowl, and square of jaw, and surrounded him with opulent possessions and women. Joseph Leyendecker, known for *Saturday Evening Post* covers, painted the prototype of "The Arrow Collar Man," who went on to outlive detachable collars and became the Arrow Shirt man. For another client, Wesson Oil, the agency's regular discussions between copywriters and artists—Hall called these sessions "The Composite Man"—produced an effort to convert American housewives from their traditional use of a shortening made from hardened animal fats to a liquid, vegetable version. Instead of verbal persuasion, the selling point became René Clarke's paintings of enticing salads dressed with Wesson as the salad oil. C & H did similar selling-by-association campaigns for Kelly Springfield tires, Sherwin Williams paint, Pierce-Arrow cars, and the laboratory of Thomas Edison ("he was some little dictator," Calkins recalled).

The agency's most celebrated campaigns, for Force breakfast cereal and the Lackawanna Railroad, combined two advertising styles first popularized in the 1890s. Trade characters such as Aunt Jemima, Cream of Wheat's black chef, and the Uneeda slicker boy of themselves made no selling arguments, but by their comfortable familiarity they reminded the public of the product, gently but persistently. In a similar mode, advertising jingles—usually placed in streetcars to catch and beguile the commuter's short attention span—did not argue the product's specific merits but did "keep its

name before the public," as the phrase had it. The jingles written by
Charles M. Snyder for the DeLong Hook and Eye clasp mentioned
the product's special feature—a "hump" in the hook that kept it attached to the eye—but left readers uninformed as to precisely what
the hump did.

> He rose, she took the seat and said,
>   "I thank you," and the man fell dead.
> But, ere he turned a lifeless lump,
>   He murmured, "Do you see that HUMP?"

It made no sense, but perhaps that in itself piqued curiosity. Every
week Snyder put a new jingle in the streetcars of eighty cities, describing some improbable situation.

> The man who takes the streetcar floor
>   To be a public cuspidor,
> Avenging fate, give him a thump,
>   Till he's obliged to See that HUMP.

("It is astonishing," Charles Austin Bates said of jingles, "how some
of the things that we think the silliest will stick in our minds for
years.")

In 1900 Artemas Ward, still in charge of advertising Sapolio, told
one of his artists, a recent Cornell graduate named James K. Fraser,
to come up with a new campaign. "Here was Sapolio, widely
known," Fraser said later. "It seemed as though it had been advertised in every conceivable manner." One night, after a late dinner of
Welsh rarebit, Fraser had a dream about a town, apparently in the
Netherlands, where all the inhabitants testified to the excellent
qualities of Sapolio. The next day Fraser started drawing the pictures and writing the jingles for a series of streetcar ads.

> This is the maid of fair renown
> Who scrubs the floors of Spotless Town.
> To find a speck when she is through
> Would take a pair of specs or two,
> And her employ isn't slow,
> For she employs SAPOLIO.

It took the public a few months to grasp the plot, but soon people
were anticipating, like the next installment of a popular serial, the

debut of another well-scrubbed citizen of Spotless Town. Toys, books, plays, and political cartoons borrowed the motif. Real towns passed resolutions to become as spotless as the one in the ads. The campaign ran for six years, the biggest success of its kind.

Force cereal, introduced by the addition of a trade character to the jingle style, was part of a revolution in American breakfast habits. The traditional morning meal for farmers and manual laborers emphasized eggs, meat, fried potatoes, and biscuits: heavy, greasy fare suitable for a day of strenuous physical work. As more Americans took up office work in cities, lighter breakfasts of grains and cereals were advertised as a logical adjustment to the more sedentary habits of the new middle class. Shredded Wheat, declared its inventor Henry Perky in 1903, "sells chiefly to the best classes. The man with the dinner pail doesn't eat it." Cereals were sold to the "best" people as a health food, good for the nervous system, bound to restore youthful health and vigor, specifically suited to brain work, and—especially—light and easily digested. "You eat too much for breakfast," said a Calkins & Holden ad for an oat product. "H-O is enough."

To launch Force, a new flaked cereal, the manufacturer hired Minnie Maude Hanff, a young woman who wrote jingles and children's articles for New York newspapers. Instead of promoting Force in the serious, almost medicinal fashion of most breakfast foods, Hanff decided to try an oblique, humorous approach. "Goodness gracious! A breakfast food isn't all life, is it?" she later explained. "People are not going to take it nearly as seriously as the advertiser wants them to. They see the ad for a single minute, and I thought far better to give them a minute's entertainment." So she created a grouchy old man who was transformed by eating Force.

> Jim Dumps was a most unfriendly man,
> Who lived his life on the hermit plan;
> In his gloomy way he'd gone through life,
> And made the most of woe and strife;
> Till Force one day was served to him—
> Since then they've called him "Sunny Jim."

A friend of Hanff's, Dorothy Ficken—still in high school—drew Sunny Jim as a portly little man, round of face and form, with an incongruous pigtail. The campaign began in March 1902 with full-page ads in Sunday newspapers. As new jingles appeared, the public learned about Jim's family, the cook, the janitor, the girl upstairs taking singing lessons.

> Jim Dumps a little girl possessed,
> Whom loss of appetite distressed;
> "I des' tan't eat!" the child would scream;
> Jim fixed a dish of Force and cream—
> She tasted it—then, joy for him—
> She begged for more from "Sunny Jim."

After a few months the campaign went to Calkins & Holden. Calkins wrote hundreds of the jingles; thousands more were sent in unsolicited by Sunny Jim's fans. A giant likeness adorned the sides of two eleven-story buildings in New York. Songs, musical comedies, and vaudeville skits were written about him. Anybody with a cheery personality and the name of James risked being called Sunny Jim. A prominent judge cited him in rendering a decision. A Force Society was organized. "No current novel or play is so universally familiar," *Printers' Ink* commented. "He is as well known as President Roosevelt or J. Pierpont Morgan."

When the Lackawanna Railroad, known mainly as a freight line, started to publicize its passenger service between New York and Buffalo, it hit on an advertising theme with the help of Mark Twain. He had ridden on the Lackawanna, Twain advised the railroad, and his white duck suit was still white. The line burned anthracite coal on all its passenger trains, not just the limiteds, so its customers arrived less sooty. The Lackawanna's advertising man, Wendell P. Colton, dubbed it the Road of Anthracite. He asked Elmo Calkins for a series of jingles on that theme. Calkins remembered a poem from his childhood, "Riding on the Rail," that onomatopoetically imitated the rhythm of a locomotive. He repeated the device for his saga of Phoebe Snow, a pretty young woman dressed all in white who evidently spent her days riding the Lackawanna.

> Says Phoebe Snow
> About to go
> Upon a trip to Buffalo:
> My gown stays white
> From morn till night
> Upon the Road of Anthracite.

As Calkins described her further adventures—eating lunch, admiring the passing landscape, being romanced by a comparably unsooted young man—Phoebe Snow came to rival Sunny Jim as an overnight phenomenon. Her richly illustrated, full-color streetcar cards adorned the walls of many college dormitories.

Spotless Town, Sunny Jim, and Phoebe Snow all charmed the public with their rhymed meter, occasional humor, and agreeable illustrations. But they did not necessarily *sell* the public. For a familiar product like Sapolio, jingles and trade characters might sustain the sales of an item already well established. For a new or reoriented product, however, customers might applaud the advertising and avoid the merchandise. "The advertising absolutely sold 'Sunny Jim' to the public, but it did not sell Force," Calkins said later. "Humor, you see, is a very good servant but a bad master." After a run of only eighteen months, the Sunny Jim jingles gave way to harder-selling conventional copy about the nutritional benefits of Force ("Hard physical work consumes fat, but hard mental work consumes Phosphates, and Nitrogen instead"). Phoebe Snow lasted longer, despite ongoing debates about her selling power, until yielding to a detailed J. Walter Thompson campaign about the Lackawanna's equipment and service.

Great popularity, it seemed, did not necessarily translate into sales. "They sound very much like productions of the silly season," *Printers' Ink* concluded after the demise of Spotless Town and Sunny Jim. "The thoughts back of them were shallow." These campaigns left Calkins & Holden with a reputation as a "pretty picture" agency producing stylish, attractive copy that might not work. Not a greedy or particularly ambitious man, Calkins regretted the reputation but went on producing the same kind of ads. "My chief satisfaction," he always insisted, "has been in improving the physical appearance of advertising." For the industry as a whole, though, the cycle was turning back to a harder sell.

❦❦

Advertising humor, 1901:
"Why is the merchant who doesn't advertise like a man in a rowboat?"
"Because he goes backward, I suppose."
"No; because he has to get along without sales."

❦❦

A classic moment in advertising history: late one spring day in 1904, the Chicago office of the Lord & Thomas agency received a note from a man waiting downstairs in the lobby. You do not know what real advertising is, the note said. If you want to know, let me come up and tell you. A junior member of the firm, Albert Lasker, was delegated to receive the caller, whose name was John E. Kennedy. In his few years in the business, Lasker had been seeking a definition of advertising that rang true. When, at three o'clock that morning, the two men finished talking, Lasker finally believed he had his definition.

Kennedy preached his advertising gospel with all the zeal of a convert. A Canadian, forty years old in 1904, at one time supposedly a member of the Royal Canadian Mounted Police, Kennedy broke into advertising as ad manager of the Hudson's Bay department store in Winnipeg in the 1890s. There he wrote flowery, unspecific copy of the kind that made Nathaniel Fowler grind his teeth ("Aye, a veritable fairyland! . . . Looking down long avenues of dress fabrics and through dreamy, hazy vistas of cloudy laces and shimmering silks, which rival in coloring and variety the wealth of summer and autumn's rich array . . ."). Kennedy sent this ad to Charles Austin Bates in New York, who ran it in his *Printers' Ink* column as an example of bad copy—too literary and general, lacking prices and definite information. "It has often occurred to me," said Bates, "that it is not a good idea to be too original." Kennedy in rebuttal claimed that his readers in Winnipeg, "tinged with English ideas of tone and business propriety," preferred high English to everyday language; and further that retail advertising needed only to bring customers to the store, where salesmen would then sell the goods.

Unpersuaded for the moment, Kennedy nonetheless did absorb the Bates dicta of treating advertising as business news to be told in a detailed, straightforward reportorial style. He passed through a series of jobs, never staying for long or taking orders well: business manager for a Montreal newspaper; writing ads for the Regal Shoe Company in Boston; promoting his own inventions, the Resilia Ventilated Shoe and the Semi-Ready Wardrobe (whereby a customer tried on a nearly completed garment, was fitted, then waited while a tailor quickly made the adjustments). In 1903 he was called in following the demise of Sunny Jim to write harder-selling copy about the "Brain-Food" nutritional benefits of Force. After a few months he moved on to Postum and then to Chicago, where he presented himself at the office of Lord & Thomas.

Advertising, Kennedy told Lasker, is "salesmanship-on-paper."
("Advertisements," Bates had said in 1896, "are printed salesmen.")
Instead of merely drawing customers to the store, Kennedy now asserted, an ad should say in print precisely what a good salesman
would say face-to-face to a customer. Instead of general claims,
pretty pictures, or jingles, an ad should offer a concrete *reason why*
the product was worth buying. Not charming or amusing or even
necessarily pleasing to the eye, a good ad was a rational, unadorned
instrument of selling: "True 'Reason-Why' Copy is Logic, plus persuasion, plus conviction, all woven into a certain simplicity of
thought—pre-digested for the average mind, so that it is easier to
understand than to *misunderstand* it." Like Bates, Kennedy warned
against aiming copy too high for the public to grasp. The average
person, he urged, was uneducated but not stupid, with a shrewd but
persuadable openness to appeals made by sensible arguments. Advertising needed to find a delicate middle ground, high enough for
rational dialogue but not over the public's head.

Lasker, who knew talent and acted quickly when he saw it, hired
Kennedy as his chief copywriter. Kennedy wrote ads in a visually
distinctive style—heavy on italics, underlining, and capital letters—
that caught the eye despite a jerky rhythm that reminded one reader
of riding in a wagon with one lopsided wheel. The style was rapidly
imitated by other agencies, leaving Kennedy to insist that reason-
why copy amounted to more than some "typographical dress."
Lasker, at least, did not mind the imitation. He trumpeted the Kennedy approach in a pamphlet, "The Book of Advertising Tests."
Over seven thousand copies were distributed, bringing in hundreds
of letters a week from inquiring manufacturers. Test your usual copy
in one city, the pamphlet challenged, against Lord & Thomas copy
in another, and then compare the results. Neither art nor literature,
"Advertising should be judged *only* by the goods it is conclusively
known to sell, at a given cost. 'Keeping the name before the people' is
wrong and 'salesmanship on paper' is right."

"We saw more clearly than ever," Lasker later recalled, "that basically it is copy that makes advertising pay." He therefore started a
copywriting school at Lord & Thomas. A section of the office was
partitioned into nine cubicles for apprentice copywriters. Kennedy,
it turned out, could not teach the group: facing an audience, he
would speak inaudibly if at all. So he taught Lasker, who passed the
message along, holding class twice a week for four or five hours a

session. The students, both at Lord & Thomas and at other agencies, then carried forth the gospels of reason-why and salesmanship on paper (the latter phrase was subsequently changed to salesmanship in print). Looking back in later life, Lasker pronounced this development "the most memorable thing in my lifetime." One of his students, J. George Frederick, went even further: this "epoch-making rebellion in copywriting," comparable (said Frederick) to Martin Luther's Reformation, "aimed at an appeal to reason and intelligence rather than the time-honored assumption that the public was a mass of dumb, driven sheep, who could be swayed with mere picture-and-catch-word."

The advertising business already suffered from historical amnesia. Although a sharp change from jingles and trade characters, in most of its elements reason-why only repeated the formulas of the Powers-Wanamaker-Bates style. But as the cycle came around it seemed new and revolutionary. After the uneven sales record compiled by the jingles, reason-why seemed particularly hardheaded, serious, and *businesslike*. Lord & Thomas spent tens of thousands of dollars to publicize its alleged discovery, declaring war on "that Goldbrick of Advertising called 'General Publicity.'" The agency rode reason-why to a position, it announced, as the largest advertising agency in America. "Mr. Kennedy is a one-idea man," the trade journal *Advertising & Selling* concluded. "But his is a great idea. . . . His style is now the foundation stone of successful advertising."

To his credit, Kennedy did not claim to have invented the copy style associated with his name: old patent-medicine ads, he said, operated on good reason-why principles. He owed his celebrity to good timing and his prickly conjunction with Albert Lasker. A large, forceful man, sure of his own opinions, Kennedy wrote to nobody else's time clock. Given an assignment, he would study the client for days, imagine the potential customers, perhaps interview a few of them, speculate about objections to the product, rebut those objections, list the article's selling points; all in avoidance of writing the copy. Finally, with a deadline hanging over him, he would sit down at home and write through the night on an ocean of coffee. He then would insist the ad be run exactly as written, even if it did not fit the page. Despite the fame and new business he brought Lord & Thomas, he was a problem. "A very slow worker," as Lasker remembered him, "because he had to work everything out by very concentrated thinking. He worked under great pressure. He was a giant physically, but mentally he would wear himself out, and there would be long periods when nothing would come to him." After less than two years—longer than most of his jobs—he departed Lord & Thomas. "Kennedy left us, for what reason I do not know," Lasker recalled, though presumably he knew the reason all too well.

Kennedy briefly ran an agency with George Ethridge, wrote for a Baltimore department store, returned to Lord & Thomas for an even shorter stay, and settled into the free-lance work that most suited his personality. He became rich—at one point, Goodrich tires paid him $20,000 a year for half his time—and insisted that he did not mind that his reputation was overshadowed by other practitioners of reason-why. "Anyone may have my share of the glory," he said in old age, "for I have over $2,000,000 worth of consolation with which to soothe my wounded feelings."

To replace him at Lord & Thomas, Lasker hired Claude C. Hopkins, who wrote in the Kennedy style but with none of his alarming habits. Hopkins worked fast: he would visit a client and then, in forty-eight hours, produce a finished campaign that would run for a year. (Lasker might wait six weeks before showing the ads lest the client think the work hurriedly done.) A timid introvert, prudent and cautious, Hopkins did not question the boss. "So far as I know," said Hopkins, "no ordinary human being has ever resisted Albert Lasker. He has commanded what he would in this world." Best of all, Hopkins had the consistent, unflagging personality of a metronome. He allowed himself virtually no diversions, no sports, music, politics, books, plays. "He lived by the clock," an associate recalled, "—each day must be fruitful. He dallied cautiously with life's dissipations and frivolities. He was always abstemious, hesitant against extremes, never permitting pleasures to interfere with his precious work." Hopkins loved work, he claimed, the way some men loved golf. He seldom left his office before midnight. He would excuse himself from bridge games and dinner parties to return to his typewriter. Weekends meant nothing to him; Sundays were the best working day because of fewer distractions. For almost two decades he toiled in Lasker's shadow, each man's personality complementing the other's. On a list of the great copywriters of all time, most students of advertising history would rank Hopkins first.

As a workaholic he was at least the logical extension of his childhood and family background. On the paternal side he came from a long line of impoverished preachers. His father, a newspaperman,

died when he was ten, and Hopkins grew up under the sway of a formidable mother. From her, he said, he acquired his "conspicuous
conservatism," by which he meant attention to work and avoidance
of vices ("The lack of that quality has wrecked more advertising
men, more business men, than anything else I know"). The mother
taught school to support her widowed family; in the evenings she
wrote kindergarten books and then spent vacations selling them on
the road. The son could not miss this example of application to
duty. As a boy in Detroit, he held jobs from the age of nine; in summer he worked sixteen hours a day on a family farm. Between his
Scotch Presbyterian mother and hard-shell Baptist grandfather he
attended five church services every Sunday. "Together they made
religion oppressive," he recalled. "Seemingly every joy in life was a
sin." Pointed toward a career in the pulpit, he started preaching at
the age of seventeen. But a year later, in a gesture of bold independence practically unique in his life, he rejected his mother's literal
fundamentalism and announced his retirement from preaching. It
meant a permanent break from his mother, whom he rarely saw
thereafter. Eighteen years old, a young man of uncommon sobriety
and self-possession, he was on his own.

In advertising Hopkins found a secular replacement for the suffo-
cating Christianity of his youth. Advertising gave him a purpose and
livelihood, and—by the totality of his commitment to it—ironically
denied him the joys for which he had left the church. Working as a
bookkeeper for the Bissell carpet-sweeper company in Grand Rap-
ids, he read a draft by John E. Powers of a promotional brochure for
Bissell. Though admiring the Powers candor and style, he decided
the brochure reflected no knowledge of the product. (Hopkins always cared more about content than style.) To prove his point Hopkins then wrote an improved version, and so began his advertising
career. Quick successes brought him to Chicago as an advertising
manager for Swift and Company.

Already, in the 1890s, he had worked out the basic elements of an
advertising philosophy. Instead of a college education or newspaper
training, he said, an adman needed practical business experience.
Mere writing skill was not required. Instead, advertising called for a
visceral, receptive alertness to popular moods and tastes. Most people, Hopkins declared, preferred pulp literature and popular music
to good classics: "We advertisers must take the world as we find it.
Our business is to win people, not to make them over." Nine-tenths

of the public would rather be intrigued than educated. So advertisers had to snag an elusive attention span with "dignified sensationalism," provocative statements that tickled but did not abuse the truth. A campaign should be built around a single overriding selling point, undiluted by a confusion of multiple claims ("You cannot chop a tree in two by hitting every time in a different place").

Hopkins thus spoke in general for the gospel articulated by Bates and, later, by Kennedy. Like them, Hopkins defined advertising as a form of salesmanship itself, not just a brass band clearing the way for the barker. "I consider advertising as dramatic salesmanship," he said in 1897. "I dramatize a salesman's arguments. . . . Advertising must be better than ordinary argument, just as a play must be stronger than ordinary life." To manufacturers, still not universally convinced of the need to advertise, Hopkins argued his case with a zeal that can only be called missionary. Advertising, he said, had the power to create new industries, change customs and fashions, build empires, sway the most intimate habits of millions of people. Not a gamble or a guessing game, advertising was an exact science that rewarded close study and long hours, the best effort a man could give it. "I steep myself in advertising," said Hopkins. "I read advertising, write advertising, think of advertising night and day."

In Chicago he went into free-lance work and made his reputation promoting a germicide, Liquozone. Instead of testimonials and reckless claims, he offered a money-back guarantee. For other clients he developed the technique of the preemptive claim, an impressive-sounding assertion that seemed to establish a product's uniqueness—though its competitors might have made the same claim had they thought of it first. He learned that Schlitz beer steam-cleaned its bottles, as did other breweries. To impress customers with the sparkling purity of Schlitz, he proclaimed that its bottles were "washed with live steam." The public, not knowing brewery procedures, bought the claim, and the advertising world took notice. One day, as Albert Lasker told the story, he ran into Cyrus Curtis on a train. Curtis, as ever a connoisseur of advertising copy, handed Lasker a magazine with the Schlitz ad and told him he should hire the copywriter. Lasker gave Hopkins a part-time food account, liked the results, and put him on the regular payroll at a thousand dollars a week.

At Lord & Thomas, Hopkins added to his weapons the techniques of mail-order advertising, in which the agency did over a third of its business. Formerly opposed to offering free samples of merchandise, he now saw that a coupon could both goad the customer into taking action and give the advertiser a precise gauge of an ad's effectiveness. A free or cheap sample, offered through the mail, made the ad seem altruistic, holding out a favor instead of threatening to part the customer from his money. Hopkins also liked the esthetics of mail order: dense copy in small type, hard reason-why arguments instead of rhetorical flights, severely functional illustrations and graphics, a packed page with small borders of white space. Mail order became the model for Hopkins. He was permanently identified with premiums and coupons.

For Quaker Oats, Hopkins had the name of its Wheat Berries product changed to Puffed Wheat, with a higher price to provide an advertising budget. After the failure of a newspaper campaign, the cereal—"shot from guns" by the manufacturing process, the ads said—reached a more affluent public through magazine advertising. (The ads featured a coupon offering a free package.) When Hopkins launched his first campaign for Pepsodent toothpaste, the disappointing coupon returns dictated a change in strategy. Reading up on dental hygiene, Hopkins discovered plaque. He decided to emphasize a beauty appeal, the pretty teeth available to customers who used Pepsodent to remove that cloudy film from their teeth. The ads showed attractive people with good teeth and offered a free sample of the toothpaste. Hopkins bought an interest in the product, the campaign took off, and he eventually made a million dollars from Pepsodent.

Within a few years he was, by reputation, "the highest paid advertising man the world has ever known." He bought land in the country outside Chicago, near the farm he had worked as a boy. On a bluff of virgin forest he built a home that he tinkered with and enlarged for the rest of his life. A half-mile of flower gardens led down to a spring-fed lake. Still afflicted with a Scotch conscience, he let his wife keep track of household expenses, the extent of which would have made him unhappy. Commuting into Chicago, he liked to arrive at six o'clock in the morning and walk through Grant Park, where he would sit down and talk to vagrants about the beauties of hard work.

At the office he had fifteen points to look for in good copy, each listed on a separate slip of paper. During the day he tacked them to the wall over his desk, a catechism for his constant guidance, and took them down every night. Not articulate in discussions, still easily shocked by the world, he remained awkward and unsophisticated in face-to-face contacts. Once he was appalled by a client meeting to discuss the advertising of toilet seats: "Gracious! Gracious!" was his comment. The antithesis of the voluble, widely acquainted Lasker, Hopkins found conversation difficult and had few friends either inside or outside the agency. "He did everything softly," an associate remembered. "Of tall, well-built physique, and with the innocent face of an eager schoolboy, he spoke softly with a trace of a lisp. But *was* he definite and convincing in his ideas of good copy!"

Alone, at his desk, he was supremely in his element. He lived to write advertising, and in that calling found the bulk of his happiness. Late in life he claimed to have worked twice as hard as anyone else in the business—and wondered whether in his dedication he had missed something. He would not advise his son to follow his example, he said: "Life holds so many other things more important than success that work in moderation probably brings more joy." Occasionally, along the way, he had allowed himself other misgivings. Addressing the Sphinx Club in New York in 1909, one of his rare public appearances, he reflected that advertising men were known by their works, but not by their names. While authors, actors, and politicians were celebrated and recognized, the adman —"who, we must contend, is the peer of them all"—toiled in anonymity, making other people famous. "Perhaps you, as I, have longed to be a Jack London," said Hopkins. "It is a happy position where one may contribute to the amusement of mankind. Such men are known and applauded. They are welcomed and wanted, for they lift the clouds of care. But those who know us, know us only as searchers after others' dollars."

At the end of this address, Hopkins said he must mention someone to whom friends and enemies alike deferred as the greatest of them all. "Ten years ago this man was an office boy, drawing ten dollars a week. No man in all the history of advertising has gone so far in a lifetime as this man has gone in ten years. When we mark where he stands at the age of twenty-eight we can only gasp to think of where forty will find him." Hopkins allowed that his employment made the tribute sound biased. Nonetheless, "a man but flatters himself as a man of breadth and discernment when he says of Albert Lasker, 'He is the advertising king.' "

Lasker, always Lasker. Surrounded by older men at Lord & Thomas, he dominated them all (and, reputations aside, made more money than anyone else, including Hopkins). He was an impossible boss, mercurial and unpredictable, forever badgering his subordinates with orders and sudden inspirations subject to recall. Every few years he would sweep through his employees, firing a certain percentage, weeding out the deadwood and keeping the survivors on their toes. His service department maintained a huge wall chart, showing due dates for the various stages of campaigns under preparation; but these dates were set slightly ahead of the actual schedule expected by the client, so that workers labored under an artificially looming deadline. Lasker ran the place in the serene confidence of "his colossal assurance," as one of his men, Fairfax Cone, remarked, "that, given the same circumstances, nothing that he was doing could be done better." He loved power and influence, and wielded more of them over a longer period than anyone else in advertising history.

Albert Lasker was a self-created personality, doubly an outsider as a German Jew among WASPs and a Texan among New Englanders and Midwesterners. The young advertising industry presented no rigid molds to break; though an apparent anomaly, Lasker had only to shape his own mold. He held together the mismatched parts of himself—an old young man of astonishing precocity who grew younger with age, a ruthless boss who fired at will but carried his people through the panic of 1907, a political and social conservative who liked high-stakes gambling, a *bon vivant* and high liver who went around the office turning off lights—in a precarious equilibrium punctuated, over his lifetime, by at least three nervous breakdowns. His omnivorous, insatiable ego oddly did not crave public recognition. He gave few interviews or public addresses and was seldom written up by the general press. Several competitors of lesser magnitude within advertising enjoyed larger reputations outside the business. "It is my eccentricity," he said in a rare moment of unguarded reflection, "or fancy—or maybe egotism—to want to be behind the throne and not on it. Even in businesses of which I was the sole owner, I've very seldom had any position but secretary. If I was not in the public eye, I felt I could cover more territory—I could be a free lance, a lone wolf, and I liked that." He wanted influence without the tinsel, power without its constrictions: nothing held him down. To his associates he was taller than his height; larger than life;

and ultimately elusive, like quicksilver spilled on a laboratory bench, flashing glints now here, now there, but hard to contain or recover. He inspired many implausible anecdotes but not much coherent analysis.

To the extent that he may be summed up quickly, he was evidently very much Morris Lasker's son. The father's ancestors lived in the village of Lask (thus the name) in the province of Poznan, then part of East Prussia, now the modern state of Poland. Eduard Lasker, elder brother to Morris, was a prominent lawyer and liberal politician in the Reichstag who first supported Bismarck, then broke with him at some risk to his career. Morris Lasker came to America in 1856, a late arrival in the emigration of German liberals after the failure of the revolutions of 1848. According to Albert, his father left Prussia "to get away from the European system that was grinding down individualism." But he was only sixteen at the time, probably motivated less by politics than by adventure. He headed west, slowly, an itinerant peddler selling goods to housewives from his wagon. When he got to Texas he stopped, spent a dozen years at various places within the state, and finally settled in Galveston in 1872. He joined a wholesale grocery firm, branched into milling and banking, made his first fortune, and built a big house.

Albert, born May 1, 1880, was the third of eight children and the second surviving son. An early photograph presents a child with a steady, knowing, eerily adult look in the eye. Growing up with privileges in a raw, unformed frontier town, he acquired a swift sense of his own possibilities. (Years later, on a visit to the nascent state of Israel, he was reminded of the Texas of his youth: "a pioneer people with all the released energy of pioneer people.") Drawn to newspaper life, at the age of twelve he launched the *Galveston Free Press,* a four-page weekly. " 'Advertise and make good' is our motto," he declared, unconsciously anticipating his future career. Many other boys—such as Elmo Calkins—started such enterprises, only to drop them quickly after an ungrateful reception. Albert kept his going for a year, delivering measured opinions on the passing scene and turning a regular profit.

Much later, after Albert's great success in advertising, Morris told his son that he had always known Albert was the special child, the logical inheritor of Uncle Eduard's mantle of achievement, high principle, and public service—an assertion perhaps more certain in retrospect, after Albert's triumphs. What seems clear, as the boy was growing up, is the tension between the two. Albert wanted to please and feel loved; Morris—domineering, crusty, in his fifties during the boy's adolescence—expected too much, doling out punishing criticism with one hand even while granting special privileges with the other. After being wiped out by the panic of 1893, Morris sent the rest of the family home to Prussia, closed up most of the big house, and lived with Albert in a single room. Night after night, Albert was awakened by a scratching sound as his worried, sleeping father compulsively shredded a rug by the bed. At that point, perhaps, the boy raised in comfort and high expectations began to feel less awed by his demanding father.

Morris retrieved his fortune, the family returned, and Albert— still in high school—became a reporter for a Galveston newspaper. He got his first scoop by posing as a telegraph messenger to obtain an exclusive interview with Eugene Debs. Once out of high school he took his first regular jobs with newspapers in New Orleans and Dallas. Wasting no time, he decided to try newspaper work in New York. His father refused permission: newspapermen, he said, drank too much.

"I was very devoted to my father," Albert later recalled, understating a bond that had included many quarrels and violent scenes. They agreed to a compromise. Albert would, for a three-month trial, join the Chicago advertising firm of Lord & Thomas, with which Morris had done some business. After three months, if not happy with the work, Albert could try New York. The son agreed to the plan, but only to go through the motions, with his mind still set on newspaper reporting. "I would be in a big city—I had never been in a city before—and have a good time," he recalled. "It would be a nice semi-vacation, and in ninety days I would be on my way to New York and my father would be satisfied."

Daniel M. Lord and Ambrose L. Thomas, both transplanted New Englanders, had started their firm in 1881. Initially they specialized in placing advertising for Christian periodicals, claiming "entire control" of the ads in four such journals. By 1898, when Albert Lasker came up from Galveston, they had followed the general shift in the business from selling space to selling clients. L & T's biggest accounts were Anheuser-Busch and a patent cathartic, Cascarets, of which Thomas was a principal owner. Young Lasker, granted entry by his father's connections, was set to sweeping floors and emptying cuspidors for ten dollars a week. Enjoying himself in the big city,

looking forward to New York, he fell into bad company and lost five
hundred dollars in a crap game. What to do? He could not confess to
Morris, and the gambler wanted his money. So Albert talked Ambrose Thomas into advancing him the money; Lasker then had to
stay and work it off. Thus advertising gained its greatest personality
by way of a gambling debt. "I never got to what I wanted to do,"
Lasker said later. "America lost a great reporter when I was forced
into other channels." And Morris Lasker, incidentally, was happy
not to lose his son to drink and the newspaper life.

After a year as an office boy Albert went out on the road as a salesman, seeking new accounts in Ohio, Indiana, and Michigan. "The
main things in my favor," he remembered, "were dedication and
energy, because I wanted to work to pay off this debt." Only nineteen years old, he landed an order on his first day. Within a few
months he had pulled in about $50,000 in new business. "I was a
young boy—and that intrigued people." At that time most of the
agency's clients wrote their own copy and then paid L & T a commission of 10 percent, or less, to place the ad. Catching the trend
already visible in other agencies, Lasker persuaded a client—a manufacturer of ear trumpets—to pay 15 percent if he provided the
copy. Lasker wrote no copy, then or later; instead he engaged a
newspaper friend to write the ad. The client liked the new arrangement and jumped its advertising budget from $3,000 to $20,000 a
month, with L & T's share growing from $300 to $3,000 a month.
Lasker became a young man to watch. By 1902 he was the star salesman, making $10,000 a year. Two years later, with that salary in-
creased fivefold, he bought a quarter interest in the firm after Lord
retired: a partner at the age of twenty-four.

As Thomas explained the phenomenon, Lasker rose so swiftly because of his thoroughness, a knack for directing subordinates, and a
"capacity to originate." Of his early innovations, the most important was the "record of results" department. Whether Lasker actually invented this department—it was started in 1900, when he
was still on the road—he nurtured and made it a prime selling point
for the agency, "the guiding spirit of our business." As part of their
contracts with L & T, clients were required to submit weekly reports
on how well their ads were doing: the number of replies to a given ad
in a given medium for mail-order campaigns, along with sales fluc-
tuations related to advertising in retail campaigns. These reports
from all the agency's clients were then collated and filed on a separate card for each medium carrying L & T ads. By 1906 this depart-

ment kept eight people busy tabulating and filing returns from over 600 clients on the pulling power of some 4,000 magazines and newspapers. The results were occasionally surprising, showing good returns from small, obscure media and poor yields from large, famous ones. Ad placement, traditionally dependent on a medium's reputation and a sixth sense of the agent's, thus acquired a more rigorous procedure. "We have a positive gauge on mediums and copy," Lasker declared in 1906, "such as is probably to be found nowhere else." When an ad failed, the advertiser normally did not know whether to blame the copy or the medium. But at L & T, the question was simplified if a dozen different campaigns all bombed in one medium. "We know copy can't be wrong with all," Lasker explained, "so the paper comes under suspicion. If it is really weak, all our advertisers are out within a month, and there is a big aggregate saving."

Once under way, the record-of-results department churned out its findings routinely, providing a steady flow of hard data with which to pick media and impress clients. Lasker could turn his mind to his real love, the preparation of copy. Given what he called his "reportorial mind," he naturally embraced Kennedy's insistence that advertising was news, to be told without distracting stylistic flourishes like jingles. " 'Sunny Jim' is dead," said Kennedy. " 'Spotless Town' is off the map." In Kennedy and Hopkins, and then a long line of successors that would include many big names in copywriting, Lasker found the men to write copy his way, simple and unadorned, with a single compelling pitch. Regarding the business as an inborn talent, like singing, he hired writers with the requisite gifts at salaries of unprecedented generosity. He expected them to produce at once—"A fellow who didn't make good with them in a hurry didn't stay around," one of his copywriters recalled—and fired them quickly if they stumbled. Lord & Thomas, Lasker always insisted, was a *copy* agency. "What goes into the space—that makes the difference," he said in 1906. "Ninety per cent of the thought, energy and cost of running our agency goes into copy. We have stated that our copy staff costs us four times as much as that of any other agency. No one has disproved this statement."

As the agency's total annual billings kept climbing—from $800,000 in 1898 to $3,000,000 in 1905 and $6,000,000 in 1912—most of the credit went to its resident boy wonder. "Mr. Lasker enjoys a degree of confidence and an initiative," *Printers' Ink* commented, "that have probably been given to no man of his few years

in publishing or advertising affairs." Physically he was unremarkable: slim, of average height, he carried himself in a tight, bristly,
erect manner that made him seem larger. His face, ruddy in tint and
framed by large ears, was set off by heavy black eyebrows and large,
glittering, deep brown eyes. He dressed well, in styles that accen-
tuated his slimness, and had a fetish about close shaves. (Sitting in a
meeting, stroking his cheek, he might discover a stray whisker and
bolt the room to have it removed at once.) Knowing how he could
affect people, he played the role of Albert Lasker with great verve
and persistence. "He projected himself all the time," Fairfax Cone
remembered.

Associates were most struck by certain qualities of his mind and
personality. Apparently he read nothing but advertising materials
and the popular press. If utterly unintellectual, his mind was
breathtakingly quick and inventive, all but giving off sparks as he
applied it to some problem. "His thoughts catch up with his words,"
one observer noted, "and overtake them, and get ahead of them—
until at last he seems to be talking on six or seven different points of
the subject at the same time." The cascading flow of language could,
if he intended, effectively quash interruptions and rebuttals. As he
rushed along, he would sprinkle his discourse with odd oral punctuation marks—grunts and "hunh" and "d'you" (short for "do you
understand?"). Whether speaking or in a brief moment of listening,
he radiated a vibrating aura of vitality, of childlike curiosity and
bubbling humor, and an unarguable certainty that he was the dominant figure in the most important business in the world.

Amid all this success, he left occasional hints of darker strains. For
a man of such apparent self-confidence, he strangely resisted working with anyone else of comparable stature. "He'd never want anybody to be too darn smart," Lou Wasey reflected. "If you got too
smart, he thought you were getting too powerful." In 1912 he
bought out his partners and became sole owner of the biggest agency
in advertising; but that same year he suffered his first breakdown
and could not speak to anyone for five minutes without weeping un-
controllably. In fundamental ways he still craved his father's approval. For years he had a recurrent dream: after some notable
achievement, he would return to Galveston in glory, riding a white
horse, and dance on his father's kitchen table. As the dream kept repeating itself, it seemed he had not yet accomplished the necessary
feat. Indeed, in 1915 his father wrote Albert that his advertising
career was "but a trifle compared with what you were destined to

accomplish to humanity at large." Not arguing the point, Albert replied, "I am keenly alive to both my intellectual limitation and my lack of profound information. . . . All I have proved thus far is that I can make money. I know that I desire to do better things with my life."

In fact, even as he wrote he was spending long hours and thousands of dollars in legal fees to defend Leo Frank, a Jew accused of murder in Atlanta. (Spared a legal execution, Frank was then lynched.) Over the next few years Lasker delved into politics, handling publicity for Republican candidates in Illinois and nationally. In June 1918 he went out to Oyster Bay to meet Theodore Roosevelt. "They tell me you are America's greatest advertising man," said TR. "Colonel," Lasker replied, "no man can claim that distinction so long as you live." Lasker even managed—perhaps at the insistence of his doctors—to fit simple diversions into his jittery style. As a boy in Galveston he had watched the Chicago Cubs in spring training; now he bought a major share of the club. Though temperamentally unsuited to golf, he added a private eighteen-hole course to his suburban estate in Glencoe. He played regular, cutthroat poker with a group of old cronies, none of them in advertising. In city cultural and political affairs he was a large presence, "the uncrowned king of Chicago."

None of this substantially diverted him from his absorption in advertising. He bestrode his trade for so long because he never lost his quivering fascination for how it worked. Late in his career, he was leaving the office one day in evening clothes, accompanied by his chauffeur. He stopped by the desk of a new employee, Walter O'Meara, later a prominent copywriter. Looking over O'Meara's copy, Lasker said he needed to follow through more, to squeeze every idea dry. O'Meara listened ("that's all you ever did when the Great Man talked"). The chauffeur reminded Lasker of the late hour. Lasker grunted and waved him away, continuing to speak. Later the chauffeur interrupted again; Lasker started to leave, had another thought, came back. He left again, walked to the end of the hall, and came back once more. His guests, doubtless rich and powerful, would wait. Albert Lasker was talking advertising.

❧❧

As advertising matured it grew more effective. The art of Calkins & Holden, the copy of Kennedy and Hopkins, and the headlong drive and executive skills of Lasker together made advertising a force that not only moved goods but also might change how people lived. Yet to stay effective, advertising could not depart too far from established public tastes and habits: consumers might be nudged but still balk at being shoved. Ads necessarily *reflected* the times, and as an independent force they helped *shape* the times. Ads and their general historical context reinforced each other, forming a circle of cause and effect that doubled back and merged together. Advertising thus was always both mirror and mindbender, with the relative proportions of these two functions depending on the particular campaign in question—on the audacity of the advertiser, the malleability of the audience, and the skill of the agency's creative staff. A complex relationship, clouded by variables and imponderables, this double-edged role defies generalization and remains the fundamental chicken-and-egg riddle in advertising history.

Fashions in advertising copy and layout thus responded to both internal and external dynamics. Internally, the cycles of soft sell and hard sell—in this era, of jingles and reason-why—unwound according to the industry's own rhythms and its perception of the public's boredom level. These internal cycles continued all through the twentieth century, in apparent independence of the external historical context. But if the beholder's eye shifts from the advertising microcosm to the macrocosm of the times, the cycles of copy style seem more a mirror, less a self-contained independent force.

The Age of Lasker coincided with the cluster of political and social reforms that historians have called the progressive era. Along with most other aspects of American life, advertising came under progressive scrutiny—an examination prodded in part by the vogue of reason-why and salesmanship in print. The old trade characters and jingles sold gently, even obliquely, with charm and humor that respected the audience. The Lord & Thomas approach banned humor and fine writing as distractions from the essential task of selling a public unworthy of much respect. "People are like sheep," said Hopkins. "They cannot judge values, nor can you and I." Reason-why thus aimed its pitch at a lower common denominator, without undue concern over ethical considerations. Hopkins advertised a Reo automobile as the "farewell car" of the inventor, Ransom E. Olds; unaware of his alleged retirement, Olds protested the deception but probably did not mind the success of the campaign. *Judicious Advertising,* the Lord & Thomas house organ, solicited ads from magazines that were then rewarded with their own contracts from

the agency. The L & T copy department ground out *Judicious Adver-*
tising articles celebrating the favored clients, "and we felt no concern
about the ethics involved," John Orr Young recalled. As Lasker's
methods became the model for the industry, advertising presented a
more obvious target for reformers.

Patent-medicine advertising, the lineal ancestor of reason-why
copy, drew first attention. Banned from the advertising columns of
the *Ladies' Home Journal* since 1892, patent medicines were exposed
by a series of outraged *Journal* articles in 1904–05. "There is no evil
in America to-day so great as this accursed passion for self-doctor-
ing," declared editor Edward Bok. He printed a Lydia Pinkham ad
asserting that "Mrs. Pinkham, in her laboratory at Lynn, Massachusetts," could heal a sick woman better than the family doctor; next
to it Bok ran a photo of Lydia's tombstone, recording her death
twenty-two years earlier. Bok also published the American label of
Mrs. Winslow's Soothing Syrup alongside the label of the product's
English version which, as required by English law, was labeled a
poison because it included morphine. *Collier's Weekly* ran a series of
exposés, "The Great American Fraud," by Samuel Hopkins Adams
which revealed chemical analyses of scores of patent medicines;
Peruna, Adams noted, was banned on Indian reservations because
of its alcohol content.

Under these and other pressures, notably from women's clubs and
the American Medical Association, Congress passed the Pure Food
and Drug law of 1906. It forced product labels to list the active ingredients. Thus Lydia Pinkham now disclosed an 18 percent alcohol
content, made more modest claims about treating a prolapsed
uterus and pregnancy problems, and made no claims at all about
kidney diseases and "all weaknesses of the generative organs of
either sex." Unfortunately the law said nothing about advertising.
The patent-medicine manufacturers fixed their labels, proclaimed
their product now "guaranteed" under the Pure Food and Drug
law, went on advertising as before, and saw total sales rise 60 percent
from 1902 to 1912. It was a typical progressive exercise, pruning
branches while ignoring the root, depending on moral appeals and
publicity instead of tough legal enforcement.

Public opinion, it was supposed, would not support the regulation
of advertising, even of its more dubious forms. Year by year, advertising grew in volume and variety, constantly extending into new
media, ever more powerful and less avoidable. As editor of the *Nation*

since 1865, E. L. Godkin had witnessed the transformation of periodical and newspaper publishing by advertising. It seemed to him, and to other observers, that advertising now held dangerous power over public opinion. When newspapers depended on subscribers for their income, Godkin noted, editorial opinions had to respect the readership. "The advertiser, rather than the subscriber, is now the newspaper bogie," said Godkin. "He is the person before whom the publisher cowers and whom he tries to please. . . . There are not many newspapers which can afford to defy a large advertiser." Patent-medicine companies inserted a clause in their lucrative newspaper contracts stipulating that the contract would lapse if any bill adverse to the business passed that newspaper's state legislature, and even—in some cases—if the newspaper printed any unfriendly editorial matter. For any newspaper depending on patent-medicine money to survive, the clause effectively muzzled its freedom of expression. For some newspapers the arrangement was more direct: anyone placing a thousand-dollar ad in Hearst's *New York Journal,* it was rumored, could expect a favorable comment on the editorial page.

Even without such arrangements, the sheer volume of advertising appeared ominous. "There is no hour of waking life in which we are not besought, incited, or commanded to buy something of somebody," Samuel Hopkins Adams warned in another *Collier's* series in 1909. "Advertising has a thousand principles, one purpose, and no morals." Mr. Dooley, Finley Peter Dunne's idiot savant, complained indignantly that he had bought his favorite magazine and found over a quarter of its pages devoted to literature. Why, he had started reading an ad only to find it was really an article! If this dangerous trend continued, he warned, people would stop reading magazines: "A man don't want to dodge around through almost impenethrable pomes an' reform articles to find a pair iv suspinders or a shavin' soap."

Granted that advertising had meant more magazines and more readers, but what about the quality of the reading matter? Mr. Dooley was sure that literature had improved ("it has more to eat"). *Harper's* and the *Century,* the leading magazines of the 1880s, held to their high standards and lost steady ground to *McClure's* and the *Saturday Evening Post,* which pitched both ads and articles at the common denominator recommended by Claude Hopkins. Democratic in political terms, this process was vulgarizing by the standards of high culture. "I doubt if you gentlemen realize how much you can do to shape the tastes of the peoples of this country," Jane Addams told an advertising group in 1913. "Advertising is being read more and more, and I am sorry to say that some of it does not have a good moral effect."

So it went, with the critics deploring and the advertisers replying that they only gave the public what it wanted. The critics could count occasional small victories. A New York woman won a $6,000 judgment from Lydia Pinkham under a state law prohibiting the use of a photograph without the subject's permission. *Collier's* was awarded $50,000 in damages after C. W. Post, stung by the criticism of Samuel Hopkins Adams, claimed the magazine was picking on him simply because he did not advertise in it. But most of the critics focused on small-time, obvious frauds and left the major advertisers alone. Even Adams recommended no legislative remedies, only more public vigilance. As Theodore Roosevelt summed up the case against advertising in 1911, it involved mainly bogus financial schemes and the old standby, patent medicines. But the Post Office had recently cracked down on financial frauds, and no "respectable" magazine now carried patent-medicine notices. As to the bulk of advertising, TR had no complaints.

Public opinion might have supported a more extended critique. At least as reflected in popular fiction and drama, advertising and its practitioners were still not well esteemed. In the character of Lancelot Todd in some early short stories by Sinclair Lewis, in the novel *The Clarion* by Samuel Hopkins Adams, and in another novel, *H. R.* by Edwin Lefevre, an odor of snake oil and Peruna still clung to the advertising business. "We don't want our fictionists to spread the notion," *Printers' Ink* commented on *H. R.*, "that advertising is chiefly a means of exploiting the public by shrewd trickery." On Broadway, the play *It Pays to Advertise* by Roi Cooper Megrue presented the business so harshly that one agency, Sherman & Bryan, ran a series of ads in rebuttal. Another play, *Nothing But Lies* by Aaron Hoffman, depicted admen as liars and crooks who sold junk with the help of a corrupt politician. If ephemeral as literature, these works took on historical significance as unanimous condemnations of advertising; no dramatists or writers of fiction yet came forward to praise the trade in their work. "Some day," *Printers' Ink* predicted in summarizing this literary situation, "the writer is going to appear who knows the ad-man as he really is . . . based on his merits rather than his buffooneries."

Advertising, which paid its way by selling and building images, had its own image problem. The combined effects of progressive critics and popular literature could not be ignored. Among themselves, ad people might cover the problem with humor. "Advertising is the most prolific producer of fiction in modern times," the freelance copywriter Frank Irving Fletcher told the Sphinx Club in 1914. "Today it is almost an axiom that in order to discover the truth of an advertisement it is necessary to read between the *lies.*" More typically, people in the business would reassure each other of their essential honesty, of the unfairness of the critiques, with language that by its overstated hyperbole revealed lingering doubts—as though advertising might be improved by the repeated assertion of its virtues.

A more promising solution was self-organization leading to self-regulation, a system of internal restraints that would wipe out the external threat of government regulation. Local clubs of admen, first organized in the 1890s, joined in 1904 in a loose national federation, the Associated Advertising Clubs of America. A catholic group of anyone in the business—agencies, advertisers, and media representatives—the AACA muddled along until 1909, when Samuel C. Dobbs of Coca-Cola took over as president. As sales manager of his company, Dobbs had already advertised Coke into first place among soft drinks; he had good reason to believe in advertising and wanted to purify it. For two years he prodded the AACA, leading up to the convention in Boston in 1911 where over one hundred local clubs adopted the slogan of "Truth in Advertising." "We are men with a mission," Dobbs told the convention, "to educate the advertisers of the country that there is but one kind of advertising that will be permanently profitable." The group formed a Vigilance Committee to discover and correct abuses. Catching the spirit, later that year *Printers' Ink* had its "model" law drafted which, passed state by state, would make fraudulent advertising a misdemeanor.

Launched on a wave of enthusiasm, these efforts soon washed ashore. The AACA could not function as a union of all the warring tongs in advertising: agencies, advertisers, and media all had different interests and constituencies. Reorganized in 1914, the AACA was splintered a year later when the big advertisers left to found their own Association of National Advertisers. The AACA did carry out useful educational work by subsidizing books and lectures about the business. But it had no power, thus no effectiveness, in raising ethical standards. It was true, AACA president Herbert Houston conceded in 1915, that the Vigilance Committee was seldom heard from: "it rests on persuasion and education in the main and not on prosecution, save as a last resort. We believe that men want to do the right thing and that it is better to point out the right thing in a friendly way rather than to do it with a club." *PI*'s model law foundered on the same well-intended sentiments. Passed in twenty-three states in ten years, it produced few convictions. "Moral suasion is the chief weapon employed," *PI* explained.

In 1917 the agencies followed the advertisers out of the AACA to start their own group, the American Association of Advertising Agencies. Bruce Bliven, later editor of the *New Republic,* then writing for *Printers' Ink,* recorded his impressions of the founding convention in St. Louis: college cheers on arrival, the $2.50 hotel room temporarily "reduced" to $6, the hunt for a souvenir cane, "the struggle to look as though you always carried one," the bored newspaper reporter sitting in the lobby making up convention anecdotes, the cute young thing "who doesn't see how you think up all those clever ads," the delegate who played golf for three of the four days and did $27,000 worth of business out on the links, the concluding pageant best appreciated in the newspaper the next day. Amid these festivities, 111 charter-member agencies managed to launch the group. It issued a list of Agency Service Standards, a Standard Rate Card, and emphasized ethics and character in its qualifications for membership.

Some of the larger agencies, having no need for the AAAA, avoided it. "We didn't see what we had to gain by joining the association," Albert Lasker later explained. "A lot of people joined the association that we didn't think had any right to be advertising agents, and we didn't want to seem to be, by being in membership with them, giving approval to them. . . . Our second reason was, we were getting a much higher price than anyone in the line, but two or three. We didn't feel it was our business to educate these others how to get the higher price." Without the largest agency and the dominant personality in the business, the AAAA for a time lacked credibility. In the 1920s, led by a few major advertising figures, the group did establish itself. But its efforts to police ethical norms hardly surpassed the old AACA's. The ANA and AAAA had their purposes, with meaningful self-regulation not among them.

As before, reformers within advertising fell back on hopeful whistlings in the dark. In 1917 Charles Austin Bates took a look at the business after a dozen years away from it. Advertising, he reported, was now conducted less on grounds of friendship, more in terms of results. Earnest young men of high ideals hoped to dignify the profession, perhaps by licensing it. "Rampant righteousness in the advertising business is nowadays more a reality than a pose," Bates concluded. "The improvement in mental attitude and moral tone is vividly apparent."

❦❦

In fact, the next cycle of advertising copy proved a more effective reform measure than any specific, intentional effort from either inside or outside the business. The new style was called "impressionistic copy" or "atmosphere advertising." It made its pitch obliquely, by suggestion or association. It featured opulent art and striking layouts, striving for an impression of effortless high quality and class (layout and typefaces did not matter, Claude Hopkins insisted, or "any meaningless picture or display," since "people read ads, like everything else, because the subject is important to them"). The new style valued dignified, elegant writing as a complement to its high visual tone. ("Style is a handicap," Hopkins insisted. "Anything that takes attention from the subject reduces the impression.") Finally, instead of the shady patent-medicine, mail-order associations of reason-why, the new style conveyed an impression of honesty and clean ethics.

In all four respects the new style merely recalled the old style of Calkins & Holden, minus the jingles and trade characters. Once again the cycle spun around and delivered a venerable, discarded approach, with modifications, to be embraced as an innovation, the latest up-to-date model. The Calkins & Holden campaigns for Arrow collars and Pierce-Arrow cars were prominent examples of impressionistic advertising. "They are almost all picture," Cyrus Curtis noted. "It's the *atmosphere* in these that sells . . . the quality that gives prestige, the little imaginative sure touches that bring the thing before you." These techniques acquired theoretical support from *The Psychology of Advertising*, an influential book by Walter Dill Scott of Northwestern University. Reason-why copy, Scott insisted, had been oversold. Customers might on occasion be directly persuaded, but more often they bought because of a suggestion at the right psychological moment: "The actual effect of modern advertising is not so much to convince as to suggest." Taking this insight further, B. L. Dunn, ad manager for Oneida Community Silver, based his campaigns on beauty and pictures aimed at the unconscious minds of consumers. "The psycho-analysts have learned this about humankind," explained Dunn, an admirer of Freud and Jung, "that nearly all the important decisions of the individual are really made *in the subconscious.*" Of course, Calkins had already reached similar conclusions without the benefit of Freud and Jung; at least in this era, advertising psychology only justified and elaborated on what people were already doing. "We have all used it," one adman replied to Dunn, but "most of that highbrow stuff is 'bunk.' "

The leading advocate of advertising by atmosphere and suggestion was Theodore F. MacManus. As the star copywriter for General Motors, he produced ads specifically tailored to a particular kind of product. Cars like Buick and Cadillac were expensive items that customers bought infrequently, usually after careful planning and scrimping. So MacManus did not try to persuade his readers to go right out and buy the product. Instead, he aimed to build a durable image of reliable quality, year after year, that would send the consumer to General Motors whenever the big decision to buy was made. "We are haunted," he said in 1910, "by the ghost of mushroom reputations; quickly made and quickly lost. We see in the background next year, and the next, and ten years thereafter." Eye fixed on the future, he scorned quick, spectacular campaigns aimed at fast sales. Instead, in the same unhurried way that two people became friends, he aimed to build a friendship based on a slow accumulation of favorable impressions. "The real suggestion to convey," he insisted, "is that the man manufacturing the product is an honest man, and that the product is an honest product, *to be preferred above all others.*"

With his most famous ad, "The Penalty of Leadership," MacManus established himself as the leader of this school of advertising. Cadillac for years had built its reputation with a four-cylinder engine. Packard, its main rival among prestige cars, then came out with an engine of six cylinders. Raising the ante, in the fall of 1914 Cadillac announced a high-speed V-8 of British design. But the V-8 was skittery at first, prone to short circuits and fires. Packard made the most of Cadillac's problems. Having built for Cadillac an aura of reliability and high quality, MacManus now had to retrieve the situation with an advertisement. One day, late in the afternoon, pacing his office and puffing a cigar, he dictated the copy to his secretary. "In every field of human endeavor," said MacManus, "he that is first must perpetually live in the white light of publicity. . . . When a man's work becomes a standard for the whole world, it also becomes a target for the shafts of the envious few." (An indirect reference to Packard's advertising the V-8's problems.) Only the best artists, writers, musicians, and inventors were paid the compliment of unfair criticism. "There is nothing new in this. It is as old as the world and as old as the human passions—envy, fear, greed, ambition, and the desire to surpass. And it all avails nothing." Any real leader was invulnerable. "That which deserves to live—lives."

The copy did not mention Cadillac by name, or the V-8, or even automobiles. The ad ran once, with no illustration and wide margins of white space around the text, in the *Saturday Evening Post* of January 2, 1915. When MacManus came to lunch at the Detroit Athletic Club on the day that issue of the *Post* appeared, he was teased by his colleagues in advertising and the car business for writing a corny, implausible piece of fluff. But it worked. Cadillac was inundated with requests for reprints. Cadillac salesmen carried copies to give to prospects. Sales boomed. For years, an annual average of 10,000 copies were sent out on request. "The Penalty of Leadership" was tacked on walls, included in sales manuals, cited in sales meetings. Periodically Cadillac would use it again in direct mail and newspaper campaigns. "The real explanation of this astonishing popularity," MacManus offered, "is that almost every man considers himself a leader and secretly suspects that he is the victim of enmity and injustice." Perhaps for this reason, the ad inspired several generations of laborers in the competitive, insecure field of advertising. Thirty years after the ad first appeared, *Printers' Ink* asked its readers in the trade: What is the greatest advertisement of all time? "The Penalty of Leadership" won overwhelmingly, with the next-favorite ad a distant second.

Its durable popularity made MacManus the Claude Hopkins of soft sell. He came from a working-class Irish Catholic family in Toledo; his most vivid boyhood memory was the celebration of Grover Cleveland's Democratic victory in 1884. He left school young to work as an office boy in a Standard Oil department. At sixteen he started reporting for a Toledo newspaper and rose quickly to be managing editor. Later he went into department-store advertising in Pittsburgh, then sales management of coffee and wholesale grocery firms, then back to Toledo and his own advertising agency. GM brought him to Detroit. After "The Penalty of Leadership" he was offered a six-figure retainer to spend half his time in a Chicago agency. But he stayed in Detroit, working in an office on the thirteenth floor of the Fisher Building, commuting—by auto, of course—to his home in Bloomfield Hills.

To spurn a chance at the advertising big league in Chicago might have mystified his colleagues. But it faithfully reflected his style both in person and in copy. "He was a true figure of mystery," an associate recalled: "always quietly aloof; invariably absent from garrulous advertising cliques; a law unto himself." He was a large man, somewhat professorial, with a high forehead and rimless glasses. Unlike Hopkins, he had a life outside the trade. He liked golf and fishing and took two vacations a year, at his home on the Georgian Bay of Lake Huron in the summer and in Nassau in the winter. He read widely, especially in political philosophy and economics, wrote books on business topics, and privately published three volumes of his own poetry. In his intellectual depth and sense of proportion he resembled Elmo Calkins: it was no coincidence that they wrote similar copy. "I look upon the public as myself multiplied," said Mac-Manus, "and I have not yet reached that stage of diffidence and humility which permits me to write myself down as an Ass." Hopkins wrote down to the public, MacManus up to it.

In most respects the two men were mirror images of each other. Hopkins stressed the importance of pretesting a campaign—"I have never spent much money on a gamble or a guess"—and claimed a scientific rigor for his efforts. MacManus wrote his copy from his own imagination, based on what he himself would like to see in ads. Hopkins summed up his methods in his book *Scientific Advertising;* MacManus replied that people were moved by suggestions that were seldom systematic or scientific. According to MacManus, reason-why consisted of "a clever and semi-scientific application of the thesis that all men are fools" and assumed "in the mass-mind an almost invariable response to certain adroit and plausible appeals." His own approach, MacManus continued, "holds the mass-mind in somewhat higher esteem," offers "appeals of a substantial and more or less virtuous character," and "maintains that while men may be fools and sinners, they are everlastingly on the search for that which is good."

No doubt Hopkins would have quarreled with these distinctions. Yet Lord & Thomas could not ignore the competition from this new school of advertising. Having ridden reason-why to the top of the business, Lasker could not accept the use of impressionistic copy and lavish art and layout. "I hated to see ... this great force dolled up like a Christmas tree, in things utterly extraneous," Lasker said later. One of his million-dollar accounts, Goodyear Tire, asked Lasker for more atmosphere, less reason-why in its ads. He refused the request and paid for his stubbornness: three of his men left Lord & Thomas—with the Goodyear account—and started their own agency, Erwin, Wasey & Jefferson, to give the client what it wanted.

In general, though, these two schools of advertising coexisted in a sniping stalemate. Reason-why did not give way to suggestion in the sudden, dramatic fashion that reason-why had pushed aside jingles and trade characters. Instead, each claimed its adherents, in large measure depending on the product to be advertised. The Hopkins style worked best for small, frequently purchased items like cigarettes, toothpaste, and soap that could be cheaply offered as samples and sent through the mail. "The products that I like to advertise most are those that are only used once," said Lasker. The Mac-Manus style was best applied to large, expensive, durable items with prestige associations, bought infrequently and seldom on impulse. Surrounded by what MacManus called "an invisible cloud of friendly, favorable impressions," the product would all but sell itself at the proper time. If Hopkins insisted that suggestion copy lacked selling punch, MacManus could as plausibly reply that reason-why lacked dignity.

Once, in the 1930s, MacManus let his partners talk him into actively soliciting a certain account. He disliked the crassness of such pursuits but went along for the presentation to the prospective client. Toward the end of the meeting the client turned to MacManus and asked if he would care to say a few words. "On what subject?" asked MacManus.

❧❧

A little more than two years after the appearance of "The Penalty of Leadership," another external event intruded on advertising's internal cycles. The United States entered the World War. Manufacturers who converted from making consumer goods to war production still wanted to keep their name familiar to the public; other manufacturers still producing consumer articles felt constrained by patriotism, or fear of reaction, from pushing nonessential articles during a time of national crisis and scarcity. For both kinds of manufacturers, the solution was advertising in the MacManus style. It kept company names and trademarks in the public eye by dropping reason-why in favor of grandiloquent essays under such headlines as "Dependability" and "Principles" and "The Truth That Embodies All Truth." By extolling the firm as an institution, in its commitment to lofty ideals, this "institutional" style of advertising maintained ad budgets without giving offense and—coincidentally—helped establish the MacManus approach.

Meantime campaigns in the more pointed, reason-why tradition helped sell the war itself. Arguing for the establishment of his Committee on Public Information, the journalist George Creel had promised Woodrow Wilson "a plain publicity proposition, a vast enterprise in salesmanship, the world's greatest adventure in advertising." Wilson bought the proposition, and the Creel Committee spawned endless divisions to shape public opinion: one to make movies, another to make posters, another to organize novelists and professors to explain the war, another to coordinate some 75,000 "Four Minute Men" in delivering brisk, exhorting speeches; and so on, endlessly. In this welter of activity, an Advertising Division under the direction of five prominent figures in the trade supervised the placing of $1.5 million worth of donated ad space and copy. Private advertisers also featured war themes and Liberty Loan appeals in their own campaigns.

At the time, the near-unanimity of public opinion on the war allowed the advertising industry a new and bolder sense of its power. "Advertising has earned its credentials as an important implement of war," *Printers' Ink* concluded. The most ubiquitous ad was written by Courtland N. Smith of the Joseph Richards agency in New York for the Red Cross. Entitled "The Greatest Mother in the World," it presented a beatific woman in a nurse's uniform as the embodiment of the Red Cross ("Seeing all things with a mother's sixth sense that's blind to jealousy and meanness; seeing men in their true light, as naughty children—snatching, biting, bitter—but with a hidden side that's quickest touched by mercy"). Artists such as Charles Dana Gibson, Howard Chandler Christy, and James Montgomery Flagg turned out posters for loan campaigns and military enlistments, for vigilance against traitors and the conservation of war materials in the home. Flagg did a famous rendering of Uncle Sam, with piercing eyes and pointing finger, declaring "I Want YOU for

U.S. Army." "A number of us," Flagg later recalled in hindsight, "who were too old or too scared to fight prostituted our talents by making posters inciting a large mob of young men who had never done anything to us, to hop over and get shot at. . . . We sold the war to youth."

Again the problem of chicken or egg: did the screaming ritual of wartime patriotism reflect the shaping of advertising, or did that advertising merely support and extend the temper of the time? In this case, probably more of the latter. Wilson explained the war as a conflict between idealism and aggression, democracy and autocracy. The public so bought this pitch that it allowed, even insisted on, the worst violations of civil liberties in American history. Even before the establishment of the Creel Committee's Advertising Division, vigilante groups of superpatriots sprang up spontaneously to root out German influences and enforce devotion to the war. The Creel Committee had only to fan these flames. One of its booklets, "The Kaiserite in America," urged the suppression of such traitorous notions as calling the conflict "a rich man's war" or "a businessman's war." A poster aimed at labor unions warned, "American industry can and will win this war for human liberty. Breeders of industrial war at home must be eliminated." So it went, with over 1,500 arrests under wartime alien and sedition acts, the censorship of the press and the mail, the renaming of German measles and dachshunds as liberty measles and liberty pups. American advertising took part in this dubious process, but it was only one voice in an overwhelming roar of enthusiasm.

"The work, as a whole, was nothing more than an advertising campaign," Creel said afterward to an advertising convention, "and I freely admit that success was won by close imitation of American advertising methods and through the generous and inspirational cooperation of the advertising profession." Before the war, he went on, "your status was anomalous. Today, by virtue of government recognition as a vital force in American life, you stand recognized as a profession." In at least one sense, which he did not intend, he was right. With national energies focused on the great crusade, the war killed off most progressive reform movements, including the critics of advertising. Applied to a cause perceived as the public good, advertising did emerge from the war in higher standing.

In general, though, advertising prospered most not during the war but during the peace. After the armistice in November 1918, manufacturers raised their ad budgets for the return to a consumer economy. Threatened by an excess-profits tax, companies needed to spend their extra income quickly, in a manner that could be justified as a business expense. So they invested lavishly in advertising: full pages in newspapers, double pages in magazines, with more illustrations and wider borders to fill the space. In only two years the total annual volume of advertising *doubled,* from $1.5 billion worth in 1918 to just under $3 billion in 1920. This surge would propel the business into the decade of its greatest influence on American life.

"The advertising man is the enfant terrible of the time, unabashed before the eternities," declared S. N. Behrman in the *New Republic* in 1919. "Even war needs him, to say nothing of Swift and Company." He was typically young, said Behrman, handsome, impeccably dressed, with sleek hair and snappy shoes. His prominence in American life made him as self-satisfied as a movie actor. "The cornerstone of the most respectable American institutions; the newspapers and magazines depend on him; Literature and Journalism are his hand maidens. He is the Fifth Estate."

THREE

HIGH TIDE AND GREEN GRASS: THE TWENTIES

When in 1931 Frederick Lewis Allen wrote *Only Yesterday,* his classic reminiscence of the 1920s, he felt obliged to begin the book with a bemused description of the far-away world inhabited by a typical American family in 1919. From a vantage point of only a dozen years later, Allen already had to describe pre-1920s life in the wondering tones of an anthropologist describing an exotic culture from the distant past. Flashing ahead, Allen wondered how his 1919 family would deal with salient aspects of the coming decade: some transient (home-run records, boxing gates, Mah-Jongg), some timeless (inflation and women's fashions), some extensions of things on hand (airplanes, cigarettes, sexuality, Wall Street, paved highways, and fast cars), some new and startling (prohibition, organized crime, jazz, radio broadcasts, tabloid newspapers, and vitamins). "Since 1919," Allen concluded, "the circumstances of American life have been transformed."

Amid these fluid circumstances, advertising took on new powers. The first national experience with total war had cracked society open, leaving broken certitudes and discarded patterns. "Are we going to rest upon the record of advertising as a factor in the war," one adman asked in 1919, "or are we going to develop it still further, to apply it to the many fields in which it can serve in reconstruction and the days of peace?" Just approaching maturity, the advertising industry stood ready with fresh patterns. New products—not merely new versions of familiar items—changed American life, down to its most intimate details, with a speed and totality that left observers groping for precedents.

Novelists and politicians agreed in describing the decade as an entrepreneurial riot. Advertising grew fat in a buyer's market, with distribution and marketing replacing production as the natural limit on industrial activity. Standing athwart the pipeline, between the factory and the consumer, advertising found a pliant audience for the gospel that the road to happiness was paved with more goods and services. More than ever before or since, American culture and American advertising converged on a single point. Advertising reached its apogee when it became hard to distinguish between ad life and real life. ("You resemble the advertisement of the man," Daisy Buchanan told Jay Gatsby in the Fitzgerald novel. "You know the advertisement of the man—.") Ad life and real life, it seemed, both offered a clean, orderly existence, a cornucopia of products and promises. Advertising would never again have it so plush: the public so uncritically accepting, the economy so robust, the government so approving; the trade at its zenith, high tide and green grass.

❧❧

The J. Walter Thompson agency led the advertising industry into this first great boom in its history. Innovative in both copy styles and the variety of services offered to clients, JWT swept past the competition into first place in total billings, an eminence it would keep for five decades. In a business normally described as ulceratingly unstable, Thompson year after year stood as an unassailable citadel, repelling successive waves of pretenders to the crown. This durable achievement belongs preeminently to Stanley and Helen Resor, husband and wife, a team of oddly matched but complementary skills and dispositions.

Advertising more than most businesses responds to the caprices and gifts of individual personalities. Especially in its creative aspects, advertising is intensely personal, depending on a particular individual's particular taste, inspiration, and sense of proportion. Most agencies in their successful periods have taken their identities from the lengthened shadows of one or two leading figures. Agencies then often stumble when the leader falters or departs. The hole at the top is not adequately filled. Even in agencies controlled by one family, dynastic successions are rare: few children of advertising figures go into the business; of those who do, even fewer work for the family agency; of these still fewer carry on with the verve and effect of the parent. For these reasons, then, finding the next generation of leaders remains a recurrent dilemma of agency management.

In the case of J. Walter Thompson, the man, after forty years in advertising he had lost touch. When W. G. Woodward, later a successful novelist and historian, went to work at JWT in 1907, he found the place years behind the times. While Elmo Calkins and Albert Lasker were making the preparation of art and copy the crucial agency functions, at Thompson the account executives still personally owned their accounts, changing copy when they pleased and treating copywriters like office boys. Thompson himself was remote and uninvolved. "Somewhere along the road to success," according to Woodward, "he had mislaid his mind and had to go on thereafter without it. He had not done any thinking in years." Thompson would make periodic inspection trips to his branch offices in Boston, Chicago, and other cities. There he would quiz employees on their command of grammar, check their appearance and deportment. At one picnic of a local advertising club he scolded his people for sipping highballs and thereby soiling the agency's image.

Meantime, and none too soon, Stanley Resor had started his fast climb to the succession at JWT. Graduated from Yale in 1901, he had returned to his hometown of Cincinnati. Before finding his metier he worked in a bank and then for a machine-tool company. Lacking technical training in machinery, he felt inadequate as a salesman of machine tools. So, as he recalled it, he looked for a job in which he could become an authority, "knowing as much as any one in the field." His older brother Walter worked for Procter & Collier, an advertising firm that functioned mainly as the house agency in Cincinnati for Procter & Gamble. With Walter's help Stanley joined the agency in March 1904 as a salesman.

There he met Helen Lansdowne, seven years his junior and one year out of high school. After a brief stint at auditing bills for Procter & Collier she left to write retail ads for a Cincinnati newspaper, then moved on again to write copy for a streetcar advertising company. Back at Procter & Collier, Stanley Resor quickly acquired a reputation for relentless drive and persistence. A hard worker who squeezed total efforts from his subordinates, he also proved himself an imaginative planner of advertising campaigns. For a window-shade manufacturer he coined the brand name BRENLIN and helped devise a method for perforating this name in the margin of the shade cloth. "At that time," he recalled, "all window shade material was unmarked, unidentifiable by the consumer, hence subject to sharp trade practices and at the mercy of straight price competition." Resor's campaign in women's magazines persuaded women to buy the higher-priced, standardized brand. For another client, the Higgin All Metal Screen Company of Newport, Kentucky, he aimed his pitch at middle-class women who previously had used cheaper wooden screens for privacy in their bedrooms. "The use of this type of screen," he noted, "was in less than three years extended to homes of the *middle* classes—before it had been confined to houses of the rich." Already, in these early campaigns, Resor had established two enduring aspects of his approach to advertising: the coining of brand names, and the education of a given social class to imitate the habits of richer people.

Resor neither then nor later wrote the actual copy. Needing a copywriter in 1907, he remembered Helen Lansdowne. He came calling at her family's home in Covington, Kentucky, across the Ohio River from Cincinnati. Her family warned her not to accept his offer: he'll work you to death, they said. The streetcar advertising firm had offered her a job in the company's main office in New York. But for the time being she agreed to work for Stanley Resor in Cincinnati. A year later he decided to move on to a larger agency. JWT asked him to manage its Chicago branch; when he declined Thompson instead hired Stanley and Walter Resor to open a branch in Cincinnati. Helen Lansdowne came along as the sole copywriter in the office.

Most Thompson clients made products to be bought by women as the ultimate consumers. "In advertising these products I supplied the feminine point of view," Lansdowne said later. "I watched the advertising to see that the idea, the wording, and the illustrating were effective for women." For Woodbury's Facial Soap, which came to JWT in 1910, she made ads that increased sales by 1,000 percent in eight years. When Procter & Gamble introduced Crisco, a vegetable shortening, in 1911, the company broke a rule of twenty years' standing and paid an outside agency, JWT, a fee to prepare the opening campaign. On five occasions Lansdowne appeared before the P & G board of directors—the first woman to do so—to explain the advertising. Over the next few years she also wrote the original ads for Yuban coffee (a name coined by Stanley Resor), Lux soap flakes, and Cutex nail polish. "I was the first woman," she claimed, "to be successful in writing and planning national, as opposed to retail, advertising." Most of these successes came after her promotion to JWT headquarters in New York in 1911.

To replace her as a copywriter in Cincinnati Resor hired James Webb Young, who would become the third key member of the team that pushed JWT to dominance in the 1920s. A schoolmate of Helen Lansdowne in Covington, he quit school in the sixth grade to go to work in Cincinnati. Eventually he wrote mail-order advertising for book publishers in New York and Chicago. On Lansdowne's recommendation he went to see Stanley Resor, "and much to my surprise," Young recalled, "he offered me a job as copywriter." Arguing that he should not change jobs just for a raise, Resor offered Young only his current salary of forty dollars a week; Young demurred until Resor came up to sixty dollars. In a few years, with Resor spending more and more time in New York, Young succeeded him as head of the Cincinnati office. Still a small operation, this branch let all hands help out in the production of ads: "Everybody had a chance to be a part of everything," said Young, "from making the plan to wrapping up the cuts for the last train that would catch a closing date."

With this young talent snapping at his heels, old J. Walter Thompson decided to retire. In 1916 a group headed by Stanley Resor bought him out for a half-million dollars; Resor succeeded him as president and started cleaning house. Though total billings stood at just under $3 million, the agency had been losing money on many small accounts. Resor cut the client list from over three hundred to under eighty, reorienting JWT permanently toward big national accounts. Anemic local branches in Toronto, Cleveland, and Detroit were closed, and unneeded employees were fired. Only eight years after joining the Cincinnati office, Resor found himself in control of the whole company. One final act of consolidation remained. At some point the professional relationship of Resor and Lansdowne turned into something more. In March 1917, at the ages of thirty-one and thirty-eight, they were married in New York.

At the agency they continued to divide the tasks as before. In general, Stanley tended to administration and client services while Helen concentrated on the preparation of ads. But informally they discussed all aspects of the business, over the dinner table or on the commuter train to Greenwich, so decisions typically emerged with no clear line of accountability to either one. Under the Resors the Thompson agency took on a certain faceless anonymity; not for them an agency star system blaring the talents of a Calkins, Hopkins, or MacManus. Advertising was not "a matter of cleverness and immaturity," said Stanley, linking the two qualities in a revealing association. "The advertising firm which is equipped to do thorough work," he insisted, "is not a loose aggregation of brilliant individuals." Though one of the celebrated copywriters of her generation, Helen Resor held no vice-presidency at the agency, gave no speeches, turned down requests for interviews. "Publicity of this kind does not appeal to me," she explained. Stanley distrusted individual opinions—except Helen's—and operated by consensus, rejecting organization charts and rigid lines of authority in favor of what he called "cross-fertilization" from assorted minds.

Like most Yale undergraduates of his day, Resor in college had been much affected by the popular lectures of the sociologist William Graham Sumner. Human beings, Sumner taught, were not favored individuals created by a benevolent deity for some special purpose, but rather faceless parts of a moiling mass bumping its way forward through the impersonal processes of evolution. They were governed not by reason but by the heedless, irrational drives of hunger, vanity, fear, and sexuality. Folkways, the mores of society, developed at the slow and steady pace of a glacier, oblivious to the deflecting efforts of governments or reform movements. Though politically individualist in embracing laissez faire economics, the Sumner viewpoint ultimately submerged the individual in the gropings and flailings of mass man.

Perhaps in college, perhaps later, Resor was also impressed by Henry Thomas Buckle's *History of Civilization in England.* Published in 1857, before the vogue of Darwinian evolution that so persuaded Sumner, the Buckle volume nonetheless also stressed the study of whole populations, not individuals. Lacking free will, humans could still best work out their own destinies, without government or church interference, according to general historical laws. Civilization depended on the distribution of wealth, which depended on population, which depended on food, which depended on climate. Buckle constructed these tiers of historical causality on endless tables of statistics, from which he with a grand insouciance inferred all sorts of human motivations. Already, by the early twentieth century, his fellow historians had spurned Buckle's Victorian certitudes.

But to Stanley Resor the book still made sense, and for years any important new employee at JWT was required to peruse it.

Echoes of Sumner and Buckle showed up in key places at JWT under Resor's management: a political economy of rugged individualism free of meddling government, an interest in the group and the mass instead of individuals, the tapping of irrational drives by advertising, and a faith in statistics to describe and predict human behavior. As the first great advertising executive from a college background, Resor aimed to create a "university of advertising," a community of scholars and experts who would give the business new standards of precision and rationality. "Advertising, after all, is educational work, mass education," he insisted. Soon after taking over he started a training course that went beyond the copywriting school taught by Lasker at Lord & Thomas. All new male employees above the clerical level spent time in the various agency departments, with some training in each, before specializing in the work that most suited them. Copywriters and artists were sent into the field, to sell behind the counter or to ring doorbells and interview housewives, in order to acquire a visceral feel for retail problems and consumer tastes.

More formal market study relied on Buckle's darling, the sifting of population statistics. Resor had set the pattern here as early as 1912. Red Cross Shoes, one of the clients he had brought to Thompson from Procter & Collier, was hobbled by a haphazard distribution pattern, in part because no one knew where the appropriate retail outlets were located. Resor commissioned a study, *Population and Its Distribution,* which listed stores by category—grocery, drug, hardware, dry goods, clothing—and by state. The volume was then expanded and updated every five years or so. The 1920 edition, 218 pages, sold for $2.50 and (according to JWT's advertisement) was used by 2,300 companies; it described the consumer population in the radius of all major metropolitan centers and presented lists of all the towns with 500 or more residents in a given state, the number of wholesale and retail stores in cities with over 100,000 residents, and so on. These and other JWT efforts, along with the concurrent investigations by C. C. Parlin of the Curtis Publishing Company, provided the hard factual basis for the development of modern marketing research.

Claude Hopkins, aiming at his lowest common denominator, had declared that advertising had no place for the college man. Stanley

Resor by contrast liked to point out the number of college graduates and doctorates on his staff. In 1922 Paul Cherington, who had taught marketing at Harvard Business School for a dozen years, became JWT's director of research. As he explained it, surplus consumer income and the burgeoning cornucopia of available goods brought special marketing problems. "Consumption is no longer a thing of needs, but a matter of choices freely exercised," said Cherington. "The consumer's dollar is not a coin wholly mortgaged to the necessary task of providing a bare living. It has in it a generous segment to be spent at the consumer's own option as to what he will buy, and when he will buy, and where." Consumer tastes—such as preferences for brown eggs in Boston and white eggs in New York—were mysteriously unpredictable and beyond the reach of common sense. So Cherington conducted endless rounds of consumer surveys. Questionnaires were drawn up, with the questions formulated "so as to secure the truthful answers with a minimum of distortion due to self-consciousness," and administered in person or by mail. A disciple of Frederick Winslow Taylor, the prophet of scientific management, Cherington then tabulated his data and came up with astringently quantified answers to the imponderables of advertising.

At least to its marketing aspects, that is. To help place the actual preparation of ads on a more scientific basis, Resor hired another former academic, the psychologist John B. Watson. As one of the founders of behaviorism, the most empirically scientific and practical-minded of psychologies, Watson claimed to have found basic techniques for predicting and manipulating human actions. In simple terms, advertising informed by behaviorism needed to exploit the bedrock human drives of love, fear, and rage. (Here Watson found common ground with Resor's old professor Graham Sumner.) "To make your consumer react," Watson promised his advertising colleagues, "it is only necessary to confront him with either fundamental or conditioned emotional stimuli."

Upon joining the agency he was sent through the usual training program. For ten weeks he made his rounds selling Yuban coffee to grocers; he spent another two months as a clerk in a department store. "I saw I would have to more or less junk my psychological training," he noted. His academic learning included nothing about industry or consumer tastes. At the same time, he was appalled by the "terrific waste" in the advertising business. "No one knows just what appeals to use," he told a fellow psychologist. "It is all a matter of 'instinctive' judgement. Whether I can establish certain principles or not remains to be seen." One of his early successes was a controlled blindfold test revealing that people could not recognize their favorite brand of cigarette; it followed that cigarettes could not be advertised by rational appeals. Watson conducted employment, intelligence, and performance tests for the agency, and made speeches about the uses of behaviorism. After a few years he was promoted to a vice-presidency and became an account executive. Given prominent office space and liberal exposure to admiring clients, Watson functioned as a persuasive example of JWT's efforts to make advertising a science. Other agencies began to speak the language of psychology. Critics grew alarmed about an insidious psychological sell.

All of this amounted to more appearance than substance. "There is one psychologist of high attainment in one New York advertising agency," a prominent adman pointed out in 1928. "So far as those familiar with many agencies know, his situation is unique." Even at Thompson, Watson had less impact than some authorities have suggested. As he acknowledged at the time, the uses of psychology in advertising had been "greatly oversold." Employment tests had little value in the selection of personnel, said Watson; better just to train people on the job. Years later, Watson recalled that agencies and clients paid little attention to their resident psychologists until the 1940s. Watson's presence at Thompson faithfully reflected Stanley Resor's vision of what an agency should be: a serious, quiet, professional place of dispassionate scholarly inquiry. But Watson had no significant original, shaping impact on the actual product of the agency. "Advertising absorbed John," James Webb Young later concluded, "without absorbing much of his psychology."

Art and copy fell under the aegis of Helen Resor, whose approach was essentially intuitive and esthetic instead of scientific. Her favorite advertising media were the Curtis flagships, the *Ladies' Home Journal* and *Saturday Evening Post*. (The October 1921 issue of the *Journal* carried ads for fourteen JWT clients.) She developed an "editorial style" of advertising that imitated the look and layout of the Curtis magazines and so caught the reader's eye by resembling nearby reading matter. In a typical Helen Resor ad, beneath a pretty painting the gently pointed selling copy gave various arguments for buying the product, and then capped the case with an offer of a free or cheap sample by mail. She thus blended the visual appeal of Calkins with the reason-why and proffered coupon of Hopkins: a powerful combination.

Her most famous ad, for Woodbury's Facial Soap, established this style with a painting by Alonzo Kimball of a handsome couple in evening dress, the man embracing the woman from the side, the woman smiling and winsomely looking away. Beneath the painting, the headline "A skin you love to touch," followed by seven paragraphs of copy. "Your skin is changing every day! As the *old* skin dies, *new* skin forms in its place. *This is your opportunity.* By using the proper treatment you can keep this new skin so active that it cannot help taking on the greater loveliness you have longed for." Then "the most famous skin treatment ever formulated": wash with Woodbury's, working the lather into the skin, "always with an upward and outward motion," rinse with warm and then cold water, and finish by rubbing the face with a piece of ice. Next the offer: for ten cents, an eight-color reproduction of the Kimball painting and a week's supply of the soap. Finally, in a corner of the page, a picture of the soap and a fine-print suggestion to "Tear out this cake as a reminder to get Woodbury's today at your druggist's or toilet counter."

It was a packed ad, no detail neglected, yet with an open, airy, uncluttered look to it. The reader's eye riveted on the headline in the center of the page. Later ads in the series appeared with different illustrations but kept that headline with its muted sexuality. "The phrase sings itself into your memory," the sober *Atlantic Monthly* commented. "The pictures of this famous series have probably been seen by more people at one time than any others ever painted." Previous ads had exploited sex and pretty women, but none with the effect and persistence of the Woodbury's campaign. From the perspective of several decades later, Albert Lasker declared the three great landmarks in advertising history to be Ayer's introduction of the open contract, his own development of reason-why, and JWT's use of sex appeal in the Woodbury's ad. (The campaign began, it should be noted, several years before Watson joined the agency and started explaining the psychological wallop of tapping irrational drives.)

Jim Young approached another indecent subject, underarm odor, in his daring campaign for a deodorant. A Cincinnati surgeon had invented Odorono after being hampered by perspiration during an operation on a hot summer day in 1907. The surgeon's daughter,

Edna Albert, started marketing the product to women. (Men kept their coats on and were expected to smell anyway.) In 1919 Young wrote an Odorono ad under the headline "Within the Curve of a Woman's Arm," thus avoiding the problem of mentioning the armpit. "It is a physiological fact," the copy went on, "that persons troubled with perspiration odor seldom can detect it themselves." In the wake of the ensuing controversy, the *Journal* of the American Medical Association warned that Odorono was dangerous. Two hundred readers of the *Ladies' Home Journal* canceled their subscriptions. "Disgusting" and "an insult to women," several female acquaintances told Young, and they promised never to speak to him again. Odorono sales went up 112 percent in a year.

Young, like Helen Resor, wrote ads from his own imagination and held no particular reverence for social scientists. He did not share what he called Stanley Resor's "somewhat naive respect for the Ph.D." When the Maxwell House coffee account came to JWT in 1928, Young remembered his days as a Bible salesman traveling through the South, when he would occasionally stay at the original Maxwell House in Nashville. Young sent a copywriter, Ewing Webb, down to Nashville to live at the Maxwell House, soak up atmosphere, and go through old newspaper files looking for anecdotes from the hotel's social history. Young and Ewing then prepared a campaign (rich with moonlight and magnolia and happy darkies playing in the background) about the hotel, the coffee, and their cheerful old-time associations. The account executive, Milt Blair, who had been trained in market data by C. C. Parlin at Curtis Publishing, had useful advice for sales planning. But the ads, Young insisted, owed little to social science. "The only 'research' done was for copy material in the files of the newspaper," he recalled. "The rest was 'intuitive,' growing out of a certain range of personal experience, out of advertising experience, out of editorial sense for what is interesting, out of people who had writing skills, and out of art and illustrative skills."

One of the most successful devices used at Thompson during the 1920s was simply an up-scaled version of an old technique, the testimonial. Despite a lingering unsavory association with patent medicines, the testimonial had never disappeared. The World War gave it a boost, as soldiers in Europe wrote home to manufacturers in praise of their razors, toothpaste, and candy. Helen Resor took this old form and gave it new credibility by obtaining endorsements from famous people, not just ordinary citizens. The breakthrough came in 1924 when Mrs. O. H. P. Belmont, the doyenne of New York society and a prominent feminist as well, gave her name to Pond's cold cream in exchange for a donation to charity. With that precedent, JWT could get other "great lady" endorsements, both in the U.S. and abroad. "Distinguished in the society of five nations," read one headline, "they trust their beauty to the same sure care." An ad in the *Ladies' Home Journal* featuring the Queen of Rumania pulled in 9,435 coupon replies; Mrs. Reginald Vanderbilt brought 10,325 replies, and the Duchess de Richelieu hit the jackpot with 19,126.

The technique worked as well for other Thompson clients. Fleischmann's Yeast was advertised as a bountiful source of vitamins and therefore a sure cure for acne, constipation, feeling tired, and other ills. The American Medical Association warned its members against attaching their names to any such dubious claims. So William L. Day, the account executive for Fleischmann's, followed the trail of Pond's to Europe and found doctors unencumbered by the AMA who would say anything at all about Fleischmann's for five hundred dollars. They stared from the pages of American magazines, typically with pointy Vandyke beards and gesturing pencils, prescribing yeast for rheumatism, headaches, old age, and even the common cold. Day, not surprisingly, concluded that the American consumer had the average mentality of a fourteen-year-old.

"Nine out of ten screen stars," announced a new JWT ad in 1927, "care for their skin with Lux toilet soap." The stars were rounded up by Danny Danker, Thompson's representative in Hollywood, a rococo Boston Irishman out of Exeter and Harvard. Known as "the Lux Playboy," a Hollywood celebrity in his own right, Danker lived on a lavish expense account and knew his way around the studios. He signed up starlets when they were unknowns, getting their names in exchange for a crateful of Lux. Then, if they made it, he put them in Lux ads for no further expense. Joan Crawford ("Never have I had anything like it for keeping the skin smooth"), Clara Bow, Janet Gaynor, and many others appeared to testify for Lux.

Appeared to testify. They had not actually spoken the words attributed to them. If they used the product at all, they did not necessarily prefer it to other products. Despite the famous names, JWT's testimonials were no more honest than others. Stanley Resor had helped found the American Association of Advertising Agencies and had written its statement of ethical standards. A pillar of unbending rectitude, he would not solicit accounts or allow speculative campaigns. He wanted to make advertising as respectable as any other profession: the JWT letterhead did not mention advertising because, he said, J. P. Morgan did not have to identify himself as a banker. Yet at the same time Resor allowed unbuttoned tactics by some of his subordinates.

The testimonials, indeed most Thompson campaigns, appealed to those irrational drives—some parlay of vanity, fear, and jealousy. "The spirit of emulation," Stanley Resor called it. "We want to copy those whom we deem superior in taste or knowledge or experience," he explained. He typically fell back on social science for an authority: "The desire to emulate is stronger in women than in men. Lombroso, the celebrated psychologist, explains it in terms of woman's ability to excite her imagination with external objects." Helen Resor probably knew it without the benefit of Lombroso. If a woman used Woodbury's she would be nuzzled by a handsome man in evening clothes. If she bought an inexpensive jar of Pond's, only fifty cents, she acquired the same cold cream that titled European nobility put on their faces. Maxwell House coffee imparted the unhurried grace of the old South.

These successes pushed the agency's total annual billings from $10.7 million in 1922 to $20.7 million in 1926 and $37.5 million by the end of the decade. In 1927 the New York office moved into the new Graybar Building, adjacent to Grand Central Station. "That we shall be the largest tenants in the world's largest office building," a house ad pointed out, "is an interesting fact to those who can remember the days when even the foremost advertising agencies needed little more than desk room." The lush two-story conference room was designed by Norman Bel Geddes. Helen Resor supervised the decor and arrangement of the executive offices on the eleventh floor. The offices with windows on the outside of the building were separated from inner offices by iron grilles, not walls, so that secretaries might partake of the view. The executive dining room was reconstructed from an eighteenth-century farmhouse in Ipswich, Massachusetts. Kettle irons swung from the fifteen-foot fireplace, and ad executives ate off pewter dishes at an antique maple table. The wrought-iron door of Watson's office told the history of printing in eighteen panels. Individual offices were lavishly appointed according to the tastes of the occupant. A tour of the floor meant a trip through architectural history.

On the northwest corner of the floor, in his seigneurial office with rich English paneling, Stanley Resor presided over this domain like a benevolent constitutional monarch. He rendered his decisions in subtle ways—a look in the eye, a nod of the head, a flick of the hand—and seldom raised his voice or gave direct orders. But nobody questioned his authority. "In appearance he had more than a touch of the aristocrat, in character and personal habits a trace of the Scotch Covenanter," Jim Young recalled. "He had the greatest tenacity of purpose of any man I ever knew." At the opposite end of the floor from Stanley's office, Helen Resor had her own turf, a wing of women copywriters whom she hired, trained, and mothered. "She encouraged me to rent paintings and sculpture from the Museum of Modern Art, to have very good clothes, to work with top decorators at home and in the office," one of her protégées, Peggy King, said later. "She was proud of us and gave us pride. She looked after us, knowing that we needed a friend in court." These women handled most of the food, soap, and cosmetic accounts that were the agency's mainstay; thus, aside from her direct line to Stanley, Helen had the clout to get the attention of the male executives at the other end of the floor.

Although a prominent voice in the AAAA, otherwise Stanley seemed an elusive figure in advertising circles. He was seldom found at the clubs and restaurants favored by Madison Avenue. Uncomfortable behind a lectern, he gave few speeches. On a normal working day he would take the 8:11 club car from Greenwich, walk through Grand Central Station directly into the Graybar Building, eat lunch in the JWT dining room, then return to Greenwich by suppertime—all without setting foot on the sidewalks of New York. "His singular quality," noted a profile in *Advertising & Selling,* "the one which pigeonholes him as an enigma and immediately accelerates interest, is that except to a few close friends so little is known about him." Even his closest associates, according to a later article in *Fortune,* could not penetrate his personality after years of working with him: "He has an iron jaw, yet he speaks softly. He has a stubborn will, yet his manner is full of deference. Few of his associates have ever seen him give way to an outburst of temper, yet no one questions that the temper is there, and could flatten the Graybar Building if it ever really slipped the leash."

He may be approached, with caution, through fictional versions of life at JWT. The novelist J. P. Marquand worked there briefly in the early 1920s. One day he, Stanley Resor, and others were meeting to try out various slogans for Lifebuoy soap. "Every day an oily coating lightly forms upon your skin," someone ventured. "It scans, it scans!" said Marquand excitedly. "Who says there isn't poetry in advertising?" Silence in the room. "John," Resor finally said, "I don't think you really have the business instinct." (Which he did not; he was shortly fired. "It seemed to me the most dreadful thing," Marquand later reflected, "to end your days putting your energy into a campaign for Lifebuoy soap—and all those Phi Beta Kappas sitting around trying to get ideas.") In the Marquand novel *H. M. Pulham, Esquire,* published in 1940, Resor appears as J. T. Bullard, the boss at the ad agency where Pulham worked. Pulham was sent out to demonstrate a soap to housewives, as Marquand had been at JWT. Bullard had his verbal tics—he said "playing with words" too often—but the portrait was not unkind, emphasizing the subject's academic tendencies. In horn-rimmed glasses and a double-breasted suit, "He looked like a professor about to deliver a lecture, except that he looked more prosperous."

Another Thompson alumnus turned writer, Richard Connell, drew a more barbed likeness in two *Saturday Evening Post* stories published in 1922 and 1923. In the first, J. Sanford Bowser, adman, was sent to a resort to be cured of what his doctor diagnosed as slogan-itis, the excessive coining of slogans. There he met an adwoman suffering the same affliction. They decided to merge. "Phrase fever is not so bad," she said, "when someone else really understands." He, sloganeering again, agreed: "Love Is Understanding." In the second story, the two were running their own agency. The staff included psychologists, at whom clients were allowed to gaze admiringly. The Bowsers addressed everyone, including each other, by last name only. (The Resors called their associates, but not each other, by last name.) Sitting in adjacent offices, the Bowsers communicated by memo. They were quarreling about what to name their son. He wanted a coined name, Yubar or Kinzo. She held out for John and finally won. (The Resors named their son Stanley.)

Fictional burlesques aside, the personal and working relationship of these two dissimilar people mystified observers. He trusted social science, she her own imagination. He was "one of the least articulate men alive," according to an admirer. She had great verbal facility, whether writing or talking. He was a listener who liked to be read to. She was a talker and constant, omnivorous reader. Diffident in manner, he hesitated when speaking, giving his listener plenty of time to interrupt. "She had a dozen ideas to the minute," Peggy King recalled, "and kept them coming so fast you couldn't possibly keep up and had to sit down afterwards with a pencil and paper and try to sort them out." He was a brain-picker and synthesizer, not flashy. "She had a brilliant feminine mind," said Nancy Stephenson, another of her copywriters, "that darted and dipped and swooped with terrifying speed and accuracy." He was slow and serious, she quick and smiling. He found his recreation outdoors, playing golf on Sunday mornings, working around the yard in Greenwich, and playing rancher at a summer home in Jackson Hole, Wyoming. She found her recreation indoors, in art and books and fashion.

What they shared was a common background of reduced circumstances, and perhaps this, more than anything else, informed the emulation style of advertising they developed. The Resor family had owned a kitchen-stove factory in Cincinnati since 1819; Stanley's father and grandfather had both spent their lives running it. At the turn of the century, new gas stoves wiped out the market for the company's wood- and coal-fired products. "I had always expected to be a manufacturer also," Stanley said in 1922; "in fact, I still have a decided liking for it, but before I left Yale the factory had passed out of our family." The young man programmed to inherit the family sinecure had to help pay his way at college by tutoring Latin students and taking summer jobs, and then went through several other jobs before finding advertising. "At the end of my first year I felt sure I was in the right work." But he had known the insecurity of falling down the class ladder and wondering whether he could climb back up.

Helen was born on a farm in Grayson, a small town in the mountains of northwestern Kentucky, the second youngest of nine children. Her mother, Helen Bayleff Lansdowne, was the daughter of a Presbyterian minister who had graduated from college and then studied for three years at Princeton Theological Seminary; thus she came from a background, for that time and region, of culture and aspiration. But when Helen Lansdowne Resor was four years old, the mother left her husband and took the children to Covington, where her two brothers lived. She had no trade, no apparent means to earn a living. She went to work for one brother as a clerk. The other brother brought food money to the home every day. With the mother at work, the oldest girl took charge of the household. The mother eventually became a librarian and sold real estate. Although never in dire poverty, the family lived carefully. The house was rented, not owned.

For young Helen, the experience of losing her father at the age of four, and then of having her mother away at work during the day, amounted to a lesson in feminism and self-sufficiency. "You're never going to get caught the way I was," the mother told her daughters. "You're going to learn how to work." When Helen graduated from high school at the age of seventeen, as class valedictorian, it was assumed that she would seek a career. Her success at JWT and her support for women's suffrage and planned parenthood may be traced directly back to the example of Helen Bayleff Lansdowne. In particular, the kind of advertising she wrote—about improving oneself, and aspiring upward to the habits of richer people—seems the logical expression of the farm girl from Grayson. In 1923 Edward Steichen photographed her hands peeling potatoes for a Jergens hand-lotion ad. "I could tell by the way she cut the potatoes," Steichen noted, "that this wasn't the first time she had done it."

❧❧

A note in *Printers' Ink* on the flood of testimonial ads:

It pays to be personal now;
It brings in the shekels—and how!
    If you want to sell drugs,
    Or Baluchistan rugs,
    Or revolvers to thugs,
    Or a spray to kill bugs—
You've got to be personal now.

❧❧

"The chief economic problem today," said Stanley Resor, "is no longer the production of goods but their distribution. The shadow of overproduction, with its attendant periods of unemployment and suffering, is the chief menace to the present industrial system." In this situation, advertising increasingly seemed a necessary part of the industrial process, one of the standard costs like labor and raw materials, instead of an afterthought tacked on if the manufacturer could afford it. Now fifty years beyond his old associations with snake oil and consumption cures, the adman could regard himself as a regular guy, just another businessman. In popular fiction of the 1920s, the adman often appeared as the hero: the copy cub who at the last minute writes a brilliant ad, snares the client, and gets the promotion and the girl.

If not exactly a hero, George F. Babbitt did offer unconscious testimony to the new power of advertising in American life. Sinclair Lewis sometimes referred to himself as a former adman ("at least they used to let me write publishers' advertising"). He made advertising a large presence in *Babbitt,* a best-seller of 1922. Not a conventionally religious man, Babbitt believed in the God of Progress and the Great God Motor. He sold real estate and composed his own ads: "Course I don't mean to say that every ad I write is literally true or that I always believe everything I say." But he did trust most of the advertising he saw. The big national brands oriented him to the universe, offering the outward evidence of inner grace. "These standard advertised wares—toothpastes, socks, tires, cameras, instantaneous hot-water heaters—were his symbols and proofs of excellence; at first the signs, then the substitutes, for joy and passion and wisdom."

Babbitt was buying not the products but what he hoped they would bring him. Advertising of the 1920s stressed the results of a given purchase—health, happiness, comfort, love, social success—and the corollary disadvantages of not having the product. The selling argument featured not the object per se but its uses. Here and elsewhere JWT established the dominant style: its food advertising offered recipes and enticing pictures of the dish ready for serving. In the *Saturday Evening Post,* overwhelmingly the biggest medium of the day, a typical ad copied the Thompson editorial format. Under the illustration, a prominent headline introduced a half-page of copy. The artwork included sumptuous paintings, ambitious photography, intricate designs and borders, and more use of color—all the frills scorned by Albert Lasker. "Beauty has been definitely injected into business," said one advocate of advertising art. "The apostles of reason-why will murmur their logical theorems in outer darkness."

These methods were applied not only to small household goods but to the ultimate consumer purchase, the automobile. Car production leaped from 2 million in 1920 to 5.5 million in 1929. Mergers and attrition cut the number of manufacturers by more than half, and the resulting economies of scale and volume sent showroom prices falling. General Motors, the ultimate merger, introduced annual model changes and, with its General Motors Acceptance Corporation, provided the structure of installment buying that brought cars within the indebted reach of most Americans. By 1925 three-fourths of car sales were by time payment. Automobile advertising, once preoccupied with reliability and mechanical details, now emphasized styling and performance, subjective and esthetic aspects which the art-conscious ads of the 1920s could exploit.

When Walter Chrysler, formerly of General Motors, bought the failing Maxwell automobile company and transformed it into his own line, he hired Theodore MacManus to help introduce the new car. The first ad, in the *Post* in December 1923, explained the pronunciation of the name (Cry-sler) and promised "important announcements" soon. More teaser ads followed in the next two weeks. Finally, with a flourish, the presentation of the Chrysler Six, available in four body styles, and a statement by Chrysler himself. It was, he explained, a long, low, powerful car, with styling like that of a custom European sedan, easily capable of seventy-five miles an hour; of course at a sensational price. The car was a hit, and a few years later Chrysler added the Plymouth and DeSoto.

The most famous car ad of the twenties was for the Jordan Playboy, a sporty open runabout manufactured in Cleveland. First run in the *Post* in June 1923, the full-page advertisement was written by Edward S. Jordan, like Chrysler the founder of his own company. The headline raised sentimental memories of the World War, when letters and dispatches from the front would be written from "somewhere in France." Beneath a drawing of the car and a cowboy on horseback sweeping down the road was the headline "Somewhere West of Laramie." At that indefinite spot in the imagination, the copy went on, "there's a broncho-busting, steer-roping girl who knows what I'm talking about." The Playboy was built for her, "the lass whose face is brown with the sun when the day is done of revel and romp and race. She loves the cross of the wild and the tame. There's a savor of links about that car—of laughter and lilt and light—a hint of old loves—and saddle and quirt." All of this from a car. Something about this jumble of the Wild West, of emancipated women, of speed and romance and adventure, caught the public. The Playboy sold well for a time, then disappeared during the Depression. But the themes of its advertising sold many other cars in the 1920s.

In this decade Detroit became the bellwether of the American economy, the biggest single industry and the key to the health of many other enterprises. A car's mechanical innards—the engine, transmission, and brakes—changed slowly, but the external shell could be fiddled with every year. Advertising sold Americans first on the need for a car, and then on the need to keep its styling up to date. By 1927 even Henry Ford capitulated: he killed his plain, reliable Model T and brought forth the Model A, better-looking and more powerful. At the end of the decade, the sociologists Robert and Helen Lynd found the residents of their typical Middletown more eager to own a car than to own a bathtub.

On a flood of advertising the twenties swept forward, gathering speed, heading toward the crash. At mid-decade *Advertising & Selling* looked back on the changes of the past few years: the leap in automobile registrations, the growth in magazine and newspaper circulations, the new amusements and diversions. "Everything has changed," *A & S* concluded, "except the calendar." At the AAAA annual meeting in October 1926, Calvin Coolidge stamped advertising with the presidential seal of approval. "It is the most potent influence in adapting and changing the habits and modes of life, affecting what we eat, what we wear, and the work and play of the whole nation," said Coolidge to general editorial approval. "Advertising ministers to the spiritual side of trade."

The most enduring effect of twenties advertising on "the habits and modes of life" involved the discovery of the human body. Long after the passing of the Jordan Playboy and the Model A, Americans were still fussing over newly acknowledged problems related to previously unmentionable bodily functions.

Halitosis: J. W. Lambert, a St. Louis druggist, had invented Listerine as a surgical antiseptic; later it was marketed for throat infections. But sales were sluggish. In 1922 Gerard Lambert, son of the founder, called in Milton Feasley and Gordon Seagrove from the firm's Chicago ad agency, Williams & Cunnyngham. The three men threw around various new uses for Listerine. How about bad breath? someone suggested. No good, they agreed, you can't refer to bad breath in polite company. No better ideas came forth, though. Lambert asked a company chemist whether Listerine had any effect on bad breath. Yes, the report came back, "Listerine is good for halitosis." Good for what? Nobody had heard of the word before, so it was adopted as a sober, medical-sounding way of referring to the unmentionable. Feasley and Seagrove returned to Chicago and wrote a series of ads. "Even your best friend won't tell you," one ad warned. This "advertising by fear"—or "whisper copy," as Feasley called it—was soon running in eighty magazines and over three hundred newspapers. Lambert and Feasley moved to New York and started their own agency. The Listerine campaign contributed catch phrases and new anxieties to everyday conversations. The headline "Often a Bridesmaid But Never a Bride" continued, with different copy and illustrations, for over three decades. After only five years of warning about halitosis, Listerine was spending an annual ad budget of $5 million and making a net profit of over $4 million. Cynical about his own success, at parties in Lambert's home Feasley would amuse people by reading his ads aloud. After his death in 1926 Seagrove came to New York and took over the copywriting. Other uses for the product were devised, but Seagrove never strayed too far from the main pitch.

Athlete's foot: Arthur Kudner, a copywriter at Erwin, Wasey & Jefferson, heard a report that a ringworm fungus, *Tinea Trichophyton,* was appearing on American feet to an alarming degree—spread, apparently, by contact in gyms and locker rooms. With the lesson of halitosis, Kudner hired a chemical research lab to find a product on the market that would combat this new affliction. He was told that Absorbine Jr., a liniment for sore muscles and insect bites manufactured in Springfield, Massachusetts, treated the fungus effectively. Kudner replaced the Latin name with "athlete's foot," his own term, and proposed a campaign to the Absorbine company. "His heart quickened at the soft fragrance of her cheeks," read a headline, "but her shoes hid a sorry case of athlete's foot." The company bought it, and so did the public.

B. O.: After Jim Young blazed the way with Odorono, the George B. Evans company of Philadelphia expanded the marketing of its Mum deodorant. An ad by the John O. Powers agency (founded by the son of John E. Powers) repeated the double-edged slogan, " 'Mum' is the word!" Accompanied by a picture of a woman with her index finger to her lips in a shushing gesture, the copy urged, "When you're getting ready for the dance, the theatre, or an evening in other crowded and close places, and you want to make sure that perspiration and its inevitable odor will not steal away your sweet cleanliness and dainty charm—'Mum' is the word!" And so on, through ten other difficult situations. The market doubled when men, too, were found to suffer from the problem. Deodorant soaps appeared for those who balked at applying a specific remedy. The problem then acquired its own name. In 1928 Everett Grady of Ruthrauff & Ryan advertised Lifebuoy soap as a cure for Body Odor, or B. O.

The laundress problem: During the war a company in Neenah, Wisconsin, had produced "cellucotton" bandages, made from wood fiber, to replace the more scarce cotton bandages to which hospitals were accustomed. Nurses in France began to use the cellucotton bandages as sanitary pads during menstruation: wartime shortages thus produced a disposable, tidier alternative to the homemade, rewashable devices that women had always used, as well as a partial solution for the postwar shortage of household servants that so perplexed the middle and upper classes. The cellucotton firm engaged the Charles F. W. Nichols agency of Chicago for the delicate task of advertising Kotex. The first ad showed a nurse attending to two wounded soldiers, who faced the reader, with two other soldiers in the background. The ad was accepted by the *Ladies' Home Journal* but then withdrawn by the agency before publication. "It was decided," the copywriter, Wallace Meyer, said later, "that men should not be featured in so intimate a discussion of feminine hygiene." The new illustration showed a soldier in a wheelchair, his back turned, attended by three women. The campaign was launched in the *Journal* in January 1921. "Simplify the laundress problem," read one headline. "Kotex are good enough to form a habit, cheap enough to throw away, and easy to dispose of," the copy went on. "They complete the toilet essentials of the modern woman." The embarrassment of asking a male druggist for the product remained. A drugstore in Watertown, Wisconsin, avoided this problem by camouflaging Kotex in a plain wrapper and putting it out on the counter, where a woman could simply pick it up, leave the money, and avoid conversation about it. Later Kotex ads included this marketing device. Once women did not have to mention the name, sales picked up. The account moved on to Lord & Thomas. The company added another disposable wood-fiber product, Kleenex. "Women are beginning to waste it," Albert Lasker said with satisfaction. "Once you can afford to *waste* a product, it's bound to be a success!"

Pink toothbrush, dry mouth, tender gums, yellow teeth, and that dingy film: Wartime military service introduced millions of Americans to the toothbrush, and they took the habit home after the peace. Ad campaigns, taking additional advantage of the halitosis scare, heralded new brands of toothbrushes and dentifrices. By one survey, only 26 percent of Americans took care of their teeth before the war. That figure rose to 40 percent by 1926 and kept climbing. "No one creation of man," Frank Presbrey, a leading adman, said of the toothbrush, "has done more to lift the individual out of the sordid slough of mediaevalism and place him on a new aesthetic plane." Some ads tried in a general way to win converts to the toothbrush. Others went directly to a specific pitch. "This is a scientific product made to serve a hygienic purpose," Claude Hopkins said of his Pepsodent campaign. "So the commercial aspect has been largely hidden in the altruistic. . . . The advertisements breathe unselfishness and service."

The list of dangers and advertising solutions went on. The regular consumption of oranges could ward off "acidosis," or low vitality (the Lord & Thomas campaign, keyed to the drinking of orange juice at breakfast, pushed per capita consumption of oranges from seventeen to sixty-seven a year). Cutex nail polish would help ensure social poise ("You will be amazed to find how many times in one day people glance at your nails," said the JWT ad. "Indeed some people make a practice of basing their estimate of a new acquaintance largely upon this one detail"). The use of Nujol laxative, another JWT account, would help maintain "a clear, radiant, youthful complexion."

Some of this attention to the body—such as toothbrushes and oranges—actually did make people healthier. The public discussion of these private matters also implied a liberation from Victorian denials of the body. On some level, these ads fitted the spirit of a decade that saw such other liberations as Flaming Youth, short skirts, the demise of the corset, open discussions of sexuality and birth control, Hollywood sheiks and vamps, and the general flouting of prohibition. Gargling Listerine did nobody much good, or much harm. It supported no bootleggers, and it made Gerard Lambert a fortune.

On a second level, this attention to bodily functions implied a repression along class and ethnic lines. It was all so clean, inhumanly clean. In this decade chewing tobacco gave way to smoking tobacco, and spittoons disappeared from public view. Kitchen and bathroom design changed from wood, cast iron, and other relatively porous materials to tile, porcelain, linoleum, and the double-shell enameled bathtub. The Siwelco noiseless toilet appeared. Sani-Flush went so far as to show a picture of a woman pouring the product into her toilet bowl. "From a mere utility," declared an ad for Crane bathroom equipment in 1925, "the modern bathroom has developed into a spacious shrine of cleanliness and health."

It was not accidental that such a vogue for cleanliness and meticulous hygiene coincided in this decade with the presence of three Republicans in the White House; drastic congressional limits and quotas on immigration; the Rotarian sensibility of the *Saturday Evening Post;* the founding of *Reader's Digest,* and such political/racial reactions as the Red Scare, the Sacco-Vanzetti case, and a rampant Ku Klux Klan. Amid these varied nativist impulses, advertising's discovery of the body made perfect sense. It projected a WASP vision of a tasteless, colorless, odorless, sweatless world. Ethnic minorities cooked with vivid spices—even garlic!—and might neglect toothpaste, mouthwash, deodorants, and regular bathing. Advertising would show these minorities how to cleanse themselves. We are, said Sinclair Lewis, "the first great nation in which all individuality, all sweetness of life, all saline and racy earthiness has with success been subordinated to a machine-ruled industrialism."

Early in 1927 the old progressive William Allen White addressed the Advertising Club of New York. American society, he said, had its revolutionists. But they were not Bolsheviks or foreigners. "The real revolutionist is the advertising man, whose stimulation of mass desire and demands results in mass production and buying," said White. "Could I control the advertising publications of this country I would control the entire land."

❧❧

In this Advertising Decade the most celebrated adman was Bruce Barton, leader of the resoundingly named agency of Batten, Barton, Durstine & Osborn. As J. Walter Thompson under the Resors carried forward the claim-and-coupon tradition of Claude Hopkins—with the addition of visual appeal—BBDO produced institutional ads for General Motors and General Electric in the image school of Theodore MacManus. Barton wrote some of this copy. In addition, as a best-selling author and confidant to presidents, he was well known to the general public, probably the only adman whom the average citizen could identify as such. This exceptional visibility made him a symbol of the advertising business and a spokesman for its purposes. Yet he came to advertising late, after a dozen years as an editor and journalist, and he remained in some sense an outsider, embracing the trade in public while keeping his distance in private.

This ambivalence apparently derived from the major influence on his life, the particular version of Christianity he learned from his father, William E. Barton, a liberal Protestant minister and biographer of Abraham Lincoln. Bruce was born in 1886 in rural Tennessee, where the father had a circuit-riding ministry. Later in life Bruce generally exaggerated the poverty of his childhood. Actually the father soon moved on to comfortable ministries in Boston and suburban Chicago. Rich or poor, Bruce remembered his parents as "the happiest and most successful people I have ever known." This well-being, he believed, derived from their religious faith. William Barton preached a Christian God both demanding and, as time went by, forgiving. With age and experience, he dealt more gently with his parishioners, showing "less interest in calling them to repentance and greater interest in cheering them up," Bruce recalled. A strong but unexacting Christianity became Bruce's own touchstone. "I am a heretic," he said, "and I do a lot of things that are forbidden by the Methodist Board of Temperance and Morals." His favorite Biblical verse about Jesus was Matthew 14:14 ("And Jesus went forth, and saw a great multitude, and was moved with compassion toward them"). "It explains Him better than any other single verse to me," Barton noted.

At Amherst College he was a big man in his class, valedictorian and voted the most likely to succeed. He left in 1907 with a fellowship for graduate work in history at the University of Wisconsin; he expected to spend his life teaching and writing American history. But his career took the first of its unexpected turns. "I was in poor health and considerably depressed as the result of a nervous breakdown," he recalled. He spent the summer after graduation as a timekeeper in a construction camp out in Montana. In this stripped-down milieu he retrieved his spirits. Instead of entering graduate school he went to New York to seek work in publishing.

He dabbled briefly in the progressive reform movements of the day. After reading Henry George's *Progress and Poverty* he announced himself a single-taxer and started going to Georgite meetings in New York. But he found always the same people and the same number of people in attendance. "Reluctantly I came to the conclusion that this was a crusade that ought to succeed but probably could never attract a sufficiently large discipleship." He worked for the publishing firm of P. F. Collier, owner of *Collier's Weekly*, the muckraking journal that ran many attacks on advertising. In supervising the firm's door-to-door book salesmen, Barton allowed methods that themselves might have attracted the notice of muckrakers. He praised one salesman who tricked housewives into unwittingly signing contracts; but he also hoped his men would "grow into the habit of being square with themselves and with the public."

One day, typically by accident, he started writing advertising. *Collier's Weekly* had been carrying double-page spreads for the parent firm's Harvard Classics, "Dr. Eliot's Five-Foot Shelf of Books," a collection of notable volumes selected by President Charles W. Eliot of Harvard. The double-pages had not been selling many books. On this particular day the superintendent of the press room told Barton he had a vacant quarter-page in that week's issue of the magazine. Barton opened one of the books "almost at random," tore out a picture of Marie Antoinette in a tumbrel, and dashed off an ad. "This is Marie Antoinette riding to her death," said the headline. "Have you ever read her tragic story?" the copy went on. "Have you ever lived through the stirring days of the French Revolution in the pages of Burke's great book—one of the wonderfully fascinating books that have made history? . . . To read these few great works systematically and intelligently is to be really well read." Even a very busy man could become learned by picking up one of the Harvard Classics for only fifteen minutes a day. Such a plan imparted not useless knowledge but the keys to real success. In this fashion "some men—who may never have been to college—nevertheless think clearly, talk more convincingly, earn more and enjoy life more than many college men." Eliot may not have intended such practical results, and the selling argument was far removed from the college boy who expected to become a history professor. But it did work: this and other ads by Barton sold 400,000 sets of the Harvard Classics.

He next edited a series of ephemeral magazines, occasionally writing an ad on demand. For *Every Week* he and a young Norman Rockwell produced a campaign for Edison Mazda light bulbs. ("We had a grand time," Rockwell said later. "He'd think up ideas on the origins of light and I'd do the illustrations.") Despite such forays into advertising, Barton still thought of himself as basically a journalist. His magazine editorials drew particular comment. In the summer of 1918 *Redbook* hired him to write editorials under an exclusive contract; the magazine promised its readers "the most American—most sensible—most helpful—best written editorials in the U.S."

Again he was drawn to advertising by happenstance. During the World War he did his bit with publicity campaigns. For the Salvation Army he coined the slogan, "A man may be down but he is never out." In the fall of 1918 he helped plan the United War Work Campaign, the fourth major fund-raising drive of the war, to benefit the Salvation Army, YMCA, YWCA, and other national welfare agencies. The planning sessions brought him the acquaintance of Alex Osborn, an adman from Buffalo, and Roy Durstine, a former newspaperman who had worked briefly at Calkins & Holden and then started his own agency in New York. Durstine was sent to Europe so the group could produce "some *real* war advertising (by one who had seen and felt and smelt the battle-front)," as Barton recalled it, "instead of the sentimental crap to which advertisers were donating hundreds of thousands of dollars' worth of free newspaper space." The campaign aimed to raise $170 million. It ran for a week in November, just as the war ended, and brought in $202 million.

Looking toward the postwar world, Barton hoped the new techniques of publicity and advertising would help bring permanent peace. "For the first time," he declared in *Collier's,* "the pen will be actually greater and more powerful than the sword." For the war had been conducted by advertising; were Woodrow Wilson's notes to the people of Europe not good, effective ads? Now nations should advertise themselves to avoid war. "I would make the peoples of the world to know each other, knowing that ultimately they would come to like each other."

For Barton and most Americans, this bubble of wartime idealism soon burst. Later he decided the socialist Eugene Debs had analyzed the war correctly: "He said that all we got out of it was influenza and the income tax." The war did have a more lasting effect on Barton, though. It pointed him toward making a career of advertising. Late in 1918 Durstine and Osborn asked him to join them in a new agency. "I had never thought of advertising as a life work," Barton recalled, "though I had—on the side—written some very successful copy." He would have no boss and could still write freelance articles in his spare time. So he agreed, expecting to retire in fifteen years and then start another career—perhaps buy a newspaper, or teach, or enter politics.

They borrowed $10,000 and opened for business on West Forty-fifth Street in January 1919. Barton was supposed to write copy and find new clients while Durstine managed the office and paid the bills; Osborn operated a branch office in Buffalo. But on the first day of operations Durstine went to bed with pneumonia, which forced him to stay away for three months, leaving matters to Barton. "I was so ignorant of the business," he said later, "that I was too ignorant to be scared." The firm lost fifty dollars in its first week and was solvent thereafter. In those early years the agency was so small that it resembled JWT's Cincinnati office under Jim Young: formal job descriptions meant nothing. "Every one of us knew what every one else was doing," Barton recalled. "Every one of us was a copywriter and an art director and an account executive and a researcher. We were always in and out of each other's offices, asking 'What do you think of this headline?' "

Granted this intermingling, Barton was still the creative star. For one of the agency's first clients, the Alexander Hamilton Institute, a correspondence school for businessmen, he wrote one of his most effective ads, "The Years That the Locusts Have Eaten." It sold the idea of hard work, the extra effort a man would need in order to study by mail at the end of the day. For the same client Barton wrote another ad that ran for seven years. "About one man in ten will be appealed to by this page," the copy began, offering a catchy hook. "The one man in ten has imagination. And imagination rules the world." In 1923 he delivered a sermon on the general need to advertise before a meeting of electrical-utility companies. Taking as his text the Biblical passage "And Pharaoh died, and there arose a new king in Egypt which knew not Joseph," Barton warned that America kept producing new generations of consumers which knew not Joseph: "They do not know the difference between a Mazda lamp and a stick of Wrigley's chewing gum. Nobody has ever told them that Ivory Soap floats or that children cry for Castoria." Therefore advertising must be constantly applied. Two decades later, BBDO was still getting requests for copies of this speech and of the "Locusts" ad for the Hamilton Institute.

Barton, Durstine & Osborn became a hot agency. New clients appeared: part of General Electric in 1920, General Motors in 1922, Dunlop Tire and the rest of General Electric in 1923, part of Lever Brothers in 1924. In hiring new employees BDO looked for college graduates with salesmen's minds and some writing ability: "The combination is not a very common one," Barton noted. He liked ads pleasing to the eye—"Beauty is the most important factor in modern advertising," he said—with quick, succinct copy. According to a running joke at the agency, Barton's tombstone would read, "He said the copy should be shorter." An entire wall of his office was covered by an enlarged photograph of a sweaty crowd at Coney Island.

It helped him keep his audience in mind. "You are not talking to a mass meeting," he liked to say. "You're talking to a parade."

Outside the agency Barton excelled at charming clients. He was a handsome man, six feet tall and well built, with delicate features, light blue eyes, and red hair turning sandy. He projected a masculine affability, speaking in a deep, well-modulated voice, moving with long strides and an athlete's grace. He resembled an evangelist sprinkling Biblical allusions to one observer; or a large brown teddy bear to another. "A remarkable personality," Roy Durstine recalled, "particularly in front of a crowd." Addressing a client meeting, he would start hesitantly, to quiet the audience and get it leaning forward. Then he would swing into his message, still very much the preacher's son. As the contact man to blue-chip clients he sold the agency well. "I think I absorb out of you a great deal of advertising and psychology which is of no use to me whatever," Boss Kettering of GM told him in proposing monthly luncheons, "so I hope I can give you a little slant on engineering which I hope will be equally useless to you."

In 1923 Edward Bok of the *Ladies' Home Journal* established a set of annual advertising awards, to be administered by the Harvard Business School and selected by a jury of experts in the trade. For the first year Barton accepted a place on the jury ("I imagine that it is fair to say that I am recognized as an authority on advertising copy"), but then withdrew when several BDO efforts were submitted. Of the nine final awards the agency won three: for a GM institutional campaign, for a series of local newspaper ads for Macy's department store, and for a market survey on behalf of the American Radiator Company. BDO printed two thousand copies of a booklet announcing these triumphs. In future competitions it did almost as well. In the seven years that Harvard-Bok prizes were awarded, Barton's agency won more than any two other agencies combined.

This success came at the cost of long hours and piled desks. "We are creating, creating, creating all the time," Barton noted. "We are sitting in with manufacturers of cars and cabbages and sealing wax, and all of them have troubles which are passed on to us—and which we must regard as peculiarly personal and important." In only a few years BDO had grown into a major agency with two hundred employees. Now ensconced on the seventh floor of 383 Madison Avenue, it shared the building with another agency, the George Batten

Company, up on the tenth floor. Batten, established since 1891, was led by F. R. Feland, a noted copywriter, and William H. Johns, who had coined the phrase "used cars" and had helped Stanley Resor start the AAAA in 1917. In 1928 the two agencies merged, under Barton as chairman and Johns as president, to form BBDO. The combined billings of $32 million made it one of the biggest shops, along with JWT and Ayer. In addition, Feland brought BDO some badly needed eccentricity. He was addicted to bourbon and horse racing; missed few Kentucky Derbies; named his fifth child Quintus Ultimus; and every Christmas gathered his children to read them Dickens' "A Christmas Carol," stopping at the point where Scrooge says, "Bah, humbug."

As Barton helped build the agency, he held to his original plan of maintaining a separate writing career. His office correspondence files from BBDO are filled with letters to his readers and publishers. Durstine ran the office with a firm hand; when he was away Barton's writing time diminished. "This has been a dry month for me in writing," he once told one of his editors, "as Mr. Durstine has been South and I have had to be a 100% advertising man." The writing let Barton retain some tie to the varied idealisms of his younger days. He turned out interviews with admirable public figures, political commentaries, short editorials, and snappy homilies about success and happy living, often with a religious moral.

Sometime in 1923 he started writing his major work, a reinterpretation of what he regarded as the conventional view of Jesus Christ. He offered the book in installments to a major magazine, which turned it down as too controversial. It was then serialized in the *Woman's Home Companion*. Barton next took the complete manuscript to Maxwell Perkins, the legendary editor at the house of Scribner. "Too advanced for us," said Perkins; the book would be "a shock to many of those that we are thinking of" and might leave "the impression of an apparent irreverence." Furthermore, "I do find it hard myself to regard business as you do."

The Man Nobody Knows was finally published by Bobbs-Merrill in 1924. Its theology owed a substantial debt to the teachings of Barton's father. The book offered a very masculine Jesus, strong from carpentry, laughing, convivial, the most popular dinner guest in Jerusalem, "the friendliest man who ever lived." He was in fact an adman: persuading, recruiting followers, finding the right words to arouse interest and create desires, in short exemplifying all the principles of modern salesmanship. "He would be a national advertiser today, I am sure, as he was the great advertiser of his own day." His parables were model ads, based on the principle that good advertising tells the news in interesting ways. "The parable of the Good Samaritan is the greatest advertisement of all time."

The book was a huge success, selling 250,000 copies in eighteen months. Catholics objected to the suggestion that Jesus had siblings, and Mary therefore was not a virgin; liberal Protestants dismissed this Jesus as too easy to follow, shorn of his rough edges and exacting standards. *The Man Nobody Knows* truly did cry out for satirization. It offered a Christianity all too appropriate to the day, Jesus Christ as George F. Babbitt. The book's excesses obscured Barton's ultimate message: not to normalize Jesus but to exalt everyday work. Modern Americans, said Barton, should not distinguish between average occupations and religious callings—both were equally idealistic and sacred. In effect, Barton was raising his own drift away from idealisms to a higher plane. But this point appeared at the end of the book and was probably lost in the preceding treatment of Jesus.

For historians looking back at the twenties, *The Man Nobody Knows* has made its author a prominent symbol of the times. Barton did outwardly seem just another go-getter and booster with a nativist affection for the "pure blooded Americans" whom he called "a great contrast to the imported stuff with which our social settlements have to work in New York and other cities." He defended business as the greatest single influence in national affairs and advertising as its handmaiden. At the AAAA annual meeting in October 1927, this celebrated authority on the real Jesus presented "the creed of a modern advertising man." I am in advertising, he said, because I believe in business, and advertising speaks for business. "If advertising persuades some men to live beyond their means, so does matrimony. If advertising speaks to a thousand in order to influence one, so does the church. If advertising is often garrulous and redundant and tiresome, so is the United States Senate. We are young, and law and medicine and theology are old."

Thus the public face. In private he was more complex, more critical of advertising, even doubtful about the general course of American civilization. In 1926 he was invited to address an advertising meeting in Philadelphia. Not wanting just to repeat "the old stuff, that advertising has reduced the cost of selling Campbell's soup," as he put it, he consulted an academic friend, George B. Hotchkiss, a marketing professor at New York University. "Between ourselves," wrote Barton, "it seems to me that a very large percent of the current advertising is merely representative of the most wasteful phases of the competitive system." When automobiles were first produced, car ads had to educate the public with hard information and technical details. "Today there is no more need of advertising the details of automobiles to the American public than there is for advertising the multiplication table." As a result "automobile advertising says nothing and has said nothing for years." The same sterility in fact marked the ads for most standardized goods. "The only new things that have been said have, in most instances, been misleading, things like the hullabaloo about vitamins, the iron in raisins, and the healthfulness of yeast." American industry produced more than consumers could absorb, so advertising had to sell products within a finite market of similar products: "We spend our vast advertising appropriations trying to steal each other's customers here in the home market, switching people from Pebeco to Ipana and from Williams Shaving Soap to Colgate's Shaving Soap."

"I have exaggerated the case a little," Barton conceded, "and, of course, shouldn't say anything like this in Philadelphia." But could Hotchkiss offer him any reassurance about the current state of advertising? Hotchkiss could. Advertising, he said, was like a noisy elevated train, obtrusive but necessary. Though the mass of advertising had little value for any particular individual, nearly all of it had a useful message for *somebody*. New housewives always needed to learn about Royal Baking Powder and Gold Medal Flour. And advertising did keep improving: better-looking, better written, "more truthful, more instructive, and of higher sales value than that of twenty years ago." Barton thanked Hotchkiss, swallowed his misgivings, and delivered a bland celebration of his trade at the Philadelphia meeting.

His closer friends knew a man who did not resemble the public personality. One of these, Harford Powel, Jr., wrote a novel during his tenure as a BBDO copywriter. The central figure in *The Virgin Queene,* published in 1928, was Barnham Dunn, senior partner at one of New York's leading ad agencies. Dunn worked in an office furnished in an elaborate colonial style. (Barton's office desk and chairs were reproductions of furniture used by George Washington.) In college Dunn had planned to teach and write, but then had sold out his real gifts to an advertising career. On the side he wrote uplifting articles and editorials. "My stuff is punk, and I know it," said Dunn. He might have written something more important, deeper and less popular, but now it was too late. At some point, he explained, as if to himself, "I knew I'd never be more than a second-rate business man and a second-rate writer—so I decided to add the two things together and be a first-rate advertising man."

If not the writer he dreamed of becoming, Barton was still a prodigious reader. At his office, across from the photograph of Coney Island, he kept shelves of books—over a thousand volumes in all, mainly history and biography, well thumbed and annotated. He still had a historian's mind and typically constructed arguments from his knowledge of history. "You and I were reared in the same sort of homes and seek the same objectives," he once told Henry Luce, "but you believe that the Kingdom of Heaven can come all at once, and I think nothing in human history supports that hope." As a representative of advertising, that most characteristic expression of the modern age, he usually defended in public "this wonderful fabric which we call modern civilization," and the "tremendous, happy, enthusiastic productivity which sets us apart from any other nation in the world." But as a reader of history he stood back from his own time and doubted. "We are children who have been dazzled with this new toy called Science," he wrote to Will Durant. "We thought it was going to give us everything, explain everything, put us on top of the universe." Yet it seemed to undermine religious faith, leaving humans lost in a mechanical and impersonal universe. Modern technology had brought more goods and services, more leisure and labor-saving devices. But had it made people happier? "We seem somehow to have lost out of our lives," said Barton, "that leisure and that dignity and that time for thought and that solid comfort" enjoyed by previous generations. Greatly impressed by Spengler's *Decline of the West* and Ortega's *Revolt of the Masses,* Barton wondered where modernity had gone wrong.

Torn by these crosscurrents, Barton was no simple Babbitt. He worked hard juggling his two careers, always pushing and driving himself forward. "The nose seems a little sharp, the lips too thin, and the whole face caught in tight effort," noted Helen Woodward, a prominent adwoman. Beneath the surface charm and cheer he was edgy, running on a tightly wound spring. For years he suffered off and on from insomnia. "One senses that underneath his apparently perfectly self-controlled exterior there is much nervous energy," a

New Yorker profile concluded. "He always seems to be at odds with himself—a hail-fellow-well-met who enjoys a burlesque show and a drink but who writes piously about churches and morals and believes in what he writes." For a short period in 1928 he checked himself into a sanitarium.

A possible explanation of his mental state at the time emerged from court proceedings a few years later. Barton's editorials occasionally described the joys of Christian marriage, of fidelity and proper morals. He presented himself as "a devoted father, extremely happy with his family," according to the *New Yorker*. Here too the contrived exterior hid a surprise. Barton had at least one extramarital affair, with a woman named Frances King, five years his junior. She said it began in Chicago in 1925 and continued after she came to New York and took a job at BBDO. He said it began only after they met at BBDO and then lasted a month, with three visits to her apartment. Both agreed that it ended in 1928. Later her husband threatened to sue Barton for alienation of affection. Barton then paid the couple $25,000 and obtained a general release from further legal action. There the matter rested until 1932, when Frances King appeared with the manuscript of a novel about an advertising man, "Roos Martin," and his callous sexual adventuring. She threatened to publish it unless Barton paid her $50,000. He sued her for blackmail, and the case was made public.

That a rich and famous married man should take a lover is hardly surprising, of course. Two circumstances made this case significant. Barton had made himself a prominent symbol of Christian morality, the author of one best-seller about Jesus and another about the Bible, *The Book Nobody Knows.* Now he seemed just another Christian hypocrite. Second, the coverage of the trial by the New York press raised doubts about the willingness of newspapers to offend any advertising figure who controlled the placing of big ad contracts. New York's tabloid newspapers routinely ran lurid stories about love nests and marital triangles. But only the two most respectable newspapers in town, the *Times* and the *Sun*, covered the trial of *Barton* v. *King.* Three other papers gave it brief and inadequate coverage. Four others—the *American, Journal, Daily Mirror,* and *Evening Post*—gave it not a word.

Barton's wife stood by him during the trial. On the stand he was asked whether he had ever proposed marriage to Frances King, as she had claimed. "No, that's ridiculous," he said. "I have been married for twenty years, very happily." The unpublished novel about Roos Martin was read to the jury; during the reading the judge visibly paid no attention, instead devoting himself to a book on his desk. King was found guilty, the first blackmail conviction in New York County in ten years, and went to jail.

The following spring Barton and his family left on an extended tour of the Far East. In India Barton wondered what he would do on his return to America. "I can, of course, continue to write to make people think that two gallons of gasoline just alike are not just alike," he confided to his diary. "But somehow it seems to me that the old day of competition, in the sense in which we have known it, is drawing to a close—that I should be laboring in the twilight of a passing era." In a few years he embarked on a political career.

Early in the 1920s, as JWT and BBDO were starting to push the advertising industry to new levels, Albert Lasker was out of the office. He had retired in 1918 to work for the Republican party and to pursue his own diverse interests. During the presidential campaign of 1920 he served as Harding's publicity manager and as head of the speech-writing department. After the victory he hoped to become Secretary of Commerce, but the job went to Herbert Hoover and Lasker was put in charge of the United States Shipping Board. Here he ran an ad campaign for passenger service that featured a coupon—"a new idea in steamship advertising," he claimed. His major task, the liquidation of an obsolete merchant marine fleet accumulated during the war, involved mass firings of personnel and controversial sales negotiations. Later came accusations that Lasker had unfairly rewarded friends with ad contracts and had tried to lobby editorial support for a ship subsidy bill in Congress by selectively buying advertising space in newspapers. After two years of "the unhappiest time of my life," as he recalled, he quit and went back to Lord & Thomas, probably with some relief.

He found the agency had grown away from reason-why and salesmanship in print. Under the direction of Claude Hopkins, L & T had established an art department, an ornament that Lasker had always scorned as unnecessary. Few new clients were appearing. Internal quarrels divided the staff. People in the New York office wanted to try the newer styles of JWT and BBDO; "they were not preaching orthodoxy, but were preaching advertising heresy," according to Lasker. To find new business Hopkins suggested buying companies and then doing their advertising; Lasker disagreed. These two men, once such a redoubtable team, could no longer work together. Hopkins departed in the spring of 1924 and started his own copywriting and counseling service. Now competitors, the two were soon fighting over the publication of Hopkins' memoirs. "I think your book is the mistake of a lifetime," Lasker told him.

At Lord & Thomas, Lasker cleaned house with the help of Ralph Sollitt, formerly his assistant on the shipping board. The whole New York office was fired. The art department was kept—"I was wrong for a long time," Lasker conceded—but subordinated. At some agencies, he noted, artists started the ad and then copywriters came up with the text to fit it. But the headline was still 90 percent of an ad, Lasker insisted. "So you must write the headline first, and then having done that the art must be the cartoon that illustrates that headline." For other new fashions, mostly the work of Stanley and Helen Resor at JWT, Lasker had even less use. Testimonials had returned, he noted acidly, "cologned and refined by the leading ladies of the land." Copy might be pretested in modest ways, but in general advertising research revealed only "that a jackass has two ears when we knew all the time that a jackass has two ears." Other ancillary services such as merchandising and sales advice lay outside an agency's responsibilities. "An agent cannot undertake to run a client's business," Lasker insisted.

In April 1925 he gathered a meeting of all his key people. "I feel sort of like a college professor facing a class," he told them. For six hours over two days he held forth: recalling his own early days and the advents of Kennedy, Hopkins, and reason-why; leaping forward, doubling back, digressing expansively, but always returning to his themes. Citing a recent Sears, Roebuck ad about Robinson Crusoe, he ridiculed image and "long haul" advertising. "Think of the shades of old Sears getting out of the grave and talking about Robinson Crusoe," he said. All those celebrated new agency services were only a "plusage" leading away from true principles. Now he was back, to lead the industry forward again, as he had done twenty years earlier. "We must agree on one gospel," he concluded. "Agreeing on that gospel, we must be consumed with a fire of energy and enthusiasm to spread it, not only for our own profit, but for service to our art and to our profession."

As it turned out, Lasker's crusade took off under a billowing cloud of tobacco smoke. In the 1920s advertising sold the cigarette habit to the American public—surely the industry's most regrettable achievement of the decade. Just before the war, cigarette companies had developed a slightly acid blend of burley and Turkish tobaccos. Unlike previous, more alkaline products, this new blend allowed practiced cigarette smokers to inhale without coughing. With this formula the R. J. Reynolds company made its Camel the first cigarette to be marketed nationally, not just regionally. The American Tobacco Company responded with its Lucky Strike, and the race was on. "It's full of flavor—just as good as a pipe," said a Lucky Strike ad. During and after the war cigarettes became the fashionable mode of tobacco consumption: less offensive than a cigar, easier to use than a pipe, more sanitary than chewing and spitting.

For these same reasons women took up cigarettes and, for the first time, became substantial consumers of tobacco. The new product crossed paths with the newly liberated woman. In 1919 *Printers' Ink,* ever on guard against advertising offenses, warned of "an insidious campaign to create women smokers." Ads for Murad and Helmar cigarettes showed Western-looking women in Turkish harem costumes, introducing the daring new idea by way of an exotic setting. More direct advertising was hardly necessary: women were assuming all the available masculine excesses anyway. Late in 1925 Bryn Mawr, a leading women's college, capitulated to circumstances by revoking a rule against smoking by students on the premises. The following year Chesterfield, through its Newell-Emmett agency, ran an ad showing a young couple sitting by a moonlit shore, a car nearby, the man lighting a cigarette, the couple's faces illuminated by the match. "Blow some my way," said the headline. A later ad for Pebeco toothpaste actually showed a woman puffing a cigarette. "My husband objected to my smoking until I began to use Pebeco," she explained.

From 1920 to 1928, while the production of pipe tobacco fell by 9 percent and that of cigars by 20 percent, cigarette production jumped 123 percent to 106 billion units a year. In this burgeoning, high-stakes market, Albert Lasker encountered a man of comparable force and ego, George Washington Hill of the American Tobacco Company. Groomed for leadership by his father, the tobacco pioneer Percival Hill, and then the absolute boss after his father's death in 1925, G. W. Hill shared Lasker's messianic faith in the power of hard-sell advertising. At his office in New York he bullied and frightened his subordinates, reminding one observer of a modern Nero. He was a small man with a round red face set off by cold, penetrating eyes under bristling, pugnacious brows. Typically he wore a blue suit, white shirt, black bow tie, and—even indoors—a strange little white hat. "His normal behavior was aggressive," recalled the publicist Edward Bernays. "He swaggered around his office, his arms swinging. At the slightest provocation he exploded, his face purpling with rage." He liked to give peculiar object lessons: discussing the need for memorable ads, he knocked a glass of water into someone's lap, saying, "See, you won't forget that"; or dragging someone to Tiffany's, flourishing an emerald necklace, and declaring that he wanted ads comparably polished; or forcing someone to hold a heavy statue while Hill loitered at his desk, then telling the poor man that his ad copy was just as heavy.

"I would not call him a rounded man," Lasker said of Hill. "The only purpose in life to him was to wake up, to eat, and to sleep so that he'd have strength to sell more Lucky Strikes. . . . It was just a religious crusade with him—which made it very difficult at times to work with a man so narrow-minded on a thing which was all out of focus." Hill smoked four packs of Luckies a day, inhaling deeply. On his desk he kept a cigarette box with Luckies in all four compartments. Nobody dared show any other brand in his presence. His Rolls-Royce had Lucky Strike packages taped in the rear window and outlines of the package in the center of each taillight. His estate on the Hudson River featured Japanese deer, black and white swans, and tobacco growing in the flower garden. He owned two dachshunds, named Lucky and Strike.

Lasker put up with this headlong monomaniac because Hill spent more money on Lucky Strikes than anyone had ever spent to advertise a single product. Lord & Thomas rode this one account back to a place among the major agencies: Lucky Strike brought in $12.3 million of the agency's total billings of $40 million in 1929. To avoid the collision of two titanic egos Lasker kept a buffer, usually Ralph Sollitt, between himself and Hill. "We would fix up a fine campaign for him, with real customer appeal and punch, and then we would have to fight continually to keep him from spoiling it," Lasker recalled. "If you let him alone, he'd get the basic idea so wrapped up in side issues and improvements that the whole idea got lost."

As the man in charge of the biggest account in all advertising, Hill usually had his way. Lasker stifled his distaste for testimonials and allowed a campaign that featured European opera stars testifying to the beneficial effect Luckies had on their singing. Other Lucky Strike testimonials followed. By this time the device had become overused and controversial. In a single issue of *Liberty* magazine in 1927 the actress Constance Talmadge endorsed eight different products, from alarm clocks to inner tubes. Queen Marie of Rumania had stopped her endorsement of Pond's after being severely criticized for it in her own country. John Philip Sousa had sued P. Lorillard over the unauthorized use of his name and photograph in a cigar ad. But under Hill's lash, Lucky Strike kept pushing the form to new extravagances. The climax came with a Luckies ad featuring the hero of a rescue at sea who allowed that smoking the cigarette helped his crew perform in the crisis. With that provocation, *Printers' Ink* started an editorial campaign against testimonials. "Do you believe that the use of purchased testimonials is good for advertising in general?" *PI* asked its readers. In response 54 said yes, but 843 said no.

Meantime Hill had provoked the entire candy industry. To keep that slender modern figure, said a Luckies ad, "Reach for a Lucky instead of a sweet." The actress Helen Hayes, among others, endorsed smoking as an alternative to eating fattening confections. The aggrieved industry fought back. "The cigarette will enflame your tonsils," warned an ad placed by a New York candy store chain, "poison with nicotine every organ of your body, and dry up your blood." "Our only purpose is to sell cigarettes," Hill replied serenely. "It is up to your industry to sell its own products." He did, he added, appreciate the publicity the candy industry had given the Luckies campaign. Old Gold cigarettes then chimed in with another contribution: "Eat a chocolate, light a cigarette—and enjoy both! Two fine and healthful treats."

Finally, in January 1930, the Federal Trade Commission stepped in and ruled that American Tobacco must stop running testimonials by endorsers who had not actually used the product, must indicate paid testimonials as such, and should no longer claim that smoking cigarettes would help people control their weight. Following that precedent, the National Better Business Bureau added its own disapproval. "The advertising industry must act and act promptly," said the BBB. "It must clean its own house or have it cleaned by an indignant public. The advertising appropriations of the American Tobacco Company have perverted the judgment and character of the advertising industry."

G. W. Hill made some adjustments and went on as before. Lucky Strike replaced Camel as the most popular brand of cigarettes.

Theodore MacManus watched the spectacle of the 1920s and was horrified. A devout Catholic who held honorary degrees from three Catholic colleges and later built his own church on his estate in Bloomfield Hills, he unburdened himself in an essay, "The Nadir of Nothingness," published in the *Atlantic Monthly* in 1928. Protestant individualism, he said, "the principle of private judgment," had separated the average citizen from his social obligations. Timeless moral standards had given way to such liberal fads as birth control, eugenics, and euthanasia. Contemporary art, literature, and philosophy all led to the same conclusion: "So far as the soul of man is concerned, modern society is quite completely and hopelessly mad."

He was no less critical of his own field. Looking back at the end of the decade, he found nothing to praise. "The cigarette has become almost a health food—certainly a weight reducer," he noted. "The humble cake of soap has risen far above its modest mission of cleansing, and confers the precious boon of beauty upon whomsoever shall faithfully wash." The automobile, a miracle of machinery, bestowed social prestige on its owner. Success and learning could be easily acquired by making the right purchases. "We are all glowing, and sparkling, and snapping, and tingling with health, by way of the toothbrush, and the razor, and the shaving cream, and the face lotion, and the deodorant, and a dozen other brightly packaged gifts of the gods." What had happened? "Advertising has gone amuck in that it has mistaken the surface silliness for the sane solid substance of an averagely decent human nature."

A powerful dissent, but probably only a minority opinion among the Americans of the time. *Advertising Age,* a new trade journal launched at the end of this decade of advertising's greatest influence, summed up in its name the industry's general opinion of itself. Outside the industry, the governor of New York doubtless spoke for many Americans: "If I were starting life over again," said Franklin D. Roosevelt, "I am inclined to think that I would go into the advertising business in preference to almost any other. . . . It is essentially a form of education; and the progress of civilization depends on education."

FOUR

DEPRESSION AND REFORM

I f the 1920s confirmed a culture defined by advertising, the ensuing Depression decade denied that culture. The swelling flow of
goods and services faltered, stuttered, finally threatened to stop
altogether. Advertising practitioners, as resident cheerleaders for the
economy, kept up appearances longer than most Americans. Eventually, even on Madison Avenue, doubts crept out from behind the
fixed smiles and brave drumbeating.

It was so unreal—such an unlikely cap on the giddy expansion of
the New Era. The Wall Street crash of October 1929 seemed at first
just another burp, leading at worst to just another recession. "There
is actually nothing wrong with the machine," Elmo Calkins said
early in 1930. "Nothing has happened but the squeezing of inflated
paper values from a lot of stocks." "What America needs," George
Washington Hill explained later that year, "is that Americans
should put their shoulders to the wheel, attend to their business and
move forward with the same confidence in America's future and development that we have always had." But the wheel would not turn
as before.

The total annual volume of advertising dropped from $3.4 billion
in 1929 to $2.6 billion in 1930 and then to $2.3 billion a year later.
Unemployment stood at 4 million workers in 1930, 8 million in
1931. "The recovery is as inevitable as the rising of the sun," said
Paul Cherington, director of research at JWT, "and we should
not be concerned with when it is coming but how to be ready for it

when it does come." Bad news kept piling up. Platoons of the unem-
ployed took to the road. Hoovervilles sprouted in dumps and railroad yards. Even some business spokesmen began to wonder out
loud.

As a major prophet of the New Era, Bruce Barton clung to the old
faith, at least in public. Instead of spreading gloom, he said in the
fall of 1931, bankers should be constructive: "If fifty men could be
found who dared to express publicly their conviction that the world
and the United States are not going completely busted, it might
turn the trick. Isn't there enough courage in Wall Street to bring this
about?" he asked Owen Young, chairman of General Electric. The
system would right itself, that is, if everyone kept whistling.

Events continued to deny this hope. The Federal Reserve Board
index of manufacturing production fell from 110 in 1929 to 57 in
1932. Another 4 million workers lost jobs in 1932. Advertising expenditures kept withering away, bottoming out at $1.3 billion in
1933, only 38 percent of the pre-Depression level. When Franklin
Roosevelt took over the White House in 1933, the banks were closed
and one worker in four was jobless. In this bleak time even Bruce
Barton was caught up in the experimental spirit of FDR's Hundred
Days. "I'm a hard-shelled old reactionary in favor of sound money
and the ten commandments and the old-time religion," he allowed,
"but it is getting to a point where a large percentage of our clients
would rather do some business even with 'phoney' money than no
business with sound money." (Later Barton went into politics as a
prominent critic of the New Deal.)

Advertising agencies had to maintain a brave front to clients and
the public even while dealing with dwindling accounts and the hard
task of cutting personnel and client services. Early in the Depression,
Stanley Resor called a meeting of the major New York agencies and
proposed a voluntary moratorium on trying to steal each other's accounts. An obvious advantage for big, established shops like JWT,
the plan was stillborn; in 1932 William Esty left Thompson and
started his own agency. Albert Lasker cut the salaries of everyone at
Lord & Thomas by 25 percent (though he still drew several million
dollars a year from the agency himself), and then later had to fire
over fifty employees, including some senior executives. BBDO tried
to carry its people through the hard times and consequently was
overstaffed. On Madison Avenue one heard stories of agencies reduced from 150 employees to 30, of copywriter salaries slashed from

$230 to $60 a week, of stenographer salaries cut from $40 to $15 a week. Supervisors found themselves back at drawing boards and copy desks.

Clients pressured their agencies for rebates and special deals, and expected more effective ads for less money. Expensive artists gave way to cheaper photographers. The ghost of Claude Hopkins rose up: louder headlines and specific, harder-selling reason-why copy returned to favor. Underclad women, formerly encountered mostly in lingerie ads, now sold bathroom, household, even industrial products. A series of nudes by Edward Steichen for Woodbury soap featured unvoluptuous women in luxurious surroundings since "it is well understood by the masses that the best people do no wrong," *Advertising Age* assured its readers. Hard times meant a hard sell. This turn of the copy cycle predictably disappointed acolytes of the MacManus tradition like Barton. "Under the lash of bad business," he said in 1934, "ideals have been abandoned, standards have sunk." The waves of "silly advertisements, dishonest advertisements, disgusting advertisements," he added, had "cast discredit upon the business and put us on the defensive."

At a time of general skepticism toward American business, this return to the more obnoxious forms of advertising did indeed leave Madison Avenue vulnerable. Advertising's continued celebration of a materialist cornucopia appeared obscene in a nation headed toward breadlines and relief rolls. Nothing worked anymore. Advertising kept repeating the old promises and predicting the return of good times. Recovery never came. The prolonged crisis made every aspect of the economic system subject to unsparing criticism. Instead of wasteful, shoddy, unnecessary frills and gadgets, said the critics, Americans in these times needed cheap, honest, durable products. If advertising did not help this reorientation, then advertising would have to be reformed or abolished or taken over by the government. Under a new label, "consumerism," a diverse and growing popular movement presented advertising with its most severe emergency since the patent-medicine days.

❧❧

The roots of the consumer movement went back to the 1920s. In odd counterpoint to the main tendencies of the decade, a few books had raised stubborn questions about the surface optimism and materialist ethos of the time. Thorstein Veblen's *Absentee Ownership* and

the Lynds' *Middletown* would often be cited as antecedents by the reformers of the 1930s. Two other books, less academic than the work
of Veblen and the Lynds, anticipated on a more accessible level the
major themes of the Depression consumerists.

First, Helen Woodward offered a critique of advertising from
within the business. As a copywriter she had sold hundreds of thousands of books through human, emotional appeals: a picture of a little girl perched on a set of O. Henry's works; or of a barefoot Mark
Twain as a boy, watching a riverboat steaming away, with the caption "He walked with kings." Later, at the Presbrey and Gardner
agencies, she became one of the first prominent woman account executives. Yet she never relinquished the radical politics of her youth.
The daughter of Polish Jews, she had grown up in a cold-water railroad flat in New York. Her father, a cigarmaker, was a socialist and
single-taxer. "Even though I have lived a bourgeois life since I've
been grown," she said later, "I was so conditioned that I can look at
business or government only through a working-class window." One
of the highest-paid women in advertising, she retired in 1924 at the
age of forty-three and went to Paris to write her book.

Through Many Windows was published in 1926. Woodward brought
the reader inside a working ad agency, a place of fevered creativity and deadlines, of alternating triumphs and disasters, "of hurrying and joshing and smoking and swearing." Copywriters, she said,
had the best minds and the sharpest insights of anyone in the business world. In another era they might have become preachers or
teachers; now they applied their passions for instructing and con-
verting to products that they themselves might not trust. Woodward
recalled her own cynical absorption in the task at hand: the thought
of persuading millions of people to buy a can of soup excited her. In
preparing the copy she truly believed it the best of all soups. Then,
the ad finished and her passion spent, she could not imagine eating
the soup herself. Caught in these pulsings of creative frenzy and
bleak recognition after the fact, most copywriters not surprisingly
burned out by the time they reached forty. They retired, or were
kicked upstairs, or started drinking heavily or playing more golf,
with plenty of time to reflect on the misuse of their talents. "In the
advertising business we thought ourselves important," Woodward
concluded. "We thought we knew what we were doing; we had our
plans for next week or next year. The realization came to me with a
slow shock that I was nothing, we were nothing. We were feathers all

of us, blown about by winds which we neither understood nor controlled." Not an evil force, advertising was simply blind, stupid, and insincere.

Your Money's Worth, a broader indictment of American salesmanship, appeared a year later. The book was written by Stuart Chase, a liberal economist fired from the Federal Trade Commission because of his politics, and Frederick J. Schlink, a mechanical engineer who had worked for the U.S. Bureau of Standards and for private industry. "We are all Alices in a Wonderland of conflicting claims, bright promises, fancy packages, soaring words, and almost impenetrable ignorance," the authors announced. Mass production had cut the manufacturer's costs while consumer prices, fattened by advertising budgets, stayed high. Brand names, instead of ensuring consistent quality, only created monopolies. Patent medicines, insecticides, and radios offered merely the most flagrant examples of endemic consumer frauds. What could the alert consumer do? The Pure Food and Drug law of 1906 did not regulate advertising. Newspapers and magazines, dependent on ad revenues, could not dare to bite the feeding hand. The federal government must step in, subject consumer goods to standardized tests, and publish the results. That done, the consumer could make intelligent, informed choices without the need for systemic changes in the American political economy.

This mix of angry accusations within an inoffensive political framework brought the book wide attention. "It is often amusing, and in some parts seriously justified," Bruce Barton conceded, "but the picture is not finished and hence is not true." Distributed by the Book-of-the-Month Club, *Your Money's Worth* sold over 100,000 copies in a dozen years. In its wake the organization Consumers Research was launched to publish test results in its monthly magazine and to lobby for the consumer. The group prospered in the Depression, growing from 1,200 members in 1929 to 25,000 in 1931 and 45,000 two years later. Looking back later, Robert Lynd could plausibly call *Your Money's Worth* "the *Uncle Tom's Cabin* of the consumer movement."

Thus the general economic crisis of the 1930s coincided with a growing restiveness among consumers. In the progressive era, critics of advertising had indicted specific abuses in a time of general prosperity. Now, in the Depression, the ante was raised: advertising itself was attacked for generally promoting waste at a time when nobody had money to spare. A few artifacts of popular culture appeared to support this more comprehensive, more radical assault. In a movie version of *A Connecticut Yankee in King Arthur's Court,* released in 1931, Will Rogers as the Yankee defined advertising for King Arthur: "It makes you spend money you don't have for something you don't want."

The astonishing success of *Ballyhoo* magazine suggested that millions of Americans agreed with that description. Started in 1931 by a publisher of pulp and movie magazines, *Ballyhoo* reached a circulation of 2 million by showing no mercy to the purveyors of advertising and publicity. It published fake ads (one for alimony insurance drew serious replies), then real ads, leaving readers to puzzle between the satires and the satirized. "If you can build a lousy mousetrap," declared one Elmer Zilch in *Ballyhoo*, "and spend $10,000,000 advertising it, the world will beat a path to your door." His associate, Harvey K. Poop the Second, was "the man who first proved statistically that four out of five have pyorrhea and that nine out of ten believe it." The magazine helpfully revealed the Ten Commandments of Advertising (number ten: "Thou *shalt* covet thy neighbor's car and his radio and his silverware and his refrigerator and everything that is his").

In 1933 F. J. Schlink published *100,000,000 Guinea Pigs,* a more radical version of *Your Money's Worth.* Written with Arthur Kallet, an electrical engineer, the book focused on foods, drugs, and cosmetics. Not only wasteful or worthless, said the authors, these products were dangerous. The book submitted grisly cases of death or disfigurement caused by misbranded or adulterated goods. *Printers' Ink,* which had brushed aside *Your Money's Worth,* could no longer ignore the growing clamor outside. "Schlink's following among the higher-brows," *PI* editorialized, "is becoming a serious menace not only to the gyps but also to the reputable advertisers." *Guinea Pigs* sold even better than its predecessor, running through thirty-two printings and over 250,000 copies in six years, thus reflecting a building public awareness of the issues it raised.

A more radical version of *Through Many Windows* logically followed. James Rorty had spent a dozen years in advertising, writing copy for BBDO and other agencies, while he concurrently pursued a career in socialist politics, appearing regularly in the journals of the Marxist left. "He was always industrious and reliable and obedient and his stuff usually pleased," Roy Durstine said of his advertising work. "Everybody knew he was pretty red. But he mostly kept his red ideas to himself or voiced them with a deprecating giggle." In

1934, safely out of the business, he published *Our Master's Voice*, a book that was part apology, part manifesto. After his first three days in advertising, he said, he had learned all that he needed to know about copywriting. He felt no pride in the millions of words of copy he had churned out: "It was all anonymous, thank heaven, and I shall never claim a line of it."

Like Woodward, Rorty found the average adman smarter and more sophisticated than most businessmen. "But in moving day after day the little cams and gears that he has to move, he inevitably empties himself of human qualities. His daily traffic in half-truths and outright deceptions is subtly and cumulatively degrading." For two generations, said Rorty, Americans had been heeding advertising like an oracle, absorbing its values, following its instructions on how to live, love, and succeed. But now, in the Depression, advertising joined the rest of the system in a deepening crisis. The coarser forms of advertising in vogue since 1929—"dowdy and blatant and vulgar"—reflected the desperate flailings of a business in trouble. "Advertising men are indeed very unhappy these days, very nervous, with a kind of apocalyptic expectancy," Rorty concluded with relish. "I venture to predict that when a formidable Fascist movement develops in America, the ad-men will be right up front."

The book sold only 3,000 copies, but it struck nerves in the jittery advertising community. "Because he writes as an ex-insider," *Printers' Ink* conceded, "Comrade Rorty is frequently damnably penetrating in his criticism. Some of his satirical thrusts are bound to make ad-men squirm." Stuart Chase greeted the book as an autopsy of a system already doomed. *Advertising Age,* more reasonably, treated *Our Master's Voice* as a symptom of the times ("all business is under fire, and advertising is an outstanding characteristic of business in the machine age"). As *Ad Age* pointed out, Rorty's quarrel was less with advertising than with capitalism itself. "Don't try to reform advertising. It is a component part of a civilization that is wrong," said Rorty in 1935. "We must apply the Marxian formula of revolution and build from the bottom."

Rorty made other advertising reformers seem temperate and conservative. After a strike at Consumers Research, Arthur Kallet left to start another group, Consumers Union. Both organizations kept growing and tormenting Madison Avenue. The consumer movement also took in women's groups such as the League of Women Voters, PTA, American Home Economics Association, and especially the General Federation of Women's Clubs. Beyond them, an unorganized mass of individuals—teachers, office workers, labor union members, liberal publicists—read the proliferating consumer literature and sympathized with the movement's goals.

The New Deal included consumer councils in the National Relief Administration and other new agencies. Some of FDR's men were willing to go further. "From some of the advertisements I have seen," said presidential confidant Harry Hopkins, "perhaps it wouldn't be a bad idea for the government to take over the advertising business." In the Agriculture Department, Assistant Secretary Rexford Tugwell agreed with plans to take the supervision of advertising from the Federal Trade Commission, which had not bestirred itself in years, and place that authority in Agriculture's Food and Drug Administration. A bill to this end, sponsored by Senator Royal Copeland of New York, started making its slow way through Congress in 1933. As originally drafted, the Copeland bill would have established grades and standards for all food products; given the agriculture secretary wide powers over the manufacture and sale of foods, drugs, and cosmetics; extended regulation from product labels to advertising; and declared any ad false if it was misleading even by implication or ambiguity.

Facing these threats, the advertising community circled its wagons. C. C. Parlin, speaking for the National Publishers Association, warned that the grade-labeling provision of the Copeland bill threatened "the very existence" of American newspapers and magazines. "The social revolution now in progress," said Bruce Barton, might leave an industry so regimented that Americans would see very little advertising, as in Hitler's Germany and Mussolini's Italy, or no advertising at all, as in Stalin's Russia. The Copeland bill so upset Albert Lasker that he gave one of his rare public speeches to predict its consequences: a lower standard of living, an end to competition, a shackled press, and—worst—advertising stripped of its drama and emotional appeal. "The average consumer," said Lasker, "would not understand a government standard if he bumped into it in broad daylight." He conceded that advertising had its abuses, but the industry could take care of itself. "We do not burn down the barn to get rid of the rats."

In hindsight such forebodings seem excessive. At the time, though, the very excessiveness showed how worried advertising people were, how real the danger of government control appeared. The uninhibited reaching for arguments however silly accurately reflected the desperate tone of the rhetoric. Advertising was already amply supplied with problems by the Depression; now would government even keep Madison Avenue from plying its trade as before? No ordinary crisis could place Albert Lasker behind a podium. The specter of the Copeland bill hung over the industry, intruding even on vacation plans. As he left for Florida in the winter of 1933–34, Lasker looked forward to the sun and the beach: "So far as I know," he confided to a friend, "no Government control has yet been declared for the sunshine there."

To stave off federal intrusion the business fell back on its old dream of self-regulation. In 1934 the Proprietary Association adopted an ethical code and set up a committee to regulate over-the-counter drugs. Advertising also began to pay more serious attention to the consumer movement. "The tide has turned against us," said W. C. D'Arcy, retiring as chairman of the board of the AAAA in 1934. "The signals show red." *Printers' Ink* agreed: "There is in progress a consumers' rebellion of a kind that almost nobody seems to have anticipated"—"a revolt that spreads without benefit of leadership or prophecy." Consumerism drew support mainly from people of relative education and cultural attainment. Even if advertising did not sell much to this sector, it could not keep offending these articulate, politically active citizens. "The crisis is here," said *PI.* "If advertisers want to continue eating regularly, they had better meet it." All through the 1930s, as the Copeland bill came up each year, the consumer movement kept expanding. Whenever an adman looked over his shoulder, there it was, measuring, admonishing, threatening.

❦❦

An advertising glossary, as published in *Ballyhoo:*

Delicate membrane	Any part of the body
Lubricate the skin texture	Put on grease
Pore-deep cleansing	Washing the face
Harsh irritants	All the ingredients of a competitor's product
Great scientist	Anyone who will sign an endorsement
Lifetime	Until the new model comes out
Exclusive	Expensive

❦❦

Raymond Rubicam stands as a persuasive argument for a great-man theory of advertising history. No one has ever gone farther in advertising by standing apart from his times and making his own self-defined way. In the Depression decade, with other agencies failing and cutting staffs, Rubicam drove his agency from nowhere to second place in annual billings, behind only J. Walter Thompson. At a time of grim hard selling, Rubicam favored stylish, indirect persuasion, well crafted and visually attractive, that even used humor to make its pitch. With the industry drawn to the esoteric new techniques of radio advertising, Rubicam trusted and emphasized the medium of print. Finally, with the Depression pushing many advertisers to resume snake-oil methods, Rubicam held out for ethical restraint and, like Stanley Resor, would not solicit clients by campaigns prepared on speculation. "When Raymond Rubicam was in the room," said Dexter Masters of Consumers Union, "one could think of advertising as a profession."

Rubicam bucked these historical waves with an exceptional range of skills. He started out as a copywriter; as a young adman he created campaigns and slogans that lasted for decades. "I did a few outstanding things," Rubicam later said of his copy work to an admiring David Ogilvy, "but was not particularly prolific or adaptable." Once his agency reached a certain size Rubicam stopped writing in favor of supervising copy. "I think I was actually better as a copy chief and idea man than I was as a personal producer," he told Ogilvy. Though Rubicam loved the sweet tortures of creating ads, as a student of his trade he also respected research, the copywriter's nemesis. He plucked George Gallup from Northwestern University to develop the methods of opinion polling. As the agency kept growing Rubicam eventually had to give up copy supervision and concentrate on administration, charming clients, and playing advertising statesman. Least comfortable in these final roles, he nonetheless performed them as well as his earlier tasks.

Previous advertising leaders had excelled at one or two functions. A man of balanced temperament and steady habits, Rubicam excelled at everything he tried, combining the copywriting talent of Elmo Calkins, Helen Resor's teaching and supervising gifts, Stanley Resor's recognition of social science, the drive and imperial vision of Albert Lasker, and the unbending ethics of Theodore MacManus. Not merely the great adman of his generation, Rubicam ultimately became one of the most complete practitioners in advertising annals. After all these feats he still retired young, two weeks past his fifty-second birthday, and enjoyed a long, fruitful retirement in Arizona, free of both the ulcers and the recriminations of many Madison Avenue veterans.

From this distance, five decades after his advertising prime, Rubicam looks nearly mythological—a man who made no serious mistakes. Nothing in his background would have predicted this paragon: no brilliant early promise, no apparent role models, no stable family life, no inspired teacher to take the boy in hand and point the way. He apparently created himself. After a series of oddly assorted jobs he found advertising, perceived that it suited him, and took off from there, typically picking his own path, not so much against as unconcerned with the advertising fashions of his time.

He was born in June 1892 of two old Philadelphia families, German Lutheran on his father's side, French Huguenot on his mother's. The family lost its import-export business after Rubicam's paternal grandfather died intestate, leaving his holdings to his deceased wife's sisters. Thereafter Rubicam's father became a trade journalist while his mother contributed poetry to *Godey's* magazine; this orientation toward print showed up in their son. When Raymond was five his father died of tuberculosis, a family scourge. The youngest of eight children, Raymond was then farmed out to various siblings and in effect lost both parents. He stayed with a sister in Ohio, a brother in Texas, and mainly with his brother Harry in Denver. These uprootings and diverse surrogate parents produced an unruly boy, restless and constantly in trouble at school. He ran away at least twice. After the eighth grade, now in Denver, he quit school and started clerking full-time in a grocery store. (Later, when asked about his college background, he might casually refer to a nonexistent "Jersey University.")

Some inchoate yearning for roots and stability drew him back to Philadelphia, a home he had barely known. At eighteen, with an ambition to write short stories after the fashion of O. Henry, he set out again. For a year he headed eastward, working occasionally as a bellhop, theater usher, movie projectionist, door-to-door salesman of colored enlargements of family portraits, and general hand on cattle cars. Perhaps in imitation of O. Henry, he sampled the lower reaches of society, riding freight cars and sojourning with hoboes; later he told his son a story about stealing an engineer's lunch. After this *Wanderjahr* he found a friendly reception among his relatives in Philadelphia. He settled into a more conventional life. His free-lance feature stories brought him a cub reporting job on a Philadelphia newspaper at twelve dollars a week. He next tried selling automobiles. But he had met a woman he wanted to marry, and his commissions provided a risky income for starting a family. "Then for the first time," he recalled, "I heard of advertising as a special business in a special world of its own." It would combine his interests in writing and selling and might pay better than a salesman's commissions.

As he set about breaking into this new field, the once wayward youth displayed hints of the spirit and persistence that would take him to the top of his profession. For the first time in his life he started *seeing* advertisements, looking for them, studying them. He wrote his own ads for two products made in Philadelphia: one in a slangy Ring Lardner sportswriter's style for a plug tobacco, and one in the dignified idiom of a Walter Lippmann editorial for a truck company. Unaware of advertising agencies, he contacted the manufacturers. "I telephoned the presidents of both companies to tell them in effect that I had jewels of great value to show them." He reached neither president, but the tobacco company did refer him to its agency, F. Wallis Armstrong. He left his ads at the Armstrong office and came back the next day. Hoping for an interview with the boss, he was told to wait.

Armstrong was an old-school tyrant, a tall, commanding figure with a loud voice who bullied his employees. "He was hated by all who worked for him," according to one of his clients, "and thoroughly despised by every space rep who ever had the misfortune to be obliged to call on him." To clients he smiled unctuously; in fact he owned shares of two leading accounts, Campbell's Soup and Whitman candy. Knowing nothing about this ogre, young Rubicam, twenty-three years old, waited out in the lobby. At mid-afternoon Armstrong rumbled forth, said he was too busy, and told the young man to come back tomorrow. Rubicam came back the next day, and the next, and the next, finally playing out this charade for nine consecutive business days. "I sat in that lobby—on a bench so hard that I can still feel it," he recalled. "On three different days the boss passed me, amazed me by calling me by name, but said he couldn't see me that day. By the ninth day going to that office had become a sort of hypnosis. But while I was full of hope each morning, I had been getting madder toward the end of each day. At the end of the ninth day, I exploded." He rushed out and wrote a furious letter to Armstrong describing his credentials and complaining of his treatment. After hand-delivering the letter he went home, feeling better. The next day Armstrong let him in: "Those ads of yours didn't amount to much," he said, "but this letter has real stuff." He was hired as an apprentice copywriter at twenty dollars a week—with the understanding that he would visit the washroom on his own time.

As an unreformed nineteenth-century adman, Armstrong gave his attention to space buying and nicking the corners off his contracts. The preparation of ads was unimportant to him. "A copywriter is a necessary evil," he said, "but an art director is a goddamned luxury." He made a special point of humiliating his employees. They could not receive personal visitors or phone calls in the office. Armstrong did not like to see them lunching together or socializing away from business. He would line up a half-dozen of his workers against the wall in his office and then menacingly ask each one, "Don't I pay you more than you're worth?" Despite these sweatshop conditions Rubicam learned his craft from two suffering copywriters at Armstrong, Wolstan Dixey and William Baer, and by studying the ads coming out of J. Walter Thompson. Rubicam's copy for Girard cigars, Blabon linoleum, and Victor Talking Machines brought him begrudged bonuses and raises, and a sample book impressive enough to let him move on. He decided to quit after Armstrong betrayed a business confidence—the last in a series of provocations. The three years with Armstrong, he said later, left him with the conviction "that a simple formula for a sound agency would be to reverse practically everything Armstrong did."

He wanted to join JWT, but it had no office in Philadelphia. Instead he went to work for N. W. Ayer, the best agency in his hometown, at $125 a week. ("Going to Ayer, eh?" Armstrong asked. "What do they want *you* for?") Wayland Ayer, still an intermittent presence at the agency he had started fifty years earlier, was an autocrat, but a benevolent one, according to Rubicam. The agency still stood for clean ethics and fair dealing: no secret arrangements with clients, friendly relations between employees, expressed appreciation for good work. After Armstrong the place was a paradise, releasing Rubicam to do his best work. He was assigned the Steinway piano account as one of his first tasks. Coasting on its reputation, Steinway had never advertised heavily. Rubicam was told to prepare three full magazine pages along the lines of previous campaigns. When the words would not flow, he looked through the file of old Steinway ads, noting that Steinways had been favored by most great pianists and composers since Wagner.

As all writers know to their frustration, the muse may not appear when bidden, but then may come when not called. Puzzling over the Steinway copy, Rubicam was distracted for a moment by a paper on his desk. "Without effort," he recalled, "the phrase formed in my mind, 'The Instrument of the Immortals.' I wrote it on a piece of yellow paper, and it looked so good that I was afraid to accept my own estimation of it. I decided to put it away in a desk drawer." A few days later it still looked good. For the accompanying photograph Rubicam posed a model resembling Franz Liszt at the keyboard in a dramatic posture, with sunlight streaming in from a window catching the pianist in sharp profile. Under the headline Rubicam added a short paragraph: "There has been but one supreme piano in the history of music. In the days of Liszt and Wagner, or Rubinstein and Berlioz, the preeminence of the Steinway was as unquestioned as it is today. It stood then, as it stands now, the chosen instrument of the masters—the inevitable preference wherever great music is understood and esteemed." The client, regarding "slogans" as undignified, would not make the ad the basis for an entire campaign. They agreed to run it once. For the first time in twenty years, a Steinway ad brought a noticeable response. The client reconsidered its position on slogans. During the 1920s, as radios and victrolas bit into piano production, Steinway sales went up almost 70 percent. "The Instrument of the Immortals" remained the Steinway hallmark for decades.

E. R. Squibb, known mainly as a manufacturer of prescription drugs, decided in 1921 to start advertising over-the-counter products. Wary of acquiring a patent-medicine tarnish, Squibb turned down the first four campaigns Ayer presented it. The assignment came to Rubicam: write an ad with no pictures, only a list of the products in small type at the bottom of the page; sell by association with the good name of Squibb. "My efforts to produce something effective are still painful in my mind," Rubicam wrote over fifty years later. "I became obsessed with the problem day and night and covered dozens of yellow sheets with headlines, both in the office and at home." He often wrote in the evening: he wasted mornings in a writer's ritual of writing avoidance and seldom produced anything until mid-afternoon. "One night at two in the morning I seemed as far away from a solution as ever and I started for bed. As I gathered

up my yellow sheets I took one more look through the mass of headlines I had written. Suddenly, two separate word combinations
popped out at me from two different headlines. One was 'Priceless
Ingredient,' the other was 'Honor and Integrity.' " He combined
them into "The Priceless Ingredient of every product is the honor
and integrity of its maker." The picky client accepted this line as the
basis for the campaign and kept it as the house slogan. When *Printers' Ink* in 1945 asked its readers to name the greatest advertisement
of all time, the two runners-up to MacManus' "Penalty of Leadership" were Rubicam's "Priceless Ingredient" and Ned Jordan's
"Somewhere West of Laramie."

In his three and a half years at Ayer, Rubicam also produced
noted campaigns for Rolls-Royce, International Correspondence
Schools, and the agency itself. Few copywriters have ever rung
so many bells in so short a time. The rising star at Ayer, he was given
an overnight 50 percent raise, to $12,000 a year, when a midwestern
agency dangled him an offer. But again he was not content. When
Wayland Ayer died in 1922 he was succeeded by his complacently
ignorant son-in-law, whose leadership was not promising. More
seriously, the agency did not appreciate the importance of art and
copy. Nobody from the creative departments was ever elected to
partnership. Ayer's man in New York used to clip Thompson ads
from magazines, bring them to Philadelphia and spread them on the
copy department floor, and ask, "Why can't we do this?" In 1923 the
agency passed over Rubicam and George Cecil, its two best copywriters, and named an older, better-connected, less able man as copy
chief. Rubicam decided again to leave. As with Armstrong, his time
at Ayer gave him definite ideas about how an agency *should* be run.

At Armstrong he had shared an office with John Orr Young, an
account and new business man with an expansive, gregarious personality. Later Rubicam helped Young move over to Ayer. The two
men and their families became close friends. One day in the spring
of 1923 Young and Rubicam went for a walk and, considering their
assets—"clients none, cash meager, hopes high"—they decided to
launch their own agency.

Young came from a small town in Iowa. After two years of college
he had started in advertising as a copywriter under Claude Hopkins
at Lord & Thomas in Chicago; Hopkins, a believer in words, did not
like the succulent pictures of oranges Young prepared for the Sun-
kist account. Young hastened his departure from L & T by passing a
satirical letterhead around the office:

LOUD & PROMISE
Badvertising

A. D. Rascal, President   Cable Address: Predatory
Fraud Hopkins, V.P.

Young then proceeded through a varied advertising résumé in Chicago and New York until meeting Rubicam at Armstrong. More experienced than his new partner, Young had the contacts for attracting clients. "I never felt that bird-of-prey instinct which has motivated some salesmen to outstanding success," he recalled. "I tried to let the prospect sell himself."

In this oblique way Young brought in Y & R's first important client. Calling at the New York office of the group of companies that later became General Foods, he asked not for the prospect's entire business but only its most troublesome product. "We dared the advertiser to split his account and give us the toughest piece," Young said later. He got Postum, a noncaffeinated beverage with anemic sales. Rubicam wrote a campaign stressing not the taste of Postum or the evils of caffeine but the soothing effect drinking Postum would have on nervous, sleepless people. The series of ads—"Why Men Crack" and "When the Iron Man Begins to Rust"—revived Postum sales, won a Harvard-Bok prize, and established Young & Rubicam as an agency. General Foods rewarded the agency with its big Grape Nuts account and promised more business if Y & R would move to New York. The agency complied in 1926, and over the next few years General Foods gave it Jell-O, Sanka coffee, Calumet Baking Powder, and other products.

With this growth the staff expanded quickly. One of the first additions was Samuel Cherr, hired away from the *New York American* to start a merchandising department at an initial salary higher than either Young's or Rubicam's. Soon known as "Mr. No," Cherr was a sharp, argumentative New York cynic. "Sam Cherr had a precious ability," one of his men said later, "to instill in people who worked for him the highest self-imposed standards of any man I ever knew." Robert Work started as an office boy when Y & R had only four employees and eventually managed the copy department on the strength of his teaching and editing skills. Ted Patrick, later editor of *Holiday,* began writing copy for the agency in 1928. Two other copywriting mainstays, John Rosebrook and Louis Brockway, were also on the payroll by 1930.

Young and Rubicam found some of their best talent in raids on their old employer, N. W. Ayer. Charles Leroy Whittier joined in

1924 and became copy chief three years later. Called "the bald eagle" behind his back in tribute to his nonexistent hairline, Whittier possessed "a quicksilver mind," according to an associate, "a many-splendored imagination, and a sarcastic contempt for the ordinary which terrified the rank and file." He later wrote a popular five-hundred-page textbook on advertising. Another copy man, Harold Sidney Ward, arrived in 1926. Known for his wit, Ward was asked one day whether he wanted coffee with his lunch. "What?" he asked. "Do you think I want to stay awake all afternoon?" Sigurd Larmon, an account executive, came over from Ayer in 1929; he would eventually succeed Rubicam as head of the agency. In 1930 Rubicam hired Vaughn Flannery, whom he regarded as the best art director in advertising, from Ayer for the huge salary of $25,000 plus a vice-presidency and a chunk of Y & R stock. Flannery called himself an Advertising Designer: not simply an artist converted to a business career, as he defined it, but a specialist with a long-standing interest in both advertising and design, resembling not a fine artist but an architect. "Like the architect," said Flannery, "he accepts the limitations of his craft and attempts to convert these limitations into more effective results."

In sum, a group of unconventional people from unconventional backgrounds. As a man of checkered origins and little formal education, Rubicam hired for talent and spirit, not the usual items on a résumé. By one reckoning, only a third of these Y & R "originals" had finished college; three had not even finished high school. When Lou Brockway arrived in 1930 he found that none of the top seven men in the agency had attended college. "I began to get an inferiority complex because I had gone to college," he recalled. Especially as compared to JWT and BBDO, the agency tolerated eccentric personalities and behavior. Rubicam himself still did little work before noon. Ted Patrick came in late, "looking like a pool-hall hustler or a retired jockey fresh out of a Damon Runyon story," took long lunches, and disappeared at odd times, usually to a tennis court. Roy Whittier, born of vaudeville parents, started appearing in shows at the age of five and learned to write by composing skits. For Postum he invented "Mr. Coffee Nerves," a cartoon figure resembling a stock mustachioed stage villain. Whittier was a passionate adopter and dropper of hobbies: horse riding, piano playing, navigation, farming, dieting. Vaughn Flannery painted racehorses and racing scenes, and later retired to his breeding farm in Maryland.

Jack Rosebrook, a Cincinnati native, was fascinated by the antebellum South. He maintained a Civil War library of over five hundred books, owned a plantation outside Charlottesville, named his son Jeb Stuart Rosebrook, and staged an annual Derby Ball, dressed in a Confederate general's uniform. He liked to be called Colonel.

As agencies went, Y & R allowed an open, friendly, informal atmosphere at the office. Many substantive conversations took place in the halls or on the run. "No one save the secretaries got in much before 9:30," Rosebrook noted; "it was folly to call a meeting before 10." Rubicam would ignore details as long as the work got done. Artists and copywriters, known for their tics and temperaments, were granted special leeway. At one point Whittier had the whole staff playing with diets. In the art department one day a secretary was telling an art director she didn't need to diet because she did ballet. To prove her point she invited the man to feel her thigh muscle. Just then Rubicam walked in with a client. "Well—artists, you know," Rubicam explained, backing out of the room.

But—a large but—the work did get done. Ted Patrick might take liberties, but he missed no deadlines. With a due date at hand, or when a client wanted changes or even an entirely new campaign, the evening sun meant nothing. Everyone available would join a "gang-up," as it was called, an intense meeting that from a blend of coffee, sandwiches, sweat, and cigarette smoke turned out ads at a furious pace. Though "we were paying no attention to the starting whistle, we were putting in many, many hours of overtime," Rosebrook recalled. "Ray loved to call gang-ups together at four in the afternoon, which meant we worked far into the night." Even on a normal day Rubicam seldom left the office before 7:30; then he might scout the premises for someone to take to dinner. One evening he found a new man in the radio department. "Good evening," he said, "my name is Rubicam." "Yeah, mine is Young," said the new man. The boss took him to dinner anyway.

The snap and pace of life at Y & R left casualties, notably one of the founders. At an early point Rubicam, still nursing literary ambitions, thought about quitting to try writing fiction. Young, knowing the source of the agency's reputation, talked him out of it, but at a price: Rubicam would take over as president with a controlling interest in the business. Thereafter the power and initiative flowed toward Rubicam. For his part, Young liked his hobbies and free time. Becoming rich, he said later, was no excuse to work day and night:

"Remember that some of the best years are passing while you prostrate yourself at the feet of the idol of Success." Rubicam's daughter
Kathleen was best friends with Young's daughter. When Kathleen
visited the Young home "Uncle Orr" would be there, with time for
the children. "Daddy was always working," Kathleen recalled.

"For some time there had been mutterings among key people that
Orr wasn't carrying his weight, yet was collecting big dividends
from his big block of stock," according to Rosebrook. "Orr was taking long vacations and not working too hard when on the job. He
complained of ill health and I think he was sincere. But I'm also
quite sure he was getting bored." A casual administrator, Young
also neglected his original task of new business. Once a prospective
client pointedly told Rubicam *not* to bring Young to a presentation.
Finally in 1934 Young was pressured out of the agency, and Sigurd
Larmon took his place as head of new business.

Of course, even Rubicam did not work *all* the time. As a cub reporter in Philadelphia he had reviewed plays, and he still loved theater. Despite his limited schooling he was well read and careful
about grammar and punctuation (one of his children received an
hour's lecture on the proper use of the semicolon). He read mysteries
for relaxation, and history, biography, and social commentary for
his mind. As a thinker he was confined by no business orthodoxy.
"Most of us in business," he told Bruce Barton, "make the mistake of
leaving critical examination of business to its enemies, and content
ourselves with defending it." An independent Republican, Rubicam
twice voted for Franklin Roosevelt. Temperamentally he liked to
thrust and parry and question any unsupported assertions. Sometimes he embarrassed the wives in a social group by provoking fierce
arguments. He liked games, playing to win with a smoking competitiveness. He golfed at a six-handicap until buying a farm in Bucks
County, Pennsylvania, where he turned his attention to breeding
Aberdeen Angus cattle and Berkshire hogs. The farm also released a
quiet, contemplative aspect to his personality. Occasionally he
would attend a Quaker meeting in Bucks County. At other times he
simply sat in a chair and meditated.

In the office, in his element, he dominated a corps of proud, headstrong talents. At intervals his associates would be seared by a quick
flare of temper. Making the presentation at a client meeting in Detroit one day, he paused momentarily for breath. One of his contact
men leaped in with "What Mr. Rubicam means to say—." Vain

about his command of language, Rubicam fired the man on the
train back to New York. But this episode was atypical. Normally he
spoke softly and treated his people with courtesy. He was a medium-sized man, five feet seven and a half inches tall and about one
hundred fifty-five pounds, with hazel eyes, an oval face, and unremarkable features. Given his track record and range of talents he
could lead by example, without raising his voice or pulling rank.
"There was nobody in the place who thought he was better than
Raymond Rubicam," said one of his copywriters. "Sometimes we'd
work a week on a trade ad," said another. "Imagine! A whole week.
It had to be just so."

Rubicam molded Y & R in his own image as a creative agency—
the lesson from his stay at Ayer. Many ads by his competitors, especially those offering testimonials or a mass of literal facts, seemed
idiotic to him. "A lot of people writing copy for advertisements," he
once said, "should be digging sewers." In a major address to the Association of National Advertisers in 1928, he insisted the trade most
needed better writers and "a zeal for good copy." At Y & R he encouraged good copy by giving creative control to the artists and
copywriters, not the administrators and account executives. At most
agencies in the 1930s a contact man could fiddle with an ad to suit
himself or a client. Y & R was the first major agency to change this
ancient tradition. Art and copy stars at Y & R were also routinely
made partners and rewarded with stock.

The Claude Hopkins school of claim and reason-why tended to
seize upon an effective pitch and then repeat it until it was used up.
By contrast, Rubicam pushed his creative departments to take
chances and try fresh approaches. He wanted a series of dissimilar,
striking ads, not simple reiteration. "The value of an idea is in inverse ratio to the number of times it has been used," he often said.
"Our job is to resist the usual." Instead of bulk and repetition,
a typical Y & R ad offered a light, skillful use of indirect headlines
and intriguing leads: a carrot instead of a cudgel. Roy Whittier's
textbook, significantly titled *Creative Advertising,* declared that a
copywriter needed imagination first, then logic. "The art of persuasion," said Whittier, meant the mustering of information so provo-
catively that people would make up their own minds, without being
pushed, in favor of the product.

In general, the Hopkins tradition trusted research and counting
while the MacManus tradition, embraced by Rubicam, trusted in-

tuition and the creative act. Here too Rubicam made his own way. During the 1920s George Gallup, a professor of advertising and journalism at Northwestern, began conducting surveys to find which specific parts of print media were most noticed by the audience. His newspaper studies, extended to fourteen newspapers and some forty thousand interviews with readers, found that people most noticed the picture page (85 percent), the most popular comic strip (70 percent), and editorial cartoons (40–50 percent). Even the lead story on the first page and the lead editorial fared less well. Women predictably ignored the sports, men the society and cooking articles. Department store ads drew 10 percent of the men, 55 percent of the women.

Much of this on reflection may have seemed common sense, but Gallup's survey of magazine readership, conducted in the summer of 1931, included surprises. He first tabulated the ads in four weeklies to find the most-used appeals. Economy and Efficiency, he found, ranked first, Quality fifth, Sex and Vanity tied for ninth and last place. Gallup's interviewers then rang 15,000 doorbells to ask which ads people remembered reading. Men, it turned out, had most noticed those ads with a Quality appeal first, then Sex. Women had responded best to ads featuring Sex, Vanity, and Quality, in that order. Thus the appeals used least frequently by advertisers actually drew the most attention from the public.

When Gallup published these results the advertising world took notice. His name, said *Advertising & Selling* in March 1932, "has rocketed into public consciousness with dramatic speed during the past year. The activities of this newcomer in the world of advertising and marketing have provided what is probably the most discussed topic of the day." Various agencies tried to hire him away from academia. In April 1932 Rubicam went to see him in Chicago. "Raymond Rubicam was far more interested intellectually in how advertising works than the other people I talked to," Gallup recalled, "and he offered me the complete freedom that I didn't think was possible in the business world." Gallup agreed to join Y & R in New York full-time at the end of the semester.

In contrast with J. B. Watson's efforts at JWT, Gallup had a perceptible effect on his agency's product. When he came up with something new, Rubicam would call a gang-up of his top people and they would pick over the finding until one o'clock in the morning. Given the demonstrated popularity of comic strips, Roy Whittier invented a cartoon character, Little Albie, to sell Grape Nuts in a sequence of pictures. The comic-strip technique was then applied to seemingly real people, engaged in an extended conversation about the product. Gallup also showed that readers preferred short paragraphs, type "widows" to leave white space at the end of paragraphs, and other type devices—italics, boldface, subheads—to break up the copy and maintain attention. Further, the audience preferred rectangular pictures, not odd shapes, and uncropped photos.

Gallup's influence extended outside Y & R, as reflected in the trade's greater use of nudity and sex appeal, a general adoption of comic-strip formats, and the appearance of other readership services. Daniel Starch, formerly director of research for the AAAA, started his own company to compete with Gallup in 1932. The brothers Thompson enjoyed a brief vogue in the 1930s with their twenty-seven points, drawn from research and guaranteed to select effective copy. Gallup stayed at Y & R for sixteen years and never regretted leaving academic life. "I had all the money I wanted available for any kind of an experiment that I wanted to conduct," he said later. "I was not asked to do a single thing that was not completely and entirely ethical." Once a client—a deodorant that brought in $2 million in annual billings—asked him to alter the results of his research to reveal the product as the best in its field. Gallup refused, and the agency resigned the account.

The addition of Gallup made Y & R unique in the business: an agency with a reputation for sharp, original copy *plus* professional, usable research; advertising as both art and science. Billings kept growing regardless of the Depression, from $6 million in 1927 to $12 million in 1935 and $22 million in 1937. New clients in these years included such blue chips as an insurance company (Travelers), an oil company (Gulf), a prestige car (Packard), a popular whiskey (Four Roses), and a drug company (Bristol-Myers). Twice in this period the agency had to announce it could take on no new accounts.

When Henry Luce started publishing *Fortune* in 1930, Y & R began a long and mutually beneficial connection with the magazine. One of the first issues carried a striking house ad written by Rubicam and designed by art director Walter Nield. Under the bold headline "IMPACT," a photograph of a man's face distorted, the eyes rolling upward, by a punch to the jaw; beneath the photo, two short paragraphs defining the headline: "ACCORDING TO WEB-

STER: The single instantaneous striking of a body in motion against another body. ACCORDING TO YOUNG & RUBICAM: That quality in an advertisement which strikes suddenly against the reader's indifference and enlivens his mind to receive a sales message." The day this ad appeared, the Hollywood producer Sam Goldwyn told his New York representative to sign up Y & R.

Other noted campaigns by the agency in these years included:

—for Travelers, a mood piece by Sid Ward titled "Thoughts at Thirty-Nine," under a drawing of a man leaning on a country fence, ruminating over his pipe, now beyond his youthful dreams and thinking ahead. "No, I'll probably never be rich. But I'm losing no sleep over it . . . for I've fixed things so I'm even surer that I'll never be poor. . . . Moral: Insure in the Travelers."

—for Arrow shirts, a series of ads that sold with humor. In one, a homely man declared, "Even I look good in an Arrow shirt." In another, written by George Gribbin, a picture of a man talking to a horse hitched to a milk wagon, with the unignorable headline "My friend, Joe Holmes, is now a horse." Joe, who had died, had always wanted to be a horse. Now he had returned in equine form. "I am now wearing a comfortable collar for the first time in my life," said the horse. "My shirt collars always used to shrink and murder me." Gee, the friend thought, I should have told him about Arrow shirts, which never shrink.

—for the Borden Company, a campaign to unify the advertising of all its varied dairy products. The solution, devised by Edward Dexter: Elsie the cow as the Borden symbol, providing (according to Dexter) "human interest, friendliness, good nature, credible persuasiveness." In one ad the milk-wagon horse returned to converse with Elsie—a sly in-joke for Y & R connoisseurs.

—for Four Roses, a visual image of the cooling refreshment of a whiskey highball on a hot summer day. Henry Lent had an idea while driving along the Merritt Parkway late one night. "Hey," he asked his wife, "what would you think of freezing four roses in a cake of ice?" "Sounds sort of crazy to me," she said. The photographer, Anton Bruehl, encountered a technical problem: when the ice froze all the way through it squashed the roses. But the roses stayed pretty when the center of the block was left unfrozen. The resulting ad ran every summer for years.

Rubicam's direct involvement in these ads may not have gone beyond approving the finished product. But he still set the tone and

▲ Lydia E. Pinkham, the Quaker housewife from Lynn, Massachusetts, whose Vegetable Compound—as marketed by her sons—became one of the first advertising success stories

◄ A typical Pinkham newspaper ad of the 1880s

J. Walter Thompson, who introduced advertising into polite magazines and founded a great advertising agency ▼

◄ Albert Lasker, publicist for reason-why copy, and the dominant figure in American advertising over the first two decades of the twentieth century

▲ John E. Kennedy, copywriter, who taught Lasker the gospel of reason-why and then briefly worked for him at Lord & Thomas

◄ Claude C. Hopkins, Lasker's prize copywriter and the main exponent of one of the two major traditions in advertising strategy

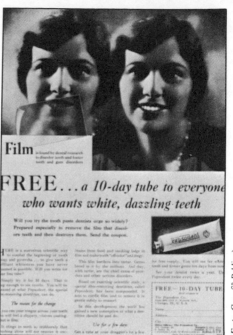

(*Foote, Cone & Belding*)

Three Lord & Thomas ads from the 1920s

(*Foote, Cone & Belding*)

(*Foote, Cone & Belding*)

▲ Helen Lansdowne Resor, the most influential copywriter of the 1920s and the first woman of real prominence in advertising; photographed around 1917, at the time of her marriage to Stanley Resor

Stanley B. Resor, who led Thompson to a position as the largest agency in the business, an eminence it would keep for fifty years ▼

James Webb Young, after Helen Resor the most noted Thompson copywriter of the 1920s; photographed in the agency's Chicago office

Through the old SOUTH he rode...
spreading the news of his discovery

Years ago Joel Cheek set out from Nashville on horseback, carrying samples of his now famous coffee blend

In his saddle-bags, Joel Cheek carried the first samples of that special blend which has now captured America—

Where the great folk of the old South gathered for banquets and balls—at the old Maxwell House in Nashville—Joel Cheek's blend was served for years

HE was a Southerner of the old South, born with an unusual sense for flavor.

Down in old Tennessee, he dreamed of a special richness in coffee—of a taste no single coffee grown could yield. To please the critical families of old Dixie he set out years ago to create a totally new shade of flavor.

For months he worked patiently and skilfully, blending coffee with coffee, joining taste with taste. Through trial after trial he persisted until he discovered it—a particular way of blending many coffees, a new, full-bodied goodness.

Soon it became the favorite coffee of the South

On horseback, Joel Cheek started out from Nashville to sell his blend. With samples in his saddle-bags, he carried the news of it through that land of good living.

From the first, his coffee won approval among the great Southern families. Long ago it became the first choice of all Dixie.

Today that extra touch of richness in Maxwell House Coffee has captured the entire country. The blend that Joel Cheek sold on horseback long ago is now pleasing more people than any other coffee ever offered for sale.

Known to the South alone until recently, Maxwell House is now by far the largest selling coffee in the United States. Seven great plants are needed to supply it fresh roasted to millions of homes from coast to coast.

A new experience in good living awaits you in the smooth, full-bodied liquor of this blend. Your grocer has it

in sealed blue tins. Maxwell House Products Company, Inc., Nashville, Houston, Jacksonville, Richmond, New York, Los Angeles, Chicago.

Radio listeners—tune in! Noted artists every Thursday—Maxwell House Coffee Radio Hour—9:00 p.m. Eastern Standard Time, 8:30 p. m. Central Standard Time...

MAXWELL HOUSE COFFEE

It is pleasing more people than any other coffee ever offered for sale

Two Thompson ads from the early years of Helen and Stanley Resor's leadership

A Skin you love to touch

Woodbury's Facial Soap

Charles Leroy Whittier, copy chief at Young & Rubicam during the agency's period of rapid growth in the 1930s ▶

▲ Raymond Rubicam, copywriter and builder of his own agency, and the major exponent of the other great tradition in advertising strategy, the antithesis of the Hopkins approach

▶ Harold Sidney Ward, copywriter and wit, author of the "Thoughts at Thirty-nine" ad for Travelers Insurance

John B. Rosebrook, student of the old Confederacy and chronicler of life at Young & Rubicam ▶

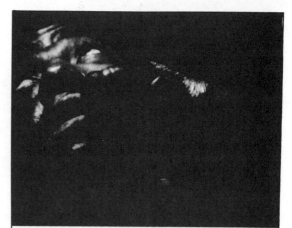

Four Young & Rubicam ads from the 1930s and 1940s

(John S. Getchell)

J. Stirling Getchell, a copywriter who loved photographs, the most important influence on the visual style of 1930s advertising; and a sad example of an adman who pursued his career with self-destructive intensity

fertile atmosphere in the creative departments. When he made Gribbin a copy supervisor, Rubicam told him never to edit someone else's copy by himself. Instead, said Rubicam, without marking up the original copy he should call in the writer for a discussion between peers, "not a critique of professor to pupil." Then the writer should make the changes himself, retaining ownership in the ad and pride in the final result.

Such delicate handling of creative egos made the agency a mecca for artists and copywriters. Two decades later, when a panel of experts picked the top one hundred copywriters in the business, twenty-four of the hundred listed major experience at Y & R and nineteen picked a Y & R ad as their favorite work. People stayed at the agency despite offers of better pay elsewhere; or if they did leave, later came back at a smaller salary. After Jack Rosebrook wrote a successful ad, "To the man who is afraid to let his dreams come true," for Rolls-Royce, Lennen & Mitchell offered him a salary of $25,000. He was then making $9,000 at Y & R. "We can't match that figure and wouldn't try to," Rubicam told him. "But Jack"— his voice trembled—"I don't want to see you leave us." ("I believe this was the only occasion in all the years I worked for and with Raymond Rubicam," Rosebrook said later, "that I ever felt close to him.") Rosebrook stayed, as did most of his associates. In its first twenty-five years nobody left the agency with an account. Y & R hired, developed, and kept its own people. "A company which must hire leaders from the outside," Rubicam once said, "either doesn't hire good employees, or doesn't train or treat them properly."

The best and the worst in advertising collided when Y & R took on George Washington Hill. Hill assigned the agency Pall Mall, its first cigarette account. Successive campaigns improved Pall Mall sales. Hill was characteristically not satisfied. He gave Rubicam a contraption with various cogs and wheels representing parts of the marketing process. Rubicam did not find the device edifying. Hill insisted that Rubicam come see him every two weeks. On these occasions he would deliver lectures about good advertising: how he entertained his grandchild by showing his watch, then his pocket knife, then his dental bridge. "The public reaction to entertainment and advertising is no different," Hill told Rubicam. "You just don't understand the advertising business." Rubicam thought he knew a little about advertising. Hill kept insisting that Rubicam replace the team working on Pall Mall with a whole new group. Three times

Rubicam complied; the fourth time he stiffened. "Most of us in Y & R had come to feel," he recalled, "that when George W. Hill was added to the innate and unavoidable difficulties of the business, the 'mix' was too much to take except in case of stark necessity. That necessity we did not have." So he called on Hill and, no doubt with relish, resigned the $3 million account. When the news reached Y & R drinks came forth and people started dancing in the aisles.

"Young & Rubicam was heaven, or next door to it, and God's name was Raymond Rubicam," one man recalled. "We were Y & R and that meant the best there was. It was more of a religion than it was an advertising agency."

❦❦

The 1930s saw the maturing of radio, the second great national medium, after magazines, to be nursed and financed by advertising. "You can't imagine," one radio pioneer, Carroll Carroll, recalled, "with what crushing surprise radio made its guerrilla attack on all advertising agencies. It caught few ready for it but all prepared to fake it."

Radio presented Madison Avenue a range of unprecedented problems: advertising with no visual aspects at all, therefore with renewed emphasis on the words, but with the addition of sounds—music, different voices, background clutter, sound effects—anything to catch and hold the ear. Though essentially verbal, radio advertising was not read. It passed through the air quickly and was gone; it could not be picked up at leisure and noticed again by the next reader. By the same token, it could move preliterate children and the one American adult in twenty who could not read. The target audience thus expanded (Ipana toothpaste helpfully referred to itself as "the one in the red and yellow tube"). Perhaps most important, radio advertising was intrusive and inescapable. One could not flip the page and skip it. The radio listener, unless willing to get up and turn the dial, was a captive audience, agreeing to hear about Pepsodent as the price of laughing at Amos 'n' Andy. Not just a sign in the subway or a distraction in a magazine, advertising now became a living voice in the home, speaking more intimately and unavoidably than ever before: "the only form of advertising that runs like a train," as a radio man put it, "that people wait for, that becomes an event or institution in their lives."

Like Young & Rubicam, radio incongruously grew and flourished in the 1930s, as though the Depression were not happening. A historian approaching this decade solely through radio shows would learn little about the economic crisis. The dance bands played happy music, and Jack Benny would have worried about money in the best of times. In this apparent paradox, perhaps, lay radio's ultimate appeal. Real life in the 1930s was hard enough to bear. When people clicked their radios on, they were seeking not reality but escape. Radio brought relief, with a message from our sponsor.

A persistent mythology has grown about the origins of American radio broadcasting. In this version radio started pure, without commercial corruption, and might have continued so but for the dark powers of Madison Avenue. Advertising, the fable goes, took this innocent maiden and turned her into a tawdry strumpet, selling herself to anyone who could pay. Instead of dispensing "good" music and entertainment, radio thereby was reduced to pandering to the "worst" (that is, most popular) in American tastes. Thus a powerful medium of great potential became just another device for selling the materialist vision of American life.

As an alternative, this mythology typically cites the British system of a radio network closely supervised by the government, with the audience paying an annual fee for the privilege of listening in. Leaving aside the practical question of whether this could have happened given the political realities of America's stronger free-enterprise traditions, this alternate scenario ignores the relative pluralism of American cultures and traditions. The dominant single aspect of early American radio broadcasting was the absence of a central authority like the BBC. Many different hands—radio manufacturers, the telephone company, nascent networks, ad agencies, advertisers, vaudeville and Hollywood talent—were stirring the pluralist stew. From this congeries of interests emerged a system of big and small networks, stations, and programs that truly reflected—for better or worse—American society. In retrospect it is hard to imagine how American radio could have developed differently.

At the start, in the early 1920s, radio so little resembled anything else that nobody knew what to make of it. Technically it came from the telegraph-telephone-wireless chain of invention, that is, verbal contact between distant individuals. At first people simply talked over the radio through microphones and headsets. It seemed most like a telephone, not like a magazine or newspaper, so it was called wireless telephone or radio telephone. The first important broadcasts—of sports or political events—were factual reports, suggesting someone calling a friend with the latest news. Radio added a new, transforming dimension when the headset became a speaker, with better fidelity and more volume than a headset designed for one pair of ears. Radio now could reach a *group* of people—a whole family, not just the teenage boy tinkering with a crystal set—and could reproduce music more pleasantly. People could half listen while otherwise engaged, and so could listen for longer periods. They might even dance to it. Thus radio came to resemble not a telephone, and not a magazine either, but with some of a magazine's attractions of diversion and variety—and perhaps its advertising potential too.

During a six-month period starting in the fall of 1921, a half-million radio sets were sold. "Who would have dreamed," *Printers' Ink* noted in the spring of 1922, "that the radio phone would today be the subject of such widespread advertising! The merchandising attention being given to this new means of communication is perfectly astonishing." The radio programs themselves carried no direct advertising; broadcasting had been started by radio manufacturers to encourage their consumer markets, and at first they sold no radio time to outsiders. American Telephone & Telegraph owned the radio patents but was prevented by its patent agreements from making radios. Seeking to profit in some way from the radio fad, AT&T considered opening the air to direct commercial messages. Such a practice, *Printers' Ink* declared in April 1922, would offend most people: "The family circle is not a public place, and advertising has no business intruding there unless it is invited." Why, said *PI,* imagine inserting "If you are under forty, four chances to one you will get pyorrhea" directly after a piano sonata! Impossible to contemplate.

AT&T decided to assume the risk. In August 1922 its New York station WEAF offered ten minutes of radio time to anyone paying one hundred dollars. A Long Island real estate firm bought the first purchased commercial in broadcasting history and quickly sold two apartments. WEAF started airing regular "reading notices," delivered in a soft-selling newsy style that deceptively resembled straight news. By March 1923 the station had twenty-five sponsors, including Macy's, Colgate, and Metropolitan Life Insurance.

PI was aghast, but in arguing against WEAF's advertising the journal revealed the real source of its opposition. If newspapers came to see radio as a rival advertising medium, *PI* warned, they would stop printing radio schedules, and radio would be hung on its own petard of commercial greed. *PI* as the established bible of advertising thus spoke for the print media. E. B. Weiss, who worked for the journal in those years, later recalled that *PI* was edited under a "balance of issue" principle: newspapers by buying ads in *PI* paid most of its bills and so received most of its editorial coverage; magazines bought the next most ads and were allotted secondary coverage; and so on through other advertisers. Though *PI* often editorially deplored advertiser control of editorial policies, it actually marched to the beat of its own advertisers. In fighting radio advertising it struck high-minded poses ("The home is a sacred place and whatever enters the home should be invited"), but it really spoke from a practical self-interest. Knowing this, the advertising community could easily shrug off its advice. Two other trade journals, *Advertising & Selling* and (after 1930) *Advertising Age,* greeted radio more fairly.

In the absence of government regulation—the Federal Radio Commission was not set up until 1927—radio made its own way, guided only by the marketplace and popular tastes. WEAF's precedent opened the air to other advertisers. Late in 1924, for example, the William H. Rankin ad agency persuaded its client Goodrich Tires to try sponsoring an hour show over a special network of nine stations. After only a few weeks and thousands of appreciative letters, Goodrich declared itself pleased with the experiment. It used only "indirect" commercials, with mention of the sponsor at the start and finish of the program; the Silvertown Cord Orchestra also incorporated a trade name. Other programs followed the same practice: the *A&P Gypsies;* the *Eveready Hour; Cliquot Club Eskimos;* and the *Palmolive Show,* with "Paul Oliver" and "Olive Palmer" as featured singers. The radio manufacturers still offered their own shows. But, as even *PI* conceded in April 1926, the best and most popular shows were underwritten by advertisers.

The signs were unmistakable. The biggest set manufacturer, the Radio Corporation of America, threw out its policies against commercial programming and, in 1926, bought WEAF from AT&T. Renaming the station WNBC, RCA under David Sarnoff then launched the National Broadcasting Company, complete with advertising rate cards. NBC hired an adman, Frank Arnold, to sell radio to the remaining skeptics in advertising. For six years Arnold traveled the country promoting radio as the fourth advertising dimension, after newspapers, magazines, and outdoor signs, the one

that added voice to eye appeal and offered advertisers a unique potential for reaching an entire household. A second major network,
the Columbia Broadcasting System, started in 1927 and was acquired after a year by the young William Paley.

When Frank Arnold started making his rounds he found many ad
agencies still resisting radio. Elmo Calkins, insulated from the new
medium by his deafness, soon retired from advertising. Even those
agencies—notably Ayer, BBDO, and JWT—that made early ven-
tures into radio embraced the new form cautiously. As late as 1928
Roy Durstine was warning against direct, intrusive ads ("listeners
ought to feel that they are invited guests"). Just as advertising was
reaching a sober respectability, radio intruded a racier show business element from vaudeville and Hollywood. "When I first joined
JWT," Carroll Carroll recalled, "everybody but us radio chickens
wore stiff collars, vests, and a serious expression. We wore soft collars, no vests, didn't get into the office until all hours of the morning,
and sometimes the socks we wore were shocking." One radio man
who sat in a meeting with Helen Resor wearing argyle socks soon
received a gift of three pairs of plain black hose.

George Washington Hill, unrestrained by respectability or any
other consideration, charged into radio with his own ideas. At an
audition for a Lucky Strike show in August 1928, he told the band to
play familiar tunes, with no distracting vocals, stretched out to at
least eight minutes to let people finish their dance. "I want real
dance music that people will like to dance by," he said, "and I don't
want their attention diverted by French horn gymnastics. Let's give
the public what the public wants and not try to educate them. We
should not be concerned about introducing new numbers and novelties." The *Lucky Strike Dance Orchestra* show was nominally produced by Hill's Lord & Thomas agency. Hill dictated the format,
chose the announcer and orchestra, and approved all the tunes before broadcast. After the show debuted over thirty-nine NBC stations in September 1928, to test radio's power Hill for a time
stopped advertising in other media. In November and December
Lucky Strike sales went up 47 percent, and radio had found another
champion. As his show evolved into *Your Hit Parade*, Hill remained
an impossible, hectoring irritant. A brusque telegram to NBC's president: "Nothing on the air is worth spending money for unless it is
unique. Nothing remains unique forever. In our opinion broadcasting systems have a definite responsibility and duty to their clients to

produce and develop effective programs. 'Wake up, chillun.' " Hill
kept a radio in every room of his house and monitored all his shows
and ads.

In his wake other cigarette companies moved into radio, shifting
their ad budgets from outdoor signs to the new medium. Camel,
Lucky Strike's main competition, sponsored weekly, then daily programs, and started to overtake Lucky Strike. Competing with essentially identical products in a lucrative market, the cigarette makers
brought their aggressive selling styles to radio, pushing it to allow
more overt commercials. The *Sir Walter Raleigh Revue* managed to
squeeze seventy references to the sponsoring cigarette into one hour:
the theme song ("rawlly round Sir Walter Raleigh") introduced the
Raleigh Revue in the Raleigh Theater with the Raleigh Orchestra
and the Raleigh Rovers; then would follow the adventures of Sir
Walter in Virginia and at Queen Elizabeth's court, with ample
mention of his cigarettes and smoking tobacco. "With all of these
interspersed credits," said *Printers' Ink,* succumbing to the radio
boom, "it is not felt that the sponsor's plugging is offensive inasmuch
as it does not depart from the spirit of the program." (Because the
program did not depart from the spirit of Walter Raleigh.) G. W.
Hill, seizing on the new medium's intrusiveness, fought back with
slogans repeated on his own shows and at intervals all through the
day: "Nature in the raw is seldom mild," "Spit is a horrid word" (in
praise of Cremo cigars, made by a spitless process), "Be happy—Go
Lucky," and later the cryptic "LS/MFT." These metronomic repe-
titions sold cigarettes, but at the price of irritating many listeners.
"A great deal of the present agitation against sponsored programs,"
an NBC man noted in 1932, "has been caused by the blatant type of
copy used in Lucky Strike."

By then the combined pressures of the networks, advertisers,
agencies, and public tastes had made radio an irrevocably commercial medium. The Crossley rating system, started in 1930 as a joint
effort of the AAAA and ANA and subscribed to by interested agencies, gave advertisers a rough measure of how many listeners they
reached. As ratings grew the networks kept charging more for air
time, and advertisers kept cutting into their print budgets to stay on
the air. As *PI* had predicted, the major newspapers retaliated briefly
by refusing to print radio schedules. But the Scripps-Howard chain
broke ranks and resumed the listings. "The faint shuffling sound
which followed," Roy Durstine noted, "was the falling in line of the

other papers." Unable to beat radio, newspapers joined it. By 1932 thirty stations were owned, and forty-three others were operated, by newspapers. Americans owned 15 million radios, of which 10 million were tuned in every day. In September 1932, NBC and CBS yielded to advertisers who wanted to specify prices on the air. The change would mean shorter ads, William Paley promised: "It has often been necessary for advertisers to use hundreds of words to compensate for the inability to crystallize the selling story into mention of the price."

Only a dozen years after the first broadcast, Madison Avenue had a baby colossus on its hands. Copywriters learned to write for the ear: simple, conversational language, repetitive and overpunctuated, with short sentences and few pronouns and sparing use of s, f, m, and n sounds hard to distinguish orally. In a more difficult adjust-ment, agencies also took on the risks and functions of theatrical pro-duction. Most of the popular shows were underwritten by a single sponsor, with its agency as the producer at facilities provided by the network. Thus new uncertainties for the agency and advertiser: when a client bought space in a magazine he knew its circulation and so could predict the impact of his ad. The variable therefore was less the medium than the particular ad's pulling power. In radio the client bought a show that unpredictably might succeed or bomb, with obvious effect on the advertiser's return. Here the variable was the medium, not the commercial—a medium that often seemed a crapshoot to an advertising business aspiring toward scientific pre-dictability. "Radio is show business and nothing else," said Dorothy Barstow of McCann-Erickson's radio department. "In the end *the show is the thing,* and all is of no avail without that mysterious brand of genius called showmanship."

Initially the two most active agencies in radio were Lord & Thomas and JWT, both large, established shops with enough power to stand between the advertisers and the networks. Lord & Thomas handled the Lucky Strike shows and, after August 1929, the *Amos 'n' Andy* show for Pepsodent, the medium's first runaway success. One month later JWT launched the *Fleischmann Yeast Hour* with Rudy Vallee, one of the first musical variety hits. Thompson's Hollywood contacts brought movie stars to the Fleischmann show and the *Chase & Sanborn Hour* and the *Kraft Music Hall,* the agency's other big variety shows on NBC. Stanley Resor was counted "among the more important ardent supporters of radio," according to an NBC internal memo. "The influence of his thought along these lines has had a far reaching effect throughout his organization." Thompson's radio director, John Reber, worked in a coveted space, an office adjacent to Stanley Resor's. With nine shows on NBC in 1933, Thompson was bringing the network more revenue than any other agency, and so was granted a private phone line to the NBC studio—a privilege extended previously only to Lord & Thomas.

In time, other, younger agencies overtook these two early leaders in radio. Raymond Rubicam, an unreformed print man, left the radio initiative at Young & Rubicam to Chester LaRoche, his executive vice-president. The agency first offered its *Radio Household Institute,* a morning show dispensing recipes and homemaking tips to housewives in fifteen-minute segments sponsored by various Borden and General Foods products. Y & R scored its first prime-time hit with a comedy variety show for Jell-O in 1934. "Jack Benny was selected because he was available," Lou Brockway recalled. More popular comedians like Will Rogers and Eddie Cantor were locked into long-term contracts. "We were very frank with our client in presenting Benny," according to Brockway. "We said he was not our first or second or third choice but he was available and he had a good, if not outstanding, record." General Foods agreed to spend $7,500 a week for production and network costs. After three months Jell-O sales picked up and the gamble was declared a success. Instead of straight commercials Benny sprinkled the sponsor's name all through the show, in a light, self-mocking style ("Jell-*O* again. This is Jack Benny speaking"). As in print, Y & R preferred a gentle pitch that tickled the consumer: a *PI* poll found that listeners overwhelmingly regarded Jell-O ads as the best, most entertaining commercials on the air. They also moved the product. As Benny pointed out, his fans "had no difficulty in learning who was sponsoring the show."

Y & R went on to produce other hits starring Kate Smith (for Calumet Baking Powder and Swansdown Cake Flour), Fred Allen (for Sal Hepatica), and Arthur Godfrey (for Lipton Tea). None of this success much impressed Raymond Rubicam. Even as radio brought in one-third of his billings, and Chet LaRoche succeeded him as president of the agency, he continued to regard radio as a vulgarizing influence, with too much time and control given over to advertising. He seldom listened to the Y & R shows. Later he hoped TV would not repeat the pattern established in radio.

A similar ambivalence surfaced among the principals at Benton &

Bowles, one of the hottest radio agencies. William Benton and Chester Bowles, who had met at BBDO, opened for business just before
the stock market crash in 1929. After nine months they faced bankruptcy. The firm was rescued by the *Maxwell House Showboat,* a variety show supervised by Bowles. It replaced the Fleischmann hour as
the top program in the Crossley ratings for 1934, and two other
B & B shows—Palmolive's operetta series and Ipana's *Town Hall*—
made the top four. All these shows integrated the sponsors liberally
into the program. On the *Maxwell House Showboat* performers spent a
lot of time drinking coffee, smacking their lips and tinkling their
cups. Maxwell House sales went up 85 percent in a year.

Though the agency's billings grew steadily to $8 million by 1934,
Benton and Bowles kept thinking about quitting the business. Instead of hiring known performers at big salaries, Benton complained, advertisers newly acquainted with show business preferred
to develop their own stars for less money. "They get a big wallop out
of adventures as impresarios, but the journey over unfamiliar
ground is pretty certain to be expensive," said Benton. "If there isn't
enough money to do the job right, radio should be left alone." Despite the agency's success, because of the Depression the partners
balked at adding staff and so had to work that much harder themselves. "We almost killed ourselves working," Bowles recalled, "because we didn't dare hire enough people." In charge of B & B's hit
shows, Bowles found himself chained to an implacable weekly grind,
with deadlines that could not be put off and pincerlike pressures from
both clients and networks. Benton quit on his thirty-sixth birthday in 1936, and Bowles followed him a few years later. Once out of
advertising, both men made a point of never listening to the radio.

Even in the new world of radio, the two basic traditions of advertising practice still operated in characteristic ways. Representing the
MacManus school, both Young & Rubicam and Benton & Bowles
made commercials with taste and subtlety, and they worried about
the ethics of a medium controlled by advertising with no central
figures—no Curtis, Bok, or Ayer—to serve as ethical guardians.
Conversely, the dominant ad agency in radio, Blackett-Sample-
Hummert, followed the Hopkins methods of hard sell and loose
principles. Hill Blackett and Frank Hummert had both trained at
Lord & Thomas under Hopkins and Lasker. By this direct succession
they brought reason-why to the new medium, inventing the soap
opera and riding it to first place among radio agencies.

The key figures at B-S-H were Hummert and his assistant, later his wife, Anne Ashenhurst. As a marital team in advertising they wielded influence comparable, for a time, to that of Helen and Stanley Resor. Like the Resors, they avoided personal publicity—to the point of hiring a press agent to keep their names *out of* the papers. Hummert in particular constructed a mysterious shell for himself. Seldom seen in public, he often worked at home, came and went through a private entrance at the agency, spoke inaudibly if at all, supposedly fired a man for talking to him in the washroom, and generally dealt with subordinates through Ashenhurst. To curious interviewers he was reticent about his early years, giving his birth date as "before 1890" and skipping past his youth. According to one story, as a young man he had ridden with the Texas Rangers for two years. These vaguely romantic origins only added to the enigma of this strange, gifted man.

Daytime radio, aside from Young & Rubicam's *Radio Household Institute,* had as yet attracted few sponsors. Housewives, it was thought, had no time to listen to the radio. In 1929 Hummert, then working at the Blackett-Sample-Hummert Agency in Chicago, decided to approach this audience not with household hints but with human interest: newspapers ran daily installments of popular, long-running stories; why not apply the device to radio? Hummert thought up the main characters and general plot lines, and turned the concepts over to Ashenhurst.

Just Plain Bill, sponsored by Kolynos toothpaste, presented the travails of a barber who had married out of his social class. *Betty and Bob,* sponsored by Gold Medal Flour, offered a feckless man, the son of wealth, married to a saintly woman who struggled to keep the family intact. *Ma Perkins,* for Oxydol detergent, was described as Just Plain Bill with skirts. As drama, these soap operas were distinguished for implausible situations, histrionic dialogue, and glacially paced plot exposition—and familiar, likable people, under dire stress, ever being threatened and rescued from peril. The stories and sponsors aimed directly at housewives and found their marks. Hummert shrewdly kept ownership of the shows himself, while B-S-H drew its percentage of the billings.

By 1933 B-S-H was handling more radio shows than any other agency. The whole operation moved to New York, headquarters of the networks. Hummert's first wife had died of cancer; afterward he and Ashenhurst began taking long walks together, talking con-

stantly, seeing each other in new ways, and they were married in
1935. They set up a factory for churning out soap opera scripts.
Writers were hired, given detailed instructions and lists of taboos,
and paid twenty-five dollars a script. Under a deadline a writer
would be sequestered in a hotel room, with food and extra typewriters brought in until the work was done. The roster of shows kept
growing, extending beyond housewives. *Jack Armstrong,* the All-
American boy, sold Wheaties to children. At the center of this empire, Ashenhurst held all the lines in her hands, speaking for her
unseen husband, deploying the platoons of writers, directors, actors,
and musicians. "She was a little girl, and pretty," Glen Sample said
later. "But she was tough, in a most lady-like manner. You should
have seen how she handled the talent." By the late 1930s the B-S-H
shows were drawing a million fan letters a week; fourteen writers delivered fifty scripts weekly, a total of about six and a half million
words a year.

For Frank Hummert this meant wealth, power, and the freedom
to ignore onerous social amenities. In 1937 he was the best-paid man
in advertising, with a base salary of $132,000, plus bonuses and his
share of the soap operas. (Stanley Resor that year made a base salary
of $90,000, Roy Durstine $84,000, Raymond Rubicam $67,500.) He
disliked his sponsors—"All clients are *pigs,*" he warned a young
David Ogilvy—and did not much care for the networks either.
When a competing aspirin made price comparisons with his own
Bayer over the air, Hummert sent a sulphurous threat to the network: "If this continues any further I personally will see to it that
every relationship between us and National Broadcasting Company
is impaired to the best of my ability and I think you know that I
usually make good on these things." NBC calmed the combatants
and negotiated a settlement, but Hummert was not mollified. He
promised future assertions of his rights to NBC, "even though it may
invite further insulting communications from you." As owner of his
shows he could, had he so pleased, have taken them over to the wel-
coming arms of CBS.

Within the boundaries of radio, the Hummerts were simply richer
and stronger than any individual, client or network, with whom
they dealt. They still took long walks together, always talking, an
empire unto themselves. Once a new president of NBC asked them
to lunch at the network. "I am afraid," Hummert replied, "that the
grandeur of National Broadcasting Company is too much for me."

Would the NBC man care to come dine with the Hummerts? Aware of the power relationship, the NBC man did.

As the leading agency in radio B-S-H could stand toe to toe with a network. For other agencies the battle with the networks over control of programming was harder. In general, agencies and sponsors produced the most popular, best-rated shows while the networks put on "sustaining" programs aimed at a higher cultural and economic class. If a sustaining show—like the *Mercury Theater* of Orson Welles—drew substantial attention a sponsor would then pick it up. The most profitable shows thus gravitated toward the agencies, leaving networks their highbrow standards and low ratings. "Rudy Vallee could sell automobiles the same as he sells yeast," noted John Royal of NBC; "Paul Whiteman could sell radio tubes just as easily as he does cheese." These shows were hits because of the performing talent, not any particular genius for show business on the part of the producing agencies. "Why," Royal wondered, "are agencies taking all our good production men to create and build their shows?" For their part, agencies complained about the regular increases in network fees for air time. As Leonard Bush of the Compton agency pointed out, print media responsible for their own editorial content justifiably raised their fees if better content brought larger circulations. But in radio the networks charged more if efforts by outside parties—sponsors and agencies—pulled better ratings, as if to say, " 'The more capable you, my customers, are, the more I will charge you for my facilities.' "

The agencies and networks collided most often over the tastes and prerogatives of the network censors. Occasionally the censors objected to an extravagant claim in a commercial. (In rebuttal, an adman gleefully submitted an NBC publicity blurb about Dorothy Lamour that read, "To see her is to look upon a scented loveliness that holds the dark flame of a tantalizing ecstasy. . . .") More seriously, the censors combed over show scripts submitted before the broadcast. To understate the matter, the censors and script writers did not like each other. "Most of the good writers," said Max Wylie, the CBS censor, "are either psychopathic dopes or female men." The NBC censor, Janet MacRorie, was known to some as "the old maid on the second floor." She watched for excessive allusions to sex, ethnic slurs, drunken women, and disparagements of God. In 1939 she detected a "trend toward sensationalism" in the Hummert soaps: "An attempt is being made to give them new life through the introduction of childbirth, illness and death, murder, breach of promise cases, murder trials and constant misunderstandings between husbands and wives. For the most part, human happiness or contentment, according to these scripts, can never be attained." *Young Widder Brown*, she added, was "a sex story, pure and simple," with too much bigamy and "intimate personal relationships between men and women."

With time the specific issues may have seemed less important, but the real stakes loomed ever larger. The agencies and networks were fighting over big money. In 1938, for the first time, radio passed magazines as a source of advertising revenue, and the gap kept widening. At the end of the decade the agencies with the most annual billings over the major networks were B-S-H ($12.1 million), Benton & Bowles ($7.7 million), Young & Rubicam ($6.5 million), Compton ($5.3 million), and JWT ($4.6 million). A few years earlier those billings alone would have sustained a substantial agency.

❦❦

Sally Rand, fan dancer, when asked to explain her success: "I owe it all to advertising," she said, and to following the principle of using plenty of white space.

❦❦

J. Stirling Getchell arced across the advertising landscape of the 1930s like a comet, appearing suddenly, soaring and falling. In his brief transit he had more impact than anyone else on the advertising styles of the decade.

Getchell was born in July 1899, the son of a silk salesman and a schoolteacher, and grew up in suburbs of New York. A case of rheumatic fever at about the age of eleven left him with a permanently weakened heart. He was nonetheless a willful, determined child. Closer to his mother, a strict disciplinarian, he rebelled against her rules and went his own way, a constant, perplexing source of worry to both parents. When he was in his teens the family bought a new Overland car. The son promptly took it apart to see how it worked. For nights on end he examined pieces of the car on the kitchen table. His father wondered if Stirling would be able to put it back together. "I don't know," said his mother, "but he's learning a lot." Too restless for much formal education, when he was seventeen he ran away to Mexico to join Pershing's troops in pursuit of Pancho

Villa. "We had a hell of a lot of fun," he later said of this episode. The following year, after the United States entered the World War, he enlisted and served overseas. In 1919 he returned with an English wife and, for some reason, decided to go into advertising.

Over the next twelve years he held a dozen jobs in advertising, sometimes quitting, sometimes being fired, always in a hurry. For his first job he claimed to be twenty-one, though he was two years younger, and had no real credentials. But the head of a small agency in New York found "something about his earnestness" compelling and hired him as a copywriter. His boss soon noticed that he wanted to learn *everything* about advertising—"not merely copy and layout, but art styles, typography, methods of engraving, merchandising— his thirst for information was insatiable." Nominally a writer, Getchell was always drawn to visual aspects. One of his first successful ads, promoting a dealer campaign for a tire company, showed a picture of a pair of shoes dominating the page, under the headline "Can You Fill These Shoes?"

After an argument over salary he moved on to agencies in Philadelphia, Toledo, Detroit, and New York, specializing in campaigns for automobiles and related industries, still the boy tinkering with the Overland on the kitchen table. In other ways, too, he remained a boy—curious and probing, headlong and reckless, charging into unknown territory without fear or much thought. He chose an important client meeting to make his first public address. At an agency picnic he went sailing for the first time, handled it, and brought the boat back to the mooring. When a fire alarm rang he chased it, driving at his usual breakneck clip. Soliciting an account near Niagara Falls one winter day, toward evening he went to the falls, climbed over the guard rail to the brink, broke off an enormous icicle and threw it into the torrent.

He sold himself well. He got his first big-league job, at Lord & Thomas in 1924, by presenting a leatherbound sample book with famous ads by Bruce Barton, Helen Resor, Raymond Rubicam, and others; he could, he explained, write similar ads if given the chance. He was hired to write for the Studebaker account. Now in the presence of major advertising figures, he studied their ways, already plotting toward his own agency. Someone not well acquainted with him advised him to slow down. "I haven't got time to do it that way," he said, referring to his bad heart. "I have to make all the money by the time I'm forty."

On to the Batten agency, where he shared an office with Chester Bowles and worked for William Benton. Firmly oriented toward the camera, he devised "microphotographs" that purportedly showed Colgate Rapid Shave lather softening a beard. (The beard was actually fine-tooth combs soaking in a bowl of lather.) For another Colgate product, Palmolive soap, the client asked Getchell to enlarge the coupon in a proposed ad. Getchell refused; the client insisted; so Getchell tore up the layout, threw the pieces across the room, and quit another job. "I've got to keep moving fast," he explained. "The doctor says I may live five, ten, or at the most another fifteen years."

Having applied on three previous occasions to J. Walter Thompson, he tried again and this time was hired. Getchell flouted JWT rules by wearing eccentric clothes, working in shirt-sleeves, and smoking in the halls. But under Bill Day's protection he became one of the resident stars. A terrifying driver himself, for Goodrich Tires Getchell without apparent irony started the Silvertown Safety League, a safe-driving crusade that eventually enrolled over 2.5 million people. To publicize it he sent a fleet of fifteen cars on a year-long tour of the country. He had photographers cover the tour as news, using perhaps one photo for every fifty taken. He trusted his instincts—"I feel it in my guts!"—and laughed at social scientists in advertising. "They talk about the wonderful research investigations they make," he said, "and how they always prove their point with statistics and all the rest of the hokum and bunk—and I'll be damned if I can find over six or seven agencies in the country that know anything at all about the biggest thing in advertising—the actual creative production of copy and layout."

When Lennen & Mitchell hired him away for $50,000 he took along his secretary, Helen Boyd, and his favorite art director, Jack Tarleton, from JWT. Within a year the three went to lunch at the Ritz and decided to start their own agency. It was early in 1931, two years into the Depression. "We figured we couldn't start at a better time," Getchell told an old friend in advertising. "Things can't get any worse than they are." Getchell mortgaged his house in Greenwich, Tarleton sold his car, and they opened for business in a two-room office. They survived the first year, in lieu of regular accounts, by undertaking special assignments for a fee. For General Tire they staged their own car accident, mussing their hair and clothes and donning woebegone expressions for the photographer. For Lydia

Pinkham, still selling her vegetable compound, they produced hard-sell ads that recalled the Pinkham copy of the late nineteenth century, showing distressed women in need of the product. "I'm sorry," one woman told her husband, "not tonight." The Pinkham family did not unanimously approve, but the company made a profit of $400,000 in 1931 after losing $260,000 the previous year.

These successes let Getchell hire a contact man, Orrin Kilbourn, as a third partner. Kilbourn's connections in the Chrysler organization brought the Getchell agency DeSoto, its first major account. Getchell produced ads stressing the style and fun ("Expect to be Stared At") of driving a DeSoto, with lavish photographs of happy young people at play. Thus the agency was given the one-shot task of introducing the new 1932 Plymouth. The bottom of the Chrysler line, Plymouth was not yet taken seriously by Ford and Chevrolet, its main competition. Getchell was challenged to change this perception while the Plymouth account itself stayed at an agency in Detroit.

Late one night, in a welter of headlines and layouts, Tarleton crossed out a few unnecessary words and came up with "Look at All Three!" Chrysler's executives were not impressed. "Why the hell do I want to sell Fords and Chevies?" asked one. But the proposed ad was included among others submitted to Walter Chrysler, and he was told the objections to it. "I don't give a damn," he said, slapping his hand on the desk, "I want to run that ad!" In final form it carried the headline in bold black type above a starkly lit photograph of Chrysler leaning over the hood of a Plymouth. The copy quoted Chrysler on the technical reasons why anyone should prefer his car over the unnamed competition. First run in April 1932, as Ford and Chevrolet were also introducing their new models, the ad drew attention by skirting the advertising industry's informal ban on competitive or comparative pitches. Getchell did not name the other two, but the reference was obvious. By June Plymouth sales had improved 218 percent over the same period the previous year. A few months later, after reviewing presentations by twenty-two agencies, Chrysler gave Getchell the entire Plymouth account. The ensuing campaign—"Plymouth sets the pace for all three"—extended the theme of the first ad. Plymouth's share of the low-priced market jumped from 16 percent in 1932 to 24 percent in 1933. The Getchell agency was declared hot.

As new accounts came its way, paced by Socony-Vacuum, the

second-largest oil company, the denizens of Madison Avenue began to speak of a distinctive Getchell visual style and approach. In ad-making—his preferred term—he started with photographs, dozens and even hundreds of them. Eventually the agency built up an enormous cross-indexed file of all kinds of pictures. Typefaces and headlines would be built around the photos, followed last by the copy. Getchell hired the best photographers (Margaret Bourke-White took shots of DeSotos) and never worried about budgets. Once, for Plymouth, he sent two models, a photographer, and a chauffeur up to Vermont. Ten days and many rolls of film later, they came back with one picture that was used. Getchell liked ads with "bounce," as he put it, that "came off the page fast." That meant tabloid formats, loud headlines, rectilinear layouts, fast and punchy copy, and photographs, above all photographs. "We believe people want realism today," he explained. "Events portrayed as they happen. Products as they really are. Human interest. People. Places. Told in simple photographs that the eye can read and the mind can understand."

As ever, the advertising cycle turned around and hailed an old device as the newest fashion. The artists who had illustrated most ads of the 1920s now fell out of favor, yielding in hard times to the cheaper camera. (Cheaper, that is, except in the hands of Getchell.) Advertising practitioners with long memories found the Getchell style familiar. "It's the same thing we used in our early days before beauty got to be in fashion," noted Helen Woodward. "The sales appeal is the same. What is new in the Getchell idea is his able use of modern action photographs. . . . This screaming, direct, ugly stuff hits the public as hard as ever."

Getchell still lived on the run and had neither the time nor the temperament for much reflection. The closest he ever came to articulating an advertising philosophy was a speech he wrote for the spring meetings of the AAAA at White Sulphur Springs in 1935. (Shy of the podium, he had someone else deliver it.) There are no rules or formulas, he declared, and then proclaimed his own. Advertising suffered from artificiality, gimmicks, and cleverness, he warned. For models we must go back to John E. Kennedy and Claude Hopkins: "They were news-minded salesmen" who visited factories and studied products "to draw out the unusual, vivid and exciting news. Then they told it in an honest, straightforward way. . . . Today, I think we have been getting away from this." Advertising, then, should just tell the news. Madison Avenue might profitably imitate Henry Luce, who dug out the facts and gave the details in *Time.* "And finally, we believe that the most priceless ingredient of all advertising is *enthusiasm.* Great ads are always written in fire."

Fire: the Getchell agency was hot in more than one sense. With the boss setting the pace for everyone else, new employees entered a crucible of frantic activities and pressures. Once Getchell hired an old friend as general manager in the hope of establishing order. "I was not very successful in bringing composure into a place where composure was against the rule," this man recalled, and he departed after a year. At creative sessions Getchell waved his hands, yelled and cursed, threatened and bullied. He might approve a campaign late at night and then change his mind the next morning, forcing everyone to start over. Addicted to speed in everything, he expected his wishes to be carried out at once regardless of the clock. Spouses waiting at home for their absent partners came to hate him. At 2:30 one morning one of his writers said he was tired and going home. "Lie down on the couch over there," Getchell replied. "Why the hell do people want to go home all the time?" Even at home his men—he hired few women—could expect a phone call at any time whatever. Most of his employees stayed briefly and quit before they were consumed, so that later many individuals could claim to have been trained by the great Getchell.

A man of medium height, with light brown hair, bulging blue eyes, pale skin and bad teeth, he always looked older than his years. His expensive suits did not hang on him well and generally looked wrinkled. He walked in a round-shouldered, forward-leaning shamble. His best features were expressive hands and a fiercely riveting gaze. His power derived not from physical gifts but a ferocious will, turned on himself as much as on others. He lashed himself through the week, collapsed on the weekend, and then returned for more. After his second marriage in 1936 he lived somewhat more sensibly. He would leave the office at seven o'clock at night, followed a few minutes later by the rest of the staff.

He let up a little, but not enough. In less than a decade he pushed his agency to billings of $10 million, with 200 employees and branches in Detroit, Kansas City, San Francisco, and Los Angeles. The price was too high. In the spring of 1940, his health weakened by stress and neglect, he contracted a blood infection caused, perhaps, by his decaying teeth. For nine months he hung on, but it led finally to subacute bacterial endocarditis, the final consequence of his childhood rheumatic fever. He died, forty-one years old, in December 1940. His one-man agency folded two years later.

In the late 1930s, a dozen years after quitting the business, Helen Woodward went back to advertising to see whether conditions had changed in response to the consumer movement. Her investigations produced a book, *It's an Art,* in effect a consumer's guide to Madison Avenue. She found advertising's attempts at self-regulation as meaningless as ever. The AAAA, for example, forbade speculative campaigns aimed at new accounts; yet everyone did them, on the pretense that the prospective client invited and paid for them. "Nobody believes a word of this," Woodward noted, "and yet in public everybody speaks of it as though it were absolute and solemn truth." Ads for cigarettes, toothpaste, cosmetics, and patent medicines remained obnoxious to Woodward. Advertising still held at least an implicit power over the editorial opinions of newspapers. Radio advertising, the robust infant, snuck pitches deceivingly into the programs. "The more I looked into advertising," she decided, "the more flimsy it seemed to be. Just as before, I found that the people in it were likable, able, and often brilliant. But with few exceptions here and there, the work they do is trivial. It's got to be because its objective is not good work, not a better standard of living, not anything except to make money."

The Copeland bill—"a queer, tottering, mindless thing," according to Woodward—finally passed Congress in 1938. It gave the Food and Drug Administration new powers over the manufacture and sale of drugs, but it mandated no compulsory grades for foods and, like the 1906 law it superseded, said nothing about advertising. Consumerists found more to praise in the Wheeler-Lea amendments to the Federal Trade Commission Act, also enacted in 1938. These amendments declared "deceptive acts of commerce" unlawful and added injunctive powers to the FTC's cease-and-desist orders. In the next two years the FTC handed down eighteen injunctions, forcing Fleischmann's Yeast to stop claiming that it cured crooked teeth, bad skin, constipation, and halitosis; Lifebuoy and Lux soaps to stop promising better, younger complexions; Ipana toothpaste to drop its pink-toothbrush campaign; Borden dairy products to cease making false claims about premiums; and others. These rulings, aimed at

major advertisers and agencies, sent tremors down Madison Avenue.
"The New Dealers have loaded the staff of the Federal Trade Commission with men who are definitely anti-advertising and anti-busi-
ness," said Bruce Barton, now a Republican Congressman. "Almost
a revolution in copywriting has come about within the last few
months," *Printers' Ink* commented. "The Commission means what it
says, and no foolin'."

As the decade ended, consumerism looked ever more formidable.
Consumers Union now claimed 80,000 members, Consumers Research 60,000. A *Business Week* survey in the spring of 1939 listed
twenty-two national consumer groups and a bibliography of forty-
five books. "Today, the consumer movement is something which
must be considered as unemotional reality," *Business Week* concluded. A Gallup poll of 5,000 adults later that year found that one
in four—and 83 percent of the teachers interviewed—had read a
consumerist book; 81 percent thought advertising encouraged people to buy things they didn't need or couldn't afford; 59 percent (87
percent of the teachers) called for stricter laws to control advertising.
An internal memo at NBC, citing these findings, warned that "the
advertiser who views this whole movement lightly is unwittingly
looking straight into the mouth of a loaded cannon."

The consumerist wave, still cresting, ran up against World War II.
As with the reform impulses of the progressive era, total war sucked
everything else into its maw. The organized consumer groups,
though still active, shifted from an emphasis on brand selection and
advertising practices to wartime conservation measures. The FTC
stopped bothering Madison Avenue; in 1944, for example, it
dropped a complaint against Listerine over its claims to ward off
dandruff and colds. Occasional critics of advertising were still heard,
in (for example) a series of *Reader's Digest* articles in 1943. But as a
political force consumerism was dead, not to revive until thirty years
later.

Advertising again offered its services to fight a world war. The
War Advertising Council was started by the industry to coordinate
these efforts. "This recruiting of men and money," Raymond Rubicam noted, "was not undertaken in a limpid atmosphere of universal agreement that it ought to be done." Within advertising, some
individuals wanted the government to pay for its advertising while
others gagged at the thought of working, in effect, for Franklin Roosevelt. Outside advertising, some insisted that writers and journal-

ists, not advertising men, should speak for the government in war-time. Madison Avenue became more cooperative after the Treasury Department ruled that regular advertising could continue during the war in "reasonable" amounts. Ultimately the industry donated about a billion dollars' worth of space and time to the war effort, and many conventional product ads included war messages, some of them dubious assertions of how the product was helping win the war. "We did not tell the truth, of course," Bruce Barton, a prewar isolationist, said of advertising's contributions. "We simply set forth in pictures and copy the Administration's argument. . . . This was sound and patriotic and moral while the war lasted."

In contrast with the first war, which saw the total volume of advertising drop, advertising expenditures grew from $2.2 billion in 1941 to $2.9 billion in 1945. (This still left the business a half-billion dollars below its 1929 peak.) Thompson added $10 million worth of billings in a single year, taking it to an international total of $72 million. Young & Rubicam came next at $43 million. Nine agencies in all could claim at least $20 million, an eminence formerly reserved for JWT. As for the economy in general, war was good business for advertising.

Two prominent admen retired during the war. For years Albert Lasker had been trying to find a successor. In the 1920s he had merged Lord & Thomas with the agency of Thomas F. Logan. "I believed that he could in time succeed me," Lasker said later. Logan died young only two years after the merger. Next Lasker made Ralph Sollitt president, but he soon retired from advertising. Lasker then tried Don Francisco, but things did not work out and Francisco left to work at JWT. Lasker held on awhile longer, "a benign lion" after a lifetime of conquest, according to one of his men, "dispensing wisdom to a new crop of hopeful conquerors." When his son Edward told him he would not continue in the business, Lasker threw in his hand. He liquidated his stock for $10 million, and three of his men reopened the agency as Foote, Cone & Belding in January 1943. (Lasker wanted the names in alphabetical sequence, but George Washington Hill insisted that *his* account executive, Emerson Foote, be listed first.)

Lasker's antithesis, Raymond Rubicam, had watched his agency double its billings since 1937, but he was not happy. "I felt like a cog in a machine, even though I was the biggest cog," he later recalled. "I had less and less to do with planning and making ads, and work-

ing internally with our own people, and more and more to do with
calling on chief executives, many of whom cared little about advertising and knew less." In addition, he had married his second wife in
1940. They had not planned a family, but a son had arrived. (Lou
Brockway sent a telegram: "Glad to learn that the Instrument of the
Immortals still contains The Priceless Ingredient.") After the grinding effort of building his agency and slighting his first family, he
now wanted more time. In July 1944 he retired to a life of good
works, real estate development, and golf in Arizona.

FIVE

THE SECOND BOOM

A downtown office building, five o'clock on a weekday afternoon. A man in a gray flannel suit emerges from his office, takes the elevator downstairs, and gets into a large two-toned automobile. He picks his way through the urban landscape before moving into the smooth flow of a divided highway, heading outward to a region of lawns and trees and split-level houses. At home he finds his wife, three children, and dinner awaiting him. Afterward the family gathers in the living room. Conversation, homework, indeed all other activity stops, as if in preparation for evening prayer. Lights are turned off. The man clicks a knob on a large wooden box. The room is bathed in a lurid, flickering, unearthly light. "And now," a voice from the box announces, "Texaco is proud to present . . ." The family stares, transfixed, as the image of a man appears, an aging vaudevillian, oddly dressed and called Uncle Miltie.

During the fifteen years after the end of the Second World War, American advertising parlayed this expansive cluster of circumstances—cars, highways, new patterns of suburban consumption, and the explosion of the ultimate ad medium—into its greatest prosperity since the 1920s. Breaking away from the long drought of Depression and wartime austerities, the gross total of advertising expenditures doubled in only five years, from $2.9 billion in 1945 to $5.7 billion in 1950. Measured against such other indices as per capita income and consumer purchases, however, advertising was only holding its own. In 1950 advertising represented 2.9 percent of consumer spending, a figure identical to that in the last prewar year of 1940.

The truly flush time was the decade of the 1950s, powered by a combination of demographics and geography. The baby boom and the drift to the suburbs meant prosperity for the construction business: over a million new homes each year, along with the necessary highways and shopping centers. Instead of packaged goods and cigarettes, the most heavily advertised products now were automobiles, as General Motors passed Procter & Gamble as the leading national advertiser. In 1956 the largest individual advertising budgets were spent by Chevrolet (at $30.4 million) and Ford ($25 million), followed by Buick, Dodge, Plymouth, Mercury, Chrysler, Pontiac, and Oldsmobile. Only Coca-Cola, at $10.9 million, broke into Detroit's hegemony over the top ten. Motor-vehicle registration leaped from 31 million in 1945 to 73.8 million fifteen years later. Since cars were essentially two-ton packaged goods, varying little beneath the skins of their increasingly outlandish styling, they demanded heavy advertising. With automobiles as the bellwether, gross advertising went up by 75 percent during the decade, faster than the growth of the GNP, personal income, or any other economic index. "The greatest boom in the history of the advertising business," *Fortune* reported in 1956, "is now entering its second decade, and is not yet running out of gas."

In 1945 *Advertising Age* started publishing annual estimates of the total billings for each agency during the preceding year. These figures, previously guarded secrets, now allowed advertising practitioners to gauge their progress against their competitors by a process as simple as checking the baseball standings. In 1947 J. Walter Thompson became the first agency to pass $100 million in billings. It was joined in this heady atmosphere by BBDO and Young & Rubicam in 1951 and then by McCann-Erickson in 1954. Yet the potential for growth seemed without limit. Only three years later, in 1957, all four agencies passed $200 million and kept climbing. By 1960 only the bottom agency in the top ten, Foote, Cone & Belding, hovered just below the previously unattainable $100 million mark.

These annual rankings were scorned by Stanley Resor of the Thompson agency. From his immovable perch at the top of the heap, he insisted that an agency's gross billings meant less than the service it might render a client. The last of advertising's great pioneers, still a driving perfectionist at the age of seventy-one in 1950, he entered his thirty-fifth year as Thompson's president with an undiminished focus and singleness of purpose. "A non-stop mechanism," one observer remarked: "His food and drink, his unremitting daily task, and the substance of his dreams is advertising. He has no hobbies, plays no games." In the sumptuous JWT offices on two floors of the Graybar Building, people moved about in an atmosphere of severe informality. Office doors were usually open—but behind iron grille gateways. The reception area was adorned not by artifacts of the trade but by hundreds of books, selected by Lewis Mumford for the agency, with their bindings colored and arranged in a way that pleased the eye. The essence of the place was stability, to a degree unknown anywhere else in the business. In the rare event of a major account loss, the agency avoided mass firings by simply finding, somewhere within its vast organization, new jobs for everyone affected. When Resor finally stepped down as president in 1955 ("the ending of an era," *Advertising Age* called it), he was succeeded by Norman Strouse, a Thompson man since 1929.

JWT continued to prosper in the 1950s in part because it dominated the international field at precisely the time American business in general was expanding overseas. During this decade American investments in Europe, for example, increased threefold to a total of $5 billion. As the first American agency with foreign offices—starting with one in Great Britain in 1899—JWT was there to serve. Well established on the continent during the 1920s, and then pushed into Latin America by General Motors accounts in the following decade, by the end of World War II Thompson was running fifteen foreign offices. Fourteen more were soon added. At Resor's insistence, these outposts were administered like a colonial empire, staffed by natives but opened and managed by Thompson men sent out from the U.S. "We want everyone to feel that geographical boundaries don't exist in a professional creative business," explained Samuel Meek, JWT's head of international operations. "We can get plenty of people there who speak the language. We like to know the men who are going to run our offices." A Thompson office anywhere in the world was still recognizably a Thompson office. A tour of duty abroad served as a kind of finishing school, a final testing, for rising talents in the organization. By 1960 JWT was billing $120 million abroad, nearly half the agency's domestic total.

Thompson's competitors among the big four were also building their foreign operations, though BBDO and Young & Rubicam essentially limited their efforts to Canada and Great Britain. Under Sigurd Larmon, Y & R kept pace by—in general—sticking to the designs of Raymond Rubicam. Though Larmon, formerly an account executive and new-business man, had no copy experience, the agency still enjoyed a reputation for treating its creative people well. "One of the great assets of this agency," said George Gribbin, the creative director, "is that a man here feels he can express himself as a writer." The heads of the art and copy departments, not top management or the client, had the final word about any ad. Operating out of the least pretentious offices of any major agency, Y & R was known for its teamwork, group management, and absence of overblown egos. When its veterans came back from the war, they all got jobs somewhere in the organization. Any employee with three years at Y & R automatically shared in a trust fund. "The agency has a distinct esprit de corps," one trade journal commented in 1949. Like Thompson, it had a small new-business department and never made speculative presentations to prospective clients. It hardly needed to: from 1945 to 1960, U.S. billings went from $53 million to $212 million.

BBDO did even better in that time, from $40 million to $235 million. By contrast with the Y & R experience, this jump took place because the agency departed sharply from its previous traditions. BBDO had always been an "institutional" agency that did advertising—as the saying went—for clients who did not really need to advertise. It handled few packaged goods, drugs, cigarettes, or toiletries. In manner and style it was restrained, gentlemanly, a little bland. Even the cadences of the full name—*Bat*ten, *Bar*ton, *Dur*stine & *Os*born—seemed measured and dignified. (That mouthful, according to Fred Allen, no admirer of ad agencies, sounded like a trunk falling downstairs.) After Bruce Barton lost his campaign for the Senate in 1940, he had returned as president and continued to set the tone for the office.

In 1946 he gave way to Ben Duffy, a very different personality. "He oozed Irish charisma," one BBDO man recalled, "and everybody oozed right back at him. He hadn't just kissed the blarney stone, he carried it with him." A first-generation Irish-American, a devout Catholic and Knight of Malta, a high school dropout who had started at BBDO as a messenger boy, he could hardly have been more unlike his predecessor. He maintained a perverse pride in having grown up in a tenement in Hell's Kitchen—"a wholesome neighborhood," he insisted. "Everybody helps everybody else. If the whole world adopted the code of Hell's Kitchen, no one would starve." As head of one of the most Republican and main-line agencies, he liked to make a point of reminding associates of his background, punctuating his conversation with bad grammar, vivid expletives, and a flaring Irish temper. His favorite baseball team was not the Yankees or Giants but the Dodgers, the scruffy Bums from Brooklyn. He brought to his work a street-smart assertiveness not previously seen on the BBDO premises. "Ben is sweet," one co-worker remarked, "and aggressive as hell." In 1948, when Foote, Cone & Belding resigned the $10 million Lucky Strike account, Duffy showed up first at American Tobacco's office and landed the prize after one meeting. Other coups followed: the $8 million Campbell's Soup account, Schenley, Lever Brothers, General Mills, Bristol-Myers, Revlon. In the Duffy style, BBDO was now lean and hard-selling.

Though no other agency approached the billings of the big four, all were touched by the general trend toward bigness. In the years after the war, clients began to expect—in some cases were induced to expect—more service from an agency than simply the preparation of ads. Agencies started hiring more people in such fields as market research, merchandising, and publicity. "Public relations is the fashion of the day, as well as the need of the hour," *Ad Age* noted in 1947. Young & Rubicam had already established a PR subsidiary; McCann-Erickson added one in 1955, Compton the following year, Benton & Bowles the year after that.

More traditional agency departments, in existence at least since the 1920s, now assumed more importance. The merchandising department performed tasks for both client and agency. For the client it helped out with product development, recommending changes in packaging, distribution, pricing, and sales presentations; for the agency, merchandising advised creatives about a product's selling points, told contact men about the client's selling operation, and recommended advertising media on the basis of the product's potential market. The traffic department cut across jurisdictional lines to keep ads moving along the production line toward publication, making schedules and enforcing deadlines for the whole process from copy calls to shipping. Badgering copywriters on one side and reassuring account executives on the other, a good traffic man was a consummate diplomat. The media department selected the right place for an ad to appear, with the help of the media bible, the Standard Rate and Data Service, which listed advertising rates, circulations, and mechanical requirements for all the significant publications and outlets. The media man estimated costs; reserved and ordered space; checked on the appearance of published ads; paid the bills; and, not incidentally, was well courted, wined and dined, by media salesmen who wanted to be his customers.

All these ancillary services cost money. With the commission system still at the traditional 15 percent, and salaries and overheads increasing, agency profit margins started to wither. In response, the prewar process of meiosis, by which ambitious young admen quit big shops to start their own operations, yielded to its polar opposite, a series of mergers and consolidations. Just before the boom of the 1950s, a few agencies were launched on the older pattern. Thus in 1946 three men from Ruthrauff & Ryan and one from Thompson split off to form Sullivan, Stauffer, Colwell & Bayles, bringing with them the Noxzema and Smith Brothers accounts from R & R. "I'd like to get out and build something up again, and have some fun at it," said one of the founders. But no major agencies were launched in this way during the 1950s, in part perhaps because of the celebrated Duane Jones case. Jones, the owner of his own medium-sized agency, sued when three of his employees took a major client and started their own shop. The $300,000 verdict won by Jones in 1952 may have had a chilling effect, at least for a time, on other such ventures.

But essentially the merger trend derived from the demand for more services. When a small, one-man agency reached billings of about $3 million—at which point the business was too big for one man, but too small to expand its services—it had to grow, merge, or cut back; staying at the same level meant going under. "Advertisers are demanding more and more from their agencies," the owner of a small Chicago shop said after selling out to a medium-sized agency. "I for one simply didn't have the manpower to deliver the research, sales analysis, package design, publicity and all the other things my clients were calling for." The same situation afflicted admen farther up the ladder. "We have a choice of underservicing accounts and losing them," said the head of a medium-sized New York agency, "or overservicing them and going broke."

By the same token, mergers and bigness meant more stability and influence for the advertising business in general. Once again observers suggested that advertising was reaching a new maturity, pointing to Eisenhower's Secretary of Defense Neil McElroy, the "first adman Cabinet officer," from a background of advertising and promotion at Procter & Gamble; or to the Vatican's naming of a patron saint of advertising, Saint Bernardino of Siena. "Advertising now compares with such long-standing institutions as the school and the church in the magnitude of its social influence," declared a noted American historian, David Potter, in 1952. "It dominates the media, it has vast power in the shaping of popular standards, and it is really one of the very limited group of institutions which exercise social control."

❧❧

In 1960 Draper Daniels of the Leo Burnett agency published in *Advertising Age* a series of vignettes on agency life. Thus on the head man:

> The sharkskin-bound deluxe edition
> Of an adman's ultimate ambition,
> He is the final word, the head,
> The man who says the last word said.
> Monarch of all, and self-reliant,
> None say him "Nay," save every client.

❧❧

As usual, the ads themselves appeared in a chaotic variety of forms and styles, making any generalization about them vulnerable. Most observers perceived a return to the hard sell, of the kind that Ben Duffy was imposing on BBDO. With general prosperity, an eightfold growth in consumer credit, and more discretionary income, markets were flooded with competing nonsubsistence items distinguishable by hardly any real competitive differences among them. Procter & Gamble in the 1950s reached the billion-dollar mark in sales, half of which came from new products launched during the decade itself. General Foods was annually selling over $300 million worth of products acquired or launched since the war. Given new products of no real novelty, along with a crowded market, the ads had to hit fast and hard.

Thus copy became shorter and more simple, with the visual aspects correspondingly more vivid, to catch the attention of a consumer distracted by more advertising messages than ever before. "We are definitely again in the age of the eye," noted Margot Sherman of McCann-Erickson. "We have less time to read, browse, meditate and muse. There is such a multiplicity of messages striking us from every side . . . that it seems sometimes that only the lightning message of a picture can strike deep and hit home when we have a moment to spare."

In advertising, as in the art world generally, photographers continued to assume the function of literal representation from the artists who worked with paint and pen. For ad artists who worked with type and camera, at least, these were interesting times. One especially well-regarded campaign, Young & Rubicam's series for Jell-O in 1953, featured large, all but shimmering photographs by Irving Penn, under the supervision of Y & R's art director Frank Sergenian. The old illustrators like Norman Rockwell did less advertising work, and even when they took commissions they now enjoyed less freedom of expression. Back when Rockwell had started in advertising, "an art director was an office boy," he recalled in 1960. "Now an art director tells you what to do and how you are to do it. The art director makes up the layout, and the illustrator is relegated to the ranks of draftsmen and copiers." The most striking ads of this period—the Marlboro man, the eye-patched patrician in the Hathaway shirt, the fortunate owner of a Polaroid camera, the woman who did (or did not) use Clairol—drew their power from a single, bold photographic image with little copy, sometimes no copy at all.

Remarkably few of these best-remembered campaigns were produced by the major old-line agencies. Most of their work—and, therefore, most of 1950s advertising—was safe and dull, without flair or distinction. The memorable ads seemed especially good because they had so little competition. In the midst of its greatest boom, even as Marshall McLuhan anointed it "the main channel of intellectual and artistic effort in the modern world," the industry underwent a round of self-flagellation. All through the 1950s, advertising people deplored a lack of creativity among both practitioners and products:

"Too many people are imitating too many other people. Too many advertisers are refusing to explore new paths. Too many advertisers are 'adapting' instead of creating." (*Ad Age,* 1952)

"There is very definitely a shortage of really creative people in advertising, and I think about the problem a lot. The account management side of the business is generally regarded today as the more glamorous side." (Fairfax Cone, 1954)

"Whether you are talking products, advertising ideas, layout treatments, package design or what have you, we are in the greatest era of monkey-see, monkey-do the world has ever known." (Sigurd Larmon, 1956)

"The creative man has lost the chip on his shoulder, the fire in his eye. Success has made him courteous, obedient, cautious. Thin tie, thin skin. He has moved to the suburbs, bought a boat, which he is careful not to rock." (Whit Hobbs, BBDO, 1959)

This litany of self-abuse voiced a general agreement that a "creativity problem" existed, but no consensus as to causes and solutions. Critics blamed the war for interrupting careers at the stage when most ad people gained their creative experience before moving on to other positions in the agency hierarchy; thus, with little creative background, they now were supervising the creative departments. Others cited a growing cult of specialization, as copywriters were hired not for a general skill at writing but for particular knowledge of a particular product. The hard sell itself cut down on the time and space available to copy, narrowing a writer's range of expression and experimentation. Even the admired visual techniques diverted attention from the written word, rewarding style at the expense of content. "In any creative form," Walter O'Meara pointed out in 1957, "when the externals become too important the form becomes degenerate." (As a novelist and old copywriter, O'Meara naturally regarded everything but language as "externals.")

Defining the problem inevitably depended on one's own bias: art or copy, creative or administrative, big agency or small. At BBDO, original thinking was encouraged by the very BBDO-like technique of "brainstorming," started by Alex Osborn in 1940 and pursued in the 1950s under his disciple Willard Pleuthner. Osborn believed in keeping what he called the "creative mind" separate from the "judicial mind." The former spouted ideas; the latter judged them and might inhibit their generation. So a brainstorming session at BBDO aimed to create an atmosphere of uncritical acceptance. A group of people, gathered from various departments and levels within the company, met in a room painted sunshine yellow "to aid inspiration." The room's pine furniture, table settings, pads and pencils were all roughly the same inspirational hue. With a problem before them, all hands thought out loud, spewing forth ideas no matter how unlikely or unconsidered. The only judgments permitted were positive ones that might allow one participant to "hitchhike" on another's suggestion. For the time being, internal rank meant nothing: everyone was equal. Only afterward would someone of judicial mind sort through the stenographic record. In 1956, 401 brainstorming sessions at BBDO produced 34,000 tentative ideas, an average of 85 per meeting; of these, 2,000 were judged "worthy of development into usable ideas."

Confronted by this deluge of inspirations, one or two individuals still had to perform the truly "creative" part of the technique, the separation of wheat from chaff. The ideas finally put to use—a soup-on-the-rocks campaign for Campbell's, adding sleighbells to Schaefer beer trucks at Christmas—may not have repaid all those free-form hours of head emptying. Critics of brainstorming, who typically came from smaller agencies with reputations for creative daring, thought it a waste of time. "Brainstorming sessions," said David Ogilvy, "are the delight of sterile loafers who would rather fritter away their day in meetings than shut their doors and get down to *work*." To such observers, brainstorming meant no solution to the creative dilemma but instead simply reflected the creative bankruptcy of the big agencies, that in their sterility they would resort to such an addled stratagem.

The most frequently cited aspect of the creative problem, market and copy research, was also—depending on the eye of the beholder—variously a source, or a symptom, or a solution of the creativity drought. That research was prospering while creativity withered was clear enough; the causal relationship between the two remained quite murky. In the 1930s George Gallup had carried out his pioneering surveys of copy readership for Young & Rubicam, an agency celebrated for creative work, without damaging the agency's reputation. JWT's Consumer Panel, launched in 1939, reported the spending habits of 5,000 families to those Thompson clients willing to pay for it, again without raising alarms about its effect on ads themselves. Research departments, where they existed, were still small, and polling and sampling techniques still rudimentary, as the 1948 presidential election showed. In what *Ad Age* called "a nightmare for the advertising and marketing business," all the major polls predicted Truman's defeat; Gallup missed the final vote by 5.3 percent, Roper by 12.3 percent. "This election," the joke went, "slowed Gallup down to a trot." Fifteen newspapers dropped Gallup's column, and Roper's business fell off by one-fifth.

But the techniques were refined, and later elections did not repeat the embarrassment. The improved methods intersected nicely with the expansion of agency services in the 1950s, as advertising people began to claim a scientific exactness for their work, basing it on demographic studies and hard statistics instead of the intuitive hunches of a lone copywriter at his typewriter. All the big agencies kept adding to their research departments; outside consultants such as Daniel Starch and Alfred Politz were prospering; the Advertising Research Foundation, started in 1953, soon acquired its own quarterly journal. Media departments, another beneficiary of the expanding agency services, now had more precise notions of the audiences the various media were reaching, and the stopping power and persuasiveness of individual ads.

Within any given agency, the ascendant researchers found little common ground with the denizens of art and copy. The former thought of advertising as a science and spoke a dense mathematical patois. The latter regarded advertising as an art, or at least a craft, that responded to one's creative muse. Given the tendencies of the day, creatives felt displaced and defensively blamed their problems on "research and other things," as Les Pearl of BBDO put it: "Merchandising men and research men are statistic-ing the creative man to death." "No one yet," said Walter Weir, "has succeeded in making an advertisement by setting in type a research report." Yet at staff meetings the marketing and research people held the floor. At Foote, Cone & Belding, as Shirley Polykoff recalled it, the creatives squirmed during meetings "of monumental monotony" run by research and marketing. "Meetings that droned on and on with such deadly sameness, they could have been syndicated. Just sign on the dotted line. And most of the advertising in the fifties reflected this dullness."

As long as research concentrated on taking statistical measurements of the effectiveness of *past* and *current* campaigns, its critics could plausibly hold the research vogue responsible for the dearth of new, creative advertising. By assaying previous efforts, in the fashion of early Gallup, this traditional form of research aimed to predict future consumer responses. The effect, George Gribbin of Y & R pointed out, was "to set molds on the way advertising ought to be done." Given the creative drought, advertising needed not old molds but new patterns. "There is more need to *break out of* the mold than to *set* the mold in which advertising ought to be contained," said Gribbin. "The molds give you faceless advertising. You need to *break* with the past to get individuality." Traditional advertising research, stressing quantified returns on old campaigns, had an implicitly conservative bias that typically urged a repeat of whatever had worked before.

A new form of research, offering qualitative analyses of *future* campaigns, promised advertisers a new tool for breaking from, instead of simply repeating, past campaigns. Motivation research (MR) replaced the older statistical techniques of polling and counting with esoteric methods borrowed from the social sciences, especially depth psychology and psychoanalysis. Instead of treating consumers as rational beings who knew what they wanted and why they wanted it, MR delved into subconscious, nonrational levels of motivation to suggest—beforehand—where ads should be aimed. "If you can't understand what goes on in people's heads," said one MR enthusiast, "how can you plan advertising that will reach them? There are things people think and believe that they won't express." Instead of clipboards and adding machines, the up-to-date ad researcher now used depth interviews, projective techniques, word-association and sentence-completion games, and thematic apperception tests.

Thus psychology enjoyed its greatest vogue among ad people since the heyday of John B. Watson's behaviorism in the 1920s. The pioneer and prime salesman of MR was a Vienna-born consultant named Ernest Dichter, a strict Freudian famous for discovering that Chrysler sold fewer convertibles than sedans because men regarded the first as a mistress but the second as a wife. Such Freudian notions did not entirely dominate the field, however. An Adlerian analyst, Herta Herzog, started doing MR research on power drives for McCann-Erickson in 1945. And the most tireless publicist of the new methods was a non-psychologist, Pierre Martineau, research director of the Chicago *Tribune*. Describing copy and statistical advocates as "very rational but very insensitive people," Martineau declared the old direct, reason-why copy approach inappropriate to an era of affluence and consumer products. With bare subsistence and economic necessity less important, advertisers had to shift their appeals to deeper levels: "It is not what is said but how it is said that influences us the most." The consumer was unconsciously searching for the symbols behind the words—if, indeed, he even read the words in a typical ad.

Martineau was an outsider who took no direct part in the production of advertising. But in the early 1950s several Chicago agencies started using MR in telling ways. Leo Burnett and Foote, Cone & Belding launched separate MR departments. Burnett's "Make mine hefty, hale and hearty" campaign for the Tea Bureau derived from a finding that tea had a virility problem. A third Chicago agency, Weiss & Geller, geared its entire operation to what it called the "social science approach to advertising." Its MR research group discovered that women bought lingerie for the approval of other women, not to please men; that men and women had different motives in buying homes; that chewing gum could not be sold to adolescents as an aid to good health. "For years," said president Edward H. Weiss, "most of us advertising executives have been too concerned with things—not enough with people; with products and not with the reasons why people bought or didn't buy." Rather than starting with the product and proclaiming its virtues, MR began with the buyers and what they wanted, even if they did not know what that was.

Ever since the early days of advertising, of course, ad people had tried to guess what their audience wanted to hear. The approach itself was less novel than the particular techniques, esoteric jargon, and especially the scientific patina that now surrounded it. Previously, advertisers had assumed that people bought products for the usual messy complex of human motives. MR, flourishing the authority of science, reduced those motives to two: sex and security. With the world ever more complex and frustrating, "we have been removed from the basic forms of security," said Dichter. "You either offer security or fail" as advertisers.

The insecurity with which some ad people greeted MR itself illustrated Dichter's point. "Strictly a gimmick," said one unimpressed adman in 1953. "It's the tool of the young man of upward mobility—the guy who will cut my throat and have my job in ten years." A year later Charles Brower of BBDO urged his peers to avoid "outside witch doctors and head shrinkers." But the trend was unmistakable. Two other big agencies, Young & Rubicam and Ruthrauff & Ryan, started using MR approaches. Another, Grey Advertising, devised a new campaign for Greyhound when it learned that Americans would accept criticism of driving in traffic, but not of the automobile itself. Thus the slogan: "Take the bus and leave the driving to us," which celebrated going Greyhound without belittling a man's wife (or mistress).

The most acute criticism of MR came from Alfred Politz, a psychologist and head of his own advertising consulting firm. He belonged to the old Claude Hopkins school of direct, reason-why copy. (In 1955 he republished Hopkins' *Scientific Advertising,* declaring in the preface that "present-day advertising research has a long way to go before it reaches the level of Claude Hopkins' contributions to efficient advertising.") As a psychologist, Politz spoke the language of the motivation researchers, and he was not impressed. A "pseudoscience," he declared, that simply gave an impression of "something scientific going on," MR was only telling advertisers what they already knew or wished to be told. The pretentious psychological gibberish served well to impress agency brass (definition of motive: "a hypothetical construct used to infer determinants of behavior") but concealed an essential vacuity. Hidden motives, extracted from *individuals* after careful, detailed psychoanalysis sessions, could hardly be inferred on a *mass* level. Yet Politz had his own hidden motive, since attacking MR meant an implicit defense of the competing work of his own firm. As Dichter said in rebuttal, Politz had "a vested interest in alternative research techniques."

The debate over MR suddenly opened up with the publication in 1957 of Vance Packard's *The Hidden Persuaders.* On the best-seller list for eighteen weeks—number one for six weeks—and with over a hundred thousand copies sold in its first year, the book was the most popular nonfiction attack on advertising since the 1930s. "Large-scale efforts are being made," Packard announced, "often with impressive success, to channel our unthinking habits, our purchasing decisions, and our thought processes by the use of insights gleaned from psychiatry and the social sciences." Though conceding that most advertisers still operated at a rational, aboveboard level, Packard then took the reader on a tour of MR's outer reaches, including hypnosis, the psychoanalysis of children, and "biocontrol," the regulation of mental processes and perceptions by electrical signals. Fully two-thirds of the one hundred biggest advertisers, said Packard, were using MR techniques. The future seemed bleakly Orwellian: "No one, literally no one, evidently is to be spared from the all-seeing, Big Brotherish eye of the motivational analyst if a merchandising opportunity seems to beckon.... But when you are manipulating, where do you stop? Who is to fix the point at which manipulative attempts become socially undesirable?"

As though to confirm Packard's grimmest predictions, a consultant named James Vicary stepped up with his technique of "subliminal" advertising. In a New Jersey movie theater, messages urging the consumption of popcorn and soda pop were flashed on the screen for a fraction of a second, too briefly to be rationally perceived; still, sales of the items went up. At a level below consciousness, people might be manipulated without realizing it. With the way prepared by *The Hidden Persuaders*, subliminals enjoyed a momentary notoriety. (They will, said Ernest Dichter, "give the whole field of motivation research a bad name.") In January 1958 Vicary offered a subliminal sampling to a Washington audience of congressmen, regulatory bodies, and the press. Nobody saw anything, but that was the point. "Having gone to see something that is not supposed to be seen," *Printers' Ink* noted, "and not having seen it, as forecast, they seemed satisfied." Vicary went ahead, planning audible subliminals for a Los Angeles radio station. But adverse public reaction kept them from the air, and in the spring of 1958 the National Association of Broadcasters banned them from the airwaves.

This six-month wonder was symptomatic of the whole issue of motivation research. Packard had obtained most of his information from interested parties like Dichter and Vicary who wanted to spread the gospel; taking their self-promoting claims literally, he therefore exaggerated the extent and importance of MR. Granted that it had launched a few well-known campaigns, but of those two-thirds of the biggest advertisers, how many made *habitual, significant* use of MR? How did the effectiveness of MR campaigns compare with similar campaigns conducted without the benefit of MR? What of MR-derived ideas that led nowhere? Packard did not address any of these questions. He thus gave a distorted impression of how typical MR and the psychological sell were of advertising in the 1950s.

"All the motivational mumbo-jumbo," said Charles Adams of MacManus, John & Adams, "all the Freud-happy figures assembled since Herr Doktor Dichter was knee-high to a couch cannot make the public's taste buds tingle nor its ego pant for a new car." "Anyone who entertains such a childlike fear," insisted another adman, "has never tried to market a product to the tough, skeptical American public." *The Hidden Persuaders* succeeded not by offering a true picture of advertising, but by itself tapping a deep unconscious motive: for a freedom-conscious America, a fear of being manipulated by dark, unseen forces. The book revealed more about the public mentality, and about public attitudes toward advertising, than about advertising itself.

🌵🌵

Draper Daniels on the research man:

> With a ton of charts and a wondrous plan
> He comes, behold, the Research Man.
> Give him four and twenty scholars,
> Give him twenty thousand dollars,
> And in two months he'll bring to view
> The facts that you already knew.

🌵🌵

Although much discussed in the 1950s, motivation research—in its emphasis on hidden, irrational drives, oblique copy, and image building—was not representative of most advertising of the time. A typical 1950s ad repeated a simple theme, with (if it appeared on TV) a crisp visual demonstration: "Wonder Bread helps build strong bodies twelve ways"; "M&M's melt in your mouth, not in your hands"; "Colgate cleans your breath while it cleans your teeth," and furthermore its Gardol shield could stop a baseball; stomach acid might burn holes in cloth but was no match for Rolaids. And the most famous of all, the Anacin ad showing three boxes in the skull of a headache sufferer: in turn, a pounding hammer, a coiling spring, and a jagged electric bolt were relieved by little bubbles of Anacin making their way up from the stomach. All these ads were created by a single agency, Ted Bates, with no use at all for MR. "What this agency has done which is different from any other agency," explained Rosser Reeves, the dominant figure at Bates, "is to apply reason to advertising." *Reason*—not unconscious strivings for sex and security.

For the 1950s, Reeves was the most influential theoretician of how advertising worked. He pictured the consumer as beset not by irrational drives but by a plethora of ad messages, engulfing him on every side, glazing his eyes and overloading his memory. To cut through this deluge, an effective ad had to offer a Unique Selling Proposition (USP), strong enough to pull in new customers, that a competitor did not or could not make. The besieged consumer could only retain one strong claim or concept from a given ad; any elaboration simply cluttered the ad to no effect. Even adding sex appeal only distracted the target. The copy and art work should not be artistic or even especially interesting. The sole criterion was effectiveness. "A hard-sell advertisement," said Reeves, "like a diesel motor, must be judged on *whether it performs what it was designed to do.* Is a wristbone ugly? An ear? Or are they beautifully functional?" The Anacin boxes-in-the-skull, Reeves later recalled, "were the most hated commercials in the history of advertising." But in eighteen months they raised Anacin sales from $18 million to $54 million.

To measure the effectiveness of its ads more precisely, Bates conducted research of the traditional interviews-and-numbers kind. Every year it contacted some 5,000 people all over the country, asking them two questions about the major campaigns of Bates' clients *and* their main competitors: first, how many people remembered a given ad; second, how many actually used the product. The "usage pull" was derived by subtracting the second figure from the first. "For the first time," said Reeves, "we have an auditing approach to advertising." The Bates surveys revealed, at least to Reeves, that the campaigns with the highest usage pull (or "penetration") were not those with the biggest budgets or most creative advertising. Rather, the most effective ads repeated a single USP, over and over; no campaign ever wore out unless a product—and therefore its USP—became outmoded. In a given product field, one's own penetration was inverse to the competition's. Penetration was a finite universe because the besieged consumer could only retain so many USPs in his head at one time. Thus a wise advertiser found a USP and stuck with it, in every medium, for years.

In creative terms, then, a typical Bates campaign was straightforward, unremarkable, even prosaic. At most agencies the creative halls were prowled by temperamental, hungry young lions under the age of forty. At Bates, one-third of the creatives were over fifty, another third in their mid-forties. "I never tried to make *interesting* commercials," Reeves said later. "Once you've found a Unique Selling Proposition, any good copywriter can write a good ad. The rest is just wordsmithing." This approach irritated critics who thought of advertising as an art. But its practical success was undeniable. Specializing in packaged goods—products to be eaten or rubbed on or smoked—the agency saw its billings soar from $16 million in 1945 to $130 million in 1960, just one notch below the big four.

During most of this growth Reeves dominated the place, writing much of the copy, overseeing everything. "At the agency," a Bates associate recalled, "Rosser worked practically around the clock. A real bonecrusher. And he had an adrenal cortex the size of a *baseball*. Pouring out ideas." He was a strong, thickly built man, an inch under six feet and 190 pounds, with a full head of dark hair and heavy-rimmed glasses. Speaking in a loud, deep voice, projecting a positive, overpowering manner, he was especially effective at client presentations, holding forth in front of an easel. His favorite sermon on the virtues of a USP was known around the agency as the Cross of Gold speech. "Rosser had a way of making the clients agree with him, *out loud*, from the moment he started to talk," according to his associate. "The clients' intellectual capacity for resisting what Rosser said just seemed to disintegrate as he talked."

Reeves was born in 1910 in Danville, Virginia, the son of a Methodist minister. Always bookish, he started writing fiction and poetry at the age of ten, publishing occasionally in little newspapers and magazines. Evidently the major influence on his early life was his father. From him the son absorbed an intellectual passion to know and understand his world; at the same time the son could not share his father's religious zeal and standards of moral conduct. "Rosser's father couldn't speak three sentences without quoting the Bible," John Lyden of Bates later recalled. "Rosser grew up in an atmosphere of significance, and developed a cosmological sense. He's always reached for the conceptual meaning, tried to get final and ultimate solutions. He needs a system; he's a Methodist turned inside out."

He enrolled at the University of Virginia expecting to become a lawyer. After encountering a gifted teacher, Stringfellow Barr, in a course on the French Revolution, he changed his mind and thought about teaching history. But in his sophomore year, following a disastrous fling at the stock market and the onset of the Depression, he had to leave school and go to work. Now intent on a career in writing and journalism, he joined a Richmond bank to edit its house organ. When the periodical was dropped Reeves transferred to the bank's advertising department. His drive and writing gifts soon pointed him toward the agency business in New York. Through one of the bank's directors Reeves made contact with the Cecil, Warwick & Cecil agency. Hired to write copy at thirty-four dollars a week, he arrived in New York in 1934, twenty-four years old.

At Cecil his boss was James Kennedy, who had trained under

Stirling Getchell at Thompson and so became the first of Reeves' mentors in the hard-sell Hopkins tradition. "He was sort of my baby—the first really brilliant writer I'd got my hands on," Kennedy said later. A headlong enthusiast by nature, with an abnormal supply of energy and unquenchable zest for widely assorted aspects of life, Reeves pounced on his new vocation. He studied the precedents, wrote piles of copy, and talked advertising late into the night over many drinks. At the same time, living in Greenwich Village, he tried the varied cultural offerings of his new home: magicians' nightclubs in Times Square, dinners at the Roosevelt and 21, gambling dens across the Brooklyn Bridge. And books, always books, especially Spengler in these years. On the model of Thomas Wolfe, another expatriate southerner in New York, he started writing a great American novel. "He already had this tremendous penetrating gaze, and these amazing hobbies," Kennedy recalled. "Here was this great feverish mind, racing a hundred miles an hour all the time. We were afraid he was going to crack up."

Reeves moved on through other advertising jobs, notably a stint at Blackett-Sample-Hummert in the late 1930s. Here, in Duane Jones and Frank Hummert, he acquired two other mentors in the Hopkins mold. Reeves never betrayed much interest in the corollary style of advertising that Raymond Rubicam was using with such success at the same time. From start to finish, with a consistency that verged on rigidity, Reeves attached himself to reason-why and claim-and-coupon. During his two years at B-S-H, he later told Hummert with pardonable exaggeration, "I learned all that I know about advertising and have been selling it ever since." John E. Kennedy's "salesmanship in print," Reeves insisted, was "still the best definition of advertising. If a copywriter isn't a salesman, then he is a bad copywriter."

In 1940 the account executive Ted Bates left Benton & Bowles with the Wonder Bread and Colgate Dental Cream accounts to start his own agency. Bates brought Reeves along as his star copy man. For the next quarter-century this odd couple would run the agency. One man had his name on the door, but the other man got most of the credit for the winning campaigns and financial success. Bates was a patrician Maine Yankee, educated at Andover and Yale, lean and taciturn in the Yankee manner, who ate lunch alone and communicated with his staff by memo. Reeves was a baroque Virginian, hedonistic and hyperbolic, who dominated any room. Each man was a walking contradiction: Bates an introverted account man, Reeves an extroverted writer. When they convened at the office, just the two of them behind a closed door, associates could only wonder how it was going. If Reeves emerged, his face hard and set, giving off sparks and smoke, then it must not have gone well. Occasionally Reeves would threaten to quit, would even start going through the motions. Then Bates would make a concession, Reeves would get at least some of what he wanted, and matters at the agency would subside into a normal routine again.

In the 1950s, even with the thumping success and demands of his advertising work, Reeves still enjoyed a capacious range of hobbies and side interests, from serious pool to more serious chess to sailing his racing sloop and piloting (and once crashing) his seaplane. Though no longer intent on writing a great American novel, he still reveled in his personal library of some eight thousand books and tried his hand at poetry. Thus a reflection on the ultimate demise of earth:

> . . . the curious end of restless man,
> Who for a second of galactic time
> Floated upon a speck of cosmic dust
> Around a minor sun.

"You surprise me," said an associate after receiving a sample of Reeves' poetry. "Verse of this intransient quality is not entirely compatible with the bow tie and the slick Madison Avenue facet with which you more usually confront me." "The poetry side of my life is a very secret one," Reeves explained, "and as a rule I don't even publish it under my own name."

(Years later, in retirement, Reeves wrote a novel about a picaresque Greenwich Village eccentric, a bearded poet in blue jeans and tennis shoes who had rejected a privileged background and family to wander the streets declaiming speculations about religion, infinity, the universe, and the purpose of life. "You could say the book is my secret self," Reeves allowed.)

None of this secret self showed up in his work at Bates. He seemed two distinct people: at home, reflective and literary, the organizer and captain of the first American chess team to tour the Soviet Union, the sort of man who could savor the quiet, deliberate pace of a sailing sloop; at work, hyperactive and relentless, booming away in his Virginia drawl, a demanding taskmaster who drove his copy-writers hard: "the prince of hard sell," and "the ultimate pragma-tist." To most of his peers in the business he was known only by his work and reputation. During the 1950s *Printers' Ink* and *Advertising Age* ran scores of profiles of advertising figures, all but a few of them less significant than Reeves; for some reason Reeves was never pro-filed. In 1962 *Time* put a dozen admen on its cover; Reeves again not among them. With his other self unknown, the man was—perhaps unfairly—equated with his work. In some quarters one heard that American advertising had only two things wrong with it: Rosser Reeves.

As ever, the industry worried about its ethical standards, and Bates ads seemed especially suspect. The Anacin ad damned plain aspirin, the unspeakable Brand X, yet promoted Anacin for having "the pain reliever doctors recommend most," that is, aspirin. Many Bates commercials featured an actor in a white coat, sounding like a doctor. The USP trumpeted for a given product might not be pecu-liar to that product. "The claims may be true for all brands, not just our own," Reeves conceded. "But we tell people about them." (Claude Hopkins, whom Reeves admired, would have approved. Years ago Hopkins had pointed out that a client's beer bottles were "washed with live steam," as were all beer bottles. Later Lord & Thomas proclaimed, "It's toasted!" of the tobacco in Lucky Strikes, as was all cigarette tobacco.)

Admen liked to think of the old buccaneering days as gone for-ever, replaced by higher ethics. The Bates approach represented a throwback. The agency continued to run commercials for Prepara-tion H over 150 TV stations, although the promotion of such "per-sonal" products was banned by the National Association of Broadcasters' television code. The NAB, a voluntary effort at indus-try self-regulation, had no enforcement power. But the Federal Trade Commission did. In the late 1950s it forced Bates to drop any "liver" claims from ads for Carter's Little Liver Pills, and issued fur-ther complaints about four other Bates campaigns: the claim of a "protective shield" in Colgate Dental Cream, the faked depiction of "flavor gems" in Blue Bonnet margarine, Life cigarette ads demon-strating its filter's superiority at holding back water (and, implicitly, tar and nicotine too), and a Rapid Shave commercial supposedly demonstrating the shaving of sandpaper that was really only a Plex-iglas mask with sand applied. Other agencies received complaints at the same time, but none as many as Bates. Not a bit contrite, at a cost of over $23,000 Reeves placed a bristling full-page rebuttal in seven major newspapers. "These crippling press indictments," he said, "rest on flimsy ground indeed—mere subjective opinion that minor props and artifices have resulted in horrendous deceits." Over the next few months, though, Bates quietly withdrew all the offending campaigns.

Still unpersuaded of his alleged crimes, Reeves replied at greater length in his book *Reality in Advertising.* First written as an extended memorandum to new Bates executives, then published by Knopf in the spring of 1961, in six months it sold thirty-two thousand copies and was translated into seven foreign languages. "Advertising began as an art," Reeves noted, "and too many advertising men want it to remain that way—a never-never land where they can say: 'This is right, because we feel it's right.' " Actually, said Reeves, advertising was a science like engineering, with some incidental esthetic potential but essentially a tool, an instrument of commerce firmly grounded in practical matters. Giving the back of his hand to motivation research ("the Freudian hoax") and *The Hidden Persuaders* ("the sheerest nonsense"), Reeves explained the USP and the Bates consumer surveys. If a client's product was identical to its competition and could not be altered to acquire a USP, the public still might be told something new about it: "This is not a uniqueness of the product, but it assumes uniqueness, and cloaks itself in uniqueness, as a claim." At all costs, admen should avoid "the most dangerous word of all in advertising—*originality,*" an esthetic conceit deadly to maintaining a proper USP. Because too many creatives liked to create, eight of ten magazine campaigns were only "show-window advertising."

While avoiding any discussion of those "minor props and artifices," *Reality in Advertising* offered a cogent, widely read defense of the Bates approach. It brought in $18 million in new accounts—and loud, varied reactions from other advertising people. Reeves, said Fairfax Cone, believes in delivering advertising "without subtlety and without concern for anyone's gentler feelings. He also proves that such advertising works. That it may annoy a great many people, he dismisses as being beside the point." "There is enough ammunition in this book," an ad critic noted, "to keep the enemies of advertising supplied for years to come."

There, perhaps, was Reeves' real sin. His hard-sell methods were scarcely atypical for the time. Cone's own agency produced the "Aren't you glad you use Dial? Don't you wish everybody did!" deodorant-soap ads, which had their own capacity to annoy. Reeves only articulated, in notably blunt terms, the conventional wisdom of the day, and thereby helped reveal to outsiders the easily bruised feelings of the advertising community. When criticized for doing this, Reeves merely pointed to his sales figures and shrugged off his critics. "Certainly some of our clients use the brute force of money to move goods," he acknowledged, "—but, oh, do they sell soap."

One day in 1958, an unknown party sent Reeves a live white duck. The duck's name was USP, a card explained: "USP can't quack as well as you can, but louder." Reeves decided the culprit was Brown Bolte, the president of Sullivan, Stauffer, Colwell & Bayles. He sent Bolte an egg in a Tiffany box, with a message. "Dear Brownie," he wrote: "What else have you laid lately?"

❦❦

Draper Daniels on the copywriter:

> NOW . . . AT LAST . . . THE NEW AMAZING
> Gem of genius slowly blazing.
> The one man who, without a doubt
> Knows what this business is about.
> The man who screams, when words are changed,
> That all the changers are deranged.
> Still, were he quieter or politer,
> He wouldn't be a copywriter.

❦❦

All the salient postwar agency tendencies—mergers and bigness; international expansion; more services; research; and plain, punchy advertising—came together with particular effect in one firm, McCann-Erickson, and its legendary president, Marion Harper, Jr. As Rosser Reeves was the characteristic theoretician and copywriter of the 1950s, Harper was the characteristic executive and empire builder, the Albert Lasker of his time.

Among its competitors in the big four, only BBDO matched the growth rate of Harper's agency. In one twelve-month period in the mid-fifties McCann added $45 million worth of new business, including the Westinghouse appliance divisions and the $15 million

Coca-Cola account. Chesterfield and Mennen soon followed. In 1957 the agency moved its main office, with 1,100 employees, into luxurious new quarters on 14 floors of a new building at 485 Lexington Avenue—"the largest office move," according to a press release, "ever made by an advertising agency." By 1959 it trailed only Thompson in domestic billings. A phenomenon in the trade, controversial for its talent raids on other firms, McCann was known variously as "the research agency" and "the organization man's agency."

Or, more pertinently, as "Harper's Bazaar." The former boy wonder of American advertising, Marion Harper was, indeed, the pluperfect organization man, utterly representative of his era. In earlier days, as one advertising veteran, William L. Day, noted in 1952, most of the major figures had vivid personalities; but now, alas, most had "no more personality than angleworms." Harper projected a calm, judicial manner, devoid of eccentricity and spontaneous emotion, icily controlled and intellectual. A big man, six feet one and a half inches tall and hefty, he looked like a college professor with his bald pate, indoor pallor, and dark, tortoise-shelled glasses. He read books at a furious pace, late at night or while pedaling a stationary bicycle in the morning, starting at the back and then working forward, always taking notes and looking for ideas that might be useful at the office. He wore a brown suit on days that he felt cheerful, a gray suit on other days ("sometimes I don't really find out how I feel until I notice what I have on"). He always ate the same lunch—a hamburger, stewed tomatoes, tea, no liquor—usually with a client or a prospect.

Lacking charm and superficial charisma, Harper dominated his agency with a superior intellect and a stupefying capacity for hard, concentrated work, sometimes thirty-six or even forty-eight hours at a stretch. Essentially shy, with no time for jokes or office gossip, he might cap one of these marathon sessions by taking a quick nap and a shower and then, steeling himself, going off to a client meeting where he typically kept silent until the end, then had the last, authoritative word. "Marion's like one of those deep-sea fish that can function only under enormous pressure," said one associate. "He creates his own deep sea." Draper Daniels, who worked at McCann briefly and did not particularly *like* Harper, later recalled that he had known two presidents and three near-presidents of the United States: "None of them impressed me more than Marion Harper, Jr.

before he passed the age of 35 and let ego and optimism dim the brilliant clarity of his mind."

Harper was a rarity in the business, a second-generation adman. He was born in 1916 in Oklahoma City, where his father was advertising director of the *Daily Oklahoman*. When he was five his parents separated. Marion Sr. moved to New York and a career with General Foods and the Compton agency. An only child, beset by asthma, raised by his religious, strong-minded mother, the son was precociously self-disciplined and self-contained. President of his Methodist Sunday school class, at ten he made his public-speaking debut by addressing the state convention of the United Daughters of the Confederacy. At fifteen, visiting his father in New York, he watched a radio show being produced at the NBC studio and became interested in radio and advertising. After graduating from Phillips Andover with honors in Bible studies, he went on to Yale, spending summers doing door-to-door consumer interviews for his father's agency, majoring in psychology as the best preparation for an advertising career. Upon graduation he made the rounds of a half-dozen agencies. "Very polite," the interviewer at McCann-Erickson noted, and he was hired as an office boy.

The agency was then in its twenty-sixth year under Harrison King McCann. A tall, laconic Scotch-Irish Yankee from Westbrook, Maine, who looked "like a farmer who had found there was money in the Maine legislature," McCann ranked with Lasker and Resor as a builder of ad agencies. He had started in the advertising department of Standard Oil; after the company was dissolved by the Supreme Court in 1911 he was invited to form an agency to service the dispersed divisions of Standard Oil. As head of his own shop McCann took no part in the production of advertising, said little in meetings, and seldom wrote a memo or business letter. A Bowdoin graduate, he found many jobs in the organization for fellow alumni. He disliked giving orders, resigning accounts, or firing people. If he promoted a man to vice-president and heard complaints from others passed over, he was liable to make them all vice-presidents. As a result his agency, more than any other, was overrun with people holding that title. But beneath the soft-spoken courtesy he had a hard Yankee shrewdness, a deft touch at top-level client contact, and a gift for driving sharp bargains. Nobody underestimated him. He reportedly made as much money in advertising as Lasker had.

When Harper started at the agency he worked in the mailroom, ran errands, and filled water carafes ("I never realized that advertising men drank so much *water*"). At the end of the day he would drop by the research department and pick any available brain. Quickly promoted into the department, with a raise to twenty dollars a week, he was assigned to develop a test to premeasure the effectiveness of copy. In two years he had it, a technique to predict the Starch effectiveness rating of an advertisement before it ran. He was made manager of copy research at twenty-six, associate director at twenty-eight, director of research at thirty. He made his department the cutting edge of the agency. "No other advertising research," he said of his efforts in 1946, "has made such a uniformly significant contribution to better advertising, particularly to placing advertising layout and design on a more effective basis." On his thirty-second birthday in 1948, McCann moved up to board chairman and made Harper his successor. He had gone from office boy to president, in this agency top-heavy with executives, in nine years.

As boss he continued to expand his old base of power. Both within the agency and at outside trade meetings he preached the social science gospel, urging the application of psychology and general semantics to the study of consumer buying motives and media selection. McCann was the first agency with its own psychological research staff. Instead of "skipping around a Maypole of creativity," said Harper, advertising people should ground their work in hard, dispassionate science: "Advertisers are not spending billions to decorate media. Their messages are not meant as ornaments." Like Rosser Reeves, he denied that advertising was an art not because he meant to denigrate advertising but because he had some sense of what *real* art amounted to. "What the audience receives from advertising is all-important," he explained. "This is not the character of the creative arts, in which the artist's inspiration is paramount, and in which there can be indifference to the audience response." (On his office wall he hung a Mexican painting of a whirling cockfight—"a history of the advertising business," he noted.)

Harper did extend one old McCann tradition, the overseas operations. Standard Oil accounts had taken the agency into Europe in the 1920s and into Latin America in the following decade. In the 1950s its international accounts included Bristol-Myers, Colgate-Palmolive, Goodyear, W. R. Grace, RCA, Nestlé, Westinghouse, and Coca-Cola; Coke had cited McCann's international capacity as one reason for shifting its business from D'Arcy. Harper had a missionary, patriotic enthusiasm for his foreign offices, citing their important role in advancing American interests, both economic and political. "International agency management is a tricky affair," *Advertising Age* commented, "traditionally shrouded in secrecy." The leading agency in Latin America and on the European continent, McCann then made the first big move into the Far East by acquiring Australia's third largest agency. By 1960 it was billing close to $100 million overseas, second only to Thompson.

In other ways Harper broke from the gentlemanly style of Harry McCann. His talent raids on other agencies provoked some discussion. ("We've invited a number of people to join us in recent years," a McCann executive replied, "but the large majority have managed to find the company's address or phone number.") More controversial was the agency's resignation, early in 1958, of its 15-year-old, $27 million Chrysler account in order to take on the $24 million Buick account, with the expectation it would lead to other GM business. In the past, BBDO had resigned Kool when it got Lucky Strike, and Benton & Bowles had dropped Bristol-Myers to add Colgate: but these cases of dropping a smaller for a larger account had a certain logic. When McCann sloughed off its larger Chrysler account—which had been producing good sales for the client—it sent shock waves through a business always worried about its stability and image. "We are not very proud of the advertising business this week," *Ad Age* editorialized. "I feel more like a huckster today than I ever felt in my life," said the president of a major agency. "It's a kind of billings-madness," said another.

The boy wonder, it appeared, had imperial ambitions, bent on overtaking Thompson not just by adding accounts but by building an empire of other agencies. In 1954 McCann had acquired the small agency of Marschalk & Pratt. "We had already organized the best agency possible along traditional lines," Harper recalled. "But my God, at 38 or whatever I was you can't have as your ambition just to be the best of whatever there already is." So instead of absorbing Marschalk & Pratt into the McCann structure, Harper maintained it as a separate entity, with its own office and identity. Over the next few years he gobbled up more agencies and in 1960 announced a rescrambling of the whole operation into a new conglomerate, Interpublic, with four initial divisions: McCann-Erickson, to handle domestic accounts; McCann-Marschalk, a second "traditional" agency; McCann-Erickson Corp. (International), to handle nearly fifty overseas offices; and the most exotic, Communications Affiliates, offering research, public relations, and sales promotion services. With this structure, Interpublic could handle competing accounts under its own corporate roof. McCann-Erickson took Standard Oil of New Jersey while McCann-Marschalk worked for Standard Oil of Ohio. "What we've done," Harper explained, "is take the management ladder and turn it to a horizontal position." Using this "Affiliate Principle," he predicted, Interpublic would reach total billings of a billion dollars by 1970.

Perhaps. Some of his clients were not so impressed. "We are not concerned with the organizational systems that Marion holds so dear," said one. "The same situation persists after these reorganizations; we see the same people and get the same service." "Marion has all these affiliates, and jiggles them around, but we don't care," said another.

At a competing New York agency, someone circulated a memo describing *its* new divisions: a World division to handle profitable accounts, a Good Time Charlie division to handle charity accounts, and a Teensy-Weensie division for smaller accounts, to be staffed by people not over five feet tall.

Draper Daniels on the plans board:

> Small Indians, come spread your beliefs
> Before the savage, painted chiefs.
> With wild war whoops and mystic dances,
> With tomtoms and hypnotic trances,
> They will burn you at the stake
> While pausing for a coffee break.
> They'll tear six months of work apart
> And stuff the pieces in your heart.
> Then, having spread their share of rue,
> Depart, and leave the work to you.

In the midst of its greatest prosperity, American advertising still had its usual complement of self-doubts and criticism, internal and external. The booming success itself bred misgivings as advertising loomed ever more pervasive in American life. Thus in 1956 Margaret Mead declared that the industry, in promoting tastes based on surveys revealing what those tastes already were, resembled "a silk-worm that spins silk out of the inside of itself and wraps itself up in it"—to the point that much of American life amounted to "not a culture of the U.S. but a culture of Madison Avenue." Others indicted the ethics and credibility of the business. "I don't believe there is a human being in the world who believes a motion picture ad," said the president of the Screen Actors Guild, Ronald Reagan, in 1950. Even *Reader's Digest,* no enemy of American business, periodically ran articles about advertising abuses.

Public-opinion polls revealed these attitudes as more than the carping of a few random critics. In 1946, 41 percent of the American people found half or more of all advertising misleading, and 54 percent said it played too much on the audience's emotions; in 1950, 80 percent complained that it led people to buy things they didn't need or could not afford, and 81 percent called for stricter government regulation; in 1952, 68 percent rejected testimonials as insincere. Despite the rumors of fat salaries, expense accounts, and high living in the business, young people spurned advertising as a career. A survey in 1958 of 11,000 high school students about their choice of occupation placed advertising and public relations eighteenth among twenty callings. "It is fashionable to joke about its silliness and unbelievability," *Advertising Age* editorialized in 1959, "and to gain attention with advertising that itself kids advertising. It is naive to the point of social ostracism to believe that advertising can be honest, decent, sensible and dignified, and worthy of public belief and trust."

Virtually all mass media presented a stereotyped notion of the adman, with some variations, none of them positive. He was crassly materialist (in the film *Will Success Spoil Rock Hunter?* the consuming goal was to acquire a gold key to the executive washroom) and none too bright (in the film *Twelve Angry Men* the adman on the jury was a stupid, simpering fool). He spoke a peculiar form of English—"Let's run this up the flagpole and see who salutes"; "Let's lay it on the couch and see what destructive tendencies it has"; "Let's smear it on the cat and see if she licks it off"—with an indiscriminate use of the suffix -wise. He dressed in a uniform. In the comic strip *Abbie an' Slats,* a young man took a job with the Button, Bustin, Stitch & Screech agency. An adman gained success, he learned, by acquiring an ulcer and by wearing a button-down shirt, knit tie, cordovan shoes, and a gray flannel suit: "They consider you a slob in the business if you dress any other way!"

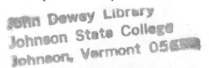

The hero of Sloan Wilson's novel *The Man in the Gray Flannel Suit* (1955) worked in public relations for a giant broadcasting company. (Wilson lived in New Canaan, Connecticut, during the novel's conception listening to admen complaining of tensions at work, and watching the commuters lined up at the station, looking like soldiers in their gray mufti.) At one point in the book, Wilson's hero, despairing of his future, thought of switching to advertising: "I'll write copy telling people to eat more corn flakes and smoke more and more cigarettes and buy more refrigerators and automobiles, until they explode with happiness." Later he criticized a speech for reducing the problem of mental health to "a cheap advertising slogan" that would "sell mental health the way they sell cigarettes!" Ultimately he stepped off the career track to spend time with his family and enjoy the rest of his life.

The Wilson book contributed a phrase to the language, but the mold for advertising fiction was set by Frederic Wakeman's hugely successful novel *The Hucksters* (1946). The central figure, Victor Norman, worked on the $12 million Beautee soap account for the Kimberly & Maag agency and its tyrannical client, Evan L. Evans. A jaded cynic at thirty-five, remote and impassive, Norman hated his work and his meaningless life: "We're all a bunch of hustlers and connivers in this business. . . . We don't steal, probably because it's bad for business, but we sure as hell do everything else for clients." An adman dealt only in appearances, skulking in shadows and deceptions. "A man's got to look bright, act like a Racquet Club member even if he isn't, have two to three simple but good ideas a year, learn how to say yes sir all the time, and no sir once in a while, and ever so often have guts enough to pound a client's desk and tell him that's the way it's gotta be." But Norman found redemption and meaning by having an affair with a married woman. Under her influence he quit the business and—in an inexplicably noble gesture—quit her too, rather than break up her marriage.

The book sold well in part because it seemed a roman à clef. The Evans character bore a physical and personal resemblance to George Washington Hill, and he shared Hill's theory of advertising, "a good simple idea" and unrelenting repetition. "All you professional advertising men are scared to death of raping the public," said Evans; "I say the public likes it, if you got the know-how to make 'em relax and enjoy it." Wakeman wrote the book while working at Foote, Cone & Belding, dealing with Hill on the Lucky Strike account, and so had the background to write an authentic "inside" version of the business. Though satirical in tone, the novel was "actually not a satire at all," its jacket copy claimed. "It just sounds that way." A number-one best-seller, with 750,000 copies in print, distributed by the Book-of-the-Month Club, condensed by *Reader's Digest,* and finally sold to MGM for $250,000, *The Hucksters* had an incalculable impact on the public perception of advertising and sent many writers to their typewriters, hoping to imitate its success.

Please Send Me, Absolutely Free . . . by Arkady Leokum, also published in 1946, had a similar theme and denouement. Gene Winter, an idealistic young man in the 1930s, drifted into advertising to make a living. Initially fascinated by the creative surge of writing "a sharp and persuasive and weighted language," he made his way upward and savored the power and wealth brought by success. He met a woman who urged him to quit and do "real writing." He tried it, failed, the woman died in childbirth, and he went back to advertising. He no longer enjoyed writing to order for a client, in a style not his own. "All imaginative work, all creative effort, had purpose. But there was none here. . . . His mind evolved wonder after wonder, but each was like a cloud. A puff of air dissolved it. Nothing remained, nothing endured." So he resigned, to an indefinite future. "It was good to feel clean and free again." Another insider, a copywriter at Lennen & Mitchell, Leokum had worked at five agencies in nine years and considered advertising "a screwy business." When his son vowed to follow him into the trade, said Leokum, "all I could think of was—over my dead body!"

Herman Wouk's first novel, *Aurora Dawn* (1947), drew on his experience as a writer for the Fred Allen radio show. The book, written before the publication of *The Hucksters,* also revolved around a soap company terrorized by a clone of G. W. Hill. The villain's ad agency, bearing the descriptive title of Grovill and Leach, was led by a man who hated advertising. Another adman, a sold-out artist, delivered a diatribe about the business: it debased the language, told lies, induced people to want things they didn't want, and cared only about selling. "Advertising blasts everything that is good and beautiful in this land with a horrid spreading mildew"—language, youth, love, nature, art. "Behold them all, yoked by advertising in the harness of commerce!" The novel's hero ultimately quit his job with a radio network and, no longer loathing himself, capered down a street shouting "Free! Free!" (Wouk later explained that he did not intend the book to be a harsh moral judgment on advertising.

"But perhaps it may be useful to raise a laugh against some of its abuses," he went on, "which are not so much monstrous or evil as just plain silly, and unworthy of an adult civilization.")

Three novels, three gleeful resignations. A slightly more sympathetic fictional version of advertising was offered by a writer, Eric Hodgins, whose direct experience in the business was limited to a brief agency tenure early in his career. In *Mr. Blandings Builds His Dream House* (1946), the copywriter hero, noted for his three-word slogan for a laxative, hated his work but kept at it. "He took a certain twisted pleasure in himself; what he had done was certainly horrible, but he was bound to admit that he had done it extremely well." So instead he sought fulfillment by building his dream house out in the country. In the sequel, *Blandings' Way* (1950), he resumed the struggle with his conscience, sometimes waking up at night and pondering his responsibility to society: "The whole country's going to pieces. Nobody's honest any more. The local community's losing its significance. The home's disintegrating. Who the hell's more responsible than an advertising copywriter? He's the guy with the tricky arguments. He's the guy who levels tastes. Is *that* the side I ought to be on?" Seeking simplicity and a return to the older virtues, he settled into his dream house and bought the local newspaper. But he was quickly tangled in a bewildering snarl of local issues, and his old life looked not so bad. The boss at his agency was gentle, dignified, and principled, and gave him back his job. "Perhaps in asking that my destiny should give me pleasure I have asked too much," Mr. Blandings concluded. If he resumed what he did best, in a world where his instincts did not mislead him, "I shall be able to scale my peak, three words at a time, three words at a time, until at last I achieve my summit."

The resignation theme was resumed in *The Glorification of Al Toolum* (1953) by Robert Alan Aurthur, a television writer. At first the hero had neither illusions nor misgivings about advertising. "Sure I believe it," he told a skeptical woman friend. "It's my job to believe it. It's my job even to instigate it, invent it, foster it, nurse it." But why? "For fifteen thousand a year plus bonuses." Any further attempt to justify himself met an impenetrable wall of anti-Madison Avenue prejudice. His redemption began with a campaign to find, and manipulate, the "most average" man in America. "The average man is completely predictable," the agency head explained. "Advertising is based on this one principle more than any other. . . .

Without this predictability our whole structure would totter." But the average man who was selected proved unmanageable, with the complexities and problems of a real human being instead of a demographic abstraction. Dealing with this supposed pigeon, the hero— nudged by his woman friend—discovered a sense of ethics that finally drove him to quit. "I never felt better in my life," he declared.

In Gerald Green's *The Last Angry Man* (1956), another Book-of-the-Month selection, Woodrow Wilson Thrasher, a vice-president at a small agency, was drowning in a morass of suburban angst and ambivalence. "Everything we do is compromise," he said to his wife in explaining why he had taken a lover. "Marriage, particularly. There are no more big risks, big thrills, big loves, and big hates. Everything is sort of medium." His work, he conceded, dealt only in fictions and illusions, more like playing house than really working. But he was conditioned too, and slogged on despite feeling compromised. (Only the boss at the agency, cushioned by a deep, unreflective ignorance, felt no compunctions about what he did.) But an outsider, an old doctor of flinty, unbudging integrity and candor, shook Thrasher out of his malaise. He gave up his lover, patched his marriage, and vowed to do better. "I'm not Woodrow Thrasher, reborn and redeemed. . . ," he decided. "I can't go off to Vermont and start a crusading daily newspaper. But I think we can settle for some minimal gains."

David Manning, the central figure in Harold Livingston's *The Detroiters* (1956), managed a similar limited moral regeneration. Livingston, a copywriter for agencies in Detroit and New York, described an advertising world of high tensions and low principle, most analogous to prostitution. Manning believed in no causes, had no ideals. "I prefer to remain a high-priced whore. The cost of living is continually rising," he said. But, someone replied, the ad business could be worthwhile and honest if one maintained a creative integrity. "My creative integrity is maintained every other week. At the bank," Manning replied. "I know what I'm being paid to do. And I do what I'm paid to do." His girl friend, a sometime hooker, reinforced the prostitution analogy. His cynicism finally started to crumble when he was asked to help acquire a big account by manipulating a friend's wife, with whom he had been having an affair and who deeply loved him. He went ahead but regretted it. "I have put ten years in this business," he reflected, "and what have I got?" Money, a car, expensive clothes. "What else is there?" At least, he concluded, he could operate more ethically. So he quit to start his own agency, to be run on cleaner lines.

Edward Stephens' novel *A Twist of Lemon* (1958) ran a full cycle from innocence through corruption and back to a chastened innocence. An account executive at Dancer-Fitzgerald-Sample, where he handled Procter & Gamble items, Stephens—like his hero, Scott Willoughby—was a Navy veteran who had taken a master's at Northwestern and then gone on to Madison Avenue. At the fictional agency Willoughby worked on a soap account for Moniter & Betts (a pun on Procter & Gamble). Initially it seemed a rational environment where one could get ahead by working hard and taking night courses on the theory and practice of advertising. But Willoughby noticed that his boss kept his job simply by dressing well and appearing to work, and that a higher executive—between nips of whiskey to allay the tension—treated the office like a giant chess game, boxing the enemy and advancing to checkmate. Willoughby himself grew addicted to power. He lost his principles, mistreated his successive lovers, stole an idea from a subordinate, developed an ulcer; and at last was himself boxed into a corner. When the pressures became intolerable, he suddenly exploded in a verbal barrage against the "cheap, phony, vicious, murderous racket" of advertising: "Double talk and the fast shuffle. Cure everything with the favorite ad-alley panacea: a large dose of semantics. Swallow the agency viewpoint and you will shit logic! . . . We are all ruined in this crazy business and we have been for a long time!" Then he collapsed, with both his ulcer and career perforated, and decided to move to Phoenix to work in a quiet, one-office agency.

And finally, two novels without neat endings. *The Admen* (1958) was Shepherd Mead's first book after he resigned a vice-presidency at Benton & Bowles. For twenty years he had come to work early and done free-lance writing, notably *How to Succeed in Business Without Really Trying,* a satire with a sharp edge. *The Admen* offered a serious, balanced treatment of agency life. The head man, Branch Torrey, was honest and decent, if unperceptive about the affair between his wife and his employee Chip Sterling. The agency president had distinguished looks, his main asset. An alcoholic copywriter kept hatching escape plans—to buy an island, or learn farming, or study fish-liver oil. When he and Sterling collaborated on an imaginative campaign, Torrey scuttled it with remarks that might have pleased Rosser Reeves: "You'll win some damned art award with it. You think I care about that? So they look at it? It's no damned good if it doesn't make 'em want to buy the thing." The final arbiter of every campaign, the emotional and intellectual heart of the whole operation, Torrey epitomized the old cliché that an ad business was only the people in it. Agencies resembled a diamond, Mead concluded, hard and glittering but with a vulnerable line of cleavage: "They could resist anything but a sharp blow, right there."

The same brittle fragility, masked by bluster, was suggested in *The Insider* (1958) by James Kelly, a vice-president with the Ellington agency in New York. "Mad Avenue," wrote Kelly. "Madmen. The Mad League where everybody in America either pitches or catches, no matter how hard he denies it. . . . An ugly place when you're down and out; a thing of beauty when you're riding high." The anti-hero, Mortimer Noyes, hung on to his account executive position because he had married the client's daughter. Utterly despicable, he lied, drank too much, cheated on his wife, did not know his children, and let others do his work. About the ad business, which he liked to think of as a game played with marked cards, he was conventionally cynical: "In this part of New York, nobody raises corn or builds houses or makes anything you can put your hand on. What they do is sell things. . . . The important thing for most of 'em is to stay popular—and stay out of real arguments. Concealing what they really think, they can think with anybody—and maybe make a sale." In the end, about to pay for his sins at last, Noyes was saved by unlikely twists in the plot and emerged triumphant and undeserving.

From these dozen novels came a remarkably consistent picture of the advertising world: false in tone, tense in pace, vacant and self-hating, overheated and oversexed. Half the novels were written by advertising men, half not. But it made no difference. The picture was the same.

Back in 1946, some advertising people had greeted *The Hucksters* as a necessary exposé, overdrawn but useful—"an expert analysis of the fundamental ill of this business," as Walter Weir put it, the paralyzing fear of losing the account hanging over some agency-client relations. Others enjoyed the attention and the milieu of big money and easy women depicted in the novels. "We knew it wasn't a true image of the business," recalled Stephen Birmingham, then a copywriter and part-time author, "but I think we rather liked being depicted that way—hard boiled and kind of glamorous." But as the years went by, and successive versions of *The Hucksters* pounded away at the same touchy points, the industry grew more sensitive. "Now it's gotten out of hand," Birmingham noted in 1957. "If you want a villain in a novel, you make him an advertising man. He's the modern version of the horse-opera city slicker." When ad people read these novels, they usually found the fictional version of Madison Avenue at odds with their own experience. "I have been in the business 20 years," said Ernest Jones of MacManus, John & Adams, "and I do not know the delightful rogues, the masters of mendacity, the boudoir athletes portrayed." "We are not rakes or devils," Edwin Cox of Kenyon & Eckhardt agreed, "nor are we romantic, as some fiction would have people believe. We are just DULL. We are being treated to large doses of moonshine."

At some point the image became self-perpetuating, as the novels piled up and reinforced each other. Thus other novelists from outside the business, having no direct knowledge of conditions, simply passed along already familiar notions of advertising life. As for the six novelists with backgrounds in the trade, it is striking that none remained in advertising. Wakeman, Leokum, Livingston, and Mead left for full-time writing careers, Stephens to teach advertising at Northwestern, Kelly to live in a Mexican village in an adobe house with no electricity or running water. So they were not "typical" advertising men, and their novels did not represent typical inside impressions of the business. Perhaps these books merely expressed the resentments and restlessness that eventually pushed their authors into other activities.

Further, to some extent these novels indicted not advertising specifically but a larger way of life, a criticism reflected by such diverse contemporary works as *Death of a Salesman, The Lonely Crowd, The Organization Man, The Exurbanites,* and *The Status Seekers.* Many writers and social critics of the day were describing the business pressures and depersonalization stalking through the advertising novels. Out in Westport or Westchester County, suburban malaise was generic regardless of how the breadwinner made his money. In the canyons of New York, admen were not the only harried executives drinking their lunches and nursing their ulcers. Seen in this broader context, life on Madison Avenue seemed not so exotic or atypical.

Finally, perhaps these novels were written to order, to fit the mold set by *The Hucksters.* Given that model, publishers and the reading public may have wanted only advertising fiction with the usual portions of sex and corruption. Ad people, insisted Robert Foreman of BBDO, were really quite normal—but "who's going to write a book or film a movie about people like that?" In the fall of 1957, James Kelly wrote an article for *Saturday Review* deploring the flood of "Madman novels" that, written solely for money, offered grim caricatures of the trade. And a year later, Kelly—apparently in deference to this commercial pressure—published his own Madman novel.

The reception of the movie version of *The Hucksters* was instructive on this point. The Norman character, played by Clark Gable, was more gentlemanly than in the book. His lady friend, played by Deborah Kerr, had been widowed in the war, so their affair was not adulterous. The language was also sanitized (Evans said "Jazz 'em up" instead of "Goose 'em"). The woman convinced Norman that he could honorably stay in advertising: "Why don't you be one of those who sells only what he believes in? Sell good things, things that people should have, and sell them with dignity—and taste. That's a career for any man, a career to be proud of." So Norman told Evans off, poured a carafe of water on his head, and lived happily ever after with the woman. But the public did not buy all this nobility. Despite a powerful cast, which included Sydney Greenstreet, Adolphe Menjou, and Ava Gardner, the movie failed at the box office. The book then came out in paperback, promoted as "The Whole Story the Movie Didn't Tell."

And yet, despite these commercial and historical factors that served to place the fictional version of advertising in a milder perspective, the novels did suggest key elements of real life on Madison Avenue. As unstable and hard to predict as ever, the business still bore out Lee Bristol's definition of an adman: "Yes, sir! No, sir! Ulcer!" On a local New York TV show in 1957, the president of Grey Advertising let slip the fact that he used Crest toothpaste; within thirty-six hours, Grey lost Kolynos as a client. In 1945, the Milton Biow agency ranked ninth in annual billings. But in 1953 Biow testified that he had paid a California lobbyist over $90,000 to get and hold the Schenley account. In three years Biow's billings dropped 50 percent, and the agency went out of business. It was, *Ad Age* commented, "another nail driven into the coffin of the irrepressible entrepreneur in the advertising agency business."

The long hours and high tensions reported in the novels were all too real. A survey in 1957 found that nine of ten ad people routinely took work home at night. "What other business has so many young men anxious to break in," asked one adman, "and so many older men anxious to break out?" An advertising career meant changing jobs every three years in one's thirties, every four years in one's forties. A study in 1956 by Life Extension Examiners of New York compared the health of executives in manufacturing, banking, and advertising. The ad people showed up worst in ten of eighteen categories, including high blood pressure, organic heart and prostate problems, and abnormal blood counts. From 1949 to 1959, at a time when the life expectancy for white males was 67.1 years, the average age at death in *Advertising Age*'s obituaries was 59.9. "It's a killing business," conceded Lou Wasey, seventy-one years old in 1956. "Most all the men who have been along with me in business— they're all dead, and they were younger than I."

The pressures were worst at the highest levels. Ben Duffy of BBDO, with a "Rolls-Royce motor in a Ford chassis," worked at a frenetic pace: "I only call home if, by happy surprise, I can get there for supper." He began to suffer from peptic ulcers when he was only twenty-eight. Eight operations for those ulcers were followed by two, perhaps three heart attacks and a debilitating cerebral hemorrhage, and essential retirement at age fifty-five. Rosser Reeves often worked ninety-hour weeks. "My kids claim they never saw me until they were about twenty-five years old," he said later. Marion Harper originally intended to retire at thirty-five and spend the rest of his life in public service. "I have been captured by what I chased," he noted. Normally he arrived home after ten o'clock at night, with his children already asleep. An avid collector of jazz records, he twice gave away his whole collection and started over. "If you have limited time," he explained, "the only way to stay current is wipe them all out and start again with the newer stuff." In 1960 he took his first vacation in twenty-two years.

When attacked by outsiders, the denizens of Madison Avenue typically defended themselves. "This whole concept of an advertising man is nothing but a lot of eggshells from eggheads," said Charles Brower of BBDO. But they revealed their more candid feelings at unguarded moments. A poll of 1,100 advertising people in 1958 found 85 percent saying they would, if given a second chance, take up the same calling; but only 8 percent said they would recommend it to their children. "In most professions," Bernice Fitz-Gibbon of Gimbel's pointed out, "parents want their children to follow in their footsteps. I have never heard of advertising people who wanted their sons and daughters to carry on in a great family dynasty."

❧❧

Draper Daniels on the traffic man:

> Alone, unloved, here he perspires,
> Caught between two spreading ires,
> The eagerest beaver of all the clan,
> The pittering, pattering traffic man.
> The ogre before him called copy resists,
> The ogre behind him called contact insists.
> Bewildered he stands, his heart all a-flutter,
> Wondering which bread carries the butter.

❧❧

Television burst onto the American scene like a delayed time bomb. The basic technology was available in the 1930s, and NBC had started regular commercial broadcasts in 1939. Suspended during the war, and then developed slowly during the adjustments after 1945, TV had a long gestation. In 1948 the FCC refused to license any new stations until problems of signal interference among the 108 existing outlets were worked out. In the following year *Printers' Ink* finally started keeping statistics on advertising revenue from television. "An advertising agency cannot ignore television," said one adman in 1950. "But television affords little profit for advertising agencies since most TV appropriations are small compared with those for other media." "We don't know yet that it pays," agreed Clarence Goshorn of Benton & Bowles. "We have a lot of fragmentary success stories, but no continuity of measurement by even imperfect scales."

Others saw the explosion coming. Ben Duffy by 1949 was spending 80 percent of his media time on TV, only 20 percent on radio. A year later, the BBDO television department had grown from 12 employees to 150, and the agency was billing $4 million in the new medium. Even under the FCC freeze the industry's total TV business went from $12.3 million (1949) to $40.8 million (1950) to $128 million (1951), a level that radio had taken 16 years to reach. The lid blew off when the freeze was lifted in the spring of 1952. New TV retail stores opened at the rate of a thousand a month. CBS television made its first net profit in 1953. A year later CBS became the largest advertising medium in the world, with a monopoly of the top-rated shows. In three years television's share of billings at the Leo Burnett agency went from 18 percent to over half. Even Benton & Bowles overcame its earlier skepticism and by 1958 was deriving 60 percent of its revenue from TV.

For Madison Avenue, television meant a new kind of advertising with its own technical problems. Dozens of big clients switched agencies to find creative departments adept at the new techniques. Like print, TV was visual; like radio, it was intrusive and had a sound track; like neither, it was kinetic, immediate, and unescapable. "On TV," the saying went, "we've got you by the eyeballs." "You can jump right into the selling copy without having to snag attention first," George Gallup pointed out. "The attention is there; so you go directly into the interest and desire-building process. . . . Bang right in with a viewer problem and solution." Instead of the frenzied tone and machine-gun delivery of radio ads, TV messages seemed to work best when cool and understated, as though the eye was more easily sold than the ear. Products could be demonstrated in use, with a spare voice-over describing the action. "Show the product and show it in use," said Ben Duffy. Young & Rubicam bragged about the "dramatic demonstration" in its early TV ads: a Goodyear tire being crushed and returning unblemished, a Remington razor taking the fuzz off a peach, a Band-Aid picking up an egg. The 1950s were "the age of the eye," as Margot Sherman noted, largely because the new toy of the period was so powerfully visual. "I don't think," said George Gribbin of Y & R, "that a television copywriter particularly needs a feeling for words." Words might clutter the ad and distract the target from *seeing* it.

In these early days—the "Golden Age" of television—the lines were blurred between ad agencies and TV networks. Many top executives shuttled back and forth between the two, changing jobs but using the same skills and contacts. With radio broadcasting as the only available model, most TV shows were produced and controlled not by a network but by an agency for a single sponsor. Shows typically bore the name of the advertiser, not the star: *Kraft Television Theater, Goodyear TV Playhouse, Texaco Star Theater.* While the sponsor and agency took charge of content, the network usually provided only facilities, air time, and occasional censorship.

This system had its own abuses and corruptions. With the technicians in a studio working for a separate employer, the network, an agency sometimes had to pay extra bribes to get special favors from the crew. With one sponsor backing an entire show, a sales pitch might be integrated into the entertainment with no clear demarcation. "A girl breaks into song," the *New Yorker* observed, "and for a moment you can't quite pin down the source of her lyrical passion. It could be love, it could be something that comes in a jar." The star of the show might don a funny hat and make the pitch, to the point of being identified with the product. Some stars found this role beneath their dignity. "Today, the sponsors pull the strings and we are the puppets," Groucho Marx complained in 1953. "Radio and television announcers have to be liars."

Sponsors sometimes interfered with shows in ludicrous ways. On the Marx show, underwritten by DeSoto, a contestant named Ford was asked to use a different name so as not to publicize the competition. On another show Rod Serling was asked to change "American" and "lucky" to "United States" and "fortunate" because the sponsoring cigarette competed with American Tobacco's Lucky Strike. Serling gave in but took his name off the script—"the only thing a writer can do in television in the way of a protest," he recalled.

On the other hand, the system of agency production and single sponsors had particular advantages. Given one advertiser and a show title often bearing its name, viewers associated a favorite show with its sponsor and—because of a "gratitude factor"—would buy the products. In 1953 twenty shows enjoyed a "sponsor identification" rating of 80 percent or better; in radio, 60 percent was considered exceptional. A star in such a stable situation might take extraordinary liberties with his advertiser. Alfred Hitchcock was famous for leading into commercials with comments ranging from sly ("Oh, dear, I see the actors won't be ready for another sixty seconds. However, thanks to our sponsor's remarkable foresight, we have a message that will fit in here nicely"), to snide ("And now as a service to you television addicts who are trying to give it up, here, before I return, is something that will certainly do the trick"), to graphic (during a shipboard story: "I feel I must move to the rail; we are about to have one of our commercials"). Bristol-Myers resisted these jabs at first, but found they helped both sponsor identification and sales. After all, Hitchcock maligned not the product but the ad. "When I bite the hand that feeds me," he said, "I really have my tongue firmly in my cheek."

More significantly, a principled sponsor with a good show could protect its integrity from other commercial interests or a network worried about ratings. Maxwell House coffee backed *I Remember Mama,* a well-crafted production stressing character and family values, for eight years; its restrained ads ran only at the start and finish, leaving the drama uninterrupted. The Kraft show put on fifty-two three-act plays a year, with production handled by the Thompson agency. Its decorous commercials emphasized recipes and information about the product, with no hard sell or repetition. The *Armstrong Circle Theater* presented documentary dramas on topical issues. "We're not seeking merely to make a quickie impression," explained Armstrong's advertising director. "What counts is the 'impact' which we feel is more important than exposure." Alcoa supported Edward R. Murrow's *See It Now* broadcasts for four years of intermittent controversy, renewing its contract even after Murrow's unsparing dissection of Joe McCarthy on the show in March 1954. "We don't think it's proper for a sponsor to influence the news," an Alcoa man said on that occasion. "It's Mr. Murrow's show. We buy what he has to offer. We expect him to attract an audience—and the kind of audience—before which we want to present our commercials."

The great virtue of this early system was its pluralism. TV production was distributed among many hands, responding to a variety of tastes and economic considerations. Maxwell House and Kraft made small, frequently purchased packaged goods; Armstrong and Alcoa (before it expanded its consumer line) made larger, more expensive products bought less often. But all were seeking a certain prestige image that depended on the quality of its own show rather than on hard, repeating ads. Instead of gross ratings, they cared most about maintaining production standards and reaching a particular audience. Therefore ratings did not yet dominate production decisions. Philip Morris dropped *I Love Lucy,* the top-rated show for three years running, because it was not attracting smokers or selling cigarettes.

All through the 1950s, the networks and agencies fought over control of TV programming. Pat Weaver of NBC led the network forces with his concept of "magazine" programming, whereby NBC sold time to many different advertisers, like a magazine, while retaining editorial control over the production. His own vehicles— *Your Show of Shows, Today, Tonight,* and *Wide, Wide World*—pioneered the new approach. "These great shows," said Weaver, never given to

understatement, "are based on the theory that if you spend money
on the show and make it so good you can get a huge audience, then
you can allocate the cost among several advertisers." A visionary
idealist, his mind overflowing with arcane historical and literary
tidbits, forever bombarding his bewildered staff with abstruse philo-
sophical memos, Weaver believed his magazine concept would improve TV, diversifying its content and pulling in more and smaller
advertisers. He came from an advertising career at Young & Rubicam and still operated within that agency's tradition of trying to
make a suspect industry more respectable.

So the battle was on. Late in 1952 CBS opened its Television City
complex in Hollywood, making its own production facilities better
than any agency's or independent producer's. Along with ABC, it
followed NBC's lead toward multiple sponsorships and network-
packaged "spectaculars" or "specials." An advertiser buying fifteen
minutes of a show paid a higher rate per minute than one buying a
whole hour. Thus four sponsors to the hour meant more revenue for
the network. As the costs of underwriting a TV show kept rising—a
process the networks assisted by increasing the price of air time—a
whole show began to exceed the advertising budgets of all but the
largest sponsors. Late in 1955, Hazel Bishop, charging NBC with
trying to dominate programming, switched its $3.5 million alloca-
tion from TV to radio and newspapers. "In this business," Bishop's
board chairman Raymond Spector explained, "most high-rated
shows have been created by independent packagers, not networks. . . . But where the nets are the only ones to decide, that's the
day when you will get government regulation."

Weaver, who parted company with NBC in 1956, proved a bad
prophet. With the networks tightening the screws, fewer—not
more—advertisers bought time: 321 in 1956, 293 the next year, 269
the next. Under the new system Ted Bates, known as "the spot
agency," set the style with its aggressive, repetitive commercials.
When one sponsor controlled a whole show, it felt responsible for the
manner and frequency of its ads. When a sponsor was just one of
many, it could avoid that responsibility. The programs themselves
declined in quality and diversity. Several well-regarded shows (the
Voice of Firestone, Armstrong-Kaiser Circle Theater, and the *Alcoa-Goodyear
Playhouse*) were canceled by their networks for low ratings, though
the sponsor in each case was satisfied and willing to continue. By
1958 the networks controlled over 75 percent of all programming,
with most decisions left to Nielsen.

The climactic struggle between the networks and agencies came over the big-money quiz shows. Relatively cheap to produce, needing only simple facilities, and easy to cancel, the *$64,000 Question* and its imitators were the last stronghold of independent production and single sponsorship. The *$64,000 Question,* developed by the Norman, Craig & Kummel agency and then sold to Revlon, achieved a 52.3 rating in the summer of 1955, the second highest in TV history to that point. It was an honest show. But too many of its successors, notably *Dotto* and *Twenty-One,* were not. Articles in *Time* in April 1957 and in *Look* the following August brought charges of collusion and slanted questions. Yet the networks, normally so interested in controlling programs owned by outsiders, were curiously incurious about these charges.

The public scandals over these shows broke in the fall of 1958, highlighted by Charles Van Doren's confession of his deceptions on *Twenty-One.* A year later, when network officials faced congressional investigators, they seemed remarkably ignorant. Asked about the *Time* article, Robert Kintner of NBC replied: "I did not read the article in *Time* in 1957, so I did not have that information." Didn't his NBC colleagues tell him about it? "No, and I would not particularly expect that." What about the *Look* article? "I do not have any knowledge; nor was it ever discussed in my presence." "I am sure," said a congressman, "that with the efficient organization that NBC has, somebody in the top echelon knew about the story in *Time,* and knew about the story in *Look.*" Surely; but somehow nobody pursued the matter.

"Isn't it rather remarkable," Frank Stanton of CBS was asked, "that it wasn't until August 8, 1958, that you had any inkling of any irregularity in the quiz shows on your network?" "I wouldn't say that I didn't have any inkling," Stanton replied, "but an inkling is a long way from something on which you can take affirmative action." Did he know about the *Time* article? "Well, I am familiar with the article, but I was not familiar with it in 1957." Was the *Look* article brought to his attention? "It was not." Was it discussed by any officials at CBS? "I do not know."

It seems impossible that Kintner and Stanton would not have known about these articles appearing in major national magazines. For years the networks had been trying to squeeze out the agencies and independent producers. Perhaps, when the first rumors of fixes appeared, the networks decided to give the outsiders enough rope to hang themselves. Then, when the inevitable scandals broke, the net-

works could self-righteously blame the outsiders and vow to be
"masters of our own house," as Stanton put it: "We propose to be
more certain in the future that it is we and we alone who decide not
only what is to appear on CBS Television Network, but how it is to
appear." So standards and practices were spelled out more carefully.
And, not incidentally, outsiders found an even colder reception at
the networks.

The decline of television quality in the 1950s was not caused by
the power of advertising over the medium. In the Golden Age, when
TV was most creative and daring, advertisers had more control over
programming than at any time since. Rather, the corruption of television is simply another chapter in the history of American corporate monopoly.

In August 1960 the previously anonymous TV critic for *Advertising
Age,* Rodney Erickson, revealed his identity and quit his column;
TV, he said, had become just another business, and he had nothing
left to say. Three months later John Crosby, the respected TV critic
for the *New York Herald-Tribune,* also turned his back on the medium:
"Television no longer deserves daily criticism on a serious level."
David Susskind, an independent producer, once had been able to
sell his ideas to dozens of agencies and advertisers. "Today you must
sell three men," he said in 1961, "because the networks control it
with a viselike grip. If these three men and their minions reject your
program conceptions, you simply don't get on the air."

Draper Daniels on the media man:

> The media man drinks lunch for free,
> His life is a loaded Christmas tree.
> And he can make a dry martini
> Vanish faster than Houdini.
> He has no brain, but it doesn't mattah
> As long as there is Standard Rate and Data.

For all the novel developments of the 1950s, in many ways this period again reinforced a cyclical theory of advertising history. The
old rhythms of hard sell–soft sell and ascendant art or ascendant
copy were still present. Agency life still rewarded the young and

fearless, and treated older people roughly. One heard the continuing arguments about whether advertising was art or science, or neither. Account executives and creative departments were still natural enemies. At conventions advertising people, as ever, damned the bad old days, praised the higher ethics of today, but still urged everyone to do better. Weary of attacks by outsiders, Madison Avenue still defended itself, a little too insistently to hide its own doubts. Early in 1956, *Fortune* sent someone to ask James Webb Young about changes in the business over the past twenty-five years. "When I told her there hadn't been any," Young recalled, "she nearly fell off her chair. But it's true."

Finally, advertising once again revealed itself as an exquisitely sensitive barometer of changes in the larger context of American society. Perhaps more quickly than any other institution, it changed with the times. The essence of the 1950s was a heady, untrammeled expansion of the American economy, with its characteristically American faith in technological progress and material benefits. For this expansion, advertising served as handmaiden, cheerleader, and publicist. "We have lived through nearly all of the Fabulous Fifties—the decade of the super highway and the supermarket, the family room and the TV dinner," said Whit Hobbs of BBDO in 1959. "The sky used to be the limit . . . but suddenly there *isn't* any limit. We can no longer even conceive what the limit might be."

SIX

THE CREATIVE
REVOLUTION

In gross volume and billings, at least, the future that Whit Hobbs
peered into held no limit at all. By 1970 J. Walter Thompson
would claim worldwide billings of $773 million. In most other
ways the 1960s meant another turn of the cycle of advertising history: from bigness and mergers back to smallness and meiosis; from
ancillary services to the creative product; from science and research
to art, inspiration, and intuition. Claude Hopkins and Albert Lasker
retreated into the shadows again as the descendants of Theodore
MacManus and Raymond Rubicam stepped forward. An ever bigger world, advertising was not really a different world.

Except in one particular. The story of advertising in the 1960s
was, more than ever, the story of its people: and the people did
change. In the previous decade someone like Rosser Reeves might
create ads that bore no resemblance to his own personality. Now, in
the sixties, gray-flannel anonymity gave way to personal expression.
The three leading figures in the new advertising—Leo Burnett,
David Ogilvy, and William Bernbach—all but signed their own
work. All three were outsiders (from Chicago, Great Britain, and
Brooklyn), and none looked or acted like the popular stereotype of
the adman. To understand these men is to understand the "creative
revolution" they spawned.

❦❦

Leo Burnett was not much to look at. Yet when people tried to
describe him they usually started with his looks, as though puzzled

that anyone with his appearance could command such respect or wield such influence in a business preoccupied with the appearance of things. He was short and pear-shaped, with sloping shoulders and a comfortable paunch. Every morning, it was said, he would don a freshly rumpled suit that would soon attract cigarette ashes and other debris. Seen head-on, his face looked lopsided, with the right ear askew; his hair was combed straight back, accentuating the pate. He had prominent lips, a jowly chin, and heavy glasses in a dark frame. Observers agreed that nobody would take him for an advertising man—but perhaps a bank teller, or a muscular librarian, or a prosperous Rotarian in town for a convention, or a tractor dealer from the plains states.

In manner he was diffident, inarticulate except on paper, lost in the advertising problem at hand. Once, deep in thought, he emerged from the train station in Chicago, entered a cab, and asked for the fifteenth floor. "I always figured that I was less smart than some people," he allowed, "but that if I worked hard enough maybe I would average out all right." On the podium he spoke quietly, his head down, with few gestures. At work, surrounded by taller, more handsome men (as *Advertising Age* once pointed out with a cheerful malice), he dominated by some inexplicable power of leadership devoid of its usual trappings. "The most imposing voice Leo Burnett can muster to this day," his copy chief, William Tyler, declared with no fear of recrimination, "is a medium-low mumble with a slight gurgling overtone."

The statement itself, along with its tone of affectionate teasing and the fact that Tyler felt free to say it in public, revealed something about life at the Burnett agency. No employee of Stanley Resor or Marion Harper would have dared make such a comment about the boss. Burnett did not mind. An oblique modesty and lack of ego marked the way he ran his agency, the style of advertising he produced, and his own ambling route to a career in the big time.

As he liked to remind New Yorkers and other foreigners, he came from a small town in Michigan. He helped out in the family's dry goods store and, after supper, watched his father lay out ads on the dining room table with a big black pencil and a yardstick on a piece of wrapping paper: "He wrote the copy right on the layout, handed it over to Charlie Clark at the newspaper next morning and waited for the customers to come in." Burnett worked as a printer's devil, taught school for a year, and graduated from the University of

Michigan in 1914. After a year as a police reporter in Peoria he wandered into advertising by way of journalism, taking a job as editor of a house organ that the Cadillac Motor Company sent to its dealers.

He thus acquired as mentor none other than Theodore F. Mac-Manus himself, only a few months after the appearance of "The Penalty of Leadership." The imperial MacManus gave little time to his client companies, even less to their junior employees: presumably Burnett's discipleship was carried on at some distance from the master. As he later recalled it, he admired MacManus' "incredibly sensitive sense of timing" and his unflinching reliance on "the power of the truth simply told." By a direct laying on of hands, his own agency would later pass on the best aspects of the MacManus tradition, its ethical standards and polite manners. Fifty years after his brief exposure to "one of the great advertising men of all time," Burnett acknowledged the debt: "I became fascinated with his thinking and his quality-mindedness and his great power of assumptiveness that he employed in his copy." By giving his work a large sweep, taking in universal symbols and common ground, Mac-Manus presumed a shared experience with his mass audience. Burnett learned that lesson best of all.

After the World War Burnett moved to Indianapolis, where he worked briefly for the Lafayette car company and then settled down in a local ad agency. He stayed put through his thirties, enjoying what he remembered as "a very happy life there," living comfortably, his salary rising to $15,000. "My three children were born there." Occasionally he sent feelers to big New York agencies, but nothing turned up, and evidently he felt no overweening ambition to move on. Finally, with his fortieth birthday approaching, he decided to leave his small pond. "I talked it over with my wife," he said later. "I thought I'd better get the hell out of Indianapolis if I was ever going to amount to anything in the ad business." He called Art Kudner of Erwin, Wasey in New York and was hired.

Still in no great hurry, at an age when many copywriters were already retired upstairs to administration and account work, Burnett went to Chicago as creative head of Erwin, Wasey's local office. In this milieu Burnett's modest horizons began to open up. Under Kudner and O. B. Winters, fellow midwesterners, the agency had been known for its institutional copy and high writing standards. During the Depression, though, creative output in Chicago suffered as the best talent was hired away by New York agencies. Burnett recognized the creative vacuum in Chicago but, typically, needed a nudge to step into it.

From his Indianapolis agency he had brought to Erwin, Wasey a copywriter named DeWitt (Jack) O'Kieffe, a gentle, bookish man who liked to read Homer and Virgil on the commuter train. In the summer of 1935 O'Kieffe told Burnett he would take a job in New York unless Burnett agreed to start his own agency. "My associates and I," as Burnett recounted it, "saw the opportunity to offer a creative service badly needed in the Middle West.... I sold my house, hocked all my insurance and took a dive off the end of the springboard." (They left just in time: a few weeks later Kudner also departed to start his own shop, taking the flagship Buick account with him.) The Leo Burnett agency was launched with $50,000, a handful of women's products accounts, and a half-dozen Erwin, Wasey people, all from the creative, none from the business side.

Burnett, at forty-four no longer an old copywriter but a young agency head, staked out his turf as a *creative* agency. "There is entirely too much dull advertising," he said in 1936, "pages and pages of dull, stupid, uninteresting copy that does not offer the reader anything in return for his time taken in reading it." Instead of the fashionable devices of contests, premiums, sex, tricks, and cleverness, he urged, use the product itself, enhanced by good artwork, real information, recipes, and humor. He never departed from this approach, but for a long time he was not heard, in particular by those dubious practitioners east of the Hudson. For over a decade his agency muddled along with billings under $10 million. The postwar expansion of agency services left him unimpressed. "A lot of it is just plain razzle-dazzle," he insisted, that threatened to turn an agency into a mere department store of marketing designed to sell a client, not the public: "we have been in thrall to the shibboleth of Bigness." The business should, he said, adopt the old-fashioned solution of simply making better ads.

Anyone running a small, creative shop might deplore the vogue of expanding services, if only from jealousy. The real test of creative zeal came in the late 1940s when the Burnett agency itself started to grow: from $10 million in billings in 1946 to $22 million in 1950 and $55 million in 1954. The little Chicago operation was now consorting with the big boys. Burnett had hired a merchandising man from Detroit, Richard Heath, and his salesmanship pushed the agency into its heady growth. A big, handsome man, with social gifts and a flair not possessed by the boss, Heath brought in most of the new business. "Leo wrote the gospel," Draper Daniels recalled, "but Dick Heath preached it to the heathen. Together they did what neither of them could have done alone." The new accounts included Pillsbury, Kellogg, Campbell Soup, the Tea Council, and a big piece of Procter & Gamble.

Thus the classic dilemma: could a big agency keep its creative spark? Through the 1950s, with the ad industry beguiled by marketing and research, Burnett kept insisting on the primacy of the product itself. "The creative men are the men of the hour," he declared in 1955. "It is high time that they were given the respect that they deserve. Agencies revolve around the men with the pencils." Instead of research, he explained, his shop relied on the copy department's imagination and a few simple principles: find the "inherent drama" in the product itself and present it believably, like a news story; use nonverbal archetypes and symbols, often drawn from American history and folklore, that easily penetrate the public mind with desires and beliefs; speak in earthy, vernacular words that project "a friendly kind of humanness," so the ad is not annoying or threatening but "fun" in a broad, human sense. None of these principles derived from research (though, if needed to pacify a client, research might be generated to "prove" them); they came from Leo Burnett's own experience in the business.

For the Minnesota Canning Company, one of its original clients, the agency created the Jolly Green Giant. This archetypal figure implicitly harked back to a folklore icon like Paul Bunyan, another amiable giant, also from the north woods. The giant hit some inexplicable, subconscious chord in the public mind, and the client rode him from regional obscurity to national prominence. When first transferred to TV he was shown walking, and he resembled a lumbering monster from a low-budget horror movie. Later, the lesson learned, he was shown pointing, bending over, HO-HO-HO-ing with his hands akimbo—but never walking. The giant became so identified with the product that the client changed its name to the Green Giant Company. The Burnett agency also made familiar, likable characters of the Pillsbury Doughboy, Tony the Tiger for Kellogg's Frosted Flakes, and others.

For its greatest success Burnett used another folklore figure, the cowboy. In 1954 a delegation from Philip Morris went looking for a new agency to push its Marlboro filter cigarette. At the Burnett agency the group was solicited by the boss in his usual diffident way. "Leo met us at the door of his office," a Philip Morris executive recalled. "He had some ads spread out on the floor around him. He didn't say much, just referred us to the ads he had done." Burnett got the account. At the time, it seemed, filter cigarettes were regarded as effeminate. So the selling problem was to promote Marlboros as a brand a man could smoke without shame. They changed the package from a mild white design to a bold red in an assertive V pattern. For the figure in the ads, the question became: "What's the most masculine type of man?" After some discussion, the answer was cowboys. The first ad, in January 1955, presented a distinctly virile cowboy with his trusty Marlboros. The market for filter cigarettes was never the same again. Later ads presented other macho sorts, drawn from various occupations, not professional models, usually with a tattoo to suggest toughness and a romantic past. Eventually the campaign returned to cowboys and stayed there, one of the longest-running successes in advertising history.

As billings kept climbing, over $100 million by 1959, and branch offices were opened, Burnett and his closest aides held absolute control of the creative output. Art and copy were produced only in the Chicago office and had to survive the harrowing sessions of the plans board, where Burnett still sat front and center. If an ad displeased him, he would look worried and his lower lip would start to protrude. People learned to judge their chances of getting work approved by what they called the Lip Protrusion Index, from one to ten: an LPI over five meant long nights ahead. As comments went around the table, an ad might begin to look tattered and threadbare, with many patches. "We have absolutely no pride of authorship here," Burnett said, putting the matter as favorably as possible. "Nobody knows for sure who produced which of our ads."

Some of his subordinates put it differently. "He was not an easy boss," Strother Cary said later. "Creative work is a spectator sport for most members of the copy department," another man maintained, anonymously. "You sit in meetings, have headings and even body copy dictated to you, and spend most of your time following through on other people's ideas." Draper Daniels wrote his exasperated doggerel about the cruelties of a plans board (see page 199) with his Burnett experience specifically in mind. Still another copywriter, his ego bruised too many times, avenged himself by imagining a session reviewing Ned Jordan's famous ad of the 1920s: "First ad presented was headlined 'Somewhere West of Laramie.' Mr. Burnett said the ad didn't tell him what happened in Laramie, and Mr. Young said he didn't care. Mr. Young remarked that the ad just 'lay there' and that it was 'flat.' Mr. Greeley pointed out that an appeal to customers who lived west of Laramie was severely limiting the market for the product, and Mr. Coulson concurred, adding, further, that Laramie wasn't a major market area. Mr. Banks said it had no TV outlet. Mr. Young suggested that the headline read, 'Now—Somewhere West of Boston.' Mr. Heath amended this to read, 'Now—At Last—Somewhere West of Boston,' and, after further study of marketing data, it was provisionally agreed that the headline should read, *'Now—At Last—Somewhere West of the Boston Metropolitan Area.'*"

Burnett drove his people hard, but so ingenuously that he disarmed all but his most aggravated employees. (In a characteristic gesture, he gleefully quoted the "West of Laramie" satire in a speech before the AAAA in 1955.) Nobody worked harder than he did. During the years when he was building the agency he kept two secretaries busy: up at five o'clock, to his study for several hours before breakfast, then the 8:13 to his office, work through the day and night, home after midnight by taxi, with papers under his arm; on weekends he buried himself in his study. "It must be disconcerting," William Tyler observed, "for three highly intelligent children to see their father only if they happen to get up for a glass of water during the night." Success included its costs and losses. According to agency folklore, Burnett's only holiday was Christmas. He watched TV and read magazines and newspapers, but mainly to monitor the ads. He had no small talk, no serious interests outside advertising.

He allowed himself two diversions. At his country home forty miles from Chicago—he liked to call it a farm—he drove a truck around the 140 acres, supervising the planting of trees and shrubs. He had an artificial lake built and named it Lake Naomi after his wife (the dam that created it she called Dam Leo). And on occasional Saturdays he would bet the horses at the Arlington track near his home. Looking like a tout, dressed in a wildly colored cap, casual clothes, black and white shoes and with a cigarette dangling from his lip, surrounded by a litter of paper, pencils, and tip sheets, he managed to get his mind off business. "You can't make an ad at a race track," he pointed out.

Well into his sixties, Burnett kept working with an undiminished love for the act of making ads. After finding his stride late in life he never broke it. From Chicago, he watched his New York competitors in the 1950s and spurned their ways. He did allow a research department at his agency, under a man named John Coulson, but referred to its consumer surveys as "finding out what Coulson's morons say." Giant Madison Avenue agencies like Marion Harper's "Interplanetary, Inc.," he suggested, appeared to review their creative output only in retrospect. He was appalled by Rosser Reeves' assertion of the dangers of originality ("sort of like having General Electric decide to come out with a theme like 'Progress is our most unimportant product' ").

In a desk drawer Burnett kept a folder filled with what he called "Corny Language." Whenever he heard an especially evocative expression he jotted it down. Three or four times a year he went through the file and wrote a memo urging the best corny harvest on his staff. Ever the evangelist, he preached "the Chicago school of advertising" in pithy little phrases. Simplicity, clarity, and people-talk. Straightforward without being flat-footed. Warm without being mawkish. The lighter the touch, the heavier the wallop. "Our sod-busting delivery, our loose-limbed stand and our wide-eyed perspective make it easier for us to create ads that talk turkey to the majority of Americans," he said. "I like to think that we Chicago ad-makers are all working stiffs. I like to imagine that Chicago copywriters spit on their hands before picking up the big, black pencils."

Even as one of the top ten agencies, because of its founder the Burnett shop still resembled a one-horse operation. He was a simple man who did simple advertising. The Burnett style offered the major alternative to the salient tendencies of the 1950s: Theodore MacManus lived on in Chicago.

❧❧

"I am an advertising classicist," David Ogilvy said in 1952. "I believe that advertising has had its great period to which I want to return it." On the office walls of his agency hung reproductions of twenty classic ads. Over the years he acknowledged creative debts to a long line of forebears, including George Gallup, James Webb Young, John Caples, Stirling Getchell, Helen Resor, Gerard Lambert, and Robert Updegraff. His real mentors, though, were the progenitors of the two broad streams in advertising history: the "image" school of MacManus and Rubicam and the "claim" school of Lasker and Hopkins. Studying both, shuttling back and forth between them, aiming to extract the best from each, Ogilvy recapitulated in his own career the history of the business.

As a man of multiple paradoxes Ogilvy was perfectly cast for this bifurcated quest. He was a very English tweeds-and-pipe Englishman with a lifelong fascination for America; a celebrated copywriter from a copy research background. A self-professed snob with a patina of Oxford culture, he displayed an incongruously uncertain grasp of grammar and spelling. He wrote his most famous ads in the image tradition but craved identification with the claim tradition. A man of definite, pungent opinions, never reluctant to express them, he was also quite susceptible to his surroundings, and a hero worshipper and seeker of father figures. In nautical terms, he once said, he lacked a deep keel: "I have always carried too much sail." He worked in advertising, that most characteristic expression of modernity, but sojourned among the Pennsylvania Amish and then retired to a twelfth-century French chateau. All of this somehow came together to comprise the dominant advertising *personality* of his time— "the most spectacular man in the agency business today," as Rosser Reeves called him in 1960.

His conflicts and his ambition derived from an ambivalent childhood. He was born near London in 1911, the fourth of five children, to an Irish mother and Scottish father. In the Edwardian fashion, his parents—both Fabian socialists and militant agnostics—extended carefully measured displays of affection or approval. "A quirk in the character of all Ogilvys," David noted years later, "makes it difficult for us to say anything pleasant about each other; we play an elaborate game of sarcastic denigration, to conceal our mutual devotion." He could not compete with his big brother Francis, who was always stronger and a better athlete and student; worse, as a young boy he could not even measure up against his sister Mary, four years older. David therefore considered himself a sissy: "I grew up to think I was a boob." The father, a kindly classical scholar, failed in business, so the family scraped by in genteel poverty.

Freudian analysis later persuaded Ogilvy that it was a problem of masculine identity. Overshadowed by a brother good at everything, drawn toward but unable to find a strong role model in his father, David was a shy, scared little boy. "There was always," he later confided to sister Mary, "an undercurrent of anti-man feelings in our family—and our Mother had it, she belittled almost all men." At age eight he was sent off to boarding school. Homesick and miserable, he read *Huckleberry Finn* and started to think about America. The book "possessed my soul to such an extent," he recalled, "that I decided to light out for the Mississippi at the first opportunity."

In adolescence he began to emerge, momentarily, from his brother's shadow. At a second boarding school he led a successful revolt against the resident bully and made better grades. He then won a scholarship that allowed him to attend Christ Church, Oxford. Here he failed. Concentrating in modern history, he botched chemistry and in general was less than diligent. So he was expelled (his brother had graduated from Cambridge with honors). "Next to flaring drunkenness and illicit love," he said later, only half kidding, "nothing appeals to Scotch sentiment so much as having been born in the gutter. I abandoned the cloistered serenity of Oxford and sought my place in the gutter."

Over the objections of most of his family—but with a key contact provided by his father—he took a job in the kitchen of an opulent Paris hotel. On his own for the first time, he toiled sixty-five hours a week for a wage of seven dollars. After work he romanced one of the salad girls, played court tennis, and on fine evenings climbed up Montmartre to watch the lights of Paris. If not quite the gutter, his year at the Hotel Majestic did provide a contrast to Oxford and left him with a fund of stories that he told for the rest of his life. When his family summoned him home he became a door-to-door salesman of cooking stoves in Scotland, quickly acquiring the skills of salesmanship. He wrote a pamphlet, "The Theory and Practice of Selling the Aga Cooker," that got him a position with the company's London ad agency, Mather & Crowther, where his brother was an account executive.

Now in his mid-twenties, he had found his métier. "I didn't have the brains to be a historian," he would recall. "Of all the things that were open to me, advertising was the best. It's the only thing in my whole life I've been any good at." His wild-oats days behind him, he settled into harness, assaulting his new profession, reading everything he could find, working until three o'clock night after night. Still infatuated with America, he subscribed to a Chicago clipping service that sent him the new ad campaigns. He then copied the best American campaigns for his British clients. With the United States

as his mecca, he talked Mather & Crowther into sending him there
for a year to study advertising techniques. Before leaving he
dropped by the National Broadcasting Company's London office,
explaining that by importing American methods he hoped to increase commercial broadcasting in England. "An unusually able as
well as attractive young man," NBC's London agent wrote home,
". . . a 'go-getter' of the best kind." Perceiving the mutual advantage
in his trip, the agent urged NBC in New York to greet him cordially.
"We will be glad to have him visit us," New York wrote back, "and
he can make himself at home with us a hundred percent."

And so, for adventure and to escape his brother's shadow, he came
to America, playing Huck Finn at age twenty-seven. When he saw
the Manhattan skyline he wept from joy. With a letter from his
cousin Rebecca West he met Alexander Woollcott, spending weekends at Woollcott's island retreat in Vermont and gaining entry to
New York's literary and artistic circles. NBC gave him the run of its
facilities: front-row seats for broadcasts, access during rehearsals, in-
troductions to agency men. He made the rounds on Madison Avenue, picking brains at will. "When I looked at Young & Rubicam
ads, or heard them on the radio, I sat in awe," he recalled. "Those
Sanka coffee ads! I was completely swept away by it all!" A conspicuously handsome young man, he apparently charmed everyone
he met.

Of these new acquaintances the most significant for his future
turned out to be Rosser Reeves, then writing copy at Blackett-Sample-Hummert. Ogilvy had arrived as an exponent of the British
image school of whimsy and soft sell. Reeves loaned him a copy of
Claude Hopkins' *Scientific Advertising* and at working lunches lectured him on the advantages of the claim approach. "My admiration for these two opposite schools tore me apart," Ogilvy
remembered. "It took me a long time to reconcile what I learned
from both of them." Those lunches also began a complex, fraternal,
highly charged relationship between the two men. Though only a
year older than Ogilvy, Reeves was farther along in the business.
When they talked advertising at this time Reeves held the floor
while Ogilvy listened. In other ways, too, Ogilvy acted as the disciple. Upon meeting Reeves' wife he declared that he wanted to meet
her sister; which he did, and shortly married her.

The yearlong foray became permanent residence. Working for
George Gallup's research organization in Princeton and Hollywood,

in three years he conducted over 400 national opinion surveys, an invaluable mass of insights on American tastes and customs. Not everything pleased him. "The more I trepan the mind of America," he told Woollcott, "the more I suspect that a return to Athenian democracy is the only way to save this country from its beastly politicians." He still had his mind on advertising. The Gallup approach—with its emphasis on news, editorial format, service, and photographs instead of artwork—showed up in his ads later and pushed him further from image to claim techniques.

Following wartime service in the British embassy in Washington, Ogilvy moved with his wife and son to an Amish farm in Lancaster County. On visits to the region Ogilvy had been drawn to its nineteenth-century "atmosphere of security and continuity." No less a fan of American flash and progress, he felt oddly at home in this unchanging, antimodern society of farmers and craftsmen. He grew a full Amish beard and settled in to raise tobacco on his hundred acres of limestone land, with a trout stream flowing through the meadow. But he was not, alas, a farmer. He lacked the strength for the heavy handwork, was mechanically clumsy, and could not learn animal husbandry. "The years we spent in Lancaster County were the richest of my life," he said later. "But it became apparent that I could never earn my living as a farmer."

Back to advertising. Even on the farm he had kept his hand in. Early in 1947 he compiled an all-star agency with James Webb Young as chairman of the board, Ted Bates as president ("he always reminds me of Robespierre"), Ben Duffy for media, Gallup in research, and Reeves in copy ("few would deny that the author of the current Raleigh campaign is in the direct line of apostolic succession from Claude Hopkins"). The roster suggested a claim orientation, as did a list of "Thirty-nine Articles of Faith" he drafted later that year for Mather & Crowther, stressing a "Basic Selling Proposition" (like the Bates USP), pretested by research, with the actual creation of the ad written off as "mere *technique.*" "Most of it is kindergarten stuff," Ogilvy advised Reeves, "but it is still badly needed even in the best British agencies."

Yet when he thought about working for an agency, his first choice was Young & Rubicam, the biggest shop in the image tradition. "But I knew that they would not hire a middle-aged rolling stone like me, so I never even applied." He therefore determined to take a Huck Finn-like leap off the raft: after being out of the business for ten years, he would start his own agency. With $6,000 of his own money and major capital from Mather & Crowther and another London firm, S. H. Benson Ltd., he set up what he called "a British advertising agency in New York." The partners offered the presidency to Reeves, who demurred, and then hired Anderson F. Hewitt, an account man with J. Walter Thompson and formerly head of Getchell's radio department. Ogilvy became vice-president in charge of research. Hewitt, Ogilvy, Benson & Mather was launched in September 1948 with a few modest British accounts. "We think," Ogilvy offered, "we are pretty good at using *small* spaces—we have to be."

The agency's early work, for clients like Helena Rubinstein and Guinness Stout, ran mainly to newsy, detailed copy in the mail-order and claim tradition. Then in 1951, for the small Maine clothing firm of Hathaway, Ogilvy tried a different approach. To sell a modestly priced line of shirts he planned an ad that would convey an atmosphere of class and expensive accessories. The model, he explained to his art director Vincent DeGiacomo, should look distinguished, perhaps like Ernest Hemingway or William Faulkner; "middle-aged, and preferably moustached. I wouldn't mind an elegant black patch over one eye. Or glasses." Years earlier, a dashing schoolmaster with an eye patch had left a stylish imprint on the ten-year-old Ogilvy. Recently he had seen a rakish photograph of Lewis Douglas, the former U.S. ambassador to Great Britain, wearing an eye patch after a fishing accident. "I have always been mildly obsessed with the things," Ogilvy later noted. Sitting in his bath one night, he decided to try the device in the Hathaway ad.

DeGiacomo picked the model, a White Russian named George Wrangell. He was, as suggested, middle-aged and mustached, with a resemblance to Faulkner. On the way to the photo session Ogilvy bought an eye patch. They shot it with and without the patch, but when they saw the proofs the decision of which to run was obvious. Ogilvy undertook the sales job on the client: "I have done something outrageously unorthodox," he wrote. The patch would give the ad a story appeal—people would wonder why he was wearing it—and make the model look "like a very real and interesting person, instead of a conventional dummy. . . . It is a small matter, but it may make a big difference." The client agreed, and "The man in the Hathaway shirt" was launched in the *New Yorker* of September 22, 1951. Soon the Hathaway factory could not keep up with the demand for its shirts.

No longer restricted to research, Ogilvy now found himself dreaming up a series of situations for his creation, many of them activities that Ogilvy in his own life would have liked to perform. In ad after ad, always in his eye patch, Hathaway shirt, and haughty look, Baron Wrangell was shown "playing the oboe, painting, conducting the Philharmonic, that kind of thing," Ogilvy recalled. "All Walter Mitty Ogilvy. Hence, the coherent image." For four years the man appeared only in the *New Yorker*, thus gaining by association a further boost up the socioeconomic scale. The campaign resembled a long-running serial, as readers would flip the pages of a new issue to see what the Hathaway man was doing this week. "We have never seen anything just like it in our whole twenty-seven years here," the *New Yorker*'s advertising manager reported. The first ad in the series had included five paragraphs of detailed, reason-why copy; by 1956 the campaign was so familiar that Ogilvy could run an ad without copy, without even the name of the product—just a photograph of the man and his eye patch. Customers were buying an image, not a sales pitch.

The success of the Hathaway man, as the client's annual sales tripled, rebutted the claim school's usual assertion that image advertising could not move merchandise. With that example, Ogilvy began to rethink the other main point of contention between the two schools, the question of ethics. Buoyed by the fame of the Hathaway ads, in the summer of 1952 he renewed his acquaintance with the grand old man of image advertising, Raymond Rubicam, living in retirement in Tucson and Boothbay Harbor, Maine. In August he spent a weekend with the Rubicams in Boothbay, sitting at his feet while Rubicam lectured on ethics. "Your remarks about Lasker and Hopkins have been very much in my mind," he wrote Rubicam a few weeks later. "Obviously you *proved* that it is unnecessary for advertisers to tell lies and bamboozle the public." But, he went on, Hopkins had written a memoir while Rubicam had not. "That is why so many of the younger generation, including myself, tend to accept the rightness of Hopkins and his ilk." Rubicam never did write his book, but for the next five years he corresponded with his new disciple, offering measured praise in exchange for Ogilvy's homage. "It is a remarkable fact," Ogilvy told him, "that the best copywriter in America should have gone on to become the greatest administrator and leader in agency history. . . . I am not in your class, either as a copywriter or in leadership."

Despite the hint of sycophancy in such declarations, Ogilvy

meant them sincerely. Rubicam was out of the business and really
had nothing but advice to offer. As both advertising classicist and
seeker of heroes, Ogilvy was always looking for the best precedents.
Rubicam now became the model. Ogilvy set as his standard what he
called "the great Y & R tradition—a tradition which defies stereotypes, but does so with perfect manners, and with no sacrifice of
'sell.' " Instead of specific claims, he aimed to build "the most favorable image, the most sharply defined *personality*" for his clients—as
he had done for Hathaway. In running his agency, Ogilvy absorbed
Rubicam's dictum that only one man could lead. As Rubicam had
done with *his* account executive partner, John Orr Young, Ogilvy
parted company with Anderson Hewitt, and the firm became
Ogilvy, Benson & Mather.

Picking up Rubicam meant putting down Rosser Reeves. In September 1952, fresh from his weekend in Boothbay, Ogilvy offered a
cyclical theory of agency history in a speech to a group of New York
ad people. A new agency, he said, full of ambition and creative dy-
namite, does great ads. As the years pass the founders grow tired,
but the agency still prospers, living on its name and contacts. "But
the agency has grown too big. It produces dull, routine campaigns.
It has become a bureaucratic sausage-machine." It starts losing clients to hungry upstart agencies, and the cycle then repeats itself.
Reeves thought he knew which old and young agencies Ogilvy had
in mind, and he offered a rebuttal two weeks later. "The theory is
hardly in accord with the facts," said Reeves, citing Thompson,
Ayer, BBDO, and "maybe fifty" other old agencies still producing
good work. A young agency, he went on, with an implicit nod
toward OB & M, was usually built around one man and so ran the
risk of being wiped out by a wayward taxicab.

"What surprises me," Ogilvy continued the argument in private,
"is that you should have said things which you don't believe. For
example, you have told me a thousand times what you really think
of N. W. Ayer and BBDO." As for running a one-man shop, the
Ogilvy staff of 107 "includes some terrific people." Instead of adding
useless collateral services, as old, overgrown agencies did, the focus
should be on preparing ads: "You used to share that view. And I
think you still do." After this public quarrel the two men remained
friends and still saw each other socially. But the professional argument created a personal breach. At parties each liked to dominate
the room. If Reeves came in a loud dinner jacket, Ogilvy appeared

in a kilt. They competed for attention, each measuring himself against the other. Reeves enlisted in the anti-Communist crusade of the day; a Bates copywriter was fired for some nebulous proletarian association. Reeves sent pamphlets to Ogilvy warning about the Red menace, but Ogilvy, a political liberal, was not persuaded. "Let's live and let live," he told Reeves; "and keep peace in the family." Even family peace eluded them after Ogilvy's divorce and remarriage. Soon, without specifically naming his former brother-in-law, Ogilvy was dismissing the followers of Claude Hopkins as "unscrupulous toughs."

Meantime his agency achieved its second notable success with another pure image campaign. When the Schweppes quinine water account came to him by way of Mather & Crowther, Ogilvy did not want it. Schweppes would at first bill only about $15,000, he noted, and it seemed to lack growth potential. He was fed up with little "shop window accounts," he pleaded with his brother Francis: "The great problem is to avoid getting bogged down in trivia." But his British partners insisted, so Ogilvy planned a newsy campaign stressing the availability of the beverage in the United States for only fifteen cents a bottle. No good, said the client. Wanting a plusher image, Schweppes suggested that Ogilvy feature its bearded advertising manager, Commander Edward Whitehead, arriving in the United States to assure that the domestic version measured up to the original. So, building on the success of "the man in the Hathaway shirt," "the man from Schweppes" started smiling his engaging smile in the *New Yorker*. Slated only to launch the campaign, the commander made such a hit that he stayed in the ads for years. "Whitehead's bearded mug," Ogilvy remarked, as mystified as anyone, "has captured the imagination of the American public." In a clean-shaven era, when the few visible beards were clipped, modest goatees, Whitehead wore a bushy, bristling thicket of hair on his face. The luxuriant growth made him as exotic in his way as the Hathaway man's eye patch. People reacted to it the same way: why is he wearing that? Who is he? This curiosity translated into increased sales for a product that many drinkers continued to find only marginally palatable.

After Hathaway and Schweppes, the agency that began in a research-oriented Hopkins mold was established as a hot creative shop with Ogilvy as the resident genius. "His place among the great advertising writers of all time is practically assured," *Printers' Ink* de-

clared in 1953. He made many speeches preaching the creative gospel and pricking the complacencies of the day. The trade press
lavished its attention on this exotic foreigner. Stanley Resor tried
to hire him to work for Thompson ("I had met the old boy at a
luncheon," Ogilvy told Rubicam, "and managed to hold my tongue
when he said that Adlai Stevenson and Averell Harriman were traitors to their class"). Still in his early forties, Ogilvy had made good
in America and was almost free of the unsparing judgments of his
family. "My brother and sisters," he noted, "are still very surprised
when someone calls me creative."

He worked seven days and six nights a week, a total of about seventy-five hours, administering and attending meetings at the office
and doing all his writing at home. Ever the Ogilvy, he seldom
praised his staff. "I was constantly badgering him to be nicer to people," one associate later recalled. In hiring he looked for people of
obvious ambition—"men with fire in their bellies"—who had studied liberal arts, not advertising, in college; he had only contempt for
undergraduate courses in advertising. Coming to the agency as a *ta-
bula rasa,* a new employee was then expected to absorb Ogilvy's very
specific rules for making ads: include the brand name in the headline, don't try to be clever, avoid analogies and superlatives, write
sentences of less than twelve words, make at least fourteen references
to people per one hundred words, avoid humorous copy, use photographs instead of artwork, and so on. Holding his people to these
precepts, he was sometimes accused of rigidity and of stifling creativity. He did, however, excel at client contact. He would call up the
client and very precisely ask for nine or thirteen or twenty-two minutes. Upon arrival he would remove his watch, place it in front of
him, and glance at it during the presentation. "And in the number
of minutes he had assigned himself," Henry Schachte of Lever
Brothers recalled, "he brilliantly delivered his obviously well-
thought-out presentation, always impressive, always helpful, and always about advertising. He had the stage, and he knew what to do
with it."

He was most at home, at his best, in writing ads. As he described
the arduous process, he first went through a long preamble. He dug
up the precedents, studying the ads of competing products for some
years back; called in the research department; assembled every conceivable fact and selling idea about the product; defined the selling
problem and campaign purposes and got the client to agree to them;

wrote out various headlines, as many as twenty for one advertisement. "At this point I can no longer postpone doing the actual copy," he noted. "So I go home and sit down at my desk. I find myself entirely without ideas. I get bad-tempered. If my wife comes into the room I growl at her." Facing the stubbornly blank page, he endured the terrors known to all writers. Sometimes the words came easily. If they did not, he learned techniques "for keeping open the telephone line to my unconscious," as he put it: "I hear a great deal of music. I am on friendly terms with John Barleycorn. I take long hot baths. I spend an hour at stool every day. I garden. I go into retreat among the Amish. I watch birds. I go for long walks in the country." Under way at last, he imagined himself giving advice to an intelligent woman at a dinner party who had asked about a certain product. Speaking in the second-person singular, as though in a conversation, he aimed a little above the average mentality. Like other writers in the image school, he assumed a certain sophistication in his audience. After four or five editing stages the copy went to the client. "If the client *changes* the copy, I get angry—because I took a lot of trouble writing it, and what I wrote I wrote *on purpose*."

Clients generally deferred to him. He carried himself like an Oxford don, the historian *manqué*, projecting his own compelling personal brand image. After two decades in the United States he still spoke British vernacular in the accents of his native West Horsley. At 4:30 each afternoon he took tea in his office. In winter he wore tweeds, in summer light-colored suits with a prominent foulard in the jacket pocket, and thick rubber-soled shoes. For inspirational music he favored Bach, Handel, and Mozart, with an occasional military march for panoply. He was comfortable in the presence of writers and intellectuals, preferring the company not of his Madison Avenue peers but of academic friends in Boston ("I wish I lived up there—I like the people better, more my type"). His *New Yorker* ads embellished this personal image of cosmopolitan taste and high culture.

Of course, the image had its cracks. The Hathaway man, after all, only embodied Ogilvy's fantasy life. His grinding work schedule left no time for serious avocations or intellectual pursuits. He seldom read novels or poetry. He read magazines—*Reader's Digest* was his favorite—but, like Burnett, did so mainly to keep up with the advertising. He played no sports or games. Though he urged "gentle manners" on his staff, he was still so shy and self-conscious about displays of affection that he would slip away from social occasions without saying good-bye. His polished copy implied a mastery of the language that his odd lapses denied. He used "ineffably" in a Hathaway ad and then could not define it ("I think it means supremely, a lot"). Again, criticized for misspelling "grisly" and using "like" as a conjunction, he dismissed grammar as "the most boring and fatuous subject on any school curriculum" but conceded that "I misuse the English language abominably."

By the standards of high English, that is. Perfect grammar and a capacious vocabulary hardly qualified a man to write advertising. If less the intellectual than he seemed, Ogilvy had a finely tuned sense of the task at hand. Hopkins and Rubicam were not intellectuals either. "The qualities which make a man effective in advertising do not necessarily include an ability to write well," he told the novelist Roald Dahl. "Most of the great advertising agents—great in the sense that their advertisements sell merchandise—are illiterate. . . . The ability to write well is generally a handicap, partly because most of the customers are uneducated housewives. Most of my copy is awful, by your standards." Measured against most advertising of the 1950s, though, Ogilvy's copy sparkled and sang.

It was, perhaps, aimed too high for its era. His fellow copywriters rushed toward Ogilvy as an oasis in the creative desert of the 1950s. He won prizes and an attentive press. But he was marked as an eccentric Englishman who could only write soft-sell pieces for the carriage trade of the *New Yorker*. His most famous accounts barely paid their way. Hathaway in four years spent only $300,000 on advertising. The agency had to bill Schweppes for annual *losses* on its account: $20,000 in 1953, $38,000 in 1954, over $25,000 in 1955. Nonetheless these campaigns seemed successful because the clients were selling a lot of shirts and quinine water. Thus imitators appeared with their own visual gimmicks: a giant nest egg in a bank ad, a horse in a liquor ad. Not flattered, Ogilvy scorned these efforts as plagiarized attempts to sell without the bother of writing any copy. "I have become the symbol for a school of advertising which I deplore," he lamented in 1956.

In its first five years the Ogilvy agency had jumped quickly to billings of $10.7 million in 1953. Looking ahead then, Ogilvy disclaimed any imperial designs. "Like Raymond Rubicam 30 years ago," he said, "we have only one ambition"—to become the best agency in America. "I'm not sure that you can combine bigness with bestness nowadays. . . . Perhaps a billing of $30,000,000 is most suitable for what I have in mind." But the agency moved sluggishly toward even this modest goal. Billings fell off to $10.1 million in 1954, then recovered slowly to $11.8 and $14.1 million in the next two years. Large, packaged-good accounts remained leery of the celebrated Ogilvy approach. By style and natural inclination he still preferred the image tradition; for practical reasons he needed to shift toward the claim tradition.

In 1956 he hired Esty Stowell as executive vice-president in charge of account management. From a hard-sell career at Benton & Bowles, Stowell set out to give OB & M a harder image. "I guess we'll all go to our graves with eyepatches on our headstones," he said later. Stowell brought in Maxwell House coffee, the agency's first big packaged good, and billings started climbing. For Ogilvy the creative task was now to combine the style and good manners of image advertising with an equally memorable sales pitch: to find that elusive best of both schools he had been seeking since 1938.

When Rolls-Royce first offered its account to OB & M in 1957, Stowell talked Ogilvy into turning it down because it would only add to the carriage-trade reputation and scare away big, fat accounts. A few months later Rolls-Royce came back with a better offer, and Ogilvy would not be dissuaded again. "I want this account more than almost any we have ever solicited," he told his partners. "Young & Rubicam had Rolls-Royce when they were our age. It did not hurt them." The initial billing was under $200,000, but his partners caved in. With the ball in his court, Ogilvy took charge of the copywriting. For four days in a row he got up at five o'clock in the morning and sweated out the copy. From twenty-six different headlines his associates picked the one that ran: "At 60 miles an hour the loudest noise in this new Rolls-Royce comes from the electric clock." (An echo from advertising history: in 1933 Charles Brower of BBDO wrote a Pierce-Arrow ad with the headline, "*The only sound* one can hear in the new Pierce-Arrows is the ticking of the electric clock." "What a fascinating thing," Ogilvy replied to Brower. "I picked up that headline from an article in a British motoring magazine.")

Beneath the soon-famous headline Ogilvy wrote long, reason-why copy, filled with the sort of facts and statistics that only a Rolls could command. Polite and stylish, but detailed and factual, with no visual gimmicks: claim and image together. It was Ogilvy's third big hit in seven years, and Rolls-Royce sold 50 percent more cars in 1958. "If only people would stop talking about the eyepatch, and Commander Beard," Ogilvy reflected. "I'm so totally sick of them; and at best they were minor tricks." But, like the patch and beard, the Rolls campaign made money for the client and not for the agency. The billing never exceeded $250,000 a year; in four years OB & M lost a total of $26,000 and then resigned the account.

It was no coincidence that Ogilvy did his most spectacular work for miserly clients. On bigger accounts, he left the creative work to his associates. They produced solid, less celebrated ads that earned more money for the agency. "I have detected in myself," he noted, "a tendency to be courageous and creative when the ads are cheap, but to take refuge in safe formulae when the budgets are big. I tend to lose my nerve." Dealing in small change, he could risk unorthodoxy with no great loss if he bombed. That dilemma raised again the question of bigness or bestness. If the agency really started to grow, would there be a collective loss of creative nerve?

As time went by Ogilvy was more willing to take that risk. From 1951 to 1957, with OB & M growing by slow increments, Rosser Reeves was taking Bates on a hard-sell wave from $28.8 to $103.4 million in domestic billings. Perhaps impressed by that example, toward the end of the decade Ogilvy gravitated once again in the direction of Reeves. He corresponded less often with Raymond Rubicam. In an article for *Television Magazine* in November 1958, he listed Hopkins, Hummert, and Reeves as his copy mentors—and did not mention Rubicam. For a time after Ogilvy's divorce from Reeves' sister-in-law, the two men did not see each other socially. They were reconciled in 1959. With that barrier removed, Ogilvy tried to identify himself with Reeves and the Bates technique of claim and repetition. "We believe the same things," he insisted. "It is grotesque, and for me almost tragic," he told Reeves, "that so many people should regard me as the leading opponent of your Reality Sell philosophy, when I am in fact your most fervent disciple." (As for Reeves, dealing from strength, he felt no corresponding urge to link himself with Ogilvy. He joked about doing a Bates ad for Anacin in the Ogilvy fashion: Cecil Beaton or Truman Capote reclining on a bed in a Viyella bathrobe, with a caption of "You'll never know you drank that gin—if you brush your teeth with Anacin.")

For most of the 1950s, though, Ogilvy stood out as a maverick strayed into a rather docile industry. At trade meetings he urged his peers to listen to their rebels and reformers, to tighten ethics and behave more professionally, and—in particular—to make better ads. To the objection that he was only singing the song of any small, creative shop, he had his rebuttal: Leo Burnett. "You people have built a very great agency," Ogilvy wrote Dick Heath, "—the only one which has my undiluted respect." (The two agencies almost merged in 1955.) Burnett in the 1950s showed, as Young & Rubicam had in the 1930s, that creative verve might coexist with bigness. As a student of advertising history, Ogilvy hoped to make the same demonstration in the 1960s. "What we're trying to do here," he explained, "is to return to the eternal verities of the advertising business. The first concern of an advertising agency should be to produce great advertising."

❧❧

When Ned Doyle, Maxwell Dane, and William Bernbach opened their agency in June 1949, the name itself hinted at a departure. No comma, dash, or ampersand, just: Doyle Dane Bernbach. They started with thirteen employees and $500,000 in billings, in a top-floor office at 350 Madison Avenue, a floor and a half above the last elevator stop.

Doyle, forty-seven years old at the founding, was the account man. From a background in magazine sales and advertising, he had grown up in New Jersey, attended Hamilton College for two years on a football scholarship, shipped to sea on a tramp steamer, and knocked around Europe before settling down to work in New York. Vaguely Runyonesque in character, he had a sharp, angular, don't-bluff-me face and addressed anyone his junior as "kid." He was bluntly honest: "There aren't enough advertisers," he said early on, "who appreciate our kind of advertising agency for us ever to get over $20 million." Dane, forty-three, handled administration and finances. A high school dropout from Cincinnati, he had worked briefly as a newspaper salesman in New York and then taken an advertising job with Stern's department store. As promotion director for *Look* in 1939 he met Doyle, the ad manager. Doyle liked him at once because, he recalled, "he was willing to do all the work and let me take the credit for it." Always mild and self-effacing, Dane looked like the popular notion of an accountant and stayed quietly in the background.

Like all the founding principals except Dane, the copy chief and art director came from jobs at Grey Advertising. Phyllis Robinson had grown up in New York, intending to be a writer. When other little girls at P.S. 50 were dreaming of becoming Ginger Rogers, she said later, she wanted to be Dorothy Parker. Interested in politics, she studied sociology at Barnard and worked in public housing before meandering into the Grey promotion department ("you know, you look back and wonder how you ever got into this thing"). Robert Gage, another native New Yorker, had studied art and design under Alexey Brodovitch of *Harper's Bazaar* and was also influenced by the designer Paul Rand. At Grey in the late 1940s Gage had developed definite ideas on how to improve advertising art. "They weren't doing straightforward work in those days," he would recall. "All little things, mished together; nothing made sense. The simplicity of a strong, graphic image with a good line that works with it is what I was looking for."

Granted this talent around him, what made DDB different was Bill Bernbach. A copywriter with a sense of design, an acute judge of competence and nurser of artistic egos, and—especially—an inspired teacher, he was the most innovative advertising man of his time. More than anyone else, he invented the creative revolution of the 1960s.

Thirty-eight years old in 1949, Bernbach was born in the Bronx section of New York. His father designed women's clothes. After attending public schools he took the subway to New York University, where he studied English, music, and philosophy, showing the easy eclecticism that would later let him range across disciplines in his advertising career. A series of nondescript jobs led to a ghostwriting position with the New York World's Fair of 1939. He then heard of an opening at the Weintraub ad agency. "I had never been in advertising," he recalled, "but I thought it might be a good idea to ghost for some products instead of people. It might be lucrative and it might be very interesting." With no background in the field, and with little interest in advertising history, then or later, he had at least an uncluttered mind open to new ideas. As a writer at Weintraub he worked with the art director Paul Rand on campaigns for Dubonnet and Airwick. They spent lunch hours touring art galleries and discussing the interplay of their two crafts, aiming to integrate those ancient enemies in the creative process of advertising.

At Grey, where Bernbach became copy chief in 1945, he recreated this symbiosis with Bob Gage. On the day they met, Gage went home and told his wife that someday he would go into business with

Bernbach: "I understood what he was talking about, and he understood me. He was very inspiring." They worked on retail campaigns—shirts, watches, liquor, fashion, soft goods—for bargain outlets on Seventh Avenue. A rigorous training, these accounts demanded speed and high volume, with severely functional graphics and immediate feedback on the day of the sale. As head of copy Bernbach interviewed prospective writers, but found most of them beguiled by the current fashions for research and scientific techniques. In 1947 he sent a memo to his boss, the first sounding of themes he would repeat for the rest of his career. "I'm worried that we're going to fall into the trap of bigness, that we're going to worship techniques instead of substance," he wrote. "I don't want academicians. I don't want scientists. I don't want people who do the right things. *I want people who do inspiring things.* . . . Let us blaze new trails."

Thus Doyle Dane Bernbach in 1949. After a few years in their elevatorless office they moved to a modest building on West Forty-third, a block and a half from Madison Avenue but farther removed in spirit. Here, even as business improved, the decor remained utilitarian, without the showy touches other agencies used to impress clients. Artists and copywriters were jumbled together on one floor. None of the principals made the usual daily trek to Westchester or Greenwich. Doyle and Dane lived in Manhattan apartments; Bernbach, still a subway rider, lived with his wife and two sons in a stucco house in the Bay Ridge section of Brooklyn. "We probably do less entertaining than any agency in the business," Bernbach conceded. "We're three guys who live very modestly and we don't cater to clients because we want the money."

All of this expressed something essential about DDB and about Bernbach's own personality. He had a strong sense of himself and a fully adequate ego. (According to one story, probably apocryphal but nonetheless revealing, he was walking down the street one day with an associate from the agency. His companion remarked on the beautiful weather. "Thank you," said Bernbach.) But his strength was the kind that did not need to trumpet itself. He walked and talked softly. Short and blocky, he had bland features, mild blue eyes, and blond hair turning gray. "Take Bernbach in the abstract," his friend the composer William Schumann noted, "and ask what his profession is, and you would never say advertising." He was utterly sane and balanced, uneccentric to the point of dullness. Once, asked if he had ever felt moved to write fiction, he said no: "I have no sores to squeeze." He prided himself on never spending evenings or weekends at the office. At the end of a normal working day he took the Sea Beach Express home to Bay Ridge. "I'm a loafer," he explained. "I work very hard during the day and then take it easy." His hobbies were predictably calm and easygoing, no sports, nothing strenuous, just reading and listening to music. His literary tastes ran to philosophy, sociology, and fiction, with a preference for versatile polymaths like Lewis Mumford and Bertrand Russell. He liked to quote a statement of Russell's: "Even in the most purely logical realms, it is insight that first arrives at what is new."

Bernbach was his own plans board. Every ad passed under his review before it left the agency. Yet he supervised with a light touch. In his office he sat with the door open at a round teak work table with five other chairs grouped around. The arrangement implied a horizontal hierarchy: we're all peers here. Easily accessible, he was called Bill by most of the staff. He still picked his people with little regard for normal qualifications, sometimes interviewing for months before making a hire, and seldom firing anyone. "We don't care about the usual things," a DDB employment ad read. "For instance, we don't particularly care what kind of accounts you've been working on. We don't care what size agency you're with now. We don't care about age, sex, college education or the other questionnaire trappings." He recognized no aptitude tests for creativity and often hired people with no advertising background. "I pull 'em in from all over the lot," he said. "And what there is to know about advertising, we teach them later."

He did his best work as a teacher. Especially in the early years, he frequently left his office to prowl the creative floor, dropping into cubbyholes to review work in progress and discuss his theories of combining art and copy in dynamic new forms. "Sometimes they hated to see me come in," he recalled, "because I would tend to get headlines for them and so on. Well, I shouldn't do that, and I learned that very early. I'd ask questions and lead them so that they did it." Instead of imposing his own personality, he tried to discover the particular talent of each individual and to give it the freedom to develop naturally. This was Bernbach's signal contribution to the practice of agency management. "Not trying to stamp them out with a cookie cutter," as Phyllis Robinson described it. "Leave them, and give them an opportunity to grow in their own way rather than try to make more of the same." "He allows for you per-

Three from the 1950s:

▲ George Gribbin, who succeeded Sigurd Larmon as head of Young & Rubicam

◀ Rosser Reeves, polymath and Hopkins disciple, whose leadership pushed the Ted Bates agency to the fastest growth of the decade

Does she...or doesn't she?

Hair color so natural only her hairdresser knows for sure!

MISS CLAIROL® HAIR COLOR BATH®
THE NATURAL-LOOKING HAIRCOLORING • MORE WOMEN USE MISS CLAIROL THAN ALL OTHER HAIRCOLORING COMBINED

◀ Shirley Polykoff's Clairol campaign for Foote, Cone & Belding

David Ogilvy, student of advertising history and best-selling author, who became famous for ads in the MacManus manner but who sought identification with the Hopkins tradition

Winter is icumen in...so keep on drinking Schweppes!

Unloading Schweppes elixir on Pier 92

Three incarnations of Ogilvy as Commander Whitehead in the Schweppes campaign—"All Walter Mitty Ogilvy," Ogilvy noted. "Hence, the coherent image."

Great new fashion: Schweppes as a <u>Soft Drink</u>

The Gun is a $2,000 Purdy from England
(The shirt: A Sea Island Cotton from Hathaway)

THIS Sea Island cotton is astounding stuff—with fibers *three times longer* than those of ordinary cotton. It is described in the advertisements as "soft as swansdown, lustrous as satin, absorbent as wool, durable as linen." It is grown on St. Vincent, Antigua, St. Kitts, Montserrat, Nevis and Barbados.

Then it travels. Between being plucked in the balmy Caribbean sunshine, and its final apotheosis in a shirt by HATHAWAY of Maine, this nonesuch among cottons has been to England and back.

The Sylex Sea Island yarn is spun with loving care by Thomas Oliver & Sons, then woven on the looms of Ashton Brothers—two of the finest mills in England. Notice the extraordinary sheen. You can almost *feel* its downy softness.

The shirts are superbly tailored, with all the famous HATHAWAY hallmarks—generously long tails, single-needle stitching, big buttons of ocean pearl. Price $15, at stores that keep up the great tradition. For the name of the store nearest you, write C. F. Hathaway, Waterville, Maine. In New York, telephone MU 9-4157.

(Ogilvy & Mather)

The Hathaway Man, as played by George Wrangell in the pages of *The New Yorker;* Ogilvy's first big success

The Rolls-Royce Silver Cloud II — $15,655 P.O.E. (Delivery costs slightly higher in Alaska and Hawaii.)

"At 60 miles an hour the loudest noise in this new Rolls-Royce comes from the electric clock"

What __makes__ Rolls-Royce the best car in the world? "There is really no magic about it — it is merely patient attention to detail," says an eminent Rolls-Royce engineer.

1. "At 60 miles an hour the loudest noise comes from the electric clock," reports the Technical Editor of THE MOTOR. The silence inside the car is uncanny.

2. Every Rolls-Royce engine is run for four hours at full throttle before installation, and each car is extensively test-driven over varying road surfaces. Every Rolls-Royce has its "History Book" — an eleven-page signed record of every operation and inspection performed on the car.

3. The Rolls-Royce Silver Cloud II is designed as an *owner-driven* car. It has power steering, power brakes and automatic gear-shift. It is very easy to drive and to park. Women handle the car with ease.

4. The finished car spends a week in the final test-shop, being fine-tuned. Here it is subjected to ninety-eight separate ordeals. For example, the engineers use a stethoscope to listen for axle-whine.

5. The new eight-cylinder aluminium engine is even more powerful than the previous six-cylinder unit. It accelerates from zero to 60 miles an hour in 11.4 seconds. (ROAD AND TRACK test report.)

6. The coachwork is given as many as nine coats of finishing paint — hand rubbed.

7. Every Rolls-Royce takes the "Monsoon Test." Windows are rolled up and the car is pelted with water and air at gale force.

8. By moving a switch on the steering column, you can adjust the shock absorbers to suit road conditions. (The lack of fatigue in driving this car is remarkable.)

9. There are three independent brake linkages. The Rolls-Royce is a very *safe* car — and also a very responsive and lively car. It cruises serenely at eighty-five. Top speed is in excess of 100 m.p.h.

10. Automatic transmission, power brakes and power steering are *standard*. So are the radio, heating and ventilating equipment, walnut panelling, seats adjustable for tilt and rake, and white sidewall tires. The Rolls-Royce people do not designate essential equipment as "optional extras."

11. The Bentley is made by Rolls-Royce. Except for the radiator shells, they are identical motor cars, manufactured by the same engineers in the same works. The Bentley costs $300 less, because its radiator is simpler to make. People who feel diffident about driving a Rolls-Royce can buy a Bentley.

PRICE. The car illustrated in this advertisement costs $15,655 at port of entry. Delivery costs slightly higher in Alaska and Hawaii.

ROLLS-ROYCE AND BENTLEY

If you would like the rewarding experience of driving a Rolls-Royce or Bentley, write or telephone the dealer listed below. For further information or complete list of U. S. dealers, write Mr. Richard L. Yorke, Vice President, Rolls-Royce Inc., Room 467, 45 Rockefeller Plaza, New York 20, N. Y.

See 1961 Rolls-Royce and Bentley Motor Cars at the International Automobile Show, New York Coliseum, April 1 to 9.

J. S. Inskip, Inc., 304 East 64th Street, New York, TE 8-6100

(Ogilvy & Mather)

Ogilvy's famous headline for Rolls-Royce

William Bernbach, successor to the mantle of Raymond Rubicam; the most innovative and respected advertising man of the 1950s and 1960s

▲ Robert Gage, art director, one of the founding creatives, along with Bernbach and Robinson, at DDB

Helmut Krone, art director for the Volkswagen and Avis campaigns ▶

◀ Phyllis Robinson, the first and most influential copy chief at Doyle Dane Bernbach

▲ Two ads in the Levy's series by copywriter Judy Protas and art director Bill Taubin ▼

▲ Bernbach's taboo-defying ad for El Al

▲ Bernbach's catty ad for Ohrbach's

Lemon.

Think small.

Eleven years ago, the first Volkswagens were imported into the United States.

These strange little cars with their beetle shapes were almost unknown.

All they had to recommend them was 32 miles to the gallon (regular gas, regular driving), an aluminum air-cooled rear engine that would go 70 mph all day without strain, sensible size for a family and a sensible price tag too.

Beetles multiply; so do Volkswagens. By 1954.

VW was the best-selling imported car in America. It has held that rank each year since. In 1960, about 155,000 Volkswagens were sold, including 35,000 station wagons and trucks.

And again in 1960, Authorized VW Dealers sold a higher average number of units than any other dealer selling any other kind of car.

Volkswagen's snub nose is now familiar in fifty states of the Union, as American as apple strudel.

As any VW owner will tell you, Volkswagen service is excellent and it is everywhere. Parts are plentiful, prices low. No small factor in Volkswagen's success.

Today, in the U.S.A. and 119 other countries Volkswagens are sold faster than they can be made. Volkswagen has become the world's fifth largest automotive manufacturer by thinking small. More and more people are thinking the same.

▲ The two most celebrated ads for the Volkswagen campaign by copywriter Julian Koenig and art director Helmut Krone ▶

Avis is only No.2
in rent a cars.
So why go with us?

We try harder.
(When you're not the biggest, you have to.)

We just can't afford dirty ashtrays. Or half-empty gas tanks. Or worn wipers. Or unwashed cars. Or low tires. Or anything less than seat-adjusters that adjust. Heaters that heat. Defrosters that defrost.

Obviously, the thing we try hardest for is just to be nice. To start you out right with a new car, like a lively, super-torque Ford, and a pleasant smile. To let you know, say, where you can get a good, hot pastrami sandwich in Duluth.

Why?

Because we can't afford to take you for granted.

Go with us next time.

The line at our counter is shorter.

◀ The first Avis ad by copywriter Paula Green and art director Helmut Krone

(Leo Burnett)

◄ Leo Burnett, heir to Theodore MacManus; leader of the Chicago style of advertising with his campaigns for Marlboro and the Jolly Green Giant

(Shirley Polykoff)

Reva Korda, who wrote Schweppes, Pepperidge Farm, and Dove copy for Ogilvy & Mather, became the agency's first woman vice-president and creative head, and later started her own agency ▼

▲ Shirley Polykoff, who did the Clairol campaign for Foote, Cone & Belding and later started her own agency

(Reva Korda)

(Advertising to Women)

Lois Geraci Ernst, president and creative director of Advertising to Women, which did campaigns for Aviance, Rive Gauche, and Jean Naté ►

**Two characteristic figures
in the aftermath of the
creative revolution:**

George Lois, art director and founder of agencies; the unbridled mustang of the advertising business

Edward N. Ney, who led Young & Rubicam into a period of mergers and acquisitions and finally toppled Thompson from its perch as the largest agency in U.S. billings

sonally to grow," said another DDB copywriter, Paula Green. "I mean he's there, he guides, and he's a tremendously perceptive man. And he lets his people go." As an application of progressive educational theory to running a creative department, the agency amounted to "sort of an adult Summerhill," as DDBer Ron Rosenfeld pointed out. Like A. S. Neill's experiment in education, it penalized people of little talent or poor self-motivation by leaving no room for excuses or buck passing. For others, for most who worked there, it offered room to take chances, express individuality, and see one's best efforts appear without the meddling of a plans board.

Bernbach taught, then, a set of general principles instead of a list of specific rules. He cited a finding by an AAAA study that 85 percent of all ads were ignored by consumers. "We can't question whether the public loves us," he said. "They don't even hate us. They are just bored with us. Business is spending its money for advertising and is achieving boredom with typical American efficiency." With more reading and viewing matter on hand than ever, and with the press of violent news and current events, an ad had to cut through the clutter with an "interrupting" idea. For Rosser Reeves, that meant taking his Unique Selling Proposition and drilling it in by repetition. Bernbach turned this approach on its head: the human psyche was bored by repetition and craved novelty, and would respond only to messages presented divertingly. "I am absolutely appalled," Bernbach declared, "by the suggestion, indeed the policy, of some agencies that once the selling proposition has been determined the job is done."

Form therefore mattered at least as much as content. But it was more than mere technique. In concert Paderewski hit a lot of wrong notes, Bernbach pointed out, yet he somehow moved his audience; Theodore Dreiser wrote an awkward prose but was still a great writer despite his shabby technique. And so, by analogy, in the art of advertising. "There are a lot of great technicians in advertising," Bernbach said in 1953, the high noon of research and science in the trade. "And unfortunately they talk the best game. They know all the rules. . . . But there's one little rub. They forget that advertising is persuasion, and persuasion is not a science, but an art. Advertising is the art of persuasion." The act of making ads thus drew on the same gifts of intuition and inspiration, creative leaps and flashes, as any other art form.

The creative act might be impeded, not helped, by the intrusion of research. In Bernbach's view, marketing surveys led to dullness and uniformity: they tested and interviewed, weighed and counted, always with a pretension of mathematical exactness, and came up with similar conclusions that belabored the self-evident. Biased toward past successes, the scientific approach tended to recommend more of the same and so discouraged innovation. "I consider *research* the major culprit in the advertising picture," Bernbach concluded in 1957. "It has done more to perpetuate creative mediocrity than any other factor." DDB did have a research department, but its employees enjoyed little power or prestige within the agency. After six years there one research man, Paul Klein, decided that Bernbach was "creative in one very limited area," the generation of copy: "His appreciation of a world outside of ad copy but inside the ad business is very limited." Trusting only the art and copy people on the twenty-fifth floor, said Klein, Bernbach was frightened of any other department. "It's something he doesn't understand and therefore it doesn't exist."

At any agency the happiness of research personnel was inverse to the happiness of the creatives. At DDB the creatives were given their head, again with a few general propositions from Bernbach. It started with the image school's tradition of respecting the audience. "It's true that there's a twelve-year-old mentality in America," Bernbach often repeated. "Every six-year-old has it. We're a smart people." So ads should convey an impression of honesty and candor, speaking an everyday colloquial language, showing photographs of people with natural, unfeigned expressions. The message should be simple and dramatic, sympathetic rather than strident or threatening. Tricky devices or cleverness for its own sake would only annoy an audience too intelligent to be fooled. "Don't be slick. Tell the truth," said Bernbach. "People get an impression, feeling, vibration about an ad long before they really look at the picture and read the copy." Above all, Bernbach told his creative department, trust your own instincts and listen to the ideas percolating up from your unconscious when the mind is relaxed, when you're walking down the street or just before falling asleep. Disregard the past. Create your own precedents. "Maybe that great philosopher–jazz musician, Thelonius Monk, hit it when he said, 'Sometimes I play things I never heard myself.' "

The ultimate expression of Bill Bernbach, the copywriter with an eye for design, was the DDB creative team. At most agencies copy preceded art, in both conception and the pecking order. (At Lennen & Newell in the 1950s, an artist once requested information on a client's industry before doing the ad. "Aren't you an art director?" asked the dumbfounded account executive.) DDB used no brainstorming or group meetings. At every level, ads were produced by an artist and writer working together as equals. "Two people who respect each other sit in the same room for a length of time," Bob Gage explained, "and arrive at a state of sort of free association, where the mention of one idea will lead to another idea, and then to another." The artist might suggest a headline, the writer a visual device: the entire ad was conceived as a whole in this exchange between disciplines.

This creative process still left blood on the floor. "We sit in a closed room and beat each other to death!" Paula Green said without undue exaggeration. "We are awfully tough on ourselves," Phyllis Robinson agreed. "The rough times for us are not when we're with the client, but when we're with each other." At its best, the process upgraded the art director to a full-blown advertising person, as concerned with the selling message as the copywriter was. It gave the creative team a sense of responsibility for their own work. "That's their property," said Bernbach. "They own it. And they walk with their heads up, and they walk with pride." The point of it all, the ad itself, thus integrated art and copy in a novel way—"the combination of the visual and the words," said Gage, "coming together and forming a third bigger thing."

During the 1950s the DDB approach yielded these celebrated campaigns:

—Ohrbach's, a bargain department store in New York, was one of Bernbach's accounts at Grey and then accompanied him to DDB in 1949. With a small media budget, Bernbach broke from retail advertising tradition, never mentioned prices or sales, but instead created an image of reliable quality at low cost. The ads exemplified the DDB integration of art and copy: a man carrying a woman under his arm, captioned "Liberal Trade-In: bring in your wife and just a few dollars . . . we will give you a new woman"; a well-tailored woman flanked by a man shattered into pieces, captioned "Clothes that make the woman without breaking the man" ("See," Bernbach explained, "the device I use to attract the reader's attention also tells the story"); a spoof of a Serutan ad with a putative doctor asking, "Do you feel dull and uninteresting? . . . You need SNIAGRAB (spell it backwards)"; and the most famous, a cat in a large lamp-shadelike hat, smoking a cigarette in a long holder, revealing cattily that her friend Joan dressed well by buying cheap at Ohrbach's. The campaign made this bargain store as familiar to New York shoppers as Macy's, which spent thirty times as much on advertising. "It's not how often ads run," Bernbach pointed out, "it's how much excitement they create."

—Success with Ohrbach's brought in another local account, the Henry S. Levy bakery of Brooklyn, with an initial billing of $40,000. An ad showed a slice of bread in three stages of consumption, captioned "New York" (one bite) "is eating" (three bites) "it up" (nearly gone). Later Judy Protas, copy, and Bill Taubin, art, did a series of ads and posters showing various non-Jewish ethnics with the explanation, "You don't have to be Jewish to love Levy's real Jewish rye." Levy's became the biggest seller of rye bread in New York.

—With its reputation spreading outside Manhattan, DDB in 1954 took on a new product, the Polaroid instant camera. For a sixty-second TV commercial, Gage and Robinson decided to risk a sentimental sell. They had recently seen the musical *West Side Story* and were impressed by the emotional compression of songs like "Maria." If it could be done in three and a half minutes, they reasoned, why not in one minute? So they created vignettes of friends and families at the zoo, after a wedding, on a train, smiling and crying with the unique help of instant photography. "People take pictures of people they love," Gage said later. "We felt," Robinson added, "it was possible to use the tenderer human emotions in advertising without getting icky; and it's a hell of a selling tool." Like the Hathaway man, the Polaroid camera became so well known it could be sold without any copy or headline. A magazine ad in 1958 showed only a nerd at the beach, Polaroid in hand, being fawned over by bathing beauties.

—El Al Israel Airlines came to DDB in 1957. At the time, Bill Taubin recalled, "airline ads were very straight and very square"—always with an airplane, seldom a full page, "and one never showed the ocean because people would be afraid of falling into it." Pondering an ad to announce El Al's new jet-prop service across the Atlantic, Bernbach got an idea walking back to the office from lunch one day. The final ad displayed a full-page photo of a stormy sea, its right border ripped and rolled like a window shade, with the headline "Starting Dec. 23 the Atlantic Ocean will be 20% smaller." El Al tripled its sales after one year at DDB.

The fame of these campaigns brought a steady growth in billings. The $8 million total in 1954 doubled in two years and then passed Ned Doyle's projected ceiling of $20 million in 1957. DDB took five of the eight gold medals awarded by the New York Art Directors Club in 1958. In its creative sparkle and fast expansion, DDB recalled the Young & Rubicam of the 1920s. Its kinetic photographs sometimes brought memories of the famous Y & R "IMPACT" ad. In client relations, Doyle claimed, "We are set up close to the early days of Young & Rubicam." And Bernbach, who bore a coincidental physical resemblance to Rubicam, later told him, "I don't think I could have quite made it without your influences. . . . You taught me the importance of saying the right things in an ad. But more than that, you taught me what later became even more essential: the importance of saying those things artfully."

Bernbach made that statement for Rubicam's eighty-fifth birthday, the sort of occasion that inspires fulsome declarations not to be taken quite literally. In most essentials DDB was sui generis, something new in the business. If Bernbach did not invent the creative team, he refined the concept and coaxed better work from it. He made the art director an equal partner with copy. His laissez-faire management style released the energies of his associates and uncovered talents previously unknown to them. They worked in a supercharged atmosphere, part creative burble, part nitrous oxide, turning out ads in a style no one had ever seen. "I don't think they really got it from anybody," said David Ogilvy, who knew the precedents. "They just sort of created an original school out of air."

In the 1950s, though, DDB—like Ogilvy, Benson & Mather—represented mainly promise for the future. Both agencies did their most famous work for small accounts. In 1959, with DDB at $27.5 million and OB & M at $25.9 million, both still qualified as medium-sized, not competing equally with the giants. Leo Burnett, at $110.5 million, was in the top ten. But none of these "creative agencies" had yet done a strikingly novel breakthrough job on a major national account.

They were, however, the critical successes of the time. In 1960 the creative directors at one hundred agencies were polled on the ten best campaigns of the past decade. Burnett won two (for Pillsbury cake and Marlboro), OB & M three (for Hathaway, Schweppes, and

Rolls-Royce), and DDB four (for Ohrbach's, Polaroid, El Al, and a small German car).

❧❧

Volkswagen was DDB's first car account, a potential road to the big time, but it brought little joy when it arrived at the agency in 1959. No chrome, no styling, no horsepower, not even an automatic transmission; worst, a relic from Nazi Germany in this agency with many Jewish employees and clients.

The creative team was Julian Koenig, copy, and Helmut Krone, art, with the counsel of Bernbach. (Krone later apportioned credit for the campaign equally among the three.) In the initial discussions, Krone wanted to make the ads as "American" as possible. Detroit was at the height of its infatuation with tailfins and overhorsed engines. It seemed impossible to sell the VW on its merits. Gradually the discussion came around to making virtues of the car's apparent deficiencies: basic and utilitarian, therefore cheap; low horsepower, therefore high mileage; ugly and unchanging, therefore well crafted and less ephemeral.

For this offbeat, oblique approach, Julian Koenig was the right copywriter. Known—to his dismay—as an Ivy League beatnik, he came from a New York family of lawyers and judges, went to Dartmouth, strayed briefly into Columbia law school, then into advertising. Before DDB he worked for an agency that kept meddling with his copy; "I learned how to handicap horses in self-defense," he recalled. He read the *Morning Telegraph* more carefully than the advertising trade press and was said to write ads at the track and at odd hours of the night. Cool and sardonic in the beat manner, he hung out with a raffish assortment of friends from sports and gambling circles.

His temperamental opposite, Helmut Krone was a first-generation German-American, the son of a shoemaker and a seamstress. He was stereotypically methodical and sober, always with his nose to his drawing board, never happy with the results. "A German son is always wrong until he's proved himself to be right," said Krone. "You tend to rework things and believe they're never good enough, because, after all, you're a 'know-nothing.'" For the VW magazine layout he and Koenig chose a conventional format of filling the page with two-thirds picture, one-third copy, with a headline in between. Certain details helped produce the feeling of simplicity and candor they wanted for the product: the picture would be "naked-looking, not full and lush" and the copy would be in an austere sans serif typeface with "widows," incomplete lines at the ends of paragraphs, to avoid symmetrically solid blocks of print. "I wanted the copy to look Gertrude Steiny," Krone explained.

For the most celebrated ad in this first series, Koenig bounced off a famous wall poster of the big-thinking 1950s. "Think small," said the headline. "Ten years ago, the first Volkswagens were imported into the United States," the copy went on. "These strange little cars with their beetle shapes were almost unknown. All they had to recommend them was 32 miles to the gallon (regular gas, regular driving), an aluminum air-cooled rear engine that would go 70 mph all day without strain, sensible size for a family and a sensible price-tag too. Beetles multiply; so do Volkswagens." Above the head and copy was an ocean of white space and a modest photo of the product. Seen against other car advertising of the time, the ad was as odd as the car. Another Koenig-Krone effort was even odder: "Lemon," said the headline, beneath a photo of an apparently acceptable VW. "This Volkswagen missed the boat. The chrome strip on the glove compartment is blemished and must be replaced. . . . We pluck the lemons; you get the plums." Instead of superlatives and subtle promises of virility and romance, the VW ads disarmingly admitted failings and gave facts in straightforward prose, sometimes with a "klitchik" at the end to sum up the case and leave the reader smiling ("It doesn't go in one year and out the other").

The campaign passed on to other creative teams, but the style of candor and mild iconoclasm remained its hallmarks. "Don't forget anti-freeze!" warned an ad in the winter of 1962. "Presented by Volkswagen dealers as a public service to people who don't own cars with air-cooled engines." Another recalled DDB's "SNIAGRAB" parody for Ohrbach's: a picture of the eight body styles VW was then making with the headline, "Volkswagen builds strong bodies 8 ways." ("I had to steal," the copywriter, John Noble, admitted. "But like Robin Hood, it didn't bother me that much. I was stealing only from the rich, Wonder Bread.")

As many observers pointed out, the campaign enjoyed the advantage of presenting a unique product of high quality. The ad-makers for once did not have to scratch around for product differences to mention. Even as daring a step as quoting the price seemed obvious when it so far undersold the Detroit competition. And DDB stopped short of total candor: no VW ad ever discussed head and shoulder room, or safety in a front-end crash. Still, in the context of the time, it was an honest ad for an honest car.

For the agency, and for the oncoming creative revolution, the Volkswagen campaign was the breakthrough. "It got so I didn't want to tell anyone outside the agency I worked on Volkswagen," John Noble recalled. "At parties they treated you as though you'd written a great novel. I felt, enough already, let's talk about something else." It was easily the most admired, most influential campaign of the early 1960s, bringing the DDB style its first truly national attention. Other agencies asked their creative departments for imitations. "In a class by itself," William Tyler, *Ad Age*'s resident critic, concluded in 1965. "It stands alone, and thus beyond critical comparisons." For years it exercised incalculable power over the collective creative unconscious of the business. In 1976 *Ad Age* asked a panel of industry professionals to name the best ads they had ever seen; Volkswagen was listed by sixty of the ninety-seven replies.

It seemed a harbinger when, in the fall of 1962, the Avis car-rental company shifted its $1.5 million account from McCann-Erickson, a hot shop in the 1950s, to DDB. Another company with a selling problem, Avis was losing money and falling farther behind Hertz. For the first ad Helmut Krone turned his Volkswagen design inside out. Instead of a small headline under a big picture, he plastered a loud headline across the top of the page—not in the middle—with a modest picture and prominent copy. "It was *not* inspired," Krone said later. "It was a mathematical solution. I made everything that was big, small, and everything that was small, big."

For the copy, though, Paula Green repeated the Volkswagen idiom of candor and self-deprecating humor. "Avis is only No. 2 in rent a cars. So why go with us?" the headline led off. "We try harder. (When you're not the biggest, you have to.) . . . we can't afford to take you for granted. Go with us next time. The line at our counter is shorter." Before approaching the client, Bernbach submitted the ad to a consumer panel for testing. It scored miserably. Americans, it seemed, only liked to associate with a winner. Bernbach sold it to the client anyway: the Avis management had agreed to run whatever he recommended.

In two years Avis increased its share of the market by 28 percent. The billing jumped to $3.5 million and then to $5 million. "We try harder" entered the language and sprouted on lapel buttons. As with Volkswagen, the campaign acquired new creative teams but kept the same spirit. "Avis can't afford television commercials. Aren't you glad?" asked an ad written by Ed Vellanti. "But business is getting better. Maybe soon, you won't be so lucky." Another copywriter, David Herzbrun, rented an Avis car and found the ashtray full of butts. His next copy told all: "I write Avis ads for a living. But that doesn't make me a paid liar. . . . If I'm going to continue writing these ads, Avis had better live up to them. Or they can get themselves a new boy." The campaign did in fact raise the client's standards for itself. It required Avis to become a first-rate company, "and this is tough to do when you really aren't a first-rate company," the Avis president admitted with DDB-like forthrightness. "Our problem today is how to continue to deliver up to the implications of our advertising."

Volkswagen and Avis brought DDB out of the small-account category. In one year it took three accounts—American Airlines, Seagram, and International Silver—away from Young & Rubicam. (At an AAAA panel in 1963, Bernbach and George Gribbin of Y & R accused each other of conducting client and talent raids.) Big-ticket business kept flowing toward DDB: Heinz, Sony, Uniroyal, Lever, Gillette, Bristol-Myers. For Mobil the agency did one of the most quoted ads of the 1960s: under a photo of a nuzzling couple driving down the highway, the headline "Till death us do part," with copy by Bob Levenson ("It may be beautiful to die for love in a poem. But it's ugly and stupid to die for love in a car"). In 1965 DDB nudged into the top ten with $130 million in U.S. billings. It still dominated the awards for art and copy and won industry polls as the best agency.

With his children grown, Bernbach finally moved in town from Brooklyn, to an apartment in the UN Plaza. But he held DDB to its idiosyncratic, winning ways. "We may not be meant for each other," the agency warned the California Avocado Board in soliciting its account. "We are known to try new and unusual things." DDB then withdrew before the final decision. Another time, a copywriter had the temperamental Bobby Fischer signed and delivered to endorse a Sony radio—but Bernbach vetoed it, explaining that "I think it's wrong to work with someone so selfish and ill-mannered."

Meantime David Ogilvy was taking *his* creative shop into the top ten with an oil account, a book, and a merger. In 1960 Shell left J. Walter Thompson and came to Ogilvy with its billing of $12.5

million, thus raising the agency's total by almost 50 percent. A
branch office was opened in Toronto to handle the account in Canada. The campaign started with dense, reason-why newspaper
copy—"Shell recommends 21 ways to make your car last longer"—
and with modest illustrations and no visual gimmicks. At Shell's
suggestion, the agency worked for a fee instead of the usual 15 percent commission on billings. The fee amounted to the actual cost of
operating the account, plus 25 percent, and approximated the current industry norm of 1 percent net on billings. In the next few years
other OB & M clients, including Sears, KLM, American Express,
and IBM, also adopted the fee arrangement. To its advocates the
method put the agency-client relation on a more professional basis,
like that of an attorney or physician, with payment for actual work
done instead of depending on what the agent could persuade the client to spend on the media budget. "The commission system is an
anachronism," Ogilvy declared.

In the summer of 1962, perhaps impressed by the success of *Reality
in Advertising* by his ancient rival Rosser Reeves, Ogilvy spent his vacation writing a book. As he set down his lists and theories of advertising, sprinkling the narrative with anecdotes, he kept bursting out
laughing. "It will probably be too indiscreet to publish," he told an
associate at the agency, "but the catharsis is doing me good. Fourteen years of discretion (humbug) have almost destroyed my soul."
He did, alas, remove the juicier client stories before sending the
manuscript to his publisher. He expected the book to sell 5,000
copies. With a final edit by the novelist Stephen Becker, and promoted by Atheneum salesmen wearing eye patches, in five years it
sold over 400,000 copies in hardcover and paperback, the best-selling advertising book ever. (Twenty years later, after a million copies,
it was still in print.)

Confessions of an Advertising Man offered ten crisp how-to-do-it chapters (on managing an agency, getting and keeping clients, writing
potent copy, and so on), with final reflections on the question
"Should Advertising Be Abolished?" The tone—iconoclastic, self-
mocking, apparently ingenuous—softened the prescriptiveness of
the message. In no fewer than sixteen lists, Ogilvy outlined a definite, specific catechism for the novitiate. At last resolving his struggle with the two schools of advertising, he came down in favor of the
claim. "I have never admired the *belles lettres* school of advertising,"
he wrote, citing "The Penalty of Leadership" and "Somewhere West

of Laramie." "I have always thought them absurd; they did not give the reader a single *fact*." He also recorded his disapproval of Rubicam's "The Priceless Ingredient." As to the best copywriters the business had seen, "In a class by himself stands Claude Hopkins. . . . By today's standards, Hopkins was an unscrupulous barbarian, but technically he was the supreme master." Ogilvy listed Rubicam second, a seeming non sequitur. "You are Claude Hopkins," Rubicam told him after receiving the book, "enriched with an intellect and an Oxford education."

The book helped attract new business—domestic billings went from $58.5 to $77 million in 1964—and made Ogilvy the only advertising man with a substantial reputation outside the trade. By now he wrote little copy, though he kept his office on the copywriters' floor and tried to stay in touch. Describing himself as "an almost extinct volcano," he still loved to read in the press "about what a good copywriter I am." In his early fifties, he found the ad business less and less appealing. He bought another farm among the Amish, then in 1967 his French chateau. From these distant vantage points, he said, "I have developed an almost uncontrollable distaste for my job: the paper, the unappreciative clients, the perpetual firefighting, the humbug."

In 1964 his agency merged with Mather & Crowther, one of its London-based parent companies, to form Ogilvy & Mather, with Ogilvy as chairman and chief executive. (His brother Francis, chairman of Mather & Crowther, had died eight months before the merger.) By this symbolic act of the son and brother absorbing the father, the new organization, with combined billings of $130 million, became one of the top ten agencies worldwide. "We felt it would be tremendous fun to go into Europe," said Ogilvy. "If God is on the side of the big battalion—and that seems to be the case—the path of wisdom lies in becoming one of the big battalions."

Leo Burnett, already one of the big battalions, had now been joined by the two other creative shops of the 1950s in the upper reaches of the billings race. The three had long admired each other's work (though Ogilvy in his Hopkins moods was not sure about Bernbach's use of humor and short copy). "I guess half of my 'Ads Worth Saving' file," Burnett wrote Ogilvy, "is composed of tearsheets of ads from your shop and Bill Bernbach's. If I weren't getting so darned old, I think I would probably start my own agency." The three also commanded the respect of their creative peers in the trade. The Copywriters Hall of Fame, started in New York in 1961, admitted one new member each year; the first four inductees were Burnett, George Gribbin, Ogilvy ("I detest awards except when I win one"), and Bernbach.

Now, in the mid-1960s, as the cycle of advertising history turned once again, their influence reached beyond the creative cells into the entire industry. The creative revolution, a phrase that appeared in 1965, drew from all three agencies. From Burnett came a tradition of gentle manners, humor, credibility, and a disdain for research. From Ogilvy, a civilized intelligence, a classiness that spoke up instead of down to the audience, and the visual style of Hathaway, Schweppes, and Rolls-Royce. From Bernbach, the creative union of art and copy, candor, the reduction of the account executive, and a looser management style. From all three, the most vital ingredient: people. With creativity the fashion of the hour, employees of these three agencies found themselves quite portable, able to move to other employers at better pay with more responsibility. The most daring split off to start their own shops, as the business entered a round of agency founding. Small "boutique" operations, specialized and determinedly creative, opened overnight in hotels and suitcases, and sometimes disappeared as fast. "I feel like an old grandmother," Phyllis Robinson remarked. "I've got all these offspring all over the place."

The forerunner of this decade's hot creative shop had been established in 1960, when Fred Papert, an account man fired by Kenyon & Eckhardt, talked Julian Koenig and George Lois of DDB into starting their own agency. In his one year at DDB Lois had won art awards for three campaigns. He was a New York street kid, a basketball junkie, explosive and profane. ("The only thing wrong with you, George," Bernbach told him, "is that your mind is in the gutter.") He had grown up in the Kingsbridge section of the Bronx, the only Greek family in an Irish neighborhood, in a third-floor apartment redolent with incense and Greek cooking. After two years at the Pratt Art Institute he started in advertising, changing jobs frequently. At DDB he found a mentor in Bernbach. "He personally revolutionized the alphabet of advertising," Lois said later. "He was a sensitive teacher and a bold leader, a man whose impact on my life is retained with respect and love."

Papert, Koenig, Lois thus was set up like a miniature DDB: art and copy teams, no plans board, few meetings, little respect for research or peripheral services, the primacy of the ad itself. Lois held his meetings walking down the hall. "You meet the other guy," he explained, "and just say blah, blah and work it out—you don't have to have a meeting or write a memo." PKL's ads also reflected the DDB style. Koenig and Lois presented a tomato being propositioned by a bottle of Wolfschmidt vodka: "You're some tomato. We could make some beautiful Bloody Marys together." A week later, the faithless bottle approached an orange: "You sweet doll, I appreciate you. I've got taste. I'll make you famous. Kiss me!" "Who was that tomato I saw you with last week?" the orange asked. To demonstrate the simplicity of operating a Xerox machine, a PKL TV commercial showed a chimpanzee making copies. A TV spot for Allerest asked, "Cat make you sneeze?" An Allerest bottle then flipped and, implausibly, sneezed.

Like Ogilvy & Mather and its fee system, PKL also held no reverence for the industry's traditional business arrangements. In 1962, with billings up to $17 million, the agency "went public" by selling stock to general shareholders, thus offending the usual view that regarded advertising as a personal-service business to be owned by its practitioners. "The concept of public ownership puts us on a par with any company that produces a product," said Lois. "The image of our business no longer has to be that of shufflers who make money because they have a slick line of talk. No pride, just talk." Older hands shook their heads. "I wouldn't want to be part of an agency that owed its primary obligation to stockholders," warned Fairfax Cone. Sixteen months later Foote, Cone & Belding also went public, followed by DDB in 1964 ("If this is the way to attract and hold good people," said Mac Dane, "you do it"), Grey in 1965, Ogilvy & Mather in 1966, and others—finally even Thompson in 1969. Public ownership made more cash available for diversification and investments and forced agencies under stockholder scrutiny to run tighter ships internally.

Multiply innovative, PKL was the first really successful new agency since Bernbach and Ogilvy had started in the late 1940s. By 1964 billings were up to $30 million and its stock had doubled from six to twelve dollars a share. With the bristly Lois setting the tone, clients were told what to do. "I make decisions on the basis of what will improve a client's sales," Lois jabbed, "not what he thinks he likes." At Madison Avenue watering holes, people told PKL stories about fistfights and pissing on a client's rug. One copywriter later sued the agency, claiming "an atmosphere of physical violence" had kept him from doing his work there. The place was known as Stillman's East, after the West Side boxing gym.

In imitation of PKL—if not in *every* respect—other new agencies sprang up. Carl Ally left PKL in 1962 and opened for business with the $1 million Volvo account. A man with "the humility of a professional lion tamer," according to *Ad Age*, Ally took on the besieged Hertz account and broke from another industry tradition, the taboo against comparative advertising. In pushing Avis, DDB had referred obliquely to the competition without calling it by name. The Ally approach, with copy by Jim Durfee and art by Amil Gargano, was more direct: "For years, Avis has been telling you Hertz is No. 1. Now we're going to tell you why." "If you were in the car rental business and you were No. 2 and you had only half as many cars to offer and about half as many locations at which to offer them, and fewer people to handle everything, what would you say in your advertising? Right. Your ashtrays are cleaner." Hertz's share of the market, down from 55 percent to 45 percent under the Avis onslaught, in six months recovered to 50 percent.

Even the old guard had to respect figures like that. The ads grew ever more daring and sacrilegious: the Statue of Liberty modeling a Talon zipper; Gunilla Knutson urging "Take it all off" for Noxzema on TV, with stripper music in the background. The hinterlands were also being heard from. In Los Angeles Stan Freberg turned out funny ads for Pacific Airlines and Chun King, and Janet Marie Carlson did revealing work for Cole bathing suits. In San Francisco Howard Gossage's agency wrote well-crafted copy for Rover cars, the Sierra Club, and Beethoven sweat shirts—and helped foist Marshall McLuhan on America. "This business has really gone crazy," Fairfax Cone confided to Leo Burnett.

❦❦

Advertising humor, ca. 1965: The receptionist at the following agencies answers the phone in this way:

"Hello Ted Bates, Hello Ted Bates, Hello Ted Bates."

"DDB, *guten Morgen,* what can we do for you?"

"Papert, Koenig, Lois. Fuck you!"

❦❦

As the cycle turned, the two dominant admen of the 1950s found the new fashions uncongenial.

A hot shop earlier, the Ted Bates agency under the direction of Rosser Reeves stumbled in the new decade. Some of the best Bates accounts—Colgate Dental Cream, Viceroy, Wildroot hair oil, Carter's Little Liver Pills, Super Anahist—were selling badly. "I think some of these problems are largely creative," Ted Bates concluded. "This will require some of the old Reeves genius in spades." Late in 1961 Reeves gave up his administrative tasks as chairman and chief executive officer to return to full-time copy. Observers soon noticed a "higher tone" in Bates efforts, with less use of the pitchman in TV spots, and an M & M commercial with a new jingle and improved production values. Bates billings nonetheless declined by $4.2 million in 1962, down to $145.8 million in the U.S.

Reeves was a proud man, committed to his USP and the dangers of too much originality. "Temporary trends do not change principles," he declared. He half-jokingly threatened to fire anyone at Bates who won a creative award for his work. At his induction into the Copywriters Hall of Fame in 1965, he suggested an award for ads that moved the product well. "It's terribly easy," he said, "for copywriters to lose sight of our one objective—which is sales." Yet by his own standard, Bates was struggling, up only $1.5 million that year. In January 1966 the agency lost the $8.5 million Mobil account to DDB, the very symbol of the creative revolution that Reeves disdained. A month later he astonished the industry by resigning, explaining that he had always wanted to retire at age fifty-five and hoped to find serenity.

Later in 1966 the effect of his departure was obvious: a Playtex girdle commercial with a woman in a slinky black evening gown walking her black panther on a city street. "Tames your figure like nothing else," said the announcer. Jeremy Gury, Reeves' successor as creative director, defined the new Bates as "a businessman's creative agency" that had overcome inflexibility: "We present the selling proposition in a sympathetic, empathetic way that involves people." "The world has changed," a Bates copy supervisor elaborated. "Now we don't hit the mule with a hammer to get his attention; sometimes we tickle him." Bates briefly employed Jerry Della Femina, a contentious young copywriter of some reputation, in an effort to improve its creative image.

If Bates could go creative, then Interpublic could rethink its giantism. In the early 1960s Marion Harper bought up agencies in the United States and abroad at a rate of better than one a month. After gobbling Erwin, Wasey, Ruthrauff & Ryan, with its $83.5 million in

billings, he finally leaped over Thompson into first place in worldwide billings. But it was growth by purchase, not by attracting new
clients and billings. Harper's horizontal affiliate system, whereby
different divisions under the Interpublic umbrella might work for
competing products, had clients worried about leaks within the organization. Nestlé took its business from McCann-Erickson in 1964
after the purchase of Erwin, Wasey brought Carnation into the family. "Bigness is an evil," a Nestlé man explained, "that strains relationships which ten years ago were very warm and close." A year
later Continental Airlines also quit McCann, citing the potential
competition of the Braniff account handled by Interpublic's Jack
Tinker Partners. Interpublic made gestures toward the new creativity: Harper hired Marvin Corwin away from DDB to head Erwin,
Wasey, and—with a nod toward Leo Burnett—McCann installed a
tiger as its Esso salesman. But troubles kept piling up. The affiliate
system cost an enormous overhead. Interpublic barely broke even in
1966, and then ran a $3 million deficit and violated its agreements
with two New York banks in 1967.

   Under fire, Harper simply damned the torpedoes. "We can't support people with little thoughts or little dreams," he said. The Interpublic fleet of five airplanes, known as the Harper Air Force,
included a DC-7 for the boss, furnished in French provincial. His
suite boasted a king-size bed, private library, and a sunken bath. He
divorced his first wife and in 1963 married the woman in charge of
Interpublic's Paris-based fashion affiliate (*Ad Age* called it the Interpublic merger of the week). They were married in Miami on a Fri-
day, honeymooned in Puerto Rico over the weekend, and were back
at their respective desks on Monday.

   At its peak Harper's empire included 24 divisions, 8,300 employees, and world billings of $711 million, heading toward the billion-
dollar General Motors of advertising he had once projected. He still
ran everything himself, passing on all major decisions. The company
simply outgrew such detailed supervision. Swallowed by his own
creation, Harper lost touch with reality and allowed some question-
able practices. He concealed his ownership of a data-processing
company, John Felix Associates; both Interpublic and the company
denied the rumors of a connection while Felix undertook confiden-
tial work for such competitors as Bates, Grey, Ogilvy & Mather, and
Foote, Cone & Belding.

   In 1967 Harper brought his former associate Robert Healy out of retirement to help sort out his financial snarls. Healy negotiated a $10.2 million lifesaving loan from Chase Manhattan. But the bank added a condition: Harper had to go. A directors' meeting in November heard a motion to replace him. With Harper abstaining, everyone else voted against him. "We see him," an Interpublic man said afterward, "as a genius with one glaring weakness: little sense of people." "We're not General Motors," said another, "and a concept of structure that suits General Motors, with its wide profit margins and unlimited potential, doesn't necessarily suit us." Healy started dismantling the empire. In two months over nine hundred employees were fired. Through pruning and grafting, the twenty-four divisions became five. Regional offices were given more autonomy. McCann-Erickson was broken into "collaboratives" with despecialized functions. Interpublic started making a profit again. As Healy by degrees turned the situation around, his steps repeated in ironic fashion the organizational message of the creative revolution: back to the little unit.

(The Harper saga grew weirder and weirder. In 1970 he joined with Ron Rosenfeld and Len Sirowitz of DDB in a creative boutique agency. "Just us kids," said Harper. "We will have the first agency that's small on purpose. . . . I passed through the other phase to come to this." Five months later his partners fired him, claiming he was inaccessible and autocratic. The IRS said he owed over a half-million dollars in back taxes; an investment scheme left him owing another million. With two law-enforcement agencies after him, he dropped out of sight in 1973. For years his lawyer in New York and his wife in London had no word from him. In 1979 *Ad Age* sent a reporter to Oklahoma City to interview his mother. The reporter was sitting in her living room when Marion Harper walked in. He lived nearby, he said, and he was broke.)

Mary Wells made the most money from the creative revolution. Schooled in copy at DDB, in management at Interpublic, she was the richest, most celebrated woman in the history of the business. She was born in Youngstown, Ohio, in 1929. At eighteen she first came to New York to be an actress. Instead she married Bert Wells, later an art director at Ogilvy & Mather, and started writing retail ads for Macy's. She spent seven years at DDB, rising to be an associate copy chief and head of new-products development. "A fantastic education," she said of that period. "Everyone cared only about how effective an ad was. No one drank. There were no aspiring novelists hiding out. No one did anything but work." She was called Bunny Wells then, a pretty, stylish woman with a sense of direction, short brown hair and large brown eyes. She attracted attention with her copy for the French tourist office ("The Basque and his beret are never separated") and a Warner's girdle ("Slip into something comfortable and take two inches off your waistline"). "She moved like a swan among brass and clients," George Lois recalled. "You could tell that Mary Wells would never end up with wrinkles in a writer's tower."

In 1963 Harper paid her a $60,000 salary to move over to Jack Tinker Partners. Now a blonde and divorced, she helped transform Tinker from a think tank into a functioning creative shop. For its major account, Alka-Seltzer, under her supervision Dick Rich and Stewart Greene did a famous campaign with variations on the theme "No matter what shape your stomach's in." (The TV jingle, by a songwriter named Sascha Burland, became a hit record that reached number thirteen on the *Billboard* chart; Howard Zieff, later a Hollywood cinematographer, shot the commercials.) For a rather obscure airline, Braniff—"I thought it was a town in Canada," said Greene—Wells put the stewardesses in Pucci outfits and painted the planes pastel shades. She was the rising star in the place, "the blond girl who jumps out of cakes," as she later put it. When Tinker had a heart attack she expected to succeed him as president. Harper was agreeable, but two partners, Myron MacDonald and Herta Herzog, threatened to resign rather than work for her. So MacDonald got the presidency instead.

A few months later Wells, Rich, and Greene left with the $6 million Braniff account and started their own agency. Aiming to build "the most profitable agency in history with the smallest possible staff," specializing in TV, she announced that WRG would only buy peripheral agency services as needed, for the time they were needed (the lesson of Interpublic). On the creative departments she lavished half the payroll, twice the proportion at most agencies, and paid generous salaries. She then pushed her people hard, the absolute boss. "She has been known to lose arguments," an associate noted, "but very seldom and only under much stress." In creative theory she still worked in the Bernbach tradition, except in one respect: she had no training program and no interest in teaching the craft. Get your experience somewhere else, she told young recruits, and then come see us. She ran a trim operation with high profit margins and phenomenal ratios of employees to billings.

For Alka-Seltzer WRG did humorous TV spots with the recurring tag lines, "I can't believe I ate the whole thing" and "Try it—you'll like it." Their progenitors—Howard Cohen, art, and Bob Pasqualina, copy—in true creative-revolution fashion then parlayed the campaign into their own agency. The lines were endlessly quoted and parodied. "I can't believe I won the whole thing," said George McGovern in accepting the Democratic nomination for president in 1972. The spots worked, according to Wells, because they showed real people in believable situations, like the people at her agency. "We're average consumers ourselves," she said. "We're *now* people. We use Alka-Seltzer, we talk like people in the commercials, we can identify with smiley situations."

To introduce a new 100-millimeter cigarette, Benson & Hedges, Dick Rich wrote a series of TV commercials showing the disadvantages of its length: popping a balloon, burning a newspaper, getting caught in an elevator door, lighting someone's beard. As Rich explained it, he wanted a Bates campaign with a DDB feeling. "What we are saying is that they're longer than king size, over and over again. We're different from other hard-sell agencies because of our flair and theatrics. And we're different from the creative agencies because we start on tougher selling premises than they do." A claim wrapped in an image, the campaign raised the sales of the product from 1.6 billion units in 1966 to 14.4 billion four years later.

The advertising business was continually astonished by Mary Wells. Forty years old in 1969, she still looked and dressed like a high-fashion mannequin. On occasion she sounded like the *Cosmopolitan* girl, favoring words like fantastic, terrific, and nifty. At client presentations, in a room full of men, she bowled them over before even opening her mouth. Then she started talking and bowled them over again, discussing marketing problems in high "masculine" discourse. At the agency she displayed a Machiavellian command of business politics. In 1969 she quarreled with Dick Rich. Rich departed, and she emerged with a new contract that made her, at $250,000 a year, the highest-paid executive in advertising. She lived a glamorous, jet-setting life with her second husband, Harding Lawrence, the head of Braniff, as they divided their time among homes in Dallas, Arizona, Acapulco, the East Side of Manhattan, and the French Riviera. (Shortly after the marriage, she had dropped the $10 million Braniff account to take TWA's $14.6 million business.)

"We are the agency of today," she said. In only five years, WRG reached $100 million in U.S. billings, the fastest growth record in advertising history. "I'm in excellent health," she said in 1969 as the youngest member of the Copywriters Hall of Fame, "and I've got impact you haven't felt yet. So don't relax."

❦❦

Powered mainly by an internal dynamic within the business, in the late 1960s the creative revolution crossed paths with an external context, the youth movements of the day. The two had in common a lack of historical memory, a disdain for authority, a visual orientation, and a way of making rules *ad hoc*. "Just as the hippies and the kids and the Negroes were now beginning to raise hell with the country," declared an advertising novel by Edward Hannibal, a former copywriter, "shaking up all the old farts and making them doubt themselves, advertising as a business was getting noise from the furnace room that it couldn't shut off any longer." The postwar baby boom was maturing, leaving unsettled campuses and seeking jobs on Madison Avenue. These young people did not leave their disrespectful notions in school; some hoped to make the creative revolution serve the larger Revolution. They were the first advertising generation raised on movies and TV, not books and magazines. "They are visual thinkers and nonreaders, for the most part," noted the poet L. E. Sissman, who wrote copy for Kenyon & Eckhardt in Boston. "Because of their lack of traditional cultural roots, they are exceedingly trend-conscious, exceedingly anxious to be with it."

They stood out if only by their hair and dress. "My God," said one executive in 1967, back in the business after four years away, "do you let clients see them?" At DDB Mac Dane circulated a memo suggesting that beards be trimmed, and that nonconformity might take a more creative mode than not wearing a shirt and necktie. "We've had some weird-looking people," Bernbach conceded in his tolerant way. "If they do the job, we hire them." At other agencies clients were taken on pointed tours of the creative departments, to see the miniskirts and jeans, to smell the incense and other suspicious odors, as though to prove how daring and *au courant* the shop was. "Obviously, pink shirts are more creative than white shirts," said Draper Daniels. "Paisley shirts are more creative than pink shirts. A blue denim shirt, or no shirt at all, is the ultimate in creativity. Beads or a locket are a sure sign of something close to genius."

These bemused reactions, along with the determined voguishness that provoked them, again revealed advertising as more a mirror than a creator of American mores. The youthquake came late to Madison Avenue, years after it bubbled up from the streets and schools. Three years after the San Francisco Summer of Love of 1965, Mary Wells made "Love Power" her slogan at WRG: "Everybody could use a little extra love these days." With the sexual revolution well under way, Phyllis Robinson dared sell a hair product with an "It lets me be me" pitch, hinting at a sex life for the young woman, against a backdrop of young clothes and rock music. In 1968, while young executives in Westport and Scarsdale were turning on, an advertising trade journal bravely ran a piece by "an adman head" about his professional use of marijuana ("It's a better way to think. . . . Grass makes for much freer association. You get twenty ideas instead of two in the same time"—though you did have to reexamine the ideas with a straight mind the next morning.)

For both the creative and youth revolutions, the pendulum was reaching the limit of its swing. During the first seven months of 1969, nearly one hundred new agencies were launched. Most of them quickly disappeared. So many creative awards were being given out by so many bodies that they lost any meaning. Ron Rosenfeld and Len Sirowitz each could claim over one hundred awards, too many for any wall. Leo Burnett withdrew from further competitions, preferring to invest the entry money in training programs. By the time *Newsweek* got around to putting the creative revolution on its cover, in August 1969, it was stale news.

As the decade ended, William Bernbach and Rosser Reeves found themselves in unlikely agreement. "I worry about everyone trying to be different for the sake of being different," said Bernbach. "Young people coming in and mistaking the facade for the real thing." "During the 1970s, I predict that the advertising narcissists will wake up," said Reeves. "Big business will return to the immutable advertising law that the agency must make the *product* interesting, and not just the advertisement itself."

SEVEN

REAL REFORM: NEW IMAGES IN THE MIRROR

n less than a decade the creative revolution gathered, prospered, and then inevitably cycled away. Nothing is more fragile than an advertising fashion. But the temporary creative revolution left behind more permanent changes in the advertising business. External events forced certain issues with long histories on Madison Avenue to surface and compel serious attention for the first time.

At the height of its powers, in the 1920s, advertising had been a primary, independent force in the molding of American culture and mores. Given a heady mix of general prosperity, a pliant consumer, an agreeable government, and an unprecedented flood of new products, Madison Avenue sold its materialist visions without hindrance. Since the 1920s, as all these circumstances changed in unfavorable ways, advertising had increasingly functioned more as mirror than mindbender, responding to American culture more than shaping it.

During the 1960s this diminished influence seemed especially obvious. The reform waves sweeping down Madison Avenue, aside from the creative revolution itself, derived less from internal dynamics within the business, more from changes in society at large. Advertising—which sometimes claimed to foreshadow and direct social change—actually lagged behind the general course of events. The advertising mirror itself, the reflective devices that the trade held up to Americans, remained stable, with the usual cyclical adjustments. What changed was American society and culture, the objects in front of the mirror. Slowly, stubbornly, the mirrored image changed too. But the time lag remained. Advertising never quite caught up.

⚜⚜

First and most enduringly, the creative revolution was also an ethnic revolution. The WASP hegemony over American culture finally broke down after decades of small losses. Madison Avenue then followed suit.

Back at the turn of the century, in the early, fluid days before advertising became big business—with the ethnic patterns of big business—Albert Lasker could rise to dominance even as a self-conscious Jew. His most celebrated copywriters at Lord & Thomas were still gentiles like John Kennedy, Claude Hopkins, and Frank Hummert. Gradually Lasker filled the top management positions at L & T with Jews—his son Edward, Sheldon Coons, David Noyes, William Sachse—whose names were less known in the trade but who wielded more real power at the agency. Outside their offices sat their Irish secretaries all in a row, Hannigan, Horrigan, Kerrigan, Finnegan, and Mulrooney. By the 1930s Don Francisco was the only non-Jew left on the L & T management committee. Occasionally Lasker would flex his advertising muscle on behalf of Jewish interests. In 1942, after the *Saturday Evening Post* ran an article entitled "The Case Against the Jew," Lasker obtained a retraction and apology from the *Post* by threatening to withdraw his ad contracts.

A few other agencies were known as Jewish shops, even if (like L & T) they did not bear Jewish names. Lawrence Valenstein opened an art studio in New York in 1917; after advertising assignments he turned it into an agency named Grey, from the color of the office walls. At first Grey Advertising specialized in drawing up monthly sales plans for department stores. From this base in retailing—a Jewish stronghold in New York—Valenstein and his associates Arthur Fatt and Herbert Strauss acquired the *Good Housekeeping* and Mennen accounts and built Grey up to general agency status.

But these were exceptions. From the 1920s through the 1950s, the major agencies like Thompson, BBDO, Young & Rubicam, Ayer, and McCann-Erickson were all known as WASP preserves, with some Jews in the creative departments but hardly any in management. In the early 1940s Charles Feldman and the gentile George Gribbin were regarded as the best copywriters at Y & R. "Since Charlie was Jewish," Draper Daniels recalled, "everyone assumed that Grib would become creative director eventually." And in fact Feldman was passed over in favor of Gribbin. Some clients, such as Lawrence Jones of Four Roses whiskey, insisted that no Jews work on their accounts. Meantime the Jewish agencies themselves were losing ground. When Lasker liquidated his interest in L & T he turned the agency over to three gentiles. In 1950 Grey Advertising ranked only twenty-eighth on *Advertising Age*'s list of the biggest shops. In 1956 the Biow Company, the largest agency run by a Jew, collapsed and went out of business.

During these years advertising thus trailed behind related fields in admitting Jews to positions of high authority and visibility. After Lasker and before the 1960s, advertising produced nobody who compared with such Jews as Swope and Guggenheim in industry; Goldwyn and Mayer in the movies; Sarnoff and Paley in broadcasting; Gimbel, Straus, and Bloomingdale in retailing; and Ochs, Meyer, and Schiff in newspaper publishing. As an avenue of mobility for Jews, advertising most resembled politics, in which—outside New York and a few other ethnic centers—only deracinated Jews could make much progress at this time. Advertising and politicians both submitted their wares to a touchy American public that might render its verdict based on the most irrational, irrelevant criteria. Better not to complicate the matter, so the argument ran, with ethnic distractions. Even if Jews helped prepare an ad, it was still pitched at a mythological middle America: a land of WASPs, white bread, and old-fashioned values.

Other ethnic minorities ran into similar problems on Madison Avenue. Ben Duffy and his assistants formed an atypical Irish Catholic enclave at BBDO that was not duplicated at the other big agencies. Tom Carnese at Ted Bates and the Toigo cousins, Adolph at Lennen & Newell and John at Biow-Beirn-Toigo, were among the few Italians to break into top management. John Toigo, from a coal-mining town in southern Illinois by way of the University of Chicago, considered his unusual background an ideal training for advertising. "We all have the same viewpoint," he explained, "all skeptical and analytical. You get that in a foreign-born home; it comes from living in two cultures at once. What's true at home doesn't make sense in school, and vice versa. You learn that truth is relative and depends on the viewpoint." But a typical advertising executive in this era sprang from an old-stock, Ivy League family in the Northeast. The club door was ajar, but just barely.

George Panetta, the son of a tailor, grew up in the Italian Mulberry Street neighborhood of New York and managed two years of college at CCNY. As a copywriter for various agencies he bucked the prevailing ethnic attitudes for a dozen years and finally unburdened himself in a novel, *Viva Madison Avenue!*, published in 1957. The narrator of the novel, George Caputo, and his buddy Joe Caruso were the only Democrats and "real" Italians at a WASP agency on "the street of the Anglo-Saxons, the great ad men." Of the two other Italians at the agency, one only acted ethnic around Caputo and Caruso, and the other told people he was part Indian and hoped to gain a vice-presidency. The dominant Anglo-Saxons seemed quite strange to Caputo and Caruso. "They look like humans, but take a long look and you'll know they're different; they're something better. They walk with their heads in the sky, not looking at anybody, just up and ahead," thinking about headlines and money. They were tall and fair, well spoken and well dressed ("no matter what we wear, we always look as if we just got off the boat"). They married only to reproduce themselves and thought nothing of going celibate for a week. "The Anglo-Saxons have very little blood, and when they don't go to bed with their wives, they make up for it by going to musical comedies, or, if there's snow in Vermont, by going skiing." They had no feelings except at Christmas, when they managed to smile at the Italians. "On Christmas if anybody was lucky enough to die, he'd have all the Anglo-Saxons at the wake, looking sorry the best they could." At the end of the novel, after losing big money to the Anglo-Saxons over the 1956 elections, Caputo and Caruso walked home along Madison Avenue, feeling more scared and small than ever. "But we're not so small that we're giving up. The Anglo-Saxons owe us something. We don't know what it is, but it's something big—America, maybe—and me and Joe, scared as we are, are determined to get it." (Panetta soon quit the business to write novels and plays full-time.)

Doyle Dane Bernbach drove the first real wedge into this serene WASP complacency. DDB came out of Grey, a Jewish agency. Bernbach and most of his early creative people were Jews. His most noted early accounts—Ohrbach's, Levy's, El Al—were Jewish clients. The atmosphere at DDB partook more of the Art Students League and the Seventh Avenue garment district than of the Ivy League and Greenwich. Most important, DDB produced ads that were unabashedly, recognizably Jewish in style and attitude. Ohrbach's, Levy's, and El Al, and later Volkswagen and Avis, were all little guys: plucky, struggling newcomers standing up to the bigger, privileged competition, using their wits and humor to avoid being squashed. The funny ads provoked smiles in the characteristically Jewish fashion of self-deprecation from strength, an oi-the-sky-is-falling-but-we-must-do-our-best feistiness. The "klitchik" at the end, a punning, ironic final line, also derived from traditional Jewish humor. As Fairfax Cone noted, Bernbach at first was regarded as "only another stand-up comedian, moved over from the night-clubs," a Jack E. Leonard transplanted from the borscht circuit. After VW and Avis, DDB was taken more seriously. Even gentiles started writing ads in a wry, colloquial, slightly apologetic idiom of folksy sophistication. If it was true that Anglo-Saxons had no feel-ings (except at Christmas), then advertising had to acquire a warmer, friendlier, more candid tone from elsewhere.

American society was at last ready for more cultural diversity. In 1960 an Irish Catholic was elected president of the United States. The gentile novelists, southerners and proletarians, who had dom-inated American fiction for decades gave way to platoons of Jewish writers: Bellow, Salinger, Mailer, Wouk, Malamud, Singer, Roth, and others. As the civil rights movement became the most pressing domestic issue, black athletes took more of the starring roles in pro-fessional sports, and black-derived musical forms and dances drew the attention of white adolescents. Jewish critics, mainly in New York, enjoyed a growing influence as arbiters of American intellec-tual life. Even the Ivy League included two Jewish college presi-dents.

The creative revolution, the newly mirrored image on Madison Avenue, thus consisted essentially of Jewish copywriters and Italian art directors, producing ads from their own ethnic traditions. Clients accepted the new approaches because they sold well. "I found that you overcome all prejudice by making money for someone," Bern-bach said later. "I just happened to have had a lot of Italians and Jews on my creative staff, and when business saw that what they did worked, business wanted them, too." Charles Piccirillo (DDB), Gene Federico (Benton & Bowles), Sam Scali (Papert, Koenig, Lois), Amil Gargano (Ally), Onofrio Paccione (Grey, then Leber Katz Pac-cione), and Stan Dragoti (Wells, Rich, Greene) were only the best known of the Italian art directors. In 1964 a photo service ran a trade ad featuring sixteen Italian art directors, announcing a special discount to anyone of the blood for that week. (After a protest by Jewish art directors, the photo service extended the discount to *all* art directors.) "It doesn't hurt to be born Italian or Jewish in the streets of the City of New York," said Jerry Della Femina, a stray

Italian copywriter. "You can't buy the experience. The copywriter is in disgrace today if he was born in a suburb of Boston, of a fairly well-to-do family." Grey burst into the top ten in 1966, adding $42.5 million in billings during the first six months of the year, claiming a client roster that included four of the five largest advertisers in the country.

The Jews and Italians in turn broke down the barriers for other ethnics: a Greek like George Lois, a Turk like Carl Ally. The newcomers were as liable to be graduates of Pratt Institute or CCNY—or, like Ron Rosenfeld of DDB, of no college at all—as of Yale or Dartmouth. One survey of five hundred advertising people in the medium-salaried range in the 1960s found that a third had attended college in New York; twenty years earlier, a personnel expert suggested, that figure would have been only 5–10 percent. The same trends were also overtaking the advertising business outside New York. In the 1950s Jerry Mander, the son of Jewish immigrants, had been spurned by an old-line agency in New York ("your hair is a little kinky," he was told; "you might want to try Seventh Avenue"). Now he worked as Howard Gossage's protégé in San Francisco.

In 1962 a Cuban, a Lebanese, and a Jew—the oldest of whom was thirty-five years old—launched the firm of Ferro, Mogubgub & Schwartz, to specialize in TV advertising. "That's a very unusual name," said an observer, "—Schwartz."

❧❧

Advertising humor, ca. 1960, at the height of Marion Harper's adventures with Interpublic: a rumor that Grey Advertising would merge with BBDO to form the Interfaith Group.

❧❧

In the course of delivering a speech at the AAAA spring meeting in 1961, Bill Bernbach unconsciously suggested the limits of the ethnic revolution. He told a story about the black jazzman Count Basie, illustrating the ambiguities of language, and concluded with the punchline: "Sure, sure, I said you is fired, but what you walking out for? YOU AIN'T *DAT* FIRED!" If Bernbach—a political liberal, a man of the most broadly humane impulses, the individual most responsible for opening Madison Avenue to ethnic diversity—could casually tell a nigger-dialect story, then what of the industry in general?

Here again advertising only reflected, and changed in response to, the given norms of the day. Historically blacks had appeared in ads playing roles familiar to the white majority: Aunt Jemima, the fat and swaddled black mammy; the Gold Dust twins, mischievous little pickaninnies; Cream of Wheat's chef, inevitably dubbed Rastus; Hiram Walker's butler, offering his whiskey bottle with a big smile; an occasional endorsement by a black entertainer or athlete. These ads, created by whites for white audiences, did unfortunately represent blacks as whites imagined them, extending but not inventing typical racial stereotypes. A few pioneer black admen started their own agencies, such as David Sullivan in New York (1943), Fusche, Young & Powell in Detroit (also in 1943), and Vince Cullers in Chicago (1956). They were limited to selling black products through black media to black consumers. At the major white agencies, apparently no black held a significant position until the 1950s.

If the armed forces and major league baseball could survive racial integration, then so perhaps could Madison Avenue. With the first stirrings of the modern civil rights movement as backdrop, a few agencies—notably BBDO—started "special markets" units staffed by blacks to sell to blacks. Clarence Holte, in charge of BBDO's black unit, for years somewhat quixotically urged the rest of the industry to follow his agency's example, to make Madison Avenue "a more colorful and creative place in which to work." Roy Eaton, the first highly visible black on the street, had credentials that could not be ignored: a Phi Beta Kappa and magna cum laude graduate of CCNY, a concert pianist with a master's from Yale, he had played at Town Hall in New York and been listed by *Who's Who* when, at the age of twenty-five, he was hired by Young & Rubicam in 1955 to work on TV commercials. He was the first black at Y & R, and probably the first at any major agency, with a creative function on general accounts. Later he went on to a long career as musical director at Benton & Bowles. Classically trained, Eaton could write and play the white man's music and so was not restricted to black ads and products.

Most blacks aiming for an advertising career did fall into the special-markets trap: claiming particular expertise at selling to blacks, they were then confined to that limited category. After closing his black agency in 1949, David Sullivan used up 1,200 résumés over the next fifteen years trying to break into a white agency. "Ardent interviews with ardent personnel people who are ardently sorry they cannot be helpful," he said, yielded only one "nearly firm" job offer;

one agency had kept him dangling for four years before hiring another black. "I'm sorry to hear that you are still limited to work in the Negro market," David Ogilvy told a black applicant. "That is too confining for you. If I ever succeed in getting you into our agency, I shall try to give you broader scope. Awfully sorry this isn't the time. I admire you greatly."

Few were hired, so few applied, so few were hired. This implacable circle of cause and effect presumably discouraged many black job-seekers from even trying Madison Avenue. For five years David McCall interviewed a copywriter a day at Ogilvy's agency; in that time he saw only three blacks, of whom he hired one, Benton & Bowles the second, and the third was "not up to our standards." In the early 1960s the Urban League found less than twenty-five blacks in creative or executive jobs at the top ten ad agencies. White personnel specialists such as Jerry Fields and Edward Stern blamed this imbalance on the applicant pool, not racial discrimination. "The color problem never really is an important one," said Fields, "because there never have been that many Negroes applying for jobs." "The Urban League has the facts exactly upside down," Stern agreed. "I have yet to meet a competent copywriter or account executive who is a Negro. There just aren't any. The problem is that Negroes do not tend to move into the advertising business." But even if true, such statements ignored the causes of the situation.

As the civil rights movement turned northward, from the plain injustice of southern laws to the murkier issues of northern housing and employment discrimination, Madison Avenue could no longer dismiss its own racial problems so easily. "There's discrimination under every rock," said Richard Clarke, a black personnel man. "Agencies shy away from hiring Negroes because they're afraid an account in the South might object." The new climate of concern, Clarke added, had its own dangers: "Now I'm afraid agencies may rush out and hire a lemon just to get out from under the criticism." In the spring of 1963 Bates hired Thomas Richardson, its first full-time black copywriter. John Small, a media analyst and buyer at Grey, later became the first black ad salesman at a major New York TV station. In the fall of 1963 the eastern conference of the AAAA held an "unprecedented" meeting on the black market with presentations by Roy Wilkins and other civil rights leaders.

Along with upgrading black employment at the agencies, the reformers pushed for more blacks, in less stereotyped roles, in the ads themselves. Here again DDB provided a model, with its local "You don't have to be Jewish to love Levy's" poster campaign in New York featuring a rainbow of people enjoying Jewish rye bread. (Malcolm X, no less, approved a Levy's poster with a smiling black child. "Take my picture by this sign," he told a photographer. "I like it.") At a national level, in the summer of 1963 Lever Brothers—one of the largest advertisers on TV, with an annual budget of $46 million—announced its intention to include more blacks in its commercials. The statement followed meetings between Lever and various civil rights groups. "We informed our agencies of our desire to take affirmative action," Lever explained, "because of our conviction that a broader cross-sectional representation of Americans in advertising today is good business." A commercial for All detergent showed Art Linkletter interviewing a black housewife about her laundry problems. After a few months Lever had received thirty-eight letters in favor of the new policy, twenty-six against it: a small response from millions of viewers, implying the matter was not even controversial. Over the next four years Lever produced and ran 167 integrated commercials for various products, with no perceptible impact, pro or con, on sales.

The Congress on Racial Equality, the most active group in this field, went on to pressure Procter & Gamble, Colgate-Palmolive, Pepsi-Cola, and other major advertisers. "What we want is for television to show things the way they are . . . just ordinary things," said a CORE spokesman. "We're not asking for anything revolutionary." The request seemed reasonable, the tone conciliatory. All parties agreed to try harder. Gordon Webber of Benton & Bowles led a special AAAA committee to prod the industry further. General Foods soon claimed that 8 percent of its commercials were integrated. Tobacco companies, based in the South, capitulated more slowly than most industries. But even they slowly came around. Charles Sterling, a black sales manager for Lorillard, found no evidence that integrated advertising improved sales to blacks—but it did serve "the education of the white reader and viewer," he said: "Advertising in this sense provides a type of social dialogue and most certainly some public relations benefits."

In the long run, of course, advertising cared more about sales than about education or social dialogue. After initial flurries of concern the situation subsided, and progress came very slowly. The New York City Commission on Human Rights monitored all the ads and commercials produced by forty agencies from September 1966 to August 1967. In that period only 1 ad of 177 turned out by Foote, Cone & Belding admitted a black. "We include minority groups whenever the situation suits the current American scene," said an FC & B man. "We do not think that forced or unnatural inclusion of any group in our advertising serves any purpose." The figures at other agencies displayed a wide range: 2 of 441 by Burnett, 3 of 683 by Dancer-Fitzgerald-Sample, 20 of 384 by Thompson, 25 of 639 by Grey, 28 of 418 by BBDO, and 39 of 245 by Young and Rubicam. For all 40 agencies the grand total was 314 of 7,430 commercials, about 4 percent. "As advertising specialists," said Frederick Frost of Y & R, the agency with the best record, "we must aver that commercials using only one presenter (or a single-family situation), and commercials hoping for immediate identity with the majority market, will necessarily and predominantly feature white performers."

Pressure, again, might bring sudden improvements. In the six months after the survey period, Foote, Cone & Belding included blacks in 11 of 73 commercials; Thompson, in 54 of 182. The federal Equal Employment Opportunity Commission held hearings about the presence of minorities in advertising in January 1968. A year later the chairman of the EEOC praised the industry for "the dramatic increase of minorities in public media advertisements." Percentages aside, the most encouraging reform involved the roles played by blacks in the ads. Instead of menials and buffoons, they were now shown in a more normal range of tasks and occupations. In fact, a sharper awareness of such considerations now ironically kept an occasional black *out of* an ad. "Some of the civil rights groups don't like it if they see a colored person playing the part of a manual worker in a commercial," said a white casting director. "They want the ads to inspire Negroes to upgrade themselves professionally. But the talent unions don't feel this way about it at all."

Agencies and advertisers could include more blacks in their product simply by deciding to do so. Efforts to upgrade black employment at white agencies, on the other hand, involved subtleties and complicating factors under nobody's control. Statistics bore out a general agreement that agencies needed to hire more blacks. In 1966, according to an EEOC study, blacks held 2.5 percent of the white-collar jobs at 64 New York agencies, compared with 5.9 percent of the white-collar positions in insurance, 6.7 percent in banking, and 5.2 percent in the city as a whole. (Blacks were 18.2 percent of the entire New York population.) A second EEOC investigation a year later found blacks in 1.9 percent of the white-collar jobs at 13 large ad agencies, again less than the 2.8 percent in publishing and 4.4 percent in broadcasting and communications.

"The thing that gets me is that everybody is so friendly," said a black Chicago personnel man after placing two of one hundred applicants in professional advertising jobs over a two-year period. "Nobody refuses to see our applicants. But then we send them out, and nothing happens." (Blacks fared better, he added, at companies with federal contracts concerned about presenting "an integrated front.") Agencies hired relatively few employees anyway, and offered less job security than more sedate enterprises, and lower salaries at the entry level. "If we could reach the top college kids, it might make a difference," suggested Mary Dowery, a black placement specialist in New York. "But these kids aren't oriented to the agency business." "The starting pay is low," agreed John Pope of the Los Angeles NAACP, "and there are better-paying jobs for Negroes these days." In 1966 Richard Clarke declared that the ranks of black executives in advertising were actually thinning: "They are leaving agencies and going into TV, or into corporate setups."

For their part, at most agencies individual heads of groups or departments hired their own people, looking for talent and compatibility with no special concern about the company's EEOC profile. A central personnel office, which might have watched the demographic breakdown of the staff more carefully, in general did not control the white-collar hiring process. Individual blacks such as William Sharp, a copy-group head at Thompson's Chicago office, might prod their agencies to seek out black talent. For several years in the late 1960s Sharp coordinated an annual thirteen-week basic advertising course for blacks in Chicago, sponsored by the local council of the AAAA. In June 1966 Thompson, with the help of Richard Clarke's firm, interviewed 117 black college graduates over a two-day period in New York. Other agencies, notably Benton & Bowles and Ogilvy & Mather, also undertook special recruiting efforts aimed at blacks. Still, few blacks worked on Madison Avenue in any category, professional or clerical. At 40 agencies in August 1967, according to a survey by the New York Commission on Human Rights, only 3.5 percent of the employees were black. Among 15 agencies with at least 300 employees, the percentages ranged from .4 at Esty and .8 at Cunningham & Walsh to 5.8 at

Grey and 8.5 at Benton & Bowles. Black employees were clustered in the lower echelons.

The murder of Martin Luther King in April 1968 forced a quick surge of concern. Two weeks later Daniel & Charles, one of the Jewish agencies, placed a full-page ad in the *New York Times*: "Who says there are no Negroes in the advertising business. I've heard of five. . . . The advertising business is one of the most racially imbalanced industries in America. . . . But we are not bigots or racists. Most of us have done nothing to cause this terrible situation. And, perhaps, that's where the blame lies. We must do something." The ad elicited three hundred letters and hundreds of phone calls in a week, offering help and suggestions. Daniel & Charles organized a scholarship program. Advertising "doesn't require a great amount of training," said Daniel Karsch, one of the agency's founders, "just a facility for expression or for drawing. Copywriting, for instance, doesn't require an enormous vocabulary."

Blacks already employed in advertising, tired of accusations of being tokens and house niggers, now acted with more militancy. In May 1968 they started the Group for Advertising Progress (GAP) in New York to tell other blacks—according to Douglas Alligood of BBDO—that "some of us have made a beginning in advertising, and to give them something to aim for." With an initial membership of about one hundred, GAP's other officers worked for Clairol, Thompson, and Foote, Cone & Belding. "We feel we have a hell of a lot in common with the Italian art directors and the Jewish copywriters," said Harry Webber of Young & Rubicam. "The first, toughest job in America is to try to make it in advertising and be black or Puerto Rican."

With some whites and blacks concurring, the pressures were turned up a notch, then another notch. "You white advertising folks are a lot happier about the progress of integration than us black advertising folks," William Sharp told an AAAA meeting in Chicago. The graduates of his basic advertising course, he said, still could not find jobs in advertising; so jobs should be guaranteed. In the fall of 1968 a twelve-week course in New York sponsored by Bates, BBDO, Interpublic, Thompson, and Young & Rubicam trained twenty-seven black and Puerto Rican women in clerical skills, with guaranteed agency jobs on completion of the course. In Los Angeles the following summer, twenty-two agencies underwrote a program for blacks and chicanos that included an advertising and marketing

course at USC and two months of employment at a sponsoring
agency. By the fall of 1969 minority employment at the 15 biggest
New York agencies had risen to 10.5 percent, led by Thompson (16.1
percent) and DDB (14.3 percent).

But as the black cause moved from integrationist to nationalist
ideals—from wanting to join white America to standing apart and
affirming one's blackness—the special-markets trap became ever less
avoidable. "We have to become black Anglo-Saxons to make it,"
said Edgar Hopper, a former account executive at FC & B. "If you
let your hair grow out, you're Rap Brown. Speak out and you're
coming on too strong." White agencies must accept blacks on their
own terms, Hopper insisted: "When you hire a black creative person, hire him for his life style, not because you want him to imitate
the white." Granted that young blacks trying to enter advertising
dressed, talked, and approached life differently from whites, William Sharp conceded; "but they're not sick, they're not crippled."
Reflecting, in part, this nationalist pride, a string of black agencies—Uniworld, Burrell, John F. Small, Zebra Associates—now appeared. By the early 1970s over a dozen such agencies were
operating nationwide. But as long as black agencies and blacks
working at white agencies argued that only blacks could understand, and sell to, their fellow blacks, then white accounts could reasonably pass them by. The nationalist case logically led back to the
notion that had kept blacks off Madison Avenue for so long: that
only whites could sell to whites.

In American society and in advertising, after the white ethnics
and blacks came women. As an equal rights issue on Madison Avenue feminism shared some affinities with the earlier assertions: a
sense of historical mistreatment by WASP males, a simmering dis-
content that boiled over in the 1960s, and a rhetoric of overdue en-
titlements. But in advertising, at least, circumstances made women a
special case not truly analogous to other subordinated groups.
Women had long if checkered traditions as workers in advertising.
At any point in its history advertising included at least a few prominent female figures. The ads themselves have always been mostly
aimed at women customers because women make a high percentage—estimated at 90 percent in the late 1800s, 80 percent more
recently—of all consumer purchases. In advertising circles the

consumer is normally referred to as "she." One of advertising's most ancient and durable clichés is the male executive who tries to clinch an argument by saying, "My wife thinks . . ."

Because of this special circumstance, advertising has—relatively speaking—allowed women room to move up its ladders. Males on Madison Avenue have often preened themselves by claiming that advertising treated women employees better than any other business or profession did. Faint praise indeed, but the generalization probably holds up over time. When in the 1960s advertising women, taking their cues from other groups, finally started speaking up and out in concerted ways, they operated from longer, fuller histories on Madison Avenue than Jews, Italians, or blacks. The most remarkable aspect of this feminist assertion was that it had taken so long to happen.

By then advertising as a field for women had been expanding and contracting in alternating rhythms for a hundred years. In the decades after the Civil War women showed up everywhere in the business. Mathilde C. Weil started working in New York advertising in 1867 and later ran her own M. C. Weil agency. Mary Compton placed ads for a drug account, Vapo-Cresoline, as early as 1870. The biggest patent medicine, Peruna, had a woman advertising manager, and another concoction, Swamp Root, employed a woman space buyer. J. Walter Thompson in the 1880s hired Alice Stoddard to sell ads and Ellen Sage, later a free-lance, to help prepare them. In the 1890s Grace Webber ran the Fisk Rubber Company's ad department, and two women edited trade journals, Grace Shaw in Chicago (*Judicious Advertising*) and Kate Griswold in Boston (*Profitable Advertising*). Mary Compton and Meta Volckmann joined Mathilde Weil in operating their own agencies in New York. At the turn of the century Minnie Maude Hanff and Dorothy Ficken created the Sunny Jim campaign for Force cereal, while the Hoffman sisters of Chicago wrote and illustrated the jingles for Swift's Silver Leaf lard. In a women's issue of *Profitable Advertising* Kate Griswold described the careers of about forty women copywriters, advertising artists, publishers, agents, advisers, and representatives. "It is evident," *Printers' Ink* commented in 1903, "that the advertising field offers many places for women of ability."

These pioneers are worth listing because they enjoyed, for a time, a range of opportunities in advertising that women would then not recover until the latter decades of the twentieth century. In these early years advertising was not yet fragmented into male and female accounts and jobs. With the business so new and formless and procedures not yet established, women—in the same way that Albert Lasker could succeed as a Jew—might hope to fill any open position. But as advertising matured the men took firmer control. Earlier in the nineteenth century, women who had formerly worked as doctors and lawyers found themselves excluded by the new medical and legal schools, licensing procedures, and trade organizations: all the paraphernalia of professionalization. Now, at the start of the twentieth century, the same process of exclusion overtook advertising. As the field gained prestige men made it more narrowly their own. The new advertising clubs and organizations in general barred women from membership or even attendance at meetings. Denied these sources of contacts and trade gossip, women started losing ground in the business.

As an unsatisfactory alternative, advertising women started their own groups. The Women's Publicity Club of Boston was apparently the first. The most durable such group was started in New York in 1912 by a process that reflected the constrictions tightening around advertising women. An editor of *Printers' Ink*, J. George Frederick, had assigned his wife Christine to investigate the marketing of trademarked goods in New York department stores. Her reports on the existing abuses had then appeared in *PI* under the pseudonym Isobel Brands. With her interest in advertising thus aroused, Christine Frederick planned to attend a lecture at a meeting of the Advertising Men's League of New York, the largest such group in the city. Her husband told her she could only sit in the balcony, behind a curtain. Unwilling to abide such indignities, the Fredericks invited all the advertising women they could locate in the city to a meeting. The resulting League of Advertising Women in turn helped spawn similar groups in Philadelphia and Chicago, and, as Advertising Women of New York, has lasted down to the present.

These groups, however useful as expressions of solidarity and support, ironically reinforced the male thrust of isolating adwomen in a separate and unequal sphere of their own. At a women's session of an advertising convention in Philadelphia in 1916, Christine Frederick amused the women in attendance (only two men were on hand) by citing a current ad showing a woman bathing with her hair down. A "mere advertising man," she said, was not qualified to write copy for women's products. In the same vein, Jane J. Martin,

president of the League of Advertising Women, told the group a
year later that women should blame themselves for the fact that female solicitors for newspapers and magazines, once so numerous,
were now hard to find: they had tried to imitate men, yet were still
expecting special privileges as women. But admen would no longer
accept women as true cohorts. Instead they indulged in ambiguous
gallantries that stranded women on their pedestals, exalted but im-
mobilized. "It is women surely who are best calculated to know
what constitutes the feminine appeal," declared Frank Irving
Fletcher, a prominent copywriter, to the League of Advertising
Women in 1918. "I want some day soon to see an agency made up
entirely of women." (That is, like the agencies run by Mathilde
Weil, Mary Compton, and Meta Volckmann in the nineteenth century.)

Wartime manpower shortages, and then the postwar economic
boom, reopened opportunities for women in advertising, helped
along by the achievement of votes for women which allowed many
feminists to turn from suffrage campaigns to professional aspira-
tions. Helen Woodward, reputedly "the highest-paid advertising
woman in New York," quit the business, but she was replaced by
other women of comparable prominence. Erma Perham Proetz, of
Gardner Advertising in St. Louis, won three Harvard-Bok prizes for
her Pet condensed-milk campaigns and later became the first
woman inducted into the AFA's Hall of Fame. Although now
mainly in clerical jobs, advertising women could still aspire toward a
wider range of positions. A survey of 617 women employees in 47
New York agencies in 1924 found only five space buyers, with a top
salary of $5,000 (compared to $7,500 for men). Twenty-two of the
617 worked as copywriters at salaries ranging from $2,300 to over
$10,000, again less than male norms. In 1926 Nedda McGrath be-
came the first woman art director at a major agency when she was
hired by Blackman. "I know of no other woman art director in the
field," she said. "I was discouraged by everyone from making the attempt and had to work perhaps harder than a man."

No doubt she did. Even agencies that made pointed appeals to
women as employees still treated them as a different species from
men. In the late 1920s BBDO ran house ads in trade magazines picturing seven or eight employees, always with at least one woman included in the group: a copywriter, an account executive, someone in
the radio department. "He does not resent women in his office or in

his contacts with clients," Bruce Barton's secretary, Louise Mac-
Leod, said of her boss; "he believes that they have a definite value
and contribute a good deal that could come from no other source."
But "of course, like all men, he prefers that they should be easy to
look at and, again like all men, a little flattery now and then is not
difficult to swallow." Then MacLeod, writing to another woman,
went on to deflect attention from men: "Women are touchy; they
take so many things as personal that never are, and, personally, I feel
that they do not have a very high sense of honor. But gradually they
are learning."

As Louise MacLeod demonstrated, the problem of women in the
ad business derived from no simple one-way male chauvinism. Men
and women generally agreed to isolate women in their own special-
markets ghetto, where their alleged intuitions and sixth senses about
the feminine gender uniquely equipped them to deal with products
for the women's market. Even most feminists in the trade accepted
this conventional wisdom. "There are few up-to-date advertising
departments, or agencies, today that do not include the woman
copywriter," wrote Ethelyn Middleton in *Advertising & Selling* in
1921. Women were no more temperamental than men, Middleton
insisted; they just displayed their emotions in different ways, and—
fortunately—thought in different ways too. "After all," Middleton
asked men in advertising, "if she did not work the woman-way
would she be of any particular use to you in advertising? . . .
When you want to flatter us you say we 'think like a man.' We don't
think we do." Sometimes, but rarely, a solitary dissent would be
heard. ("Intelligence is neuter," insisted Sara Hamilton Birchall of
Kenyon & Eckhardt in 1928. "Until we bring to business an impersonal intellectual honesty, men may send us roses, but they will not
grant us recognition as their business equals.") Otherwise this consensus continued to allow women a small, restricted piece of Madison Avenue.

J. Walter Thompson, regarded in this era as the best agency for
women, epitomized this double-edged concept of a woman's place.
Helen Resor made it the only big agency with a feminist near the
top. As early as 1918, JWT ran a house ad trumpeting its "staff of
women" with degrees from Columbia, Chicago, and Seven Sister
schools, turning out campaigns for Yuban, Libby, and other products. During the 1920s and 1930s the Women's Copy Group controlled most of the agency's bellwether soap, food, drugs, and

toiletries accounts. "It is one of the most competitive businesses," JWT's Ruth Waldo said of advertising in 1931; "and when competition becomes sharp, prejudices are thrown overboard, and anyone who can be a real help is given a hearty welcome."

"We were pretty liberated, even by today's standards," Marjorie Smeltzer recalled in 1981. "But equality women did not have!" The more important women at JWT wore hats in the office, to distinguish themselves from unhatted secretaries and subordinates. New male employees went through a training program, starting in the mailroom and proceeding through all departments so that men could find jobs right for them. Women had no such program; they started low, as secretaries or researchers, and then hoped to be noticed. Nancy Stephenson, hired as a secretary, was allowed to try writing radio commercials for Pond's. For six months she did her normal work during the day and wrote copy at night. Promoted to junior copywriter, she was assigned to share an office with three men. "On my first day," she said later, "they were all behind their copies of the *New York Times* and not one said good morning to me. It took about three weeks before I could get any kind of acceptance."

Copy styles, accounts, and even office perks were all rigidly segregated by gender. Though salaries were not much discussed, most of the women copywriters believed they were paid less than men. The executive dining room, with its colonial furnishings, at first served only men and their male clients. After prolonged agitation Helen Resor and Ruth Waldo were allowed to bring in their female executives one day a week—on which occasion men were excluded. Only vice-presidents were given keys to the executive washroom. Since in these years no woman, not even Helen Resor, made vice-president, all JWT women shared a common washroom. "It was a rather social place," Marjorie Smeltzer noted. "Often there a writer would run into Helen Resor, elbow propped up on the cosmetic shelf under the mirrors. She would be holding forth on some subject or giving instructions to almost anyone who crossed her path." In her free-association style she jumped from topic to topic, recommending a recent newspaper or magazine article, urging her writers to test their market value at other agencies, warning them not to let their hair go gray. She wanted to dye her own white hair, she said, but "Stanley would kill me if I did." A poignant tableau: the most powerful woman in advertising, standing in a common washroom, regretting that her husband would not let her change hair color.

Local retail work, especially in New York, gave advertising women their best opportunities during the decades between the wars. In 1931 12 of 27 (44.5 percent) New York department and specialty stores had female advertising managers; outside New York this figure stood at 27 percent. Mary Lewis of Best & Company earned a salary of $44,266 in 1934, making her the highest-paid businesswoman in the country that year. A high school dropout, she had started writing copy for Macy's as a teenager. When her boss left for the war she took over his job as advertising manager, breaking many rules but getting results. When the man came back after the war they quarreled, and she departed to work at Best's. Margaret Fishback wrote copy at Macy's for fifteen years and Bernice Fitz-Gibbon, the best known of this group, held forth at Macy's (where she coined "It's smart to be thrifty"), Wanamaker's, and Gimbel's ("Nobody, but nobody, undersells Gimbel's"). The legendary Fitz eventually reached a salary of over $100,000. A large, commanding woman, she hired only Phi Beta Kappas, paid them low as trainees, and worked them hard. She taught her women to use fresh, crisp, colloquial language, never an "item" or "event" or "slashed." When anyone submitted inept copy she assembled her whole staff and read it aloud, with sarcastic emphasis. "I think the girls have some advantages in copywriting," she said later. "They are more likely to talk and write in specifics; men in generalities and abstractions."

Retail ads, presenting a flood of hard facts and prices, were nothing if not specific. For women the retail field offered a small pond, true, but a friendly one. "Today they dominate many aspects of the business," said Kenneth Collins of Gimbel's in 1937. "At least half the jobs men still hold in the retail structure could be filled just as adequately or more adequately by women." Retail itself could not give a copywriter national exposure, and its rigid conventions might restrict a creative imagination. But as a copywriting school it developed and rewarded speed, accuracy, and basic selling instincts. A woman in retail could gauge her success by counting the house every day. "Those daily ads are like the bar exercises in ballet," said one of Fitz-Gibbon's protégées, who later went on to a big agency. "Anyone interested in advertising should never go into an agency first. They'll never learn enough, fast enough."

Aside from retail work, though, the Depression meant another contraction of advertising jobs for women. As agencies cut staffs the women went first. Married women with apparently secure jobs were often asked to give way to needy men. When *Advertising Age* started publishing in 1930 it ran a weekly story on "Women in Advertising," with a photograph and description of a particular woman. The women covered mostly worked outside New York and Chicago, and included few big names. For two years the feature appeared in each issue, then occasionally for a while, then not at all. Apparently *Ad Age* ran out of subjects. In hard times those women who managed to keep their jobs in advertising often did so at the cost of relinquishing their dreams of moving up. "The nearest I ever came to fulfilling my one ambition of really getting ahead," said a secretary to an account executive in 1935, "was when the president of the firm remarked that it was too damn bad my head wasn't on a man's shoulders!" "All you get out of years in the business world," a stenographer added, "is a terrific bitterness for things as they are. How many girls I know who have let burning ambition become cynical indifference."

A few women did surface during the Depression. Louise Taylor Davis, who wrote campaigns for Eagle Brand condensed milk, became the first woman copy supervisor and vice-president at Young & Rubicam. Ophelia Fiore sold Fels Naphtha for Y & R with warnings of "Tattletale Gray." Dorothy Barstow produced the *Dr. Christian* soap opera for McCann-Erickson and married Harry McCann in 1939. None of these women was prominent among advertising feminists. The membership list of Advertising Women of New York in 1936 did not include Davis, Fiore, Barstow, Helen Resor, or Anne Hummert. Visible advertising feminists, such as Dorothy Dignam of Ayer, tended to work in less visible jobs. The most successful advertising women, basking in their success (and perhaps polishing apples), generally denied discriminations against women on Madison Avenue. "The jobs that women hold are held because they are better fitted to hold them," Barstow declared in 1934. "There aren't very many women executives in advertising agencies, because there is not very much need for women executives in advertising agencies." "There are still functions in advertising to which women are entirely unsuited," another woman added in 1937. "They can not, for instance, with the simple grace that men can, go out and drink themselves under the table angling for accounts."

With the Second World War the advertising field again opened up for women. In this war American involvement lasted over twice

as long as in the First World War, with proportionally more men
mobilized. So women were hired and promoted as never before in
American industry. In 1944 Ruth Waldo became the first woman
vice-president at Thompson. Jean Wade Rindlaub wrote a noted
"Back Home for Keeps" series of ads for Community Silverplate
and then became BBDO's first woman vice-president, also in 1944.
"Women have made their greatest strides in advertising during wartime," she said later. (Advertising, she added, was "exceptionally
good" for women: "There is less ceiling, more opportunity.") Shortly
after the war, 58 of 123 major advertisers surveyed claimed to em-
ploy women in "responsible" (above clerical) positions; 12 of the 58
said they had done so only since Pearl Harbor.

When the men came back from the war, in many industries
women were sent home to mother the baby boom. In advertising,
apparently, women at least held on to their gains. They still con-
tended with a predictable range of male prejudices. "Their work is
scrutinized and passed on by men outside the department," said one
national advertiser in explaining the problems of female copywriters, "and these men seem to be uniformly convinced that the
work is inferior only because it was produced by a woman. We have
tested it—the same work, submitted by a man, is approved." A poll
of advertising women in 1949 found 59 reporting they were paid
more, 315 the same, but 455 less, than men for similar work. Women
still mainly handled women's products, worked mostly in copy and
research, and included few art directors or contact people. "Much as
I hate to say it, women do not make good account executives," an
agency president noted in 1957. "If you add a man-versus-woman ri-
valry, you get nothing but trouble. Advertising men resent women
who compete with them on their own level." Women seldom worked
on the lucrative liquor, cigarette, and automobile accounts. Until
1958 a woman model could not even *appear* in a liquor ad. As in
business generally, women were often the brains behind their bosses.
When Martin Mayer researched his best-selling book *Madison Avenue,
U.S.A.* in 1957, he encountered a recurrent situation at agencies:
"The man had the title and salary, but to get the answers you often
had to ask the woman who sat at the next desk or in the next room."

Nonetheless, advertising women could also cite signs of stability,
even of progress. Margaret Divver, promoted to assistant advertising
manager at John Hancock Insurance during the war, got the top job
in 1948 ("Congratulations," another woman in advertising wrote

her, "on winning the *title* for the job you already have!"). The Chicago office of Foote, Cone & Belding, which had been treating male employees to an annual country club outing for years, in 1948 extended the favor to its women. In the 1950s three women, the first of their gender, were elected to the New York Art Directors Club. Women were even paid the ambiguous compliment of a novel about an adwoman, *The Joys She Chose* (1954), by "Matthew Peters," a pseudonym.

More seriously, in the fifteen years after the war many agencies followed earlier precedents by electing their first women vice-presidents: Ruthrauff & Ryan; McCann-Erickson; Dancer-Fitzgerald-Sample; Foote, Cone & Belding; D'Arcy; Grey; Sullivan, Stauffer, Colwell & Bayles; Ayer; Lennen & Newell; and others. As before, women especially made their marks in copywriting. Mary Fillius of the Weintraub agency launched the durable "I dreamed I was . . ." campaign for Maidenform. At Bates, Alicia Tobin coined the Colgate slogan "Cleans your breath while it cleans your teeth." Catherine Haynie O'Brien of Foote, Cone & Belding came up with "Aren't you glad you use Dial? (Don't you wish everybody did!)."

Another woman at F C & B, Shirley Polykoff, created a whole new market for hair coloring. Also part of the ethnic revolution, she had grown up in Brooklyn, the daughter of Russian Jewish immigrants. "It was from the magazine advertisements that we really learned how to be truly American," she said later. "How a home should look. How a table should be set. How to dress. How to be well groomed." After training in retail advertising she was hired by FC & B in 1955. She was quickly assigned the Clairol account because, said the copy chief, "you're the only one around here who can write that kind of schmaltz." At the time only 7 percent of all women admitted to coloring their hair. Despite Helen Resor's efforts among the women at JWT, the practice by reputation appealed only to actresses and society women, or those of dubious moral probity. So Polykoff devised a campaign for women who wanted to change their hair without admitting it: "Does she . . . or doesn't she? Only her hairdresser knows for sure." *Life* magazine at first turned it down as sexually suggestive, but then relented when a poll of its female employees found no awareness of a double entendre. In six years Clairol sales went up 413 percent, and up to half of all adult women started improving on nature.

At this time, of the big agencies McCann-Erickson seemed the most enlightened place for women. In 1960 six of its one hundred vice-presidents were women, the highest proportion in advertising. Whatever his other failings, Marion Harper did respect women. His first wife worked in the agency's research department for several years after their marriage ("I was working so much it was the only way we could see each other"). Dr. Herta Herzog, a psychologist, was a prominent advocate of motivation research on the staff. "There she was," one woman recalled, "not only achieving but with all of McCann-Erickson at her feet. She was the Great Authority at the agency."

Of the women vice-presidents, Margot Sherman was the central figure. A summa graduate of Michigan and the mother of two children, she chaired the agency's creative plans board and supervised three hundred employees. She also risked her position by speaking out, as an *important* adwoman, in unmistakably feminist terms. (That she could do so without paying for it again reflected how conditions had improved since the 1930s.) Admen, she told the Women's Advertising Club of Chicago in 1953, typically regarded a woman's decision as merely a whim, and they would describe an accomplished woman as "clever" instead of "sound" or "capable." If her husband were transferred to another city, she said, she would go along; but if McCann wanted to send her to California she could not expect him to move. Yet advertising still offered the best career chances to a woman. "Women's essentially strong and sound position in advertising," she summed up in 1955, "is the result of a calculated, disciplined and talented response to inevitable male prejudice. Exactly the way women have always gotten along and enjoyed themselves in a man's world. You keep your voice serene . . . even though a man may raise *his*. You show your wit and reasoning first . . . and your new hat second. . . . A woman has to do a *little better* than any man with the same talents in the same situation in order to do as well as he from the point of salary, recognition, and respect."

Even before the 1960s, then, women were strongly if unequally established in the business. The creative revolution only improved on existing conditions, though not all the creative agencies accepted women. Leo Burnett included no women among its forty-five vice-presidents, and the agency's annual outing was still a stag affair of golf, booze, and poker. "They aren't usually required to work quite as hard as men," Burnett himself said of adwomen. "Generally they are weaker at basic planning and plotting strategy, less able to take responsibility and work on their own ... and are emotionally less fitted for the give-and-take of the daily agency operation." But, he added in a remarkable non sequitur, "our policy is to pay for value received, and without sexual discrimination."

But women were prominent at most creative agencies. Here again DDB led the way: Phyllis Robinson supervised a creative staff with women such as Mary Wells, Paula Green, Judith Protas, Lore Parker, and Rita Selden. "I've never encountered any difficulty," Robinson said as a woman in advertising. "None at all." At Ogilvy's agency Lucille Goold made vice-president in 1955 and Reva Korda wrote copy for Schweppes, Dove, and Pepperidge Farm, among others. Trained by Fitz-Gibbon at Gimbel's, Korda upon arriving at the agency found she could do a day's expected work in an hour "because I was working with Gimbel's speed, Gimbel's concentration, and the specter of Fitz peering over my shoulder." Margaret Hockaday's agency produced the noted "As long as you're up, get me a Grant's" campaign for a scotch account, and Janet Marie Carlson's Cole swimsuit ads sold with a most unladylike sex appeal.

After a century of fluctuating receptions, women in advertising now found some old barriers and clichés coming down. "The legends are all wrong," said David McCall in 1962. "The outstanding women in advertising are a pretty hard-nosed bunch. They are realistic, practical, down-to-earth. They call a spade a spade. They keep noticing that the emperor has no clothes on—and they say so. My fellow man, on the other hand, is very apt to be a wildly romantic and impulsive fellow." When DDB hired Marcella Rosen in 1962, Ned Doyle introduced her at a client meeting as "the first goddamned woman account executive we've ever had." A few years later Benton & Bowles was known as an agency willing to hire women as art directors. The old demarcations were disappearing.

Thus Wells, Rich, Greene: the demographically typical creative agency, founded by a woman and two Jewish men. An only child, Mary Wells had grown up in Youngstown, Ohio, expecting to break molds. "Mother started me in the theater at the age of five," she recalled, "hoping I wouldn't grow up and marry a steelworker." ("I have succeeded," she later told her mother, "because you expected me to.") After she reached New York her career recapitulated the history of advertising women since the war: trained in retail at Macy's, hired at McCann-Erickson by Margot Sherman ("a rather remarkable woman," according to Wells), then at DDB by Phyllis

Robinson ("I would buy a used car from Phyllis Robinson"). Sailing
along, in 1966 she started the first *hot* agency, then—quickly—the
first *major* agency ever headed by a woman. At WRG she surrounded
herself with men, except for her assistants, a series of hardworking
women who organized her life and tended to her miscellaneous
needs. All steel and velvet, with her conspicuous good looks and
charm masking a predatory will, she represented a throwback to the
leading adwoman with no complaints about men. "The idea about
American men trying to keep women down in business is a bunch of
hogwash," she said. "I've never been discriminated against in my
life, and I think the women who have experienced it would have
anyway—no matter if they were men, or cows, or what have you."
Only "the nuts and the kooks," she added, "are screaming like
babies."

By the late 1960s, as reflected in this bristling comment by Wells,
the general revival of American feminism had hit Madison Avenue.
Once again the advertising world lagged behind society at large.
Betty Friedan's *The Feminine Mystique*, the key document, was published in February 1963. One chapter, "The Sexual Sell"—though
overstated because of Friedan's too literal acceptance of Ernest
Dichter's claims for motivation research—indicted advertisers and
agencies, with "those deceptively simple, clever, outrageous ads and
commercials," as the overpowering perpetuators of the feminine
mystique: "it is their millions which blanket the land with persuasive images, flattering the American housewife, diverting her guilt
and disguising her growing sense of emptiness." One month after
the book appeared, Advertising Women of New York ran a conference with two hundred members of women's clubs. After the adwomen defended advertising in the morning, the clubwomen
attacked it in the afternoon. "As long as people buy, you'll see this
kind of ad," Jean Rindlaub said of offensive copy. "We aren't simon
pure any more than anyone else," said Margot Sherman. "We are a
reflection of the U.S., of all of you." Asked about ads that specifically demeaned women, Sherman dismissed them as probably the
work of men.

When criticized by outsiders, adwomen too naturally tended to
defend the profession. But in the next few years a small feminist
pocket of women from various agencies became apparent on Madison Avenue. Jo Foxworth of Calkins & Holden campaigned against
what she called "second sexism" in advertising (the phrase a reference to Simone de Beauvoir's *The Second Sex*). "We have thumpingly

conclusive proof," said Foxworth in 1965, "that there's no such thing as job gender." She urged women to help each other, to stop favoring male subordinates, to be ambit'ous, "to grow up to an emotional acceptance of our own capabilities." Jane Trahey, schooled in retail at Neiman-Marcus in Dallas and the boss of her own New, York agency since 1958, declared that a woman needed "almost a neurotic devotion" to her career, probably excluding marriage, to succeed. ("If you want something and you are a woman, you must wear the Avis button.") Margaret Carson of Foote, Cone & Belding and Myra Janco of the Draper Daniels agency spoke out in similar terms in the mid-1960s. "I'd like to make one thing clear. I'm not a feminist," Bernice Fitz-Gibbon wrote in 1966. But "there's dire dark discrimination against letting the female copywriter stand in the highest advertising places of this world."

Yet—the old refrain—relatively speaking, the ad business did respect female employees, a situation that cut two ways. It might, by dangling hints of power and money, encourage women to expect even more from a revolution of rising expectations. And it might discourage needed reforms in the presence of so extravagant a success story as Mary Wells. "I didn't feel put upon until I read this book," said Franchellie Cadwell of Cadwell Davis in reviewing Caroline Bird's *Born Female* in 1968. Granted "some remnants of prejudice against women," Cadwell allowed; but what about Mary Wells? "The plight of working women is hard to get worked up about," Cadwell concluded. "It's too bad this book wasn't written ten years ago. It might have been more timely."

Then, in a striking metamorphosis, Cadwell became the most militant advertising feminist. At a time of consciousness-raising, nobody's was raised further than Cadwell's. "Establishment-thinking men equate their own masculinity with a woman being relegated to a subservient position," she said in 1970. "The typical advertising guy doesn't want to acknowledge this." She made the rounds of advertising trade meetings to deplore the portrayal of women in commercials: stealing each other's soap, being instructed in floor cleaning by Arthur Godfrey, being rescued from the shame of dirty clothes by a white tornado, chatting with a little man in the toilet bowl, arguing with doves. "Advertising has let the female consumer get away from them, and get way ahead of them," she summed up. "The mass of women has been revolutionized—only advertising to women hasn't."

Amelia Bassin made her name as advertising director of Fabergé

and then, in 1970, started her own agency. She accepted an award as
Advertising Woman of the Year from the American Advertising
Federation in 1970 with a crackling feminist speech. Anyone who
knew women only from ads, she said, would have to regard them as
hysterical, adorable, masochistic, dangerous, sex-maddened idiots.
Mary Wells was "the perfect example of the kind of woman who
should be leading women," yet one never heard a word from her. "I
can well believe Miss Mary never got discriminated against," Bassin
observed. "There is no privileged class in the world to compare with
that of beautiful women. . . . It's difficult to tell if success has spoiled
Mary Wells; but boy, is she ever spoiling success!" Nobody laughed
at the black movement, so why did feminism seem so funny? It
would do everybody good, she told her audience in conclusion.
"Most of all, it will be ever so good for your profits, and that ought
to grab you, if nothing else will."

Again the question: advertising as mirror or mindbender? The
subordinate status of women surely predated national advertising.
But even so, current advertising, as Friedan argued, now crucially
reinforced the unequal sexual status quo. Women's liberation implied a new woman in the ads. "The dilemma in which the modern female finds herself," said Myra Sparkman, a Los Angeles
ad-woman, "is due, to a large extent, to the unreal world of the
feminine created by the image makers—the admen." Acting from
their peculiar, limited masculine ideas of female character, Sparkman went on, admen had produced a monster, "an object-product-
chattel symbol," simultaneously idealized and ravaged. When published in *Advertising Age*, Sparkman's remarks brought "a wave of
agreement" in letters to the editor.

Of course, adwomen too had helped create the monster. In 1964
Jane Trahey had done a controversial ad for a New York department store: a photograph of twenty-eight products and a blonde in a
bikini (labeled "From Germany"), with all the objects advertised as
available for sale at the store. An industry group condemned the ad,
and Trahey wondered why. ("It was very naughty," David Ogilvy
told her, "but it was also very *witty*.") Now, in the early 1970s, Trahey presented a slide show of objectionable ads that made women
into sex objects; another consciousness raised.

Outside the business, the National Organization for Women and
Ms. magazine undertook full campaigns to improve female images
in advertising. "Advertising is a very important form of education,"

said Gloria Steinem. "It is estimated that 40 percent of all of our
subcultural intake comes from advertising." *Ms.* would not accept
ads for unsound products like vaginal deodorants. NOW stickers
proclaiming "This ad insults women" were slapped on offending
billboards. Shirley Polykoff's Clairol campaign had received the dubious honor of a NOW Barefoot & Pregnant award. But after attending a NOW meeting about advertising, Polykoff said, "I didn't
know I was so much for them." At another NOW session, for one
hundred Ogilvy & Mather executives, the lowest-consciousness prize
went to Rosenfeld, Sirowitz & Lawson's Geritol ad ("My wife, I
think I'll keep her"). "You helped the blacks to be represented more
realistically," a NOW official told the admen; "help us, too."

The more pronounced one's feminism, the harder to see and acknowledge progress. But changes did happen. According to one
careful study of magazine advertising from 1959 to 1971, the portrayal of women as sex objects diminished sharply during the period,
but women were still presented as dependent on men. In the ad
business itself women continued to inch forward. Mary Ayres of
SSC & B became in 1971 the first woman on the AAAA board of
directors. The women at JWT's New York office—no longer the best
place for females in advertising—included five TV producers, ten
account executives, fourteen art directors, thirty-one copywriters,
and (in 1973) the agency's first woman senior vice-president, Char-
lotte Beers. And most remarkably, a few maverick admen sounded
like feminists. "Too many advertising people are insulated from the
revolution," said Jack Roberts of Carson/Roberts. "We must get
behind human liberation, rather than lagging behind."

The white ethnics, blacks, and women transformed the face, as
well as the body and soul, of American advertising. Even after the
cycle turned and the creative revolution grew unfashionable, advertising still looked different, in both its people and its products. It
more truly reflected American society, then undergoing its own
parallel transformations.

In this new world the old issues of advertising regulation looked
different too. Ever since the consumer movement of the New Deal
era had subsided into World War II, advertising had held off its critics with a promise of meaningful self-regulation. This promise—to
make ads more honest and informative, to safeguard the consumer,

to benefit the public—had always veiled the industry's real motive
in the matter, to protect its own free-enterprise freedoms and to
stave off governmental interference. "We have a demand to justify
advertising now as a social force. What a nuisance," said James
Webb Young at the founding of the War Advertising Council in
1941. "If we do not meet it we will be damaged. If we do not work
together, we will not meet it." After the war this group, its name
shortened to the Advertising Council, was underwritten by the
AAAA and ANA as a joint public-relations voice of the industry. It
sponsored ads for blandly unobjectionable causes, urging people to
vote, donate blood, drive carefully, support the Red Cross, and not
to start forest fires or cause pollution; all of them estimable efforts,
presented under the pointed aegis of the Advertising Council, "a
voluntary, non-profit business group," as it described itself, "organized for the sole purpose of helping the country."

Not exactly. Advertising characteristically dealt in appearances,
never more so than in examining its own ethics and presenting its
case as an industry to the public. Though overflowing with vivid individuals and opinions, the business lacked a tradition of internal
dissent. Reformers within advertising risked being dismissed as
heretics and gadflies, disloyal, not team players. Even so substantial
a figure as Bruce Barton felt constrained to defend advertising in
public and keep his private doubts to himself. Granted that advertising could find sufficient reasons for presenting a solid, prickly
hedge to outsiders. Routinely attacked along a wide political spec-
trum by everyone from novelists to members of Congress, advertising found few defenders away from Madison Avenue. With no
cavalry hoving into view, admen clustered together and fired back.
But in doing so they only renewed the efforts of outside reformers.

Thomas D'Arcy Brophy, for example, ranked as one of advertising's true statesmen. As president and then chairman of Kenyon &
Eckhardt from 1937 to 1957, he pushed advertising toward higher
ethics and gave huge blocks of his time and money to outside phi-
lanthropies. On occasion he expressed remarkably heterodox opinions. ("Free enterprise or capitalism calls itself a profit system," he
said in accepting a *Printers' Ink* award in 1953, "yet it has limited its
profits to a relatively few. It has not given profits to the majority of
the people.") Even Brophy, however, bristled unbecomingly when
outsiders attacked advertising. In 1949 John Benson of the AAAA,
in an article for *Advertising & Selling*, proposed an advertising code of

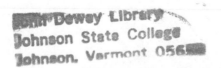

ethics. A few weeks later, speaking on a program with Brophy at a meeting in Michigan, Colston Warne of Consumers Union cited the Benson proposal in the course of a broadside against advertising; so Brophy then told Benson he should not have made his ideas public, as potential ammunition for the enemy. Again, in 1957, after a professor at Gonzaga University named John Paul Sisk published an article about motivation research in the magazine *America*, Brophy—a Gonzaga alumnus—asked the college's president, "What can we do about Mr. Sisk?" Dismissing the article as untrue and bordering on the sensational, Brophy warned the president that the offending professor had responsibilities to the school, "and, conversely, the University must take some responsibility for his public utterances." If someone of Brophy's undoubted integrity and generosity could so easily abuse academic freedom and free speech, what did that imply about the advertising business in general?

After the war the consumer movement, though less newsworthy, did not disappear as an organized force. To the contrary: with the advertising novels and the furor over *The Hidden Persuaders* maintaining a steady bombardment of Madison Avenue, the circulation of *Consumer Reports* grew from 80,000 before the war to a half-million by 1950, then nearly a million by 1961. The magazine continued to test products, publish the results, expose the failings of advertisers and agencies, and run no ads itself. The members of Consumers Union—75 percent college-educated, 98 percent owners of automobiles—paid special heed to evaluations of electric appliances and audio equipment. Now far from its proletarian origins, the group had, as Colston Warne noted, been "kicked into the middle class," the traditional stronghold of consumerism.

Meantime the ad business still maintained a charade of self-regulation while typically deploring the dangers of socialistic inroads by big government. One AAAA effort in the late 1940s to collect and outlaw objectionable ads collapsed in general disinterest. In the 1950s the National Association of Broadcasters banned TV commercials with men in white coats pretending to be doctors. Agencies got around it with background shots of hospitals, displays of medical and dental equipment, stacks of purported medical reports. Another AAAA attempt to police offensive ads reviewed 107 reported cases over a two-year period. Of these only ten—including Jane Trahey's ad offering a blonde for sale—were found distasteful. Even in these cases, enforcement measures were timidly inadequate.

In the 1960s, with most forms of received wisdom under scrutiny, the advertising community at last broke up into real arguments over regulatory policy. The seamless facade shattered. Presidents Kennedy and Johnson provided the initial goads with such appointments as Paul Rand Dixon to head the Federal Trade Commission, Esther Peterson to oversee consumer affairs in the Labor Department, and Newton Minow and then E. William Henry as chairmen of the Federal Communications Commission. All quickly provoked advertising people into debates over governmental intrusions. Minow added a phrase to the language by calling TV programming "a vast wasteland." One night President Kennedy watched the movie *PT-109,* about his war exploits, on TV and was appalled by the number of commercial interruptions. "Why do you let them put so many commercials on?" he asked Minow. "It's cheap! Cheap! Cheap! I want a rule that limits the number of commercials." Minow replied that he needed more FCC commissioners with consumerist loyalties.

As in the progressive and New Deal eras, at a time of general reform impulses advertising again found itself besieged. But this time key advertising figures at an early point joined the chorus of outside reformers. The Young Turks of the business predictably lamented the sins of the fathers—the work of the bigger, older agencies. "Is advertising worth saving?" asked Howard Gossage. "From an economic point of view, I don't think that most of it is. From an esthetic point of view, I'm damn sure it's not; it is thoughtless, boring, and there is simply too much of it." Fred Papert of Papert, Koenig, Lois urged that "weasel-wording and half-truths" be eliminated from TV commercials. "I think that packaging bills and regulations are fine things," he added. "A great deal of advertising is deceptive and misleading."

Two of the most powerful, respected men in advertising joined these younger critics in inviting more federal regulation. For years Fairfax Cone had been scolding his peers at trade meetings, to little effect. By 1961 he had lost faith in the feckless reform gestures of the AAAA, ANA, and AFA. "All three of these organizations," he confided to Leo Burnett, "are cursed with weak leadership, if, indeed, it can be called leadership at all, and I think a new approach is needed." Though Cone's agency drew over half its billings from TV, he blamed most of advertising's problems on television commercials: their noise, intrusiveness, deceptions, and irrelevant visual gimmicks. So he took his case directly to William Henry at the FCC. "The great mass of television viewers," he wrote Henry, "are treated to an almost continuous program of tastelessness which is projected in behalf of competitive products of little interest and only occasional necessity (headache remedies, stomach powders, etc.)." Again, in an article for *Fortune* in 1965, he declared that advertisers must bear half the blame and most of the consequences for the mediocrity of TV.

In his best-selling *Confessions*, David Ogilvy called for the replacement of commercial television with a system of pay-TV. William Henry passed the suggestion along in a major speech in September 1963. The speech was fine, Ogilvy then wrote Henry, though three of his biggest clients were furious with him for in effect comforting the enemy. "When, I wonder," Ogilvy asked Henry, "will the FCC really get tough on broadcasters at renewal time? And *when* will the Commission get specific?" Later Ogilvy called in public for the FCC to reduce the flood of TV commercials. "This is a very unpopular opinion on Madison Avenue," he noted. "There are a few others who hold it, and they're not all bolsheviks, either."

The bitter debate over cigarette advertising benefited from, and added to, this more pluralist atmosphere on Madison Avenue. The tobacco industry had responded to the first authoritative health alarms in the 1950s by pushing filter cigarettes. (Some filtered brands, in using stronger tobacco to overcome the filter, actually inflicted more harmful elements on the smoker.) In the ensuing filter wars—"one of the most vicious running advertising dog fights in our advertising history," according to Rosser Reeves—the competing brands all claimed the best combination of good taste with low tar and nicotine. Still the medical evidence against smoking piled up. After *Reader's Digest* published another warning in 1957, BBDO resigned the magazine's $1.6 million account; observers inferred the influence of BBDO's $15 million American Tobacco account. Two years later, when Arthur Godfrey said that smoking made him feel bad, Lorillard stopped sponsoring his show. Other cigarette companies pressured magazines not to run ads for Bantron, a smoking deterrent.

After the landmark surgeon general's report in January 1964, the *New Yorker* and other magazines banned cigarette advertising. David Ogilvy, whose brother died of lung cancer after a lifetime of heavy smoking, and William Bernbach announced their agencies would no longer accept cigarette accounts. Emerson Foote, active in the American Cancer Society since 1945, resigned as chairman of McCann-Erickson in protest against its continued handling of cigarettes. "I do not ordinarily believe in the Government's butting into people's private lives," he said. "Cigarette smoking just simply happens to be such a colossal exception that ordinary rules must be changed." CBS told its producers to minimize smoking in network shows, and Frank Stanton urged the network to prohibit cigarette commercials.

Under such pressures the tobacco industry made a few concessions. It adopted an advertising code in 1964 that stopped pitches aimed at young people and outlawed claims that smoking would improve health, ease tensions, or enhance social or sexual success. At the same time the industry, the third largest advertiser on network television, kept increasing its TV budgets, to a total of over $200 million. Through the Tobacco Institute it kept dispensing millions of dollars for research designed to show the harmlessness of smoking. Its lobbyists and congressmen tried to defeat or cripple any extension of federal regulation. But the industry was meeting more skeptics on Madison Avenue. "I think a lot of people in advertising don't like to work on cigarette accounts," said William B. Lewis, formerly of Kenyon & Eckhardt, now of the American Cancer Society. "We have had many creative people from the agencies moonlighting for us on Society material."

In March 1969 two extraordinary editorials in *Advertising Age* suggested a decisive shift among advertising people. "During the past five years, the tobacco industry has pursued a course of conduct suited to its own purposes," said *Ad Age*. "This has resulted in a series of legal disasters for the entire advertising community." The FTC had mandated a health warning on packages and in ads, and had established a laboratory to test and publish data on competing brands; the FCC had ruled, under the fairness doctrine, that stations running ads for cigarettes must also run rebuttals; political pressures were moving toward a ban on cigarette commercials in broadcasting. Suppose, now, if these measures were extended to all advertising. . . "Tobacco advertising may be a hefty tail for the advertising business, but it is still the tail," *Ad Age* concluded; "and it is time it stopped trying to wag the dog."

A few holdouts remained. "If a product can be sold in this country, a company should be able to advertise it," said Mary Wells, whose work for Benson & Hedges had sent her agency flying. A broadcast ban, she said, would be "unfair, un-American, and undemocratic," even "terrifying." No use. In March 1970 Congress removed cigarette ads from TV and radio as of the following January. (The cigarette companies transferred their billings to print and outdoor advertising. Cigarette sales reached new records.)

The cigarette controversy, involving many careers and big money, was only one part of the revived consumer movement. Forcing a major advertiser off the air gave some sense of the new power of consumerism. In most ways the revived movement struck familiar themes. Again it drew most of its troops from women, especially housewives, and thus coincided with the resurrection of American feminism. Again it appealed mainly to people of some education and sophistication and so missed the working classes that needed it most. Again it gave much attention to advertising reforms. Among ad people, new versions of Helen Woodward and James Rorty appeared: Samm Sinclair Baker and Terry Galanoy wrote revealing confessional books about their sins in the ad business. ("The general approach of admen," Baker warned, "is based on *the permissible lie*.") But in significant ways this third wave of consumerism covered new ground. In Ralph Nader it had a compelling central figure who never slept and never let up. On Madison Avenue more leaders accepted consumerism more quickly. And in the public at large it gathered more attention and more support than ever before.

In 1961 Paul Rand Dixon, as chairman of the FTC, had announced to the general distress of advertisers his intention to enforce the laws against false advertising. "The industry cannot police itself," Fairfax Cone agreed. "The FTC is just reaching for more authority to do what it's supposed to do." But after some initial rumblings the FTC did not bother advertising much. In 1969 Nader and his associate Aileen Coward asked fifty-eight advertisers to substantiate their claims. The forty replies included one retraction and thirty-nine answers deemed inadequate by Nader and Coward. They therefore petitioned the FTC to require such substantiations. The FTC agreed. Invoking previously unused authority, it called on industries to submit data as to safety, performance, efficacy, quality, and comparative prices. The FTC went on to examine the intent, not just the literal truthfulness, of claims, and to require affirmative disclosure and corrective ads to balance previous lies. *Ad Age*'s fears about the precedents established in the cigarette case were coming true, with interest. The historic failure of advertising self-regulation had brought its own punishment. "I am, and always will be, a great exponent of truth in advertising," said Charles Brower of BBDO. "But it *was* more fun when you could lie a little!"

The industry in 1971 made a final gesture toward cleaning its own house. The AAAA, ANA, and AAF, with funding by the Council of Better Business Bureaus, launched the National Advertising Review Board to serve as the appeals level of the National Advertising Division of the BBB. A complaint about the honesty of a given ad went to the NAD; complaints regarding taste or social responsibility, more difficult matters to adjudicate, went right to the NARB. For each case it heard the NARB appointed a review panel with three members representing advertisers, one from an agency, and one from the public. No one from the media took part, overtly to avoid conflicts of interest. Despite this imbalance the system worked effectively, mainly because the ad business took it seriously. Complaints at first came mainly from consumers, later more from competing advertisers. In 10 years 1,854 cases were heard, of which 42 percent resulted in modified or discontinued campaigns. The NARB could not impose fines or other penalties. Its order to stop an offending ad often came after the campaign had already run its natural course, so the ruling meant nothing. Still, it improved enormously on the previous record of advertising self-regulation. Over its first decade no advertiser refused to accept an NARB verdict. With over twenty federal agencies now involved in the regulation of advertising, Madison Avenue had to be careful.

❧❧

Johnny Carson on the *Tonight* show, 1963: "Mr. Minow says there are too many commercials on television. I think he is dead wrong. I'll have more to say on this after this word from our sponsor."

❧❧

By its nature concerned with the present and future tenses, advertising has no historical memory. Cycles in art and copy styles reappear with new names to be greeted as innovations. Among observers of the American scene, discussions of advertising in our national life always lack a historical dimension.

This historical amnesia accounted for the peculiar drift of the noisiest advertising controversy of the late 1960s, the question of political advertising. A book by Joe McGinniss, *The Selling of the President 1968*, started the initial arguments. A newspaper reporter, McGinniss had managed to work for months in the upper reaches of Nixon's advertising and media staff without being detected. His book then recounted what he had seen and heard. As a print journalist ("Print is for ideas"), McGinniss did not approve television's domination of the campaign. "The age of the columnist is over," he quoted Nixon's man Frank Shakespeare, formerly of CBS, as saying. "TV is carrying our campaign." His print bias aside, though, McGinniss did not draw many lessons but simply reported damning quotations and episodes. From these, McGinniss (implicitly) and his offended readers (explicitly) derived two main conclusions: that advertising techniques and moralities were uniquely influential in the 1968 election, and that political discourse was thereby uniquely compromised.

Neither conclusion stands up to historical examination. The first politician to tack a sign on a tree or distribute a handbill was, of course, engaged in political advertising. The first extended discussion of advertising in politics, however, occurred during the presidential campaign of 1916. In the spring a four-page insert was placed in the *Saturday Evening Post* and other magazines by the Erickson agency urging a GOP draft of Theodore Roosevelt. "Instead of relying on the uncertain results of a press-agentry campaign," *Printers' Ink* commented, "the men behind the movement decided to get quick, co-ordinated action through the ungarbled and definite medium of paid advertising." The fall contest between Charles Evans Hughes and Woodrow Wilson featured novel advertising techniques by the Democrats. The Hanff-Metzger agency put quarter-page ads, under the headline "Yes! or No! Mr. Hughes?," asking his positions on issues, in the newspapers of cities in which he was due to speak. For the Republicans, the Batten agency concentrated in states east of the Mississippi. Wilson won the election out West. As the *Wall Street Journal* noted afterward, Hughes won where he advertised heavily and lost elsewhere. "The advertising method has made great gains," declared *Printers' Ink*, "and greater gains are still to come." Early in 1917 Congress for the first time considered the regulation of political advertising.

The lesson learned, in 1918 the GOP recruited Albert Lasker to help out with publicity. Then an isolationist bitterly opposed to the League of Nations, at the 1920 Republican convention he tried to get Hiram Johnson nominated for president. Afterward, reconciled to the candidacy of Warren G. Harding, he supervised publicity and speech-writing, and performed other tasks during the campaign. (He was sent to pay off one of Harding's mistresses with $20,000, plus monthly retainers, in exchange for her silence. The woman and her husband were then dispatched on a trip around the world to get them out of the country.) Hoping to be well rewarded for such services, Lasker was disappointed with his job at the Shipping Board. He was, however, part of Harding's poker cabinet, the inner circle that met to drink and gamble together, and he often appeared in public with the presidential party. Lasker stayed active in Republican affairs well into the 1930s.

Other prominent admen followed him into politics. The winning slogan in the 1924 presidential election—"Keep Cool With Coolidge"—came from Henry T. Ewald of the Campbell-Ewald agency in Detroit. In 1920 Bruce Barton's admiring articles about Coolidge, a fellow Amherst man, had helped him to the vice-presidency. In 1928, after his withdrawal, Barton had then become an early advocate of Herbert Hoover and had written parts of Hoover's acceptance speech at the convention. "A political campaign is largely an advertising campaign," said *Advertising Age* in 1930, citing a recent election in which the winner outspent the loser on advertising by ten to one. In 1936 Hill Blackett of Blackett-Sample-Hummert directed publicity for the Republican presidential campaign. Barton served two terms in Congress in the late 1930s. "Salesmen should really make excellent congressmen," he said during his first campaign. "They know people. If you really want to find out about people, try selling them something."

So many admen took part in the 1940 campaign that Madison Avenue itself became an issue. Wendell Willkie's public supporters included Barton, Blackett, Raymond Rubicam, Stanley Resor, Harry McCann, Chet LaRoche, Stirling Getchell, John Orr Young, Lou Wasey, and others in the trade. "These are the boys," declared Dorothy Thompson, the liberal columnist, over CBS radio, "who have perfected the technique of 'selling' the American people anything on the shelves." Now, she said, they were using the familiar methods of hard selling ("The idea is first to create the fear, and then offer a branded antidote") to elect a president. Roosevelt had no admen behind him, Thompson pointed out, and she was supporting him "because I am at long last fed up with the glib copy-

writers who think you can slug this nation into an election." Barton
found himself part of an ongoing joke as audiences responded jeer-
ingly to FDR's litany of the isolationist congressmen, "Martin, Barton, and Fish," who had obstructed his efforts to help the enemies of
Hitler. Expecting a close race in his own run for the Senate, Barton
lost by over 400,000 votes and went back to BBDO.

During the war Chester Bowles conspicuously headed the Office
of Price Administration in Washington, becoming familiar to the
public as a leader of the consumer struggle against wartime inflation. When peace came he retired from advertising and ran for governor of Connecticut in 1948. A Madison Avenue connection did
not help his reputation. "Mr. Bowles is an advertising man," Senator Robert Taft had declared, "and is not concerned with facts." But
from his years of directing radio operations at Benton & Bowles, he
knew the techniques of broadcast advertising: quick, short messages,
repeated in a dense blanket of "spots" at the right moment. Bowles
won the governorship by this first application of sophisticated radio
advertising methods to politics. (In 1949 he appointed his old partner William Benton to a vacated Senate seat.)

Rosser Reeves then masterminded the first national use of broadcast political spots. Already known for his TV work at Bates, he was
approached by a group of Republican oilmen in the summer of
1952. A special unit—launched by a fund-raising party at 21,
Reeves's favorite New York restaurant—was set up to operate sepa-
rately from BBDO, the main GOP agency for the presidential campaign. From the Gallup polling organization Reeves learned the
three issues most on the public's mind: political corruption, the high
cost of living, and the war in Korea. Reeves wrote twenty spots on
each issue, making the same points over and over in different words.
After watching Eisenhower give major televised speeches, and not-
ing the technical flaws, Reeves and his associates brought him into a
TV studio in September. They changed the lighting, improved the
makeup, removed his glasses, and put him in different clothes. In
one day he did forty twenty-second TV spots; the following day he
recorded twenty-five more for radio.

A voice: "Mr. Eisenhower, what about the high cost of living?"

Eisenhower: "My wife, Mamie, worries about the same thing. I
tell her it's our job to change that on November 4."

"The man is very good," Reeves noted professionally. "He handled himself like a veteran actor."

Initially a secret project, news of the spot campaign appeared in press reports and provoked controversy even before it aired. The Republicans had all the money but no real candidate, said George Ball of the Stevenson staff: "Found with this dilemma, they have invented a new kind of campaign—conceived not by men who want us to face the crucial issues of this crucial day, but by the high-powered hucksters of Madison Avenue." Americans should not make political choices, he added, the same way they selected cigarettes and chewing gum. Nonetheless the spots were run in twenty key states during the last two weeks before election day, at a total cost of $1.5 million. Concurrently BBDO ran longer, more conventional political ads in all media. In the aftermath of Ike's landslide, it seemed that politics had entered a new age in 1952. Never again would a whistlestop campaign make much difference in national elections.

As if to underscore the point, the Republican National Committee kept BBDO on a retainer after the election for media advice as needed. For a TV panel presentation by four cabinet officers in June 1953, BBDO supervised the cue cards, charts, and graphs, and put the politicians through two rehearsals. "We're a regular account," said a presidential assistant of BBDO's efforts, "and when you get to kicking around the appropriations, it's a valuable account." In late 1955 BBDO signed contracts to provide over $2 million worth of radio and TV advertising in the coming elections. Meantime, according to reports, the opposition could not find an agency willing to antagonize its big clients by working for the Democrats.

In his acceptance speech at the Democratic convention of 1956, Adlai Stevenson warned that his opponents would use "shows, slogans, and the arts of advertising" to snare voters. "The idea that you can merchandise candidates for high office like breakfast cereal," said Stevenson piously, "—that you can gather voters like box tops—is, I think, the ultimate indignity to the democratic process." Bald hypocrisy. The Democrats had finally managed to hire an agency—Norman, Craig & Kummel—which had then redesigned the set at the convention and had helped engage singers and performers. The ten-member delegation from N C & K was described by *Advertising Age* as "one of the most significant of the Democratic convention's smoke-filled rooms." A noted copywriter, Walter O'Meara, joined the staff as copy chief for the Democrats. In the presidential campaign that fall the GOP spent $2.7 million, the Democrats just under $2 million, on radio and TV advertising. The Democrats spent less on advertising only because they raised less money. Rosser Reeves had again offered to produce spots for the Republicans, but he was turned down, perhaps because of all the controversy in 1952.

In 1960 the Democrats again tried to associate the enemy with insidious advertising methods: "a barrage of bland ballyhoo," as Frank Church put it in keynoting the Democratic convention, "the kind that results when government is run by hucksters not unaccustomed to selling inferior products by wrapping them in bright packages." Actually professional political advertising had long since become a bipartisan technique. It hardly guaranteed success; a man from BBDO applied the Lazy Shave light powder makeup that doomed Nixon in the first TV debate. But nobody, apparently, could now avoid a media campaign, especially on TV. "There is just no substitute for the magic of television," said William Proxmire, the liberal Democrat from Wisconsin. "I got more response and comments on my scheduled television appearances," agreed Walter Judd, the conservative Republican from Minnesota, "than from all other campaign techniques I used, even though these other techniques took infinitely more time and effort."

In 1964 the Leo Burnett agency produced "In your heart, you know he's right" for Goldwater's primary campaign. "Yes, far right," the joke ran, and Burnett was replaced before the fall showdown. Actually the Democrats generated the most controversy in this election with their own spots by Doyle Dane Bernbach. Well staffed with liberal Democrats, DDB created a special campaign group within the agency. "I think we have a great product," said Bernbach, "the easiest account we ever got." The first spot aired offered an angelic three-year-old girl picking the petals from a daisy and counting backward from ten; the sound track shifted to a Voice of Doom continuing the countdown, ending in a missile firing and exploding, a warning from President Johnson about the Bomb, and a final admonition: "The stakes are too high for you to stay home." The Republicans howled in protest, and Johnson ordered the daisy spot off the air. But DDB continued other spots, hardly less power-

ful, and spent $2.2 million on the campaign. Total advertising bud-
gets that fall amounted to $8.5 million for the Democrats, $16 million for the Republicans. The Democrats nonetheless carried off a
huge victory.

Thus by 1968 the record showed a long involvement of presidential candidates with Madison Avenue. The man with the more professional advice sometimes won, as in 1920, 1952, and 1964, and
sometimes lost, as in 1936 and 1940. The significance of Madison
Avenue's presence seemed unclear; the elections of 1920, 1952, and
1964 were all landslides that could hardly have gone differently.
The candidate with the larger ad budget usually won, but not always—in 1964 the Democrats were outspent nearly two to one.
The Republicans as the party of business had older, stronger ties to
Madison Avenue, so they had pioneered in bringing advertising into
the political process. But by 1968 no party or candidate dared ignore
the power of advertising, a bipartisan, universal presence.

The Nixon administration was often described as a public relations or advertising operation, "a J. Walter Thompson production,"
in Ralph Nader's words. Five key Nixon operatives did come from
JWT: H. R. Haldeman, the chief of staff; his assistant, Laurence
Higby; Ron Ziegler, the press secretary; and two special assistants,
Dwight Chapin and Ken Cole. Chapin had quit Thompson in 1966
to work for Nixon, then an unannounced candidate, as his personal
aide in charge of schedules, meals, and wardrobe. William Safire, a
public relations man, wrote speeches for Nixon; Jeb Magruder, from
a background in marketing, worked on improving the administration's image. "It seemed to me," noted Herbert Klein, an old Nixon
operative bypassed in the White House, "that half of the President's
staff considered themselves experts on press and public relations. . . .
On too many occasions, interest in promotion of a program exceeded interest in details of substance."

Especially after Watergate, Nixon's problems were frequently
blamed on an advertising mentality. Perhaps; but in a particular
way. The Thompson men around him had worked as account executives and managers, not as copywriters. They knew how to handle
clients or personnel problems, not how to write or sell a campaign,
or how to sense the public mood. "As a professional PR man," Safire
noted, "Haldeman was merely a good adman." The Nixon White
House resembled not an ad agency itself but a touchy client and his
account men, bouncing around the same room, unable to escape

each other. Nixon behaved like the client, an especially weird, headlong, unpredictable, impossible client: George Washington Hill in the White House. Trailing after him, picking up after him, his account-executive assistants existed at his pleasure, tried to please him, but had constantly to balance what he wanted done with what the public would bear. Occasionally (not often enough) Haldeman would nod, scribble some loony mission on his yellow pad, and then "forget" to do it. This wobbly structure collapsed when the staff grew too close to the client, too far from the public.

That a president should include advertising and public relations people in his inner circle was not, by now, an aberration. Aside from the early precedent of Lasker in the Harding White House, Kennedy had Larry O'Brien, and Johnson had Jack Valenti. (As, later, Carter had Gerald Rafshoon and Reagan had James Brady and Michael Deaver.) The question remains of who was corrupting whom by these involvements. As Raymond Rubicam had pointed out in 1936, advertising people might acquire deceptive tricks by reading the average political platform: "If you want to learn the arts of misleading and overpromising there is no better source to learn." Even before the Watergate crisis, when had American politics ever been conducted in the open air of rational discourse? Long campaign speeches had always been reduced to a single phrase—"The Cross of Gold" in 1896; "He kept us out of war" in 1916—no more enlightening than a TV spot campaign. The long and bloody history of American political corruption predated the intrusion of advertising. In the case of politics, once again, advertising only reflected given procedures and standards.

EIGHT

THE 1970s:
THE CYCLE NEVER STOPS

As the technical aspects of the creative revolution subsided, a student of advertising cycles might have predicted the trade's future in the 1970s. In style, back to hard sell, science, and research—an emphasis, as Rosser Reeves anticipated, on the product instead of the ad. In organization, a shift from the creative departments to management, from little boutiques to bigness and mergers, from vivid personalities to corporate anonymity. In sum, a fast trip in a time machine back to the 1950s.

After a decade as the hottest agency in advertising, Doyle Dane Bernbach entered the 1970s by losing its first major account. For Alka-Seltzer DDB had produced a popular TV ad in 1970: a winsome new bride, played by Alice Playten, cooking indigestible meals for her husband, spinning visions of marshmallowed meatballs and poached oysters until he reaches for more Alka-Seltzer. Everyone liked and laughed at the spot, but the client's market share kept falling. Late in 1970 Alka-Seltzer moved the $20 million account from DDB to Wells, Rich, Greene. "We will be more product oriented," Mary Wells announced, "and try to explain more clearly what Alka-Seltzer does."

As the economy fell into recession in 1971, most large agencies—including Thompson, McCann, Young & Rubicam, Bates, and BBDO—suffered losses in total domestic billings. But at DDB, after

314

its years of fat, consistent gains, such reversals looked more significant. A loss of $15 million in U.S. billings in 1971 was then followed
by a stampede of departing clients. Lever Brothers, Whirlpool,
Sara Lee, Quaker Oats, Cracker Jack, and others left, amounting
to a total account loss of about $33 million in 1972. Again in 1973,
a decline in U.S. billings, of almost $11 million. These figures were
somewhat balanced by DDB mergers with smaller agencies and
overseas growth. Still, the essential DDB selling point—a gift for attracting new business with fresh, effective ads—could now be
doubted for the first time.

"We've never lost our creative flame," said Oscar Lubow for the
agency. "We have seventeen of the greatest creative wizards in the
industry right here. Not one of them *only* supervises. They make
ads." Of all the DDB people who had left to start their own shops,
said Lubow, only one (Mary Wells) had really made it. Others now
wanted to come back to DDB. (But a few months later Lubow, too,
quit DDB to return to his consulting firm.) In March 1974, after the
$10 million Uniroyal tire account was lost, Bill Bernbach and Joe
Daly moved upstairs to make room for a new president, James Heekin, who announced his intention to improve DDB's account service
and marketing department: "I see my job as getting our fine creative
department and other departments working in concert." Only five
months later, Heekin also quit under pressure.

Bernbach had always prided himself on hiring carefully, training
people well, keeping them happy, and seldom firing anyone. DDB
now incredibly was just another agency, afflicted with the usual
personnel instabilities, subject to the normal, implacable cycles of
advertising fashions. Once in a losing streak, an agency found its
troubles compounded by the simple *reputation* of being in a losing
streak. The scent of blood attracted more sharks. In 1971 DDB had
done a TV commercial, an instant classic, for Life cereal, a ten-
year-old product with low visibility. Two boys, confronted with the
dubious prospect of a cereal "supposed to be good for you," pass it
on to younger brother Mikey ("he hates everything"). But Mikey
likes it, and so did consumers, as the spot pushed Life sales up by 20
percent. But—the sharks descending—in 1974 the Life account
moved from DDB to BBDO. Recognizing a good vehicle, BBDO
kept running the Mikey commercial with periodic updatings. For
DDB it meant yet another account loss.

Other creative agencies lost accounts, or became conservative, or disappeared. Howard Gossage's agency in San Francisco was dissolved in 1971, two years after the death of the founder. "It now seems impossible," explained Jerry Mander, keening over both the agency and the hopes of his generation, "to run a profitable agency in the way we had tried to run this one, which is by emphasizing public service work and those commercial jobs which were not inconsistent with our personal views." In 1972 Mary Wells lost *her* first big account: after several years of declining sales, American Motors took its $22 million worth of business elsewhere. Various problems were reported at Tinker; at Leber Katz; and at Papert, Koenig, Lois. As the creative shops grew, and then fought to maintain themselves in the constrictions of a recession, they faced the old dilemma of reconciling creative daring with growth, of staying original while working on big, boring packaged-goods accounts. "When you get to be management something happens to you," Carl Ally noted. "Because when you are down there you want permissiveness and when you're up here you want discipline."

Nothing could bridle George Lois. He had already quit Papert, Koenig, Lois—blaming the evils of growth and corporate caution— to start his second agency, Lois Holland Calloway. With the winds on Madison Avenue now blowing against him, he blamed this Thermidor to the creative revolution on a vaguely defined "them," the old regimes who could not understand. "They'll never understand why we work fourteen hours a day and they'll never understand the loosey-gooseyness of the way we like to work," he said in 1971. "They don't like the way we work, the way we talk, the way we dress. They don't know anything about advertising or how great advertising is created. They hold this business down." A few years later Lois quit his agency amid rumors of fiscal problems and quarrels with his partners. He joined another shop as president, stayed for sixteen months, was fired. "An ad agency is a business," said one of his former associates. "George ought to know that by now." Lois then launched his third agency, Lois Pitts Gershon. At a time in his career when anyone of his talent, drive, and reputation should have reached a peak in power and salary, Lois was still confined to the lower reaches of advertising. His course offered a melancholy example for other children of the creative revolution who would not (depending on one's viewpoint) grow up or sell out.

The creative revolution's two departures in fiscal affairs were also under more exacting scrutiny. Some two dozen agencies had followed the lead of PKL in selling shares of the business in stock to the general public. By 1969 five of the top ten agencies—Thompson; Foote, Cone & Belding; DDB; Grey; and Ogilvy & Mather—had gone public. But the public did not rush to buy pieces of ad agencies. Stock prices of the public agencies generally stayed at or below their original levels. Labor-intensive rather than capital-intensive, advertising did not benefit greatly from the financial advantages of public ownership. "In retrospect," George Lois said of his experience at PKL, "public ownership was the catalyst for destroying our partnership. People became rich quick and choked up. They started to think, 'We now have obligations to our stockholders.' " "It hasn't done us much harm," David Ogilvy concluded, "and it hasn't done us much good, either, except that it has forced us to manage our own affairs a little more efficiently." Starting in 1974, several agencies (notably Grey and Wells) bought back their common stock and returned to private ownership. Only the largest publicly owned shops had the cash reserves and management depth to ride out the unpredictable storms on Wall Street. The rest of advertising resumed a conception of itself as a service business trading on talent, not capital.

The traditional method of agency compensation, the 15 percent commission on media billings, also held off challenges. A fee system, publicized when Ogilvy took the Shell account on that basis, had later advanced when American Tobacco, with accounts totaling $50 million, had insisted on a similar arrangement with its two agencies in 1965. After a year American Tobacco announced a resultant saving of $1.5 million, and other clients took notice. But the practice did not take hold. General Foods tried it for two years and returned to commissions, preferring that arrangement for its well-established brands. For a new product, a fee might offer an agency more definite payment than a percentage of uncertain future media budgets. For most products, most of the time, the commission did in a rough fashion reward effective advertising and punish the rest. So the old arrangement still prevailed in perhaps three-fourths of all agency-client dealings. "With change so much a part of life," *Advertising Age* commented in 1979, "it's remarkable how the 15 percent commission system continues to flourish."

❧❧

The advertising reforms of the 1960s held up better than the creative revolution in the new decade. At a time of administering and executing instead of crusading, the winnowing process shook out some chaff but left a solid—perhaps permanent—core of changes in the way advertising had always done business.

One new reform impulse appeared in the early 1970s. Building on the precedents of advertising's responsibilities toward blacks and women, the needs of another group, children, were asserted, in this case not by themselves. TV advertisers were spending over $200 million a year pitching products (mainly toys, cereals, and candy) at children. According to child psychologists, just starting to accumulate a body of academic research in this field, the average child saw twenty thousand thirty-second spots a year, or a total of over three hours a week. Children under the age of eight generally could not distinguish between a commercial and the program: anything on TV was simply absorbed uncritically. Not until the sixth grade were most children skeptical about the truthfulness of ads. Kids presented advertisers a uniquely receptive audience, a simple matter of selling candy to a baby.

Concern about what TV was doing to their children led a group of women in Boston—Peggy Charren, Evelyn Sarson, and others— to form Action for Children's Television (ACT). Among its efforts, ACT petitioned regulatory agencies to limit and improve commercials aimed at kids. A request that the FCC ban daytime drug advertising as harmful to children was denied after hearings on the grounds of inadequate scientific evidence. But ACT and its allies could claim significant victories: a withdrawal of vitamin ads appealing to children, a reduction of commercials during weekend children's programs, a ban on hosts or stars making pitches and thus blurring the separation of ad and program, a provision for public service spots about good nutrition habits, a prohibition of appeals urging children to ask their parents to buy the product, and a stipulation that commercials may not exaggerate the size or speed of a toy. As ACT grew to 20,000 members and an annual budget of $400,000, Peggy Charren stayed on the job, the Ralph Nader of children's television.

Another new reform figure by his excesses helped tarnish the credibility of more serious critics of advertising. In a remarkably silly series of books, a journalism professor named Wilson Bryan Key warned consumers of subliminal sexual manipulations by Madison Avenue. It was a new version of *The Hidden Persuaders, sans peur* and *sans* research. Key claimed to see the word "sex" embedded craftily in Ritz crackers, in Norman Rockwell's first *Saturday Evening Post* cover in 1917, in almost anything that Key looked at long enough. Sexual embedding, Key declared with a grand sweep, had been used "in every political campaign of any magnitude in the United States and Canada for at least twenty-five years—if not much, much longer." The reader might have wondered how he had managed to examine all those campaigns. No contrite advertising artist ever came forward to confess writing in all those three-letter words—because it did not happen, save in the minds of Key and his admirers. His books sold well, testifying to the continued public suspicion of advertising and a willingness to believe the most ridiculous charges against it.

Key's flailings notwithstanding, the new regulatory apparatus, especially the Federal Trade Commission and the industry's own National Advertising Review Board, held advertising to unprecedented standards of honesty and disclosure. The FTC ordered Listerine to spend $10 million on corrective advertising ("Listerine will not help prevent colds or sore throats or lessen their severity") and directed Anacin to spend $24 million on ads explaining the product would not relieve tensions, as previously claimed. On occasion competing advertisers helped the feds out by blowing a whistle on each other. Heinz soups, trying to break into Campbell's domination of the soup market, told the FTC about faked ad photographs that BBDO had produced for Campbell: a bowl of soup with marbles in the bottom, pushing the vegetables to the surface and making the soup look chunkier. The FTC forced BBDO to stop the deception. A few years later Campbell bought a quantity of Heinz ketchup for a restaurant subsidiary and found mold in some bottles. Campbell patriotically informed the Food and Drug Administration, which seized 224 cases of Heinz ketchup.

The regulatory net now held advertising so tightly that even some of its former advocates had second thoughts. "I guess we deserved this; we failed to regulate ourselves," said David Ogilvy. "But we are now overregulated. The whole thing has become a farce." In the late 1970s, amid a general trend toward deregulation in Washington, the federal grip on advertising loosened somewhat. Testimonial ads still flourished despite FTC disapproval. The Supreme Court in a 1976 case gave advertising legal standing (and protection) under the first amendment. Concurrently a series of articles in legal and economic journals described advertising as an aid, not a hindrance, to competition. In 1980 Congress removed the FTC's power to stop "unfair" advertising, restricting the commission to the regulation of "deceptive" ads.

These developments meant a relative, not an absolute, retreat from the regulatory standards of the early 1970s. Measured against the pre-Nader era, advertising still was closely policed from both within and without. Consumerism had moved from publicity campaigns to government institutions. The consumer movement, less visible nationally, still operated effectively in local groups. Consumer-protection legislation, now less popular, gave way to emphases on consumer redress, education, and cooperative buying.

Advertising's continued efforts toward ethnic and gender pluralism brought similarly mixed returns. Blacks appeared in 5 percent of all TV ads in 1967, 13 percent in 1976, but still showed up more often in public service and promotional spots than in regular product ads. A few blacks reached rarefied levels of advertising management. William Sharp left Thompson in 1972 to run Coca-Cola's advertising department. Later he chaired the AAF and became a founding partner of a general-market agency in Atlanta. Ronald Sampson, the highest-ranking black at a major agency, was a management supervisor and partner at Tatham-Laird & Kudner in Chicago. But in general the employment of blacks in advertising at best remained stable. From 1970 to 1974, according to an AAAA study, minority employment at 38 large agencies went from 8.9 to 9.9 percent overall, but dipped from 4.6 to 4.2 percent at professional/managerial levels. The AAAA annual meeting in 1975 was told that fewer blacks were reaching the top jobs in advertising: integrating the ads, said Winthrop Jordan, a black adman, had led to "a degree of self-deception in that many advertising executives think that now they've done their bit." Blacks filed charges of employment discrimination at most of the top twenty agencies during the 1970s.

For complex, arguable reasons blacks and advertising work did not mesh well. Afro-American culture has been essentially oral and aural, without strong reading and writing traditions. Blacks have made their greatest impact on American life in sports and music—partly because of white expectations, but more because sports and music flow logically from black culture and require few literacy skills. By contrast advertising, even TV advertising, is written and rewritten and worried over down to the last comma. Media, marketing, and contact work also reward advanced language skills. The minority employment programs of the late 1960s typically took people from black cultures and, with the best intentions, dropped them into an alien advertising milieu. "The ghetto experience of which our trainees are products," said Roberta Kirwan, a counselor for DDB's minority effort, "does not foster such middle-class attributes as punctuality, literacy, regular attendance, concern with procedure and acceptance of long-term goals." Of 110 graduates from William Sharp's basic advertising course in Chicago, only 16 were still employed in advertising in 1975. Jerry Della Femina's attempt to teach an advertising class to blacks left him frustrated by a culture gap: "I had trouble because they live in a different world than I do. They can write black, they can't write white."

Like many white agencies launched at the height of the creative revolution, the black agencies suffered high mortality rates in the 1970s. John F. Small's shop approached a breakthrough in 1970 when it won a million-dollar general (that is, not black) Singer account. "Now the black man is ready to compete as an entrepreneur on the same basis as whites," Small declared. But five years later Small went under after the Navy withdrew its $1.7 million minority-recruiting account because the agency was "unable to complete its contract obligations." Zebra Associates folded in 1976 amid bizarre charges that Joan Murray, one of the agency principals, had hired two men to assault an associate. Other black agencies succumbed for different reasons. "It's one thing to have the mind and intelligence to run a business," explained Joyce Hamer, a black adwoman, "and another to be trained in the skill. So people didn't spend enough time with finance or other line areas."

The more durable black agencies stayed within their special market. Uniworld of New York claimed a glossy client list—RCA, General Motors, Gillette, AT&T, Heublein, Avon, R. J. Reynolds—for which it did ads aimed at blacks. "We have to concentrate on our niche," said Byron Lewis of Uniworld. Thomas Burrell's agency in Chicago, the biggest black shop, billed just under $20 million in 1980. It won a Clio award for a Coca-Cola spot showing black street kids do-wopping the Coke theme. Burrell won another Clio for a McDonald's ad depicting a black family reunion, with the cause of the son's absence—often a sensitive issue in black families—left deliberately vague. "Our values, what motivates us, our fears, our aspirations, are cultural or at least culturally derived," said Burrell. "And you've got to come from that culture to know what those variables are." No doubt. Yet that specialness held blacks to a separate and unequal place in American advertising.

Women started from stronger positions than blacks, and they

continued to fare better on Madison Avenue in the 1970s. Raised in the same culture as white males, and indeed traditionally adept at reading and writing, women had literacy skills at least equal to men's. With time they acquired the necessary male habits of command and self-assertion as well. Pressured from inside and outside agencies, sex roles and female images in the ads kept improving, with occasional strong women and nurturing men, female executives and male baby-sitters. "In general," *Ms.* magazine commented, "advertisers have shown a willingness to change, an increased understanding that women's interests far exceed 'feminine' products." Exxon, Sony, Gillette, Breck, AT&T, and American Express were described as especially enlightened. Print ads, targeted at particular readerships, were more progressive than TV commercials aimed at a more general audience. Unfortunately, as Franchellie Cadwell noted, the most offensive ads often tested and sold the product well. If one showed a woman giving a speech, or driving a race car, or sweating over a hot stove, Cadwell pointed out, the last usually brought the best sales response. Cadwell suggested a consumer boycott of products using sexist appeals: "You can sit at an agency and write and produce all the liberated commercials you like, but women have got to help."

Even Mary Wells developed a kind of feminist consciousness. She still did not like "militant libbers," as she called them, and she regretted that her eminence kept clients from flirting with her ("It was more fun when they thought I was a sexy blonde"). But her success in a man's world was by itself a feminist statement. She had sought, and achieved, a higher salary than that of any man she knew. "I'm not a feminist, not in the serious, activist sense," she said in 1976, "but I have a very strong feminist feeling about things like the Equal Rights Amendment and salaries. I feel strongly about the unfairness that exists. A lot is changing, though; a lot more women are coming into this business and they are very good, very useful." She praised her female account executives. Yet she promoted no women to the board of directors or to top management at her agency, and associated mainly with men away from work as well. "I really don't have girl friends," she said. Several women were qualified to head branch offices of the agency, she explained, but she would not let them because male clients could not stand it—their "chauvinism" kept them from dealing comfortably with a woman of authority. Thus, in the hands of Mary Wells, a feminist viewpoint demanded that women be treated differently.

No other woman duplicated the Wells saga, but advertising still abounded in female success stories. In 1973 Reva Korda became creative head at Ogilvy & Mather ("It was about time I got it"). After another woman filed a sex-discrimination charge against O & M in 1976, the representation of women in professional jobs at the agency leaped in six years from 40 to 57 percent. Women bossed the creative departments at four other major agencies in the mid-1970s. At one time, Shirley Polykoff noted in 1975, she could tell her associates they misunderstood women because they were men; "now you can't say that any more because there are so many women in the business." Polykoff, Jane Trahey, Janet Marie Carlson, Paula Green, Jo Foxworth, Lois Geraci Ernst, Faith Popcorn, Joyce Hamer, Jacqueline Brandwynne, and Adrienne Hall and Joan Levine all ran their own agencies. Joyce Hamer often sent a white male to represent her agency at initial client presentations. "For the first few meetings," she explained, "they can tell the boys' jokes and get it out of the way."

By the late 1970s, letters to the editor of *Advertising Age* submitting sexist ads came as often from men as from women. Two prominent advertising feminists, Jane Trahey and Anne Tolstoi Wallach, wrote advertising novels in which the heroine was menaced not by male chauvinists but by scheming female associates. The biggest of the new female-headed agencies, Advertising to Women, reached billings of nearly $50 million in 1980. Under the creative direction of Lois Geraci Ernst, the agency presented strong but sexy women selling Jean Naté ("Take charge of your life"), Rive Gauche (a woman driving alone through the night, "having too much fun to marry"), and Aviance perfume ("It's going to be an Aviance night"). "It took seven to eight years," Ernst said of marketing men, "for them to figure out that women aren't home polishing their floors any more." What of feminist criticisms that her ads reinforced a notion of woman as sex object? "If women's lib doesn't like it," said Ernst crisply, "that's tough."

❧❧

The 1970s most resembled the 1950s in copy style and management practices. Hard sell became appropriate for the tighter economic climate at the start of the decade. Creative awards no longer guaranteed jobs and promotions. Agencies instead sought marketing MBAs, people who understood the nuts and bolts of pricing, distribution, and packaging. Instead of rubbing their muses, artists and copywriters were handed the selling idea, with suggestions on how to present it. "Today, thank God, we are back in business as salesmen instead of pretentious entertainers," said David Ogilvy. "The pendulum is swinging back our way—the Hopkins way."

The prophets of the new gospel, "positioning," were Al Ries and Jack Trout of Ries Cappiello Colwell (later Trout & Ries). Of course, nothing in advertising was *really* new: as a concept, even as a term, positioning had been worked out in the late 1950s by various divisions of General Foods. Ries and Trout resurrected the concept and made it their trademark. As a small agency with no industry leaders among its clients—in 1975, at $13.7 million, it ranked 125th among all agencies—Ries naturally sought a strategy for new or marginal products, hoping to improve their market shares. That meant a quick, simple, aggressive pitch to slice through the fatter competition: a classic hard sell. "Positioning is thinking in reverse," said Ries and Trout. "Instead of starting with yourself, you start with the mind of the prospect. . . . Changing minds in our overcommunicated society is an extremely difficult task. It's much easier to work with what's already there." The first, most crucial decision was naming the product—something memorable, with a chance of becoming eponymously generic. Next, Ries and Trout urged, find one specific selling argument (like the USP of Rosser Reeves) and keep running it past the point of agency boredom. Matter, not manner, made the difference. Humor and esthetics only diverted attention from the selling concept. Positioning, in sum, turned the creative revolution inside out. "Today, creativity is dead," declared Ries and Trout. "The name of the game on Madison Avenue is positioning."

More specifically, positioning implied comparative advertising— naming the competition and drawing a favorable comparison. Another ancient technique, comparative advertising had been used obliquely by Getchell's "Look at All Three," more directly by DDB and Ally in the Avis-Hertz wars of the 1960s. The major agencies and trade groups had discouraged its use, overtly because it was deemed unsporting, more pertinently because it offered a potent weapon to small, upstart competitors. NBC dropped its ban on such ads in 1964, but the other two networks would not follow suit. To consumers and the FTC, though, comparative pitches offered the potential of more specific, informative advertising: hard, verifiable facts instead of puffing generalities. In 1972, after threats of FTC lawsuits over restraint of trade, ABC and CBS caved in, and the AAAA fell into line two years later.

Ries and Trout embraced comparative ads as the best way to "position" a product against the competition. Their own agency stayed small, with no well-known campaigns to its credit. ("If we're so smart," Ries asked in 1979, "why aren't we rich?") But bigger agencies made comparative advertising the most characteristic technique of the 1970s. Taking aim at Coke, 7-Up more than doubled its sales with an "Uncola" theme. Tylenol, "for the millions who should not take aspirin," became the biggest nonaspirin pain reliever. Scope, which did not taste "mediciny," bit deeply into Listerine's market share and forced it to produce a better-flavored mouthwash. After Coke replied to Pepsi with "It's the real thing," Pepsi riposted with hidden-camera, blind taste tests against Coke that doubled its market share within a year. Catching the wave it had helped generate, in 1976 DDB resumed its "We try harder" campaign for Avis after a hiatus of seven years.

The comparative approach still favored an underdog taking on a leader. Its use therefore carried inherent limitations. Federal Express overtook Emery with a comparative campaign by Ally, then changed to more conventional ads once it reached first place. For consumers comparative ads meant a hard sell, but a more honest, more entertaining hard sell than the old Hopkins techniques. Consumers enjoyed the spectacle of advertisers scrapping in public, naming names and predicting disaster for the enemy like boxers trying to build up a gate, often in a funny, aren't-we-daring? style. The feds looked on tolerantly, stepping in only when someone made a dubious claim against a competitor. Even the most stringent federal regulator of advertising, the Bureau of Alcohol, Tobacco & Firearms in the Treasury Department, started allowing light-beer manufacturers to compare calorie levels. Comparative advertising thus melded a traditional hard sell with a consumerist viewpoint. By 1980 one commercial in four on ABC television was drawing pointed comparisons.

The management style of the 1970s repeated the giantism of the 1950s, with a few key adjustments. Here a new management team at Young & Rubicam provided the model for the industry. When Edward Ney, a Y & R veteran since 1951, took over as chairman and CEO in November 1970, he inherited an agency—in the waning days of the creative revolution—with a bloated staff, high expenses, and a low rate of growth. Ney pared the New York office by a third, down to 1,200 employees, and installed Alex Kroll as creative director and Alexander Brody as head of international operations. This trio then led the agency into a period of astonishing growth. Kroll guarded Y & R's traditional reputation for good creative work. "We remain manic about creative discipline," he insisted. But, in contrast with the 1960s, "discipline" now mattered as much as "creative." "We believe that creativity is tactical," said Kroll; "it should be measured by the cold, gritty eye of the marketplace, not by the vibes you get in a screening room. We want our advertising to be judged by consumer take-away, not peer applause."

Ney oversaw an ambitious program of growth by mergers and acquisitions. Instead of selling Y & R stock to the public, Ney raised the money for this program by internal manipulations of agency stock and retirement programs; he thus insured himself more freedom and privacy from outsiders. Building toward what he called "a wide horizontal range of commercial persuasion," in 1973 Ney bought Sudler & Hennessey, an agency specializing in health-care advertising, and Wunderman, Ricotta & Kline, specialists in direct marketing. With the addition of their combined $62 million in billings Y & R pushed past Thompson in total U.S. billings, knocking JWT off the perch it had held since the 1920s. In the next few years Ney gobbled up regional agencies in the Midwest and Southwest, and other shops specializing in retailing and sales promotions. This expansion climaxed in 1979 when Y & R acquired Marsteller, with its billings of $306 million, and replaced Thompson as the leader in world billings as well.

Marion Harper, in penurious retirement in Oklahoma, enjoyed a kind of vindication. His vision of Interpublic as a gigantic holding company of agencies was being copied, to great success, a decade after his departure from Interpublic in disgrace. But Ney took the basic concept and avoided Harper's crucial mistakes of hubris and self-indulgence. A man of controlled ego and few apparent eccentricities, Ney kept his own role in perspective. He inspired few Ed Ney stories. "The throw-away line about me," he said, "is that I'm really a glorified personnel manager. Well, there's a lot of truth in that." Where Harper had held too much authority in his own hands, Ney delegated power to his top people, who included few yes-men. "Some CEOs don't want terribly strong people around them," Ney explained. "I feel just the opposite. Strong advisers can do more than just coexist with a strong leader. They can make him. . . . Sure, I have a point of view on things, but I listen. I'd be a bloody idiot if I didn't and maybe they'd even vote me out." The same principle of decentralized authority extended to Y & R's acquisitions. Ney bought healthy operations, not crippled enterprises in need of overhauls. So he let them run themselves if they stayed out of trouble. "They have to be autonomous," he said. "We're not going to tell a successful company how to run their business."

Other agencies followed the trend, making the 1970s a decade of mergers. Interpublic bought Campbell-Ewald and SSC & B. Ogilvy took Scali, McCabe, Sloves, the hottest new agency of the 1970s. Wells, Rich, Greene bought Gardner. Bates absorbed Campbell-Mithun. The three biggest public relations firms were acquired by Thompson, Y & R, and Foote, Cone & Belding. By the end of the decade no major independent agencies remained on the West Coast. "There's a certain malaise among small agencies today," said James Heekin, now a partner in a small consulting firm. "They've lost their entrepreneurial confidence. They see God on the side of the big battalions. They don't want to be the last guy off the beach, so they figure they should get aboard."

Especially from the mid-1970s on, billings at the top agencies and total advertising expenditures increased faster than the GNP, even faster than inflation or any other economic indicator. In a time of generally stuttering economic growth, advertising enjoyed remarkable, almost giddy leaps upward. Total spending on advertising grew from $19.6 billion in 1970 to $54.6 billion in 1980; TV as usual led the way, from $3.6 billion to $11.4 billion. In 1970 world billings at the top ten agencies ranged from Thompson's $773 million to Grey's $230 million. Ten years later, thirteen agencies—led by Y & R at $2.3 billion—exceeded Thompson's total in 1970. Eleven agencies had realized Harper's old dream of becoming billion-dollar operations.

The cycle turned. As the excesses of the creative revolution had led to hard sell and corporate growth, those developments in turn now redirected attention to the creative product. "How puny our courage and how poor our spirit," said Mary Wells. "What a bore advertising is becoming." TV advertising relied on pretesting methods—especially the telephone inquiries of the Burke service —that favored hard, rational content and strong reason-whys. A commercial with a low Burke score would not make it to national exposure. As in the 1950s, advertising lost creative verve when it regarded itself as a rational, quantifiable science. Ads came to resemble each other: vignettes and slices-of-life showing people enjoying the product; print ads for cigarettes with three cigarettes protruding from an apparently unopened package; takeoff shots for airlines; soap ads of people happily lathering as though they were not bathing alone; naked women in bath-oil spots; macho sportsmen in beer ads; pet-food commercials with a pet and a bowl of the product.

"There were fewer gee-whiz ads, commercials, and campaigns last year than for any year I can remember," said William Tyler, the resident critic at *Advertising Age*, in 1977. "The industry is waiting for the next creative giant to shake us all up." In 1978 Jane Trahey sold her agency and quit the business. "Most advertising these days is so bad I don't really believe it," she said. "I wonder about the sanity of clients. How can they buy such pulp?" "If you believe creativity is the heart of our business," agreed Alvin Hampel of Benton & Bowles, "then what we're seeing is a case of cardiac arrest."

The business, *Advertising Age* announced in 1980, was on the verge of "a new creative revolution." *Plus ça change* . . .

❦❦

An enterprise that spent $54.6 billion a year could reasonably expect to wield great power. Yet the volume and ubiquity of advertising actually worked against its effectiveness: a paradox that denied common sense. As communications research has shown, when the gross total of ads increases people screen it more finely. At some point the screaming cacophony simply becomes white noise—background clutter from which few individual messages stand out. According to one study by the AAAA, an average consumer was exposed to 1,600 ads a day; of these 80 were consciously noticed, and only 12 provoked some reaction. Most recent polls of public opinion about advertising have found neither approval nor disapproval but just indifference, a lack of interest.

This is the central irony of advertising history: over the course of the twentieth century, advertising has grown and prospered and yet has lost influence. From its peak as an independent force in American life in the 1920s, advertising has been caught in a tightening vise between two contrary forces. Regulation by the government and (finally) by the industry itself has gradually limited Madison Avenue's freedom to lie. When restricted, more or less, to the truth, advertising lost some of its most powerful, frightening devices. Yet even as advertising grew less deceptive, the public grew ever more sophisticated and skeptical. A Gallup Poll in 1976 asked Americans to rate the honesty and ethical standards in eleven fields of work. The bottom five categories proved to be business executives, senators, congressmen, labor-union leaders, and—dead last—advertising executives. Increasingly regulated on one side and increasingly scorned or ignored by consumers on the other, advertising has been shooting smaller weapons at a more garrisoned target. Along with most other contemporary American institutions, advertising now has trouble finding anybody to believe it.

At the same time, as a purely economic force advertising remains a dynamic, necessary part of American consumer capitalism. Good advertising can still make a new or obscure product successful, as surely as bad advertising can doom another product. In an economy pitched more to discretionary services, less to necessary goods, advertising becomes even more crucial in guiding purchases. Even if we deplore advertising as a cultural influence, we can hardly avoid its role in how we spend our money.

In regard to advertising's broader cultural impact—the power to create and shape mass tastes and behavior—outsiders are generally more impressed than those inside the business with the alleged influence of Madison Avenue. "As a practitioner of advertising," David Ogilvy noted in 1962, "I believe it is nothing more than a tool of salesmanship, which *follows* mores but never leads them. The public is *bored* by most advertisements, and has acquired a genius for ignoring it." Outsiders see only the smooth, expertly contrived finished product, often better crafted than the programming and editorial matter it interrupts. Insiders know the messy process of creating an ad, the false starts, rejected ideas, midnight despair, the failures and account losses and creative angst behind any ad that finally appears. In particular, the insiders know that no successful ad can stray very far from where the audience already lives. The ad must be fitted to the audience, not the other way around. "Advertising doesn't manipulate society," said Carl Ally in 1977. "Society manipulates advertising. Advertising responds to social trends. Agencies respond to advertisers. It's that simple."

Thus the favorite metaphor of the industry: advertising as a mirror that merely reflects society back on itself. Granted that this mirror too often shows our least lovely qualities of materialism, sexual insecurity, jealousy, vanity, and greed. The image in the advertising mirror has seldom revealed the best aspects of American life. But advertising must take human nature as it is found. We all would like to think we act from admirable motives. The obdurate, damning fact is that most of us, most of the time, are moved by more selfish, practical considerations. Advertising inevitably tries to tap these stronger, darker strains.

One may build a compelling case that American culture is—beyond redemption—money-mad, hedonistic, superficial, rushing heedlessly down a railroad track called Progress. Tocqueville and other observers of the young republic described America in these terms in the early 1800s, decades before the development of national advertising. To blame advertising now for these most basic tendencies in American history is to miss the point. It is too obvious, too easy, a matter of killing the messenger instead of dealing with the bad news. The people who have created modern advertising are not hidden persuaders pushing our buttons in the service of some malevolent purpose. They are just producing an especially visible manifestation, good and bad, of the American way of life.

GLOSSARY
OF ABBREVIATIONS

AA	*Advertising Age*
AAAA	American Association of Advertising Agencies
AACA	Associated Advertising Clubs of America
AAF	American Advertising Federation (see AFA)
AFA	American Federation of Advertising (see AAF)
ANA	Association of National Advertisers
B & B	Benton & Bowles
BBB	Better Business Bureaus
BBDO	Batten, Barton, Durstine & Osborn
B-S-H	Blackett-Sample-Hummert
C & H	Calkins & Holden
FC & B	Foote, Cone & Belding (see L & T)
JWT	J. Walter Thompson
L & T	Lord & Thomas (see FC & B)
NAB	National Association of Broadcasters
NAD	National Advertising Division, BBB
NARB	National Advertising Review Board
O & M	Ogilvy & Mather (see OB & M)
OB & M	Ogilvy, Benson & Mather (see O & M)
PI	*Printers' Ink*
PKL	Papert, Koenig, Lois
WRG	Wells, Rich, Greene
Y & R	Young & Rubicam

THE TEN LARGEST AGENCIES
IN U.S. BILLINGS
1945–1980

As Compiled by *Advertising Age*

All billings are stated in millions of dollars.

1945

J. Walter Thompson	$78.0
Young & Rubicam	53.0
N. W. Ayer & Son	41.0
BBDO	40.0
McCann-Erickson	40.0
Ruthrauff & Ryan	32.0
Foote, Cone & Belding	31.0
Dancer-Fitzgerald-Sample	25.0
Biow Company	22.0
Compton Advertising	21.0

1950

J. Walter Thompson	$130.0
Young & Rubicam	92.0
BBDO	87.0
N. W. Ayer & Son	79.0
McCann-Erickson	67.0
Foote, Cone & Belding	61.0
Ruthrauff & Ryan	45.0
Benton & Bowles	44.0
Grant Advertising	40.0
Kenyon & Eckhardt	38.0

1955

J. Walter Thompson	$172.0
Young & Rubicam	166.0
BBDO	162.5
McCann-Erickson	132.0
N. W. Ayer & Son	92.0
Leo Burnett	69.2
Foote, Cone & Belding	68.0
Benton & Bowles	68.0
Kenyon & Eckhardt	68.0
Ted Bates	59.2

1960

J. Walter Thompson	$250.0
BBDO	234.8
McCann-Erickson	225.0
Young & Rubicam	212.0
Ted Bates	130.0
Leo Burnett	116.7
Benton & Bowles	114.0
N. W. Ayer & Son	110.0
Dancer-Fitzgerald-Sample	100.7
Foote, Cone & Belding	99.6

1965

J. Walter Thompson	$317.0
BBDO	277.1
Young & Rubicam	276.0
McCann-Erickson	259.0
Foote, Cone & Belding	178.6
Leo Burnett	174.8
Ted Bates	169.2
N. W. Ayer & Son	135.6
Dancer-Fitzgerald-Sample	134.6
Doyle Dane Bernbach	130.0

1970

J. Walter Thompson	$438.0
Young & Rubicam	356.4
BBDO	324.4
Leo Burnett	283.6
Ted Bates	254.0
Doyle Dane Bernbach	249.7
McCann-Erickson	246.5
Grey Advertising	180.0
Foote, Cone & Belding	179.0
William Esty	170.0

1975

Young & Rubicam	$476.6
J. Walter Thompson	432.8
Leo Burnett	400.0
BBDO	369.9
Ted Bates	280.2
Foote, Cone & Belding	275.3
Ogilvy & Mather	266.1
D'Arcy-MacManus & Masius	234.0
McCann-Erickson	230.8
Doyle Dane Bernbach	228.2

1980

Young & Rubicam	$1,333.7
J. Walter Thompson	918.9
Ogilvy & Mather	837.1
BBDO International	806.4
Foote, Cone & Belding	749.3
Leo Burnett	734.6
Ted Bates	720.3
Doyle Dane Bernbach	671.0
Grey Advertising	524.9
Dancer-Fitzgerald-Sample	505.0

ACKNOWLEDGMENTS

First, I owe thanks to the families of several leading advertising figures for discussing their distinguished relatives with me. Bettina Rubicam, Kathleen Rubicam Witten, and Stephen Rubicam filled in gaps in my understanding of Raymond Rubicam. Therese Lansdowne Duble and Helen Resor Hauge provided vital insights about Stanley and Helen Resor. Mildred Locke Getchell and John S. Getchell helped me recover the elusive Stirling Getchell.

At the agencies, Mark Stroock of Young & Rubicam and Cynthia G. Swank of J. Walter Thompson were extraordinarily helpful, responding quickly and fully to my repeated requests for information and materials. I am also indebted to Cary Bayer of Doyle Dane Bernbach, Donna McGirr of Batten, Barton, Durstine & Osborn, and Robert J. Koretz of Foote, Cone & Belding.

James Kennedy shared his material on Stirling Getchell with me. Kerry W. Buckley sent me his article on John B. Watson's advertising career. Of the many librarians and archivists who helped me, I am particularly grateful to Barbara Kaiser and the staff of the State Historical Society of Wisconsin, the main repository of manuscript materials on advertising.

Robin Straus, my literary agent, had confidence in this project when I wasn't sure about it. At William Morrow she sold the book to senior editor Harvey Ginsberg, who in his promptness, generosity, and acute editorial eye has been a model for me of how editors ought to treat authors. Several friends of mine lent a hand with various phases of the book. Katherine Ransel, Brenda Englebretsen, and Patricia Johnston assisted my research. Anne Copeland provided significant criticisms and research suggestions, and she also put up with the variable temperament of a writer in the throes of composition.

334

Finally, I must express my appreciation to Rosser Reeves and David Ogilvy. These two men, among the most influential advertising practitioners of the past four decades, represent contrasting traditions in advertising strategy and copy. Their own relationship, dating back to the late 1930s, has survived family quarrels and profound differences in politics, intellectual tastes, personalities, and styles. One might write the entire history of American advertising in the form of a dialogue between Reeves and Ogilvy. They helped this book by opening their private papers to me, providing research leads, and offering extensive critiques of what I wrote about them. Both men are in fact historians *manqués,* and this history of their profession would be much poorer without their contributions.

MANUSCRIPT COLLECTIONS

Advertising Women of New York Papers, State Historical Society of Wisconsin, Madison.

Bruce Barton Papers, State Historical Society of Wisconsin, Madison.

William B. Benton Papers, Regenstein Library, University of Chicago.

Thomas D'Arcy Brophy Papers, State Historical Society of Wisconsin, Madison.

Fairfax M. Cone Papers, Regenstein Library, University of Chicago.

Dorothy Dignam Papers, Schlesinger Library, Radcliffe College and State Historical Society of Wisconsin, Madison.

Margaret Divver Papers, Schlesinger Library, Radcliffe College.

Christine Frederick Papers, Schlesinger Library, Radcliffe College.

E. William Henry Papers, State Historical Society of Wisconsin, Madison.

William Bennett Lewis Papers, Mugar Library, Boston University.

Bernard Lichtenberg Papers, State Historical Society of Wisconsin, Madison.

Wallace Meyer Papers, State Historical Society of Wisconsin, Madison.

Newton N. Minow Papers, State Historical Society of Wisconsin, Madison.

National Broadcasting Company Papers, State Historical Society of Wisconsin, Madison.

David Ogilvy Papers, Manuscript Division, Library of Congress.

Frederic Papert Papers, John F. Kennedy Presidential Library.

Irna Phillips Papers, State Historical Society of Wisconsin, Madison.

Lydia E. Pinkham Papers, Schlesinger Library, Radcliffe College.

Rosser Reeves Papers, State Historical Society of Wisconsin, Madison.

J. Walter Thompson Archives, New York City.

John B. Watson Papers, Manuscript Division, Library of Congress.

Alexander Woollcott Papers, Houghton Library, Harvard University.

ABBREVIATIONS OF SOURCES

A & S	*Advertising & Selling*
AA	*Advertising Age*
BP	Bruce Barton Papers
JAR	*Journal of Advertising Research*
NBCP	National Broadcasting Company Papers
NYT	*New York Times*
OP	David Ogilvy Papers
PI	*Printers' Ink*
PIM	*Printers' Ink Monthly*
PP	Lydia E. Pinkham Papers
Rowell	George Presbury Rowell, *Forty Years an Advertising Agent 1865–1905* (1906)
RP	Rosser Reeves Papers
Wood	James Playsted Wood, *The Story of Advertising* (1958)

CHAPTER NOTES

CHAPTER ONE

Page 13. Agency of 1870s: *PI,* April 21, 1927.

14. "Young man": *PI,* March 18, 1903.

14. "to the fact": *AA,* May 31, 1930.

15. "Why, I can": *PI,* May 3, 1893.

15. "Everybody liked": *PI,* April 21, 1927.

15. "I thoroughly understood": Wood, p. 148.

16. "I can advertise": A. D. Crabtree, *The Funny Side of Physic* (1874), p. 80.

17. "Started Trade in 1860": Rowell, p. 389.

17. St. Jacob's Oil: *PI,* March 22, 1893.

17. "Encouraging Reports": Charles H. Pinkham, "Advertising" (1953), p. 25, MS in vol. 328, PP.

18. "I really believe": Dan Pinkham to Will Pinkham, n.d., file 3118, PP.

18. "a kind of religious": Sarah Stage, *Female Complaints* (1979), p. 35.

18. "We have published": *Warren* (Ohio) *Tribune* to Lydia Pinkham, October 5, 1882, PP.

18. "As long as": H. P. Hubbard to Charles Pinkham, April 24, 1885, PP.

18. "They seem to think": H. P. Hubbard to Will Pinkham, October 21, 1880, PP.

19. "It seems as if": William James letter in *Nation,* February 1, 1894.

19. "I stand ready": H. P. Hubbard to Charles Pinkham, August 15, 1885, PP.

19. "This man Hubbard": *Chicago Mirror* to Lydia Pinkham, August 1882, PP.

20. "Among publishers": Charles Austin Bates, *Good Advertising* (1896), opposite p. 230.

20. Rowell codes: Rowell, p. 165.

21. "The book created": Rowell, p. 164.

21. "thinks of work": Rowell, p. 443.

Page 22. "a woman of refinement": *PI,* March 8, 1923.

22. "vile diseases": *PI,* October 18, 1899.

22. Royal Baking Powder: *PI,* June 28, August 23, 1893.

23. Sapolio: *PI,* March 18, 1903.

23. "The shades of night": *PI,* September 3, 1931.

24. "Through steady": *PI,* March 26, 1925.

24. Douglas shoes: *PI,* January 2, 1895; September 7, 1898; August 7, 1901; and September 25, 1924.

25. "The idea clung": Joseph H. Appel, *The Business Biography of John Wanamaker* (1930), p. 39.

26. Powers' birth: *NYT,* April 22, 1919.

26. "Grand Depot is mispronounced": *PI,* November 18, 1915.

26. "That was the discovery": *PI,* October 23, 1895.

26. "My talking style": ibid.

27. "Liked to tell": *PI,* November 18, 1915.

27. "a great, rough": Appel, op. cit., pp. 86–7.

27. "look better than": ibid., p. 88.

27. "You are the most": *PI,* May 29, 1907.

27. "We didn't always agree": *PI,* November 18, 1915.

27. "He is the biggest coward": *PI,* October 26, 1892.

28. "What is it for?": *PI,* July 16, 1936.

28. "the model and ideal": Claude C. Hopkins, *My Life in Advertising* (1927), p. 38.

28. "I don't care": *PI,* August 28, 1895.

28. E. C. Allen: *PI,* August 5, 1891; Frank Luther Mott, *A History of American Magazines* (1938), 3: 37–9.

29. Thompson in restaurant: *A & S,* December 26, 1928.

30. "too easily discouraged": Rowell, p. 145.

30. "This advertising came": Thompson in *Appleton's,* May 1908.

30. "was amazed": ibid.

31. "I have succeeded": J. W. Thompson to Lydia Pinkham, September 13, 1883, PP.

31. "No man is more": *PI,* November 24, 1909.

31. "the most wonderful": *A & S,* December 26, 1928.

31. "The prime business quality": *PI,* November 24, 1909.

32. "That's what made me": Edward W. Bok, *A Man From Maine* (1923), p. 220.

32. "It is not expense": *The Americanization of Edward Bok* (1921), p. 202.

32. "I figured": Bok, *Man From Maine,* p. 70.

32. "the psychology of publicity": *Americanization of Bok,* p. 148.

33. "I want business men": *PI,* October 28, 1896.

33. "One might almost": Edward Bok in *Cosmopolitan,* October 1902.

33. "The magazine was taken": Thompson in *Appleton's,* May 1908.

Page 34. "contributed to the journalism": Henry Steele Commager, *The American Mind* (1950), p. 73.

34. "The publishing germ": George Britt, *Forty Years—Forty Millions* (1935), p. 54.

35. "We deal direct": ibid., opposite p. 39.

35. Magazine circulations, 1885 and 1905: Mott, op. cit. (1957), 4:8.

35. "We had one copywriter": *PI*, October 13, 1927.

36. "Writers of advertisements": *PI*, March 26, 1925.

36. Prudential and Gibraltar: *PI*, December 5, 1918; Earl Chapin May and Will Oursler, *The Prudential* (1950), pp. 118–20.

36. "The man who knows": Nath'l C. Fowler, Jr., *Fowler's Publicity* (1897), p. 34.

36. "I will agree": Bates, op. cit., p. 35.

36. "There is nothing": ibid., after p. 599.

36. "My God!": *PI*, May 1, 1919.

37. "I worked for that": Earnest Elmo Calkins, *And Hearing Not* (1946), p. 159.

37. "so much like": *PI*, June 28, 1927.

37. "Wanamaker-Powers-Gillam": Bates, op. cit., pp. 30, 39.

37. "Advertisers should never": ibid., pp. 256, 440.

37. "the most complex": ibid., pp. 49, 88.

37. "my particular specialty": ibid., after p. 599.

38. "What we could do": *PI*, November 21, 1906; and see *PI*, March 16, 1916.

38. "The men in the business": *PI*, December 2, 1926.

38. "Every enterprise": *PI*, July 28, 1938.

39. Uneeda campaign: *PI*, April 19, 1899.

39. Volume of advertising: *PI*, October 23, 1953.

39. "It appears to me": *PI*, July 5, 1893.

39. Russell Conwell: *Fowler's Publicity*, p. 72.

CHAPTER TWO

41. "The desirability": *PI*, February 8, 1893.

41. "They came from": Nath'l C. Fowler, Jr., *Fowler's Publicity* (1897), p. 733.

41. "vocabulary and images": Earnest Elmo Calkins, *"Louder Please!"* (1924), p. 42.

41. "I was born": *PI*, April 30, 1914.

42. "Mr. Bates beamed": Calkins, op. cit., p. 156.

42. "let's cut out": ibid., p. 158.

42. "Ethridge knew": Earnest Elmo Calkins, *And Hearing Not* (1946), pp. 170–71.

Page 42. "He was a business man": Calkins, *Louder,* p. 191.

43. "I place all my advertising": *PI,* June 26, 1953.

43. "They have produced": *PI,* March 16, 1904.

43. "that combination of text": *PI,* July 17, 1907.

44. "the finest art work": *AA,* November 5, 1956.

44. "unrestrained imaginative": *PI,* March 30, 1911.

44. Arrow and Wesson: *PI,* March 18, 1960.

44. "he was some": Calkins, *Hearing,* p. 255.

45. "He rose, she took": *Fowler's Publicity,* p. 191.

45. "It is astonishing": Charles Austin Bates, *Good Advertising* (1896), p. 201.

45. "Here was Sapolio": *PI,* February 19, 1902.

45. "This is the maid": Julian Lewis Watkins, *The 100 Greatest Advertisements* (1949), p. 12.

46. "sells chiefly to the best": *PI,* December 9, 1903.

46. "You eat too much": *PI,* November 12, 1902.

46. "Goodness gracious!": *PI,* September 17, 1902.

47. "No current novel": ibid.

47. Twain and Lackawanna: *PI,* June 3, 1903.

47. Calkins and Phoebe Snow: Calkins, *Hearing,* p. 225.

48. "The advertising absolutely": *PI,* February 11, 1915.

48. "Hard physical work": *PI,* September 16, 1903.

48. "They sound very much": *PI,* July 29, 1908.

48. "My chief satisfaction": *A & S,* April 1, 1932.

48. "Why is the merchant": *PI,* January 9, 1901.

49. "Aye, a veritable": *PI,* March 21, 1894.

49. "It has often occurred": ibid.

49. "tinged with English ideas": *PI,* April 11, 1894.

50. "salesmanship-on-paper": *PI,* September 6, 1905.

50. "are printed salesmen": *PI,* July 28, 1938.

50. "True 'Reason-Why' Copy": *PI,* September 6, 1905.

50. wagon with one lopsided wheel: *A & S,* January 25, 1928.

50. "typographical dress": *PI,* April 11, 1906.

50. "Advertising should be judged": *AA,* June 24, 1935.

50. "We saw more clearly": *PI,* July 29, 1926.

51. "the most memorable": Albert D. Lasker, "Reminiscences" (Columbia Oral History Collection, 1950), p. 48.

51. "epoch-making rebellion": *Masters of Advertising Copy,* ed. J. George Frederick (1925), p. 25.

51. "that Gold-brick of Advertising": *PI,* September 6, 1905.

51. "Mr. Kennedy is": *A & S,* July 1909.

51. Kennedy and patent medicine ads: *PI,* April 11, 1906.

51. Kennedy's working methods: *A & S,* February 8, 1928.

Page 51. "A very slow": Lasker, op. cit., p. 49.

52. "Anyone may have": John E. Kennedy to F. C. Kendall, n.d., enclosed with Kendall to Claude C. Hopkins, June 22, 1927, box 25, RP.

52. "So far as I know": Claude C. Hopkins, *My Life in Advertising* (1927), p. 98.

52. "He lived": *PI,* October 6, 1932.

53. "The lack of that": Hopkins, op. cit., p. 1.

53. "Together they made": ibid., p. 9.

53. "We advertisers must": *PI,* October 30, 1895.

54. "You cannot chop": *PI,* February 12, 1896.

54. "I consider advertising": *Fowler's Publicity,* p. 114.

54. Hopkins on advertising's power: *PI,* January 20, 1909.

54. "I steep myself": *Fowler's Publicity,* p. 115.

54. Lasker and Curtis on train: *PI,* August 19, 1926.

55. "the highest paid": *PI,* January 20, 1909.

55. Hopkins' fifteen points: *AA,* October 17, 1938.

56. "Gracious! Gracious!": *PI,* October 6, 1932.

56. "He did everything": *A & S,* May 20, 1937.

56. "Life holds so many": Hopkins, op. cit., pp. 4–5.

56. "who, we must contend": *PI,* January 20, 1909.

56. "Ten years ago": ibid.

57. Lasker's firings: *Advertising Agency,* July 1952.

57. Lasker's wall chart: *AA,* May 21, 1962.

57. "colossal assurance": Fairfax M. Cone, *With All Its Faults* (1969), p. 110.

57. "It is my eccentricity": Lasker, op. cit., pp. 122–23.

58. "to get away from": Albert D. Lasker, *The Lasker Story* (1963), p. 57.

58. "a pioneer people": Lasker, "Reminiscences," p. 164.

58. " 'Advertise and make good' ": John Gunther, *Taken at the Flood* (1960), p. 30.

59. "I was very devoted": Lasker, "Reminiscences," p. 7.

59. "I would be": ibid., p. 11.

59. "entire control": Lord & Thomas to Lydia Pinkham, September 5, 1882, PP.

60. "I never got": Lasker, "Reminiscences," p. 13.

60. "The main things": ibid., p. 32.

60. "I was a young boy": ibid., p. 34.

60. "capacity to originate": *PI,* April 18, 1906.

60. "the guiding spirit": ibid.

61. "We have a positive gauge": ibid.

61. "reportorial mind": Lasker, "Reminiscences," p. 31.

61. " 'Sunny Jim' is dead": John E. Kennedy, "Intensive Advertising" (Associated Business Publications, 1940), p. 9.

Page 61. "A fellow who didn't": *AA,* January 9, 1956.
61. "What goes into": *PI,* April 18, 1906.
61. "Mr. Lasker enjoys": ibid.
62. "He projected himself": interview with Fairfax Cone, 1962, tape 4, page 6, in box 140, Cone Papers.
62. "His thoughts catch up": William Hard in *Collier's,* March 10, 1923.
62. "He'd never want anybody": *AA,* January 9, 1956.
62. Lasker's dream: Gunther, op. cit., p. 28.
62. "but a trifle": ibid., p. 89.
63. "I am keenly": ibid., p. 90.
63. "They tell me": Lasker, *Lasker Story,* p. 57.
63. "the uncrowned king": James P. Warburg, "Reminiscences" (Columbia Oral History Collection, 1952), p. 1,594.
63. "that's all you": *AA,* December 26, 1955.
64. "People are like": Hopkins, op. cit., p. 116.
64. Hopkins and Olds: *AA,* September 24, 1932.
65. "and we felt": John Orr Young, *Adventures in Advertising* (1949), p. 31.
65. "There is no evil": *Ladies' Home Journal,* April 1905.
65. Effect of 1906 law: Sarah Stage, *Female Complaints* (1979), pp. 170, 177.
66. "The advertiser": Godkin in *Atlantic,* January 1898.
66. Policy of *N.Y. Journal:* Will Irwin in *Collier's,* June 3, 1911.
66. "There is no hour": S. H. Adams in *Collier's,* May 22, 1909.
66. "A man don't want": F. P. Dunne in *American Magazine,* October 1909.
66. "I doubt if you": *PI,* December 5, 1913.
67. TR on advertising: *Outlook,* April 15, 1911.
67. "We don't want": *PI,* November 25, 1915.
67. "Some day": *PI,* March 21, 1918.
68. "Today it is almost": *PI,* March 26, 1914.
68. "We are men": H. J. Kenner, *The Fight for Truth in Advertising* (1936), p. 23.
69. "it rests on": *PI,* September 23, 1915.
69. "Moral suasion": *PI,* June 16, 1921.
69. Bliven on convention: *PI,* June 17, 1917.
69. "We didn't see": *PI,* October 13, 1927.
70. "Rampant righteousness": *PI,* February 8, 1917.
70. "impressionistic copy": *PI,* October 26, 1911.
70. "any meaningless picture": *Masters,* ed. Frederick, p. 118.
70. "Style is a handicap": Hopkins, op. cit p. 121.
70. "They are almost": *PI,* January 22, 1914.
70. "The actual effect": Walter Dill Scott, *The Psychology of Advertising* (2nd ed., 1917), p. 83.
71. "The psycho-analysts": *PI,* March 28, 1918.

Page 71. "We have all used": *PI,* April 18, 1918.
71. "We are haunted": *PI,* July 21, 1910.
71. "The real suggestion": *Masters,* ed. Frederick, p. 83.
71. Background of Cadillac ad: *PI,* October 16, 1964.
72. MacManus teased by colleagues: *PI,* December 7, 1945.
72. "The real explanation": *PI,* February 21, 1929.
72. *PI* poll, 1945: *PI,* September 28, 1945.
73. "He was a true figure": *PI,* November 8, 1940.
73. "I look upon": *A & S,* March 31, 1932.
73. "I have never spent": *Masters,* ed. Frederick, p. 119.
73. "a clever and semi-scientific": ibid., p. 78.
74. "I hated to see": Lasker, *Lasker Story,* pp. 48–9.
74. "The products that": Gunther, op. cit., p. 154.
74. "an invisible cloud": *PI,* February 10, 1927.
74. "On what subject?": *AA,* December 7, 1964.
75. "a plain publicity": Mark Sullivan, *Our Times* (1933), 5:425.
75. "Advertising has earned": *PI,* December 12, 1918.
75. "Seeing all things": Watkins, op. cit., pp. 38–9.
76. "A number of us": *AA,* June 14, 1930.
76. "The Kaiserite in America": *PI,* May 23, 1918.
76. "American industry can": *PI,* January 31, 1918.
76. "The work, as a whole": *A & S,* September 27, 1919.
77. Advertising volume, 1918–20: *PI,* October 23, 1953.
77. "The advertising man": S. N. Behrman in *New Republic,* August 20, 1919.

CHAPTER THREE

78. "Since 1919": Frederick Lewis Allen, *Only Yesterday* (1931), p. 1.
78. "Are we going to rest": *PI,* January 2, 1919.
79. "You resemble": F. Scott Fitzgerald, *The Great Gatsby* (1925), p. 119.
80. "Somewhere along the road": W. G. Woodward, *The Gift of Life* (1947), p. 175.
80. "knowing as much": Stanley Resor affidavit, March 19, 1924, J. Walter Thompson Archives, New York.
81. "At that time": ibid.
81. "The use of this type": ibid.
81. Family warned Helen: interview with Therese Lansdowne Duble, January 4, 1983.
81. "In advertising these products": Helen Resor affidavit, March 20, 1924, Thompson Archives.
82. "I was the first woman": ibid.
82. "and much to my surprise": JWT Newsletter, September 25, 1924.

Page 82. "Everybody had a chance": ibid.

82. Resors' discussions at dinner: interview with Helen Resor Hauge, January 3, 1983.

83. "a matter of cleverness": *PI,* November 29, 1923.

83. "The advertising firm": *PI,* December 17, 1925.

83. "Publicity of this kind": Helen Resor affidavit.

83. Resor and Sumner: interview with Helen Resor Hauge.

83. Resor and Buckle: James Webb Young in *Saturday Review,* December 8, 1962.

84. "Advertising, after all": *PI,* December 17, 1925.

84. JWT ad for 1920 edition: *PI,* March 18, 1920.

85. "Consumption is no longer": *A & S,* February 22, 1928.

85. "so as to secure": *A & S,* June 30, 1926.

85. "To make your consumer": Kerry W. Buckley in *Journal of the History of the Behavioral Sciences,* July 1982.

85. "I saw I would have": J. B. Watson, "The Ideal Executive," MS in Watson Papers.

85. "No one knows": Buckley in *Journal,* July 1982.

86. "There is one psychologist": Roy S. Durstine in *Forum,* January 1928.

86. "greatly oversold": *PI,* April 7, 1927.

86. Watson's later recollection: Otis Pease, *The Responsibilities of American Advertising* (1958), p. 171n.

86. "Advertising absorbed John": James Webb Young, *The Diary of an Ad Man* (1944), p. 120.

86. "editorial style": *PI,* April 11, 1929.

87. "The phrase sings itself": *Atlantic,* October 1919.

87. Lasker on three landmarks: Young, op. cit., p. 101.

87. Invention of Odorono: *PI,* October 6, 1927.

88. "Disgusting": Julian Lewis Watkins, *The 100 Greatest Advertisements* (1949), pp. 30–1.

88. "somewhat naive": Young in *Saturday Review,* December 8, 1962.

88. "The only 'research' ": James Webb Young to Stanley Resor et al., January 6, 1959, State Historical Society of Wisconsin.

88. World war and testimonial: *PI,* March 17, 1921.

89. Responses to Pond's ads: Carroll Rheinstrom, *Psyching the Ads* (1929), pp. 37–9.

89. Day on consumer mentality: *PI,* April 21, 1932.

89. "Nine out of ten": Watkins, op. cit., pp. 82–3.

89. Danny Danker: *AA,* July 10, 1944 and December 7, 1964.

90. "The spirit of emulation": *PI,* April 11, 1929.

90. JWT billings: *AA,* December 7, 1964.

90. "That we shall be": *PI,* April 21, 1927.

91. "In appearance he had": Young in *Saturday Review,* December 8, 1962.

Page 91. "She encouraged me": *JWT News,* January 10, 1964.
        91. "His singular quality": *A & S,* November 25, 1931.
        91. "He has an iron jaw": *Fortune,* November 1947.
        92. "Every day an oily coating": Millicent Bell, *Marquand* (1979), pp. 112–13.
        92. "It seemed to me": *Time,* March 7, 1949.
        92. "He looked like": J. P. Marquand, *H. M. Pulham, Esquire* (1940), p. 129.
        92. "Phrase fever": Richard Connell in *Saturday Evening Post,* April 29, 1922.
        92. Second story: Richard Connell in *Saturday Evening Post,* June 24, 1923.
        92. "one of the least articulate": *AA,* December 7, 1964.
        93. "She had a dozen": *JWT News,* January 10, 1964.
        93. "She had a brilliant": ibid.
        93. "I had always expected": Earnest Elmo Calkins, *The Advertising Man* (1922), p. 132.
        93. "At the end": ibid., p. 133.
        94. "You're never going": interview with Therese Lansdowne Duble.
        94. "I could tell": Edward Steichen, *A Life in Photography* (1963), n.p., chap. 9.
        94. "It pays to be personal": *PI,* October 10, 1929.
        94. "The chief economic problem": *An Outline of Careers,* ed. Edward L. Bernays (1927), p. 25.
        95. Adman in fiction: *PI,* May 19, 1921.
        95. "at least they used": *PI,* January 27, 1921.
        95. "Course I don't mean": Sinclair Lewis, *Babbitt* (1922), p. 46.
        95. "These standard advertised": ibid., p. 95.
        95. "Beauty has been": *PI,* April 5, 1928.
        96. "important announcements": *Saturday Evening Post,* December 8, 1923.
        96. "there's a broncho-busting": *Saturday Evening Post,* June 23, 1923.
        97. "Everything has changed": *A & S,* August 11, 1926.
        97. "It is the most potent": *PI,* November 4, 1926 and *Literary Digest,* November 13, 1926.
        97. Listerine and halitosis: *New Outlook,* January 1935.
        98. "whisper copy": *PI,* September 9, 1926.
        98. Listerine profit: *PI,* November 10, 1927.
        98. Kudner and athlete's foot: *New Outlook,* January 1935.
        98. "When you're getting": *PI,* August 4, 1921.
        99. "It was decided": Note by Wallace Meyer, September 21, 1960, Meyer Papers.
        99. Kotex in plain wrapper: ibid.

Page 99. "Women are beginning": John Gunther, *Taken at the Flood* (1960), 155.

100. Survey of dental care: George B. Hotchkiss to Bruce Barton, May 26, 1926, BP.

100. "No one creation": *Outlook,* January 4, 1922.

100. "This is a scientific": *PI,* June 7, 1923.

100. "acidosis": Stuart Ewen, *Captains of Consciousness* (1976), p. 156.

100. "You will be amazed": *Ladies' Home Journal,* April 1920.

100. "a clear, radiant": *Ladies' Home Journal,* January 1922.

100. "From a mere": E. S. Turner, *The Shocking History of Advertising!* (1953), p. 213.

101. "the first great nation": Sinclair Lewis in *Nation,* March 6, 1929.

101. "The real revolutionist": *NYT,* January 13, 1927.

102. "the happiest": Bruce Barton to Will Durant, June 18, 1931, BP.

102. "less interest": Barton to George A. Buttrick, December 15, 1931, BP.

102. "It explains": ibid.

102. "I was in poor": *PI,* January 28, 1932.

102. "Reluctantly I came": Barton to Tax Cumings, October 16, 1958, BP.

103. "grow into the habit": *PI,* February 4, 1915.

103. Barton and Marie Antoinette: Barton to J. L. Watkins, December 7, 1948, BP.

103. "We had a grand": *AA,* March 7, 1960.

103. "the most American": *PI,* August 1, 1918.

103. "A man may be down": Leo P. Ribuffo in *American Quarterly,* summer 1981.

104. "some *real* war": Barton to C. H. Brower, May 11, 1953, BP.

104. "For the first time": Barton in *Collier's,* December 14, 1918.

104. "He said that all": *New York Telegram,* August 17, 1928.

104. "I had never thought": Barton to C. H. Brower, May 11, 1953, BP.

104. "I was so ignorant": Barton to Norman Cousins, May 17, 1961, BP.

105. "Every one of us": Barton speech, February 1954, box 61, BP.

105. "About one man": *100 Top Copy Writers,* ed. Perry Schofield (1954), p. 31.

105. "They do not know": Barton speech, June 1923, box 78, BP.

105. "The combination": Barton to Donald Wilhelm, January 26, 1926, BP.

105. "Beauty is the most": *NYT,* May 3, 1927.

105. "He said the copy": Louise MacLeod to W. P. Maloney, January 20, 1944, BP.

106. "You are not talking": Louise MacLeod to Alex Osborn, February 17, 1948, BP.

Page 106. Barton as evangelist: *Nation,* November 5, 1938.

106. Barton as teddy bear: *A & S,* September 20, 1931.

106. "A remarkable personality": Roy S. Durstine, "Reminiscences" (Columbia Oral History Collection, 1949), p. 41.

106. "I think I absorb": C. F. Kettering to Barton, May 16, 1928, BP.

106. "I imagine": Barton to Wallace B. Donham, June 9, 1924, BP.

106. "We are creating": Barton to T. S. Trebell, March 12, 1925, BP.

107. F. R. Feland: Charlie Brower, *Me, and Other Advertising Geniuses* (1974), pp. 95–7.

107. "This has been": Barton to William L. Chenery, March 21, 1925, BP.

107. "Too advanced": Maxwell Perkins to Barton, April 8, 1924, BP.

107. Theological debt to father: Ribuffo in *American Quarterly,* summer 1981.

107. "the friendliest man": Bruce Barton, *The Man Nobody Knows* (1924), p. 58; next two quotations from ibid., pp. 140, 143.

108. Barton on average occupations: ibid., p. 179.

108. "pure blooded Americans": *A & S,* February 10, 1926.

108. "the creed of a modern": *PI,* November 3, 1927.

108. "the old stuff": Barton to George B. Hotchkiss, May 17, 1926, BP.

109. Hotchkiss reply: Hotchkiss to Barton, May 26, 1926, BP.

110. "My stuff is punk": Harford Powel, Jr., *The Virgin Queene* (1928), p. 110; next quotation from ibid., pp. 104–5.

110. "You and I": Barton to Henry Luce, March 4, 1941, BP.

110. "this wonderful fabric": *PI,* October 29, 1925.

110. "tremendous, happy, enthusiastic": *PI,* October 3, 1929.

110. "We are children": Barton to Will Durant, June 18, 1931, BP.

110. "We seem somehow": *A & S,* July 8, 1931.

110. "The nose seems": *Nation,* November 5, 1938.

110. "One senses": *New Yorker,* November 1, 1930.

111. "a devoted father": ibid.

111. Frances King on affair: *NYT,* July 28, 1933.

111. Barton on affair: *NYT,* July 21, 1933.

111. Newspaper coverage of trial: George Seldes in *New Republic,* October 26, 1938.

111. "No, that's ridiculous": *NYT,* July 21, 1933.

112. "I can, of course": Barton diary, April 21, 1934, box 148, BP.

112. "a new idea": *PI,* June 21, 1923.

112. Accusations of Lasker: *PI,* December 18, 1924.

112. "the unhappiest time": Albert D. Lasker, "Reminiscences" (Columbia Oral History Collection, 1950), p. 122.

112. "they were not preaching": Albert D. Lasker, *The Lasker Story* (1963), p. 65.

Page 113. "I think your book": Albert D. Lasker to Claude Hopkins, May 27, 1927, box 25, RP.
113. "I was wrong": Lasker, *Lasker Story,* p. 89.
113. "So you must": ibid., p. 89.
113. "cologned and refined": *A & S,* April 8, 1925.
113. "that a jackass": Lasker, *Lasker Story,* p. 108.
113. "An agent cannot": *PI,* September 16, 1926.
113. "I feel sort": Lasker, *Lasker Story,* p. 9; next three quotations from ibid., pp. 80, 72, 121.
114. "It's full of flavor": *"Sold American!"* (1954), p. 54.
114. "an insidious campaign": *PI,* April 17, 1919.
114. "Blow some my way": Watkins, op. cit., p. 77.
114. "My husband objected": *PI,* October 25, 1928.
114. Tobacco production, 1920–28: *PI,* June 13, 1929.
115. Hill as Nero: Fairfax M. Cone, *With All Its Faults* (1969), p. 116.
115. "His normal behavior": Edward L. Bernays, *Biography of an Idea* (1965), p. 379.
115. "See, you won't forget": interview with Fairfax Cone, 1962, tape 5, page 26, in box 140, Cone Papers.
115. Hill at Tiffany's: *Life,* September 23, 1946.
115. Hill and statue: *PI,* October 18, 1946.
115. "I would not call": Lasker, "Reminiscences," p. 114.
115. Lucky Strike billings at L & T: *PI,* June 20, 1929 and *AA,* December 20, 1930; Gunther, op. cit., p. 163 is wrong on this point.
115. "We would fix": *AA,* June 9, 1952.
116. *PI* re testimonials: *PI,* March 21; April 18, 1929.
116. "The cigarette will enflame": *New Republic,* February 13, 1929.
116. "Our only purpose": *PI,* December 27, 1928.
116. "Eat a chocolate": *Nation,* March 13, 1929.
116. "The advertising industry": *PI,* February 27, 1930.
117. "Nadir of Nothingness": *Atlantic,* May 1928.
117. "The cigarette has become": *PI,* March 28, 1929.
117. "If I were starting": *PI,* June 18, 1931.

CHAPTER FOUR

118. "There is actually": *Review of Reviews,* March 1930.
118. "What America needs": *PI,* August 7, 1930.
118. "The recovery is": *PI,* January 15, 1931.
119. "If fifty men": Bruce Barton to Owen Young, October 1, 1931, BP.
119. "I'm a hard-shelled": Barton to Arthur Ballantine, March 28, 1933, BP.
119. Resor proposal: Chester Bowles, "Reminiscences" (Columbia Oral History Collection, 1963), p. 37.

Page 119. Agency reductions: *Nation,* December 20, 1933.
120. "it is well understood": *AA,* July 20, 1936.
120. "Under the lash": *PI,* July 5, 1934.
121. "He walked with kings": *A & S,* November 1916.
121. "Even though I have": Helen Woodward, *Three Flights Up* (1935), p. 165.
121. "of hurrying and joshing": Helen Woodward, *Through Many Windows* (1926), p. 200; next quotation from ibid., pp. 385–86.
122. "We are all Alices": Stuart Chase and F. J. Schlink, *Your Money's Worth* (1927), p. 2.
122. "It is often amusing": *PI,* November 3, 1927.
122. Lynd on *Money's Worth: Business Week,* April 22, 1939.
123. Rogers on advertising: *PI,* May 7, 1931.
123. "If you can build": E. S. Turner, *The Shocking History of Advertising!* (1953), p. 243; next two quotations from ibid., p. 243.
123. "Schlink's following": *PI,* January 11, 1934.
123. "He was always": *A & S,* May 10, 1934.
124. "It was all anonymous": James Rorty, *Our Master's Voice* (1934), p. 219; next three quotations from ibid., pp. 19, 209, 394.
124. "Because he writes": *PI,* May 10, 1934.
124. Chase on Rorty: *Nation,* May 26, 1934.
124. "all business": *AA,* May 26, 1934.
124. "Don't try to reform": *AA,* October 14, 1935.
125. "From some of the": *AA,* December 16, 1933.
125. "the very existence": Arthur M. Schlesinger, Jr., *The Coming of the New Deal* (1959), p. 357.
125. "The social revolution": *AA,* June 30, 1934.
125. "The average consumer": *AA,* September 29, 1934.
126. "So far as": Albert D. Lasker to M. H. Aylesworth, December 26, 1933, file 15–67, NBCP.
126. "The tide has turned": *PI,* May 31, 1934.
126. "There is in progress": *PI,* March 15, 1934.
126. "The crisis is here": *PI,* April 5, 1934.
126. Advertising glossary: Turner, *Shocking History,* p. 243.
127. "When Raymond Rubicam": Dexter Masters, *The Intelligent Buyer and the Telltale Seller* (1967), p. 222.
127. "I did a few": Raymond Rubicam to David Ogilvy, April 16, 1954, OP.
128. Rubicam's youth: interview with Bettina Rubicam, Stephen Rubicam, and Kathleen Rubicam Witten, August 25, 1981.
128. "Jersey University": *AA,* February 28, 1949.
128. Rubicam's trip East: *Current Biography* (1943), p. 638.
128. Stealing engineer's lunch: interview with Stephen Rubicam.
129. "Then for the first": *AA,* February 9, 1970.

Page 129. "I telephoned the presidents": ibid.
129. "He was hated": *AA,* October 31, 1966.
129. "I sat in that lobby": *Current Biography* (1943), p. 638.
130. "Those ads of yours": *AA,* February 9, 1970.
130. "A copywriter is": *AA,* February 16, 1970.
130. "Don't I pay you": *AA,* March 2, 1970; next two quotations from ibid.
131. "Without effort": *AA,* July 7, 1975.
131. "My efforts": *AA,* July 28, 1975; next quotation from ibid.
132. *Printers' Ink* poll: *PI,* September 28, 1945.
132. "Why can't we": *AA,* July 28, 1975.
132. "clients none": John Orr Young, *Adventures in Advertising* (1949), p. 37.
133. "LOUD & PROMISE": ibid., p. 106; next two quotations from ibid., pp. 65, 44.
133. "Mr. No": John B. Rosebrook, "Madison Avenue Legacy" (MS, 1962, at Young & Rubicam, New York), p. 50.
133. "Sam Cherr had": Stanley Arnold, *Tale of the Blue Horse* (1968), p. 21.
134. "a quicksilver mind": Draper Daniels, *Giants, Pigmies, and Other Advertising People* (1974), pp. 63–4.
134. "Do you think": Rosebrook, op. cit., pp. 56–7.
134. "Like the architect": *PI,* December 17, 1931.
134. Y & R college grads: Rosebrook, op. cit., p. 58.
134. "I began to get": *PI,* May 15, 1950.
134. "looking like a": Daniels, op. cit., p. 88.
135. "No one save": Rosebrook, op. cit., p. 36.
135. "Well—artists": *PI,* May 24, 1946.
135. "we were paying": Rosebrook, op. cit., p. 37.
135. "Good evening": *AA,* July 25, 1977.
135. Rubicam assumes presidency: Rosebrook, op. cit., p. 49.
136. "Remember that some": Young, op. cit., p. 189.
136. "Daddy was always": interview with Kathleen Rubicam Witten.
136. "For some time": Rosebrook, op. cit., p. 199.
136. "Most of us": Raymond Rubicam to Bruce Barton, July 25, 1945, BP.
136. "What Mr. Rubicam": Rosebrook, op. cit., p. 107.
137. "There was nobody": *AA,* March 22, 1965.
137. "Sometimes we'd work": *PI,* July 17, 1953.
137. "A lot of people": *AA,* January 18, 1930.
137. "zeal for good copy": *PI,* November 8, 1928.
137. "The value of": Charles L. Whittier, *Creative Advertising* (1955), p. 7.
137. "The art of persuasion": ibid., p. 34.
138. Gallup newspaper studies: *A & S,* March 31, 1932.

Page 138. Gallup magazine studies: *PI,* March 24, 1932.

138. "has rocketed into": *A & S,* March 16, 1932.

138. "Raymond Rubicam was": George Gallup, "Reminiscences" (Columbia Oral History Collection, 1972), p. 39.

138. Gallup effect on Y & R: Rosebrook, op. cit., p. 137.

139. Thompson 27 points: *PI,* February 27, 1948; and see W. S. Townsend to Bruce Barton, June 26, 1935, box 67, BP.

139. "I had all": Gallup, op. cit., p. 53.

140. "Thoughts at Thirty-Nine": *100 Top Copy Writers,* ed. Perry Schofield (1954), p. 33.

140. Joe Holmes: *AA,* March 22, 1965.

140. "human interest": Schofield, op. cit., p. 122.

140. "what would you think": ibid., p. 54.

149. "not a critique": *AA,* July 25, 1977.

149. 100 top copywriters: Daniels, op. cit., p. 97.

149. "We can't match": Rosebrook, op. cit., p. 101.

149. "A company which must": *AA,* May 29, 1944.

149. "The public reaction": *AA,* May 29, 1978.

150. "Most of us": *AA,* February 22, 1960.

150. "Young & Rubicam was heaven": Daniels, op. cit., pp. 38–9.

150. "You can't imagine": Carroll Carroll, *None of Your Business* (1970), p. 8.

150. "the only form": Alexander Kendrick, *Prime Time* (1969), p. 115.

152. "Who would have dreamed": *PI,* April 13, 1922.

152. "The family circle": *PI,* April 27, 1922.

152. *PI* warning of radio as rival: *PI,* February 8, 1923.

153. Weiss re *PI* policy: *AA,* April 3, 1972.

153. "The home is a sacred": *PI,* April 24, 1924.

153. *PI* conceded: *PI,* April 1, 1926.

154. "listeners ought to feel": Roy Durstine in *Scribner's,* May 1928.

154. "When I first": Carroll, op. cit., p. 242.

154. "I want real": "Lucky Strike Audition," MS, August 30, 1928, file 2–28, NBCP.

154. "Nothing on the air": G. W. Hill to M. H. Aylesworth, February 2, 1932, file 6–16, NBCP.

155. "With all of these": *PI,* April 24, 1930.

155. "A great deal": Don Gilman to M. H. Aylesworth, March 3, 1932, file 6–16, NBCP.

155. "The faint shuffling": Durstine in *Scribner's,* May 1928.

156. "It has often been": *AA,* September 17, 1932.

156. Copywriting for ear: *The Advertising Agency Looks at Radio,* ed. Neville O'Neill (1932), p. 69.

156. "Radio is show": *PI,* February 8, 1931.

Page 156. "among the more": D. S. Shaw to R. C. Patterson, Jr., May 17, 1934, file 32–65, NBCP.

157. "Jack Benny was selected": *Y & R International Report,* autumn 1975.

157. *PI* poll: *PI,* May 13, 1937.

157. "had no difficulty": *PIM,* October 1934.

158. "They get a big": *AA,* March 5, 1932.

158. "We almost killed": Bowles, op. cit., p. 25.

159. "before 1890": *AA,* August 16, 1943.

159. Hummert and Texas Rangers: Thomas Whiteside, *The Relaxed Sell* (1954), p. 41.

159. B-S-H leading radio agency: *PI,* May 11, 1933.

160. "She was a little": *AA,* May 7, 1962.

160. Hummert salary, 1937: *AA,* April 17, 1939.

160. "All clients are": David Ogilvy, *Confessions of an Advertising Man* (1963), p. 65.

160. "If this continues": E. F. Hummert to M. H. Aylesworth, February 1, 1934, file 24–16, NBCP.

160. "even though it": E. F. Hummert to M. H. Aylesworth, February 16, 1934, file 24–16, NBCP.

160. "I am afraid": E. F. Hummert to Niles Trammell, October 31, 1940, file 74–78, NBCP.

161. "Rudy Vallee could sell": John Royal to R. C. Patterson, Jr., September 10, 1934, file 23–60, NBCP.

161. "The more capable": Leonard Bush to Niles Trammell, September 6, 1939, file 67–37, NBCP.

161. "To see her is": Clinton S. Ferris to Niles Trammell, February 1, 1936, file 44–39, NBCP.

161. "Most of the good": Max Wylie to John Howe, June 25, 1940, Benton Papers.

161. "the old maid": *New York World-Telegram,* January 28, 1938.

161. "An attempt is being": Janet MacRorie to Lenox Lohr, January 25, 1939, file 66–46, NBCP.

162. Agency radio billings, 1940: *AA,* January 13, 1941.

162. "I owe it": *AA,* May 19, 1934.

162. Getchell's rheumatic fever: interview with Mildred Locke Getchell, February 19, 1983.

162. "I don't know": ibid.

163. "We had a hell": *AA,* July 31, 1967.

163. "something about his": *PI,* December 27, 1940; next two quotations from ibid.

163. Getchell and sample book: James Kennedy and Jack Tarleton, "The Ad Man" (MS in custody of James Kennedy), p. 13.

163. "I haven't got": ibid., p. 12.

Page 164. Colgate "microphotographs": *AA,* July 22, 1974.

164. "I've got to keep": *A & S,* January 1941.

164. Getchell at JWT: Kennedy and Tarleton, "Ad Man," pp. 37–8.

164. "I feel it": Charlie Brower, *Me, and Other Advertising Geniuses* (1974), p. 44.

164. "They talk about": *PI,* December 27, 1940; next quotation from ibid.

165. Pinkham profits: Charles H. Pinkham to Lydia P. Gove, February 16, 1932, PP.

165. Tarleton and headline: James Kennedy's notes on Getchell.

165. "Why the hell": *AA,* September 4, 1961; next quotation from ibid.

165. Plymouth sales: *AA,* September 17, 1932 and February 17, 1934.

166. "came off the page": Kennedy's notes on Getchell.

166. "We believe people": *AA,* March 18, 1948.

166. "It's the same": Helen Woodward, *It's an Art* (1938), pp. 87–8.

166. "They were news-minded": *AA,* March 18, 1948.

167. "I was not very successful": *AA,* April 1, 1946.

167. "Lie down": *A & S,* January 1941.

167. Getchell description: Kennedy and Tarleton, op. cit., pp. 38–9.

167. Getchell after second marriage: Kennedy's notes on Getchell.

168. Cause of Getchell's death: *PI,* August 21, 1959.

168. "Nobody believes": Woodward, op. cit., p. 31; next two quotations from ibid., pp. 10, 377.

169. "The New Dealers": Richard S. Tedlow in *Business History Review,* spring 1981.

169. "Almost a revolution": *PI,* August 25, 1938.

169. "Today, the consumer": *Business Week,* April 22, 1939.

169. Gallup poll re consumerism: *AA,* October 30, 1939.

169. "the advertiser who views": Ken Dyke to Margaret Cuthbert et al., March 25, 1940, file 76–11, NBCP.

169. "This recruiting": *While You Were Gone,* ed. Jack Goodman (1946), p. 426.

170. "We did not tell": Bruce Barton to James Webb Young, September 19, 1946, BP.

170. Agency billings: *AA,* June 5, July 3, 1944.

170. "I believed": Albert D. Lasker, "Reminiscences" (Columbia Oral History Collection, 1950), pp. 46–7.

170. "a benign lion": *AA,* July 15, 1963.

170. Hill's insistence: *AA,* December 24, 1973.

170. "I felt like": *AA,* July 1, 1974; next quotation from ibid.

171. Rubicam and second family: interviews with Stephen Rubicam and Kathleen Rubicam Witten.

CHAPTER FIVE

Page 172. Total ad expenditures: *PI,* October 23, 1953.

173. Largest ad budgets: *Fortune,* September 1956.

173. "The greatest boom": ibid.

174. "A non-stop mechanism": *Fortune,* November 1947.

174. "the ending": *AA,* July 11, 1955.

174. "We want everyone": *AA,* March 9, 1959.

174. "We can get": *AA,* March 16, 1959.

175. "One of the great": Martin Mayer, *Madison Avenue, U.S.A.* (1958), p. 68.

175. "The agency has": *A & S,* December 1949.

175. "He oozed Irish": Charlie Brower, *Me, and Other Advertising Geniuses* (1974), p. 6.

176. "a wholesome neighborhood": John McCarthy in *Catholic Digest,* May 1955.

176. "Ben is sweet": *PI,* November 1, 1957.

176. "Public relations is": *AA,* March 10, 1947.

177. "I'd like to get": *AA,* October 27, 1947.

177. "Advertisers are demanding": *PI,* January 10, 1958.

177. "We have a choice": Mayer, op. cit., p. 101.

178. "first adman Cabinet": *PI,* August 16, 1957.

178. "Advertising now compares": David M. Potter, *People of Plenty* (1954), p. 167.

178. "The sharkskin-bound": *AA,* February 8, 1960.

179. "We are definitely again": *AA,* February 9, 1959.

179. "an art director": *AA,* March 7, 1960.

179. "the main channel": Marshall McLuhan in *Commonweal,* September 11, 1953.

179. "Too many people": *AA,* September 22, 1952.

179. "There is very": *PI,* April 2, 1954.

180. "Whether you are": *AA,* December 17, 1956.

180. "The creative man": *AA,* July 6, 1959.

180. "In any creative": *PI,* January 18, 1957.

180. "creative mind": *AA,* February 27, 1956.

181. "Brainstorming sessions": *PI,* November 29, 1957.

181. "a nightmare": *AA,* November 8, 1948.

181. "This election": *AA,* November 15, 1948.

182. "research and other": *AA,* January 21, 1957.

182. "No one yet": *PI,* March 14, 1952.

182. "of monumental": Shirley Polykoff, *Does She . . . Or Doesn't She?* (1975), p. 72.

182. "to set molds": *PI,* March 6, 1959.

Page 183.   "If you can't": *PI*, July 19, 1957.
   183.   "very rational": *AA*, June 3, 1957.
   184.   "social science approach": *AA*, March 29, 1954.
   184.   "For years": ibid.
   184.   "we have been removed": *Business Week*, June 23, 1951.
   184.   "Strictly a gimmick": Robert Graham in *Reporter*, October 13, 1953.
   184.   "outside witch doctors": *AA*, October 25, 1954.
   184.   "Take the bus": *PI*, February 7, 1958.
   185.   "present-day advertising": *PI*, April 1, 1955.
   185.   "pseudo-science": *AA*, September 19, 1955.
   185.   "a hypothetical construct": *AA*, February 15, 1960.
   185.   "a vested interest": *AA*, September 19, 1955.
   185.   "Large-scale efforts": Vance Packard, *The Hidden Persuaders* (1957),
            p. 3.
   185.   "No one": ibid., pp. 236, 240.
   186.   "give the whole": *Newsweek*, October 14, 1957.
   186.   "Having gone": *PI*, January 17, 1958.
   186.   "All the motivational": *AA*, June 9, 1958.
   186.   "Anyone who entertains": *PI*, August 8, 1958.
   187.   "With a ton": *AA*, March 7, 1960.
   187.   "What this agency": Mayer, op. cit., p. 47.
   188.   "A hard-sell advertisement": *AA*, December 21, 1959.
   188.   "were the most": Thomas Whiteside in *New Yorker*, September 27,
            1969.
   188.   Bates research methods: *AA*, February 14, 1953.
   188.   "For the first time": Rosser Reeves, *Reality in Advertising* (1961), p. 12.
   188.   Ages of Bates creatives: *AA*, September 19, 1955.
   188.   "I never tried": Whiteside in *New Yorker*, September 27, 1969.
   188.   "Once you've found": Mayer, op. cit., p. 123.
   189.   "At the agency": Whiteside in *New Yorker*, September 27, 1969.
   189.   "Rosser's father couldn't": Martin Mayer, "The Story of Ted Bates
            & Company" (unpublished MS, 1965), p. 121.
   190.   "He was sort of": ibid., p. 122.
   190.   "He already had": ibid., p. 123.
   190.   "I learned all": Rosser Reeves to Frank Hummert, May 19,
            1960, RP.
   190.   "still the best definition": Rosser Reeves to Ruth L. Laguna, Septem-
            ber 6, 1957, RP.
   191.   "the curious end": Rosser Reeves, *Popo* (1980), p. 87.
   191.   "You surprise me": Kenneth Arrington to Rosser Reeves, January
            22, 1956, RP.
   191.   "The poetry side": Rosser Reeves to George Roche, October 23,
            1962, RP.

Page 191. "You could say": *Publishers' Weekly,* August 1, 1980.

192. "the prince": ibid.

192. "the ultimate pragmatist": Whiteside in *New Yorker,* September 27, 1969.

192. *Time* cover with admen: *Time,* October 12, 1962.

192. "The claims may be": *Business Week,* October 10, 1959.

193. "These crippling press": *Time,* February 8, 1960.

193. "Advertising began": Reeves, *Reality,* p. 153; next five quotations from ibid., pp. 70–1, 55, 114, 50.

193. "without subtlety": *PI,* June 16, 1961.

193. "There is enough": *Newsweek,* April 17, 1961.

194. "Certainly some": *Business Week,* October 10, 1959.

194. "USP can't quack": *AA,* November 10, 1958.

194. "Dear Brownie": *AA,* December 1, 1958.

194. "NOW . . . AT LAST": *AA,* February 1, 1960.

195. "the largest office move": *AA,* January 28, 1957.

195. "no more personality": *PI,* July 25, 1952.

195. "sometimes I don't": Spencer Klaw in *Fortune,* January 1961.

195. "Marion's like": ibid.

195. "None of them": Draper Daniels, *Giants, Pigmies, and Other Advertising People* (1974), pp. 120–21.

196. "Very polite": *AA,* February 28, 1949.

196. "like a farmer": *AA,* December 22, 1958.

197. "I never realized": *AA,* February 28, 1949.

197. "No other advertising": *AA,* November 25, 1946.

197. "skipping around": Klaw, op. cit.

197. "What the audience": *AA,* October 31, 1960.

197. "a history of": *Newsweek,* March 30, 1964.

198. "International agency management": *AA,* July 30, 1956.

198. "We've invited": *AA,* April 28, 1958.

198. "We are not very proud": *AA,* February 17, 1958; next two quotations from ibid.

198. "We had already organized": Klaw, op. cit.

199. "What we've done": *Newsweek,* March 30, 1964.

199. "We are not concerned": *AA,* January 18, 1960.

199. "Marion has all these": Klaw, op. cit.

199. Competing agency's divisions: *AA,* January 25, 1960.

199. "Small Indians": *AA,* February 22, 1960.

200. "a silkworm that": *AA,* April 30, 1956.

200. "I don't believe": *PI,* July 7, 1950.

200. Polls re advertising: *PI,* March 7, September 5, 1952.

200. Survey of high school students: *AA,* October 20, 1958.

200. "It is fashionable": *AA,* December 14, 1959.

Page 200. "Let's run this": *AA*, January 21, 1957.

200. "They consider you": *PI*, January 20, 1956.

201. "I'll write copy": Sloan Wilson, *The Man in the Gray Flannel Suit* (1955), p. 180; next quotation from ibid., p. 201.

201. "We're all": Frederic Wakeman, *The Hucksters* (1946), p. 7; next three quotations from ibid., pp. 88, 11, 24.

202. "a sharp and persuasive": Arkady Leokum, *Please Send Me, Absolutely Free . . .* (1946), p. 121; next two quotations from ibid., pp. 309, 337.

202. "a screwy business": *PI*, August 9, 1946.

202. "Advertising blasts": Herman Wouk, *Aurora Dawn* (1947), p. 110; next quotation from ibid., p. 231.

203. "But perhaps it": Herman Wouk, *Aurora Dawn* (1956 edition), p. 8.

203. "He took a certain": Eric Hodgins, *Mr. Blandings Builds His Dream House* (1946), p. 119.

203. "The whole country's": Eric Hodgins, *Blandings' Way* (1950), pp. 46–7; next quotation from ibid., p. 314.

203. "Sure I believe": Robert Alan Aurthur, *The Glorification of Al Toolum* (1953), p. 45; next two quotations from ibid., pp. 97, 241.

204. "Everything we do": Gerald Green, *The Last Angry Man* (1956), p. 180; next quotation from ibid., p. 490.

204. "I prefer": Harold Livingston, *The Detroiters* (1956), p. 207; next two quotations from ibid., pp. 207, 327.

205. "cheap, phony, vicious": Edward Stephens, *A Twist of Lemon* (1958), pp. 444–45.

205. "You'll win some": Shepherd Mead, *The Admen* (1958), p. 306; next quotation from ibid., p. 227.

206. "Mad Avenue": James Kelly, *The Insider* (1958), p. 367; next quotation from ibid., p. 257.

206. "an expert analysis": *A & S*, June 1946.

206. "We knew it wasn't": *Holiday*, December 1957.

207. "I have been": *AA*, July 13, 1959.

207. "We are not rakes": *AA*, April 28, 1958.

208. "who's going to write": Robert L. Foreman, *The Hot Half Hour* (1958), p. 13.

208. "Madman novels": *Saturday Review*, September 21, 1957.

208. "Why don't you be": *PI*, July 11, 1947.

208. "The Whole Story": *AA*, June 14, 1948.

208. "Yes, sir!": *PI*, December 9, 1949.

208. "another nail driven": *AA*, April 16, 1956.

209. 1957 survey: *PI*, May 11, 1957.

209. "What other business": *PI*, February 15, 1952.

209. 1956 study: *PI*, February 10, 1956.

209. *AA* obituaries: *AA*, February 15, 1960.

209. "It's a killing": *AA*, January 9, 1956.

Page 209. "Rolls-Royce motor": *PI,* November 1, 1957.

209. "I only call": *Time,* March 6, 1950.

209. "My kids claim": *Publishers' Weekly,* August 1, 1980.

209. "I have been captured": *Newsweek,* March 30, 1964; next quotation from ibid.

209. "This whole concept": *AA,* February 9, 1959.

209. 1958 poll: *Newsweek,* October 20, 1958.

209. "In most professions": *AA,* May 5, 1948.

210. "Alone, unloved": *AA,* February 15, 1960.

210. "An advertising agency": *PI,* April 21, 1950.

210. "We don't know": *AA,* June 5, 1950.

210. TV ad volume: *PI,* March 21, 1952.

211. "On TV": *Business Week,* October 10, 1959.

211. "You can jump": *PI,* November 6, 1953.

211. "Show the product": *Business Week,* June 11, 1949.

211. "dramatic demonstration": *AA,* September 6, 1954.

211. "I don't think": Mayer, op. cit., p. 132.

212. "A girl breaks": *New Yorker,* February 19, 1955.

212. "Today, the sponsors": *PI,* January 9, 1953.

212. "the only thing": *Problems and Controversies in Television and Radio,* ed. Harry J. Skornia and Jack William Kitson (1968), p. 390.

212. "Oh, dear": *AA,* March 5, 1956.

212. "And now": *AA,* September 16, 1957.

212. "I feel": *PI,* July 18, 1958; next quotation from ibid.

213. "We're not seeking": *PI,* May 1, 1959.

213. "We don't think": *AA,* March 15, 1954.

213. "These great shows": *AA,* June 22, 1953.

214. "In this business": *PI,* November 18, 1955.

214. "the spot agency": Whiteside in *New Yorker,* September 27, 1969.

214. Network control, 1958: *AA,* March 31, 1958.

215. "I did not read": House Committee on Interstate and Foreign Commerce, *Investigation of Television Quiz Shows* (1960), pp. 1042–43; next four quotations from ibid., pp. 1054, 1093, 1097, 1090.

216. Erickson quits: *AA,* August 8, 1960.

216. "Television no longer": *AA,* November 14, 1960.

216. "Today you must": A. Frank Reel, *The Networks* (1979), p. 71.

216. "The media man": *AA,* May 3, 1960.

217. "When I told her": Mayer, op. cit., p. 21.

217. "We have lived": *AA,* July 6, 1959.

CHAPTER SIX

219. "I always figured": *AA,* July 1, 1963.

219. Taller, more handsome men: *AA,* August 7, 1950.

Page 219. "The most imposing": *A & S,* September 1949.

219. "He wrote the copy": *AA,* September 4, 1961.

220. "incredibly sensitive": *AA,* November 7, 1955.

220. "the power of the truth": Cliff Knoble, *Call to Market* (1963), p. 297.

220. "one of the great": *AA,* April 12, 1965; and see *PI,* October 16, 1964.

220. "a very happy": *AA,* April 12, 1965; next quotation from ibid.

221. "My associates": *PI,* January 1, 1954.

221. "There is entirely": *PI,* May 14, 1936.

221. "A lot of it": *PI,* October 29, 1948.

222. "Leo wrote": Draper Daniels, *Giants, Pigmies, and Other Advertising People* (1974), p. 220.

222. "The creative men": *AA,* October 17, 1955.

222. "inherent drama": *A & S,* September 1950.

222. archetypes and symbols: *AA,* February 8, 1982.

222. "a friendly kind": *AA,* November 7, 1955.

223. "Leo met us": *PI,* September 5, 1958.

223. "What's the most": ibid.

223. Lip Protrusion Index: *AA,* March 5, 1973.

223. "We have absolutely": *AA,* August 7, 1950.

223. "He was not": *AA,* March 5, 1973.

223. "Creative work is": *AA,* May 22, 1961.

224. "First ad presented": *AA,* November 7, 1955.

224. "It must be": *A & S,* September 1949.

224. "You can't make": *AA,* October 27, 1969.

225. "finding out": Daniels, op. cit., p. 198.

225. "sort of like": *AA,* April 17, 1961.

225. Pithy phrases: *AA,* February 18, 1963; April 12, 1965; October 16, 1961.

225. "Our sod-busting": *AA,* October 23, 1967.

225. "I am an advertising": *PI,* September 26, 1952.

226. "I have always": *AA,* March 15, 1976.

226. "the most spectacular": Rosser Reeves to Henry Robbins, November 4, 1960, RP.

226. "A quirk in the": *Flagbearer,* March 20, 1964, OP.

226. "I grew up": Spencer Klaw in *Fortune,* April 1965.

226. "There was always": David Ogilvy to Mary Ogilvy, July 9, 1956, OP.

227. "possessed my soul": *Ladies' Home Journal,* December 1966.

227. "Next to flaring": Ogilvy to Alexander Woollcott, August 18, 1938, Woollcott Papers.

227. "I didn't have": *AA,* March 15, 1976.

228. "An unusually able": F. B. Bate to John F. Royal, January 17, 1938, file 63–16, NBCP.

Page 228. "We will be glad": Royal to Bate, January 31, 1938, file 63–16, NBCP.

228. Ogilvy and Woollcott: Ruth Gordon, *Myself Among Others* (1971), p. 7.

228. "When I looked": Thomas Whiteside in *Harper's,* May 1955.

228. "My admiration": Ogilvy to Leo Burnett, July 27, 1964, RP.

228. "It took me": *AA,* March 15, 1965.

229. "The more I": Ogilvy to Alexander Woollcott, May 26, 1942, Woollcott Papers.

229. "atmosphere of security": Ogilvy to Alexander Woollcott, September 14, 1942, Woollcott Papers.

229. "The years we spent": David Ogilvy, *Blood, Brains & Beer* (1978), p. 124.

229. Ogilvy's all-star agency: *A & S,* February 1947.

229. "Most of it": Ogilvy to Rosser Reeves, July 22, 1947, RP.

229. "But I knew": Ogilvy to Bernard Soll, December 9, 1963, OP.

230. "We think": Ogilvy to Paul K. Randall, June 7, 1948, OP.

230. "middle-aged": Ogilvy to Vincent DeGiacomo, March 5, 1951, OP.

230. "I have always": Ogilvy to Lawrence S. Kubie, January 26, 1953, OP.

230. "I have done": Ogilvy to Ellerton M. Jetté, May 17, 1951, OP.

231. "playing the oboe": Ogilvy to Roald Dahl, July 27, 1964, OP.

231. "We have never": Raymond Bowen to Ellerton M. Jetté, April 17, 1952, OP.

231. "Your remarks": Ogilvy to Raymond Rubicam, September 4, 1952, OP.

231. "It is a remarkable": Ogilvy to Rubicam, April 1, 1954, OP.

232. "the great Y & R": *AA,* February 23, 1953.

232. "the most favorable": *AA,* November 14, 1955.

232. "But the agency": *AA,* September 8, 1952.

232. "The theory is hardly": *AA,* September 22, 1952.

232. "What surprises me": Ogilvy to Rosser Reeves, September 24, 1952, OP.

233. "Let's live": Ogilvy to Reeves, April 12, 1954, RP.

233. "unscrupulous toughs": Ogilvy to Victor Schwab, January 3, 1956, OP.

233. "shop window accounts": Ogilvy to Francis Ogilvy, March 7, 1952, OP.

233. Newsy campaign: Ogilvy memo, May 20, 1953, OP.

233. Schweppes suggested Whitehead: F. C. Hooper to Ogilvy, February 24, 1953, OP.

233. "Whitehead's bearded": Ogilvy to F. C. Hooper, July 2, 1953, OP.

233. "His place among": *PI,* November 20, 1953.

Page 234. "I had met": Ogilvy to Rubicam, March 28, 1955, OP.

234. "My brother": *Television Magazine,* November 25, 1958.

234. "I was constantly": Klaw, op. cit.

234. "men with fire": *AA,* October 22, 1962.

234. Ogilvy's rules: *AA,* May 13, 1957.

234. "And in the number": *AA,* February 10, 1975.

235. "At this point: Ogilvy to Ray Calt, April 19, 1955, OP.

235. "I hear a great deal": *AA,* October 22, 1962.

235. "If the client": Ogilvy to Ray Calt, April 19, 1955, OP.

235. "I wish": Ogilvy to Kythé Hendy, July 3, 1955, OP.

235. "gentle manners": *AA,* January 4, 1960.

235. Ogilvy shy: *AA,* June 25, 1973.

236. "I think it means": *AA,* February 16, 1953.

236. "the most boring": Ogilvy to George H. Smith, September 16, 1955, OP.

236. "The qualities": Ogilvy to Roald Dahl, November 9, 1953, OP.

236. "I have become": Ogilvy to Ernest A. Jones, April 10, 1956, OP.

236. "Like Raymond Rubicam": *PI,* November 20, 1953.

237. "I guess": *AA,* April 8, 1963.

237. "I want": Ogilvy to Esty Stowell et al., December 2, 1957, OP.

237. *"The only sound": Vanity Fair,* March 1933.

237. "What a fascinating": Ogilvy to Charles Brower, August 21, 1958, OP.

238. "If only people": Ogilvy to Maurice A. Needham, May 22, 1958, OP.

238. "I have detected": Ogilvy to William Tyler, January 23, 1956, OP.

238. Ogilvy listed mentors: *Television Magazine,* November 25, 1958.

238. "We believe": Ogilvy to S. H. Britt, February 1, 1960, RP.

238. "It is grotesque": Ogilvy to Rosser Reeves, August 22, 1960, OP.

238. Reeves joked: Reeves to H. A. Dingwall, Jr., November 13, 1958, RP; and see Reeves to Ted Bates, March 7, 1958, August 24, 1960, RP.

239. "You people": Ogilvy to Richard Heath, December 6, 1954, OP.

239. "What we're trying": *PI,* November 20, 1953.

239. "There aren't enough": *DDB News,* June 1, 1969.

239. "he was willing": *Madison Avenue,* August 1959.

240. "you know": *AA,* July 15, 1968.

240. "They weren't doing": *DDB News,* June 1974.

240. "I had never": *Communication Arts Magazine,* January 1971.

241. "I understood": *AA,* July 10, 1967.

241. "I'm worried": *AA,* February 1, 1960.

241. "We probably do": *AA,* August 2, 1954.

241. Apocryphal story: *AA,* August 23, 1976.

Page 241.   "Take Bernbach": Mel Gussow in *New York,* October 10, 1965.

241.   "I have no sores": *DDB News,* June 1974.

242.   "I'm a loafer": *Madison Avenue,* April 1971.

242.   "Even in the most": *PI,* July 31, 1959.

242.   "We don't care": *AA,* March 25, 1963.

242.   "I pull 'em in": *AA,* April 5, 1965.

242.   "Sometimes they hated": *Communication Arts Magazine,* January 1971.

242.   "Not trying to stamp": *DDB News,* June 1974.

242.   "He allows for": *Marketing/Communications,* May 1969.

251.   "sort of an adult": *PI,* July 23, 1965.

251.   "We can't question": *AA,* May 4, 1964.

251.   "I am absolutely": *Dun's Review,* July 1964.

251.   "There are a lot": *PI,* January 2, 1953.

252.   "I consider *research*": *PI,* March 29, 1957.

252.   "creative in one": *AA,* June 26, 1961.

252.   "It's true": *AA,* July 5, 1971.

252.   "Don't be slick": *AA,* November 8, 1965.

252.   "Maybe that great": *AA,* May 4, 1964.

253.   "Aren't you": George Lois with Bill Pitts, *George, Be Careful* (1972), p. 35.

253.   "Two people": *AA,* November 19, 1962.

253.   "We sit": *Marketing/Communications,* May 1969.

253.   "We are awfully": *AA,* October 20, 1958.

253.   "That's their property": *AA,* November 1, 1965.

253.   "the combination": *DDB News,* June 1974.

253.   "the device I use": *PI,* January 2, 1953.

254.   "It's not": *AA,* August 14, 1961.

254.   "People take pictures": *AA,* January 16, 1978.

254.   "We felt": Robert Glatzer, *The New Advertising* (1970), p. 38.

254.   "airline ads were": *DDB News,* June 1, 1969.

255.   "We are set up": *AA,* August 2, 1954.

255.   "I don't think": *AA,* July 25, 1977.

255.   "I don't think": *AA,* March 15, 1965.

255.   Poll of creative directors: *AA,* August 15, 1960.

256.   Krone apportioned: *AA,* October 14, 1968.

256.   "I learned how": *AA,* April 25, 1966.

256.   "A German son": *AA,* October 14, 1968: next two quotations from ibid.

257.   "I had to steal": *DDB News,* June 1974.

258.   "It got so": *DDB News,* June 1979.

258.   "In a class": *AA,* June 14, 1965.

258.   1976 panel: *AA,* April 19, 1976; and see *AA,* April 30, 1980.

258.   "It was *not*": *AA,* October 14, 1968.

Page 259. "and this is tough": *AA,* November 22, 1965.

259. AAAA panel, 1963: *PI,* May 3, 1963.

259. "We may not": *AA,* August 7, 1967.

259. "I think it's wrong": *AA,* November 8, 1976.

260. "The commission system": *AA,* November 21, 1960.

260. "It will probably": Ogilvy to David McCall, August 23, 1962, OP.

260. "I have never": David Ogilvy, *Confessions of an Advertising Man* (1963), p. 111; next quotation from ibid., p. 114.

261. "You are Claude": Rubicam to Ogilvy, October 10, 1963, OP.

261. "an almost extinct": *AA,* February 3, 1964.

261. "about what a good": *AA,* March 15, 1965.

261. "I have developed": Ogilvy to George Gribbin, April 6, 1964, OP.

261. "We felt": *AA,* November 23, 1964.

261. "I guess half": Leo Burnett to Ogilvy, April 29, 1963, OP.

262. "I detest": *AA,* April 29, 1963.

262. "I feel like": *AA,* July 15, 1968.

262. "The only thing": Lois, op. cit., p. 64.

262. "He personally": ibid., p. 65.

263. "You meet": *AA,* March 4, 1963.

263. "The concept of public": *AA,* June 1, 1964.

263. "I wouldn't want": Lois, op. cit., p. 119.

263. "If this is": *AA,* July 27, 1964.

263. "I make decisions": *PI,* May 3, 1963.

264. "an atmosphere": Jerry Della Femina, *From Those Wonderful Folks Who Gave You Pearl Harbor* (1970), p. 74.

264. "the humility": *AA,* September 28, 1964.

264. "This business": Fairfax Cone to Leo Burnett, June 7, 1966, Cone Papers.

264. "Hello Ted Bates": Della Femina, *Pearl Harbor,* pp. 143–44.

265. "I think some": Ted Bates to William Kearns, February 7, 1961, RP.

265. "higher tone": *PI,* April 20, 1962, and *AA,* August 20, 1962.

265. "Temporary trends": Rosser Reeves to Julian V. Pace, May 16, 1966, RP.

265. "It's terribly easy": *AA,* April 12, 1965.

265. "a businessman's creative": *AA,* November 20, 1967.

266. "Bigness is": *AA,* July 6, 1964.

266. "We can't support": *AA,* April 15, 1963.

266. *AA* re Harper marriage: *AA,* November 18, 1963.

266. Concealed ownership of Felix: *AA,* January 15, 1968.

267. "We see him": *AA,* February 12, 1968.

267. "We're not General": *Business Week,* December 2, 1967.

267. "Just us kids": *AA,* March 2, 1970.

267. Harper debts: *AA,* September 17, 1979.

Page 267. Reporter in Oklahoma City: *AA,* September 3, 1979.
     267. "A fantastic education": *AA,* April 5, 1971.
     268. "Everyone cared only": Philip Siekman in *Fortune,* August 1966.
     268. "The Basque and": *AA,* August 13, 1962.
     268. "Slip into something": *AA,* June 11, 1962.
     268. "She moved" Lois, op. cit., pp. 60–1.
     268. "I thought it": *AA,* January 27, 1969.
     268. "the blond girl": *AA,* April 17, 1967.
     268. Wells passed over at Tinker: *AA,* April 7, 1969.
     268. "the most profitable": *AA,* April 18, 1966.
     268. "She has been": *AA,* July 1, 1968.
     269. "We're average consumers": Hank Seiden, *Advertising* (1976), p. 51.
     269. "What wc are saying": *AA,* July 1, 1968.
     270. "We are the agency": *Newsweek,* October 3, 1966.
     270. "I'm in excellent": *AA,* June 2, 1969.
     270. "Just as the hippies": Edward Hannibal, *Chocolate Days, Popsicle Weeks* (1970), p. 162.
     270. "They are visual": *Atlantic,* July 1971.
     270. "My God": *PI,* May 12, 1967.
     270. "We've had some": *AA,* September 29, 1969.
     270. "Obviously, pink shirts": ibid.
     271. "Everybody could use": *AA,* May 13, 1968.
     271. "It's a better way": *Marketing/Communications,* January 1968.
     271. *Newsweek* cover story: *Newsweek,* August 18, 1969.
     271. "I worry": *AA,* September 29, 1969.
     271. "Big business": *AA,* January 19, 1970.

CHAPTER SEVEN

     273. Irish secretaries at L & T: Fairfax M. Cone, *With All Its Faults* (1969), p. 127.
     273. Lasker and *Post:* John Gunther, *Taken at the Flood* (1960), pp. 266–67.
     273. "Since Charlie": Draper Daniels, *Giants, Pigmies, and Other Advertising People* (1974), p. 77.
     273. Jones and Jews: John B. Rosebrook, "Madison Avenue Legacy" (MS, 1962, at Young & Rubicam, New York), p. 155.
     274. "We all have": *AA,* March 7, 1955.
     275. "the street of": George Panetta, *Viva Madison Avenue!* (1957), p. 6; next five quotations from ibid., pp. 6, 44, 121, 185, 250.
     275. DDB as ethnic pioneer: see, in general, Ruth Ziff, "Ethnic Penetration into Top Managerial Positions in Advertising Agencies" (Ph.D. dissertation, CUNY, 1975).
     276. "only another stand-up": *Marketing/Communications,* July 1970.

Page 276. "I found that": *Print,* January–February 1977.

276. Photo service ad: *AA,* November 23, 1964.

276. "It doesn't hurt": Jerry Della Femina, *From Those Wonderful Folks Who Gave You Pearl Harbor* (1970), p. 252.

277. Survey of 500 people: *NYT,* February 25, 1966.

277. "your hair": Jerry Mander, *Four Arguments for the Elimination of Television* (1978), p. 14.

277. "That's a very": *AA,* June 11, 1962.

277. Interfaith rumor: Edward Buxton, *Promise Them Anything* (1972), p. 77.

277. "Sure, sure": *AA,* May 29, 1961.

278. "a more colorful": *AA,* October 31, 1966.

278. "Ardent interviews": *AA,* March 9, 1964.

279. "I'm sorry": David Ogilvy to John P. Davis, March 25, 1957, OP.

279. "not up to": *PI,* November 29, 1963.

279. "The color problem": *AA,* April 22, 1963; next two quotations from ibid.

280. "Take my picture": George Breitman, *The Last Year of Malcolm X* (Schocken edition, 1968), p. 98.

280. "We informed": *PI,* September 13, 1963.

280. "What we want": *AA,* August 19, 1963.

280. General Foods claim: *AA,* July 1, 1968.

280. "the education of": *AA,* February 19, 1968.

281. "We include minority": *AA,* March 25, 1968; next two quotations from ibid.

281. "the dramatic increase": *AA,* January 13, 1969.

281. Black roles in ads: *AA,* April 11, 1966, and Keith K. Cox in *JAR,* April 1970.

281. "Some of the": *AA,* February 5, 1968.

281. EEOC study, 1966: *AA,* January 22, 1968.

282. EEOC study, 1967: *AA,* October 30, 1967.

282. "The thing that": *AA,* October 17, 1966.

282. "If we could": *AA,* January 9, 1967.

282. "The starting pay": *AA,* October 17, 1966; next quotation from ibid.

282. Survey August 1967: *AA,* March 25, 1968.

283. "Who says there": *NYT,* April 15, 1968.

283. "doesn't require": *Newsweek,* April 29, 1968.

283. "some of us": *AA,* May 27, 1968.

283. "We feel": *AA,* May 4, 1970.

283. "You white advertising": *AA,* May 5, 1969.

284. Black employment, fall 1969: *AA,* November 3, 1969.

284. "We have to": *AA,* October 28, 1968.

284. "but they're not": *AA,* May 5, 1969.

Page 285. "It is evident": *PI*, February 18, 1903.

286. Fredericks and League: J. George Frederick to Jo Foxworth, March 3, 1964, Frederick Papers.

286. "mere advertising man": *PI*, June 29, 1916.

286. Martin to League: *PI*, December 6, 1917.

287. "It is women": *PI*, January 24, 1918.

287. "the highest-paid": *AA*, January 20, 1975.

287. Survey of 617 women, 1924: *PI*, May 1, 1924.

287. "I know of": *AA*, November 1, 1930.

287. "He does not": Louise MacLeod to Catharine Oglesby, November 9, 1928, BP.

288. "There are few": *A & S*, February 5, 1921.

288. "Intelligence is neuter": *A & S*, March 7, 1928.

288. JWT house ad re women: *PI*, September 19, 1918.

289. "It is one": *Careers in Advertising,* ed. Alden James (1932), p. 307.

289. "We were pretty": *AA*, March 16, 1981.

289. "On my first": *AA*, October 14, 1963.

289. "It was a rather": *AA*, March 16, 1981; next quotation from ibid.

290. Women ad managers, 1931: *AA*, November 28, 1931.

290. Mary Lewis salary: *AA*, May 27, 1935.

290. Fitz-Gibbon as teacher: *AA*, March 29, 1982.

290. "I think the girls": *AA*, April 24, 1967.

290. "Today they dominate": *Literary Digest,* March 13, 1937.

290. "Those daily ads": *AA*, August 25, 1958.

291. "The nearest": *PI*, October 10, 1935.

291. "All you get": *PI*, October 31, 1935.

291. AWNY membership list: vol. 11, Advertising Women of New York Papers.

291. "The jobs": *A & S*, July 5, 1934.

291. "There are still": *Literary Digest,* March 13, 1937.

292. "Women have made": *AA*, December 23, 1963.

292. Survey of 123 advertisers: *PI*, October 25, 1946.

292. "Their work": *PI*, November 1, 1946.

292. 1949 poll: *PI*, June 3, 1949.

292. "Much as I hate": Stephen Birmingham in *Holiday,* December 1957.

292. "The man had": *AA*, April 21, 1958.

292. "Congratulations": Margot Sherman to Margaret Divver, November 10, 1948, Divver Papers.

293. "It was from": Shirley Polykoff, *Does She . . . or Doesn't She?* (1975), p. 10; next quotation from ibid., p. 19.

294. Women veeps at McCann: *PI*, February 26, 1960.

294. "I was working": *PI*, April 18, 1958.

294. "There she was": Helen Dudar in *Ms.,* December 1978.

Page 294. Sherman in Chicago, 1953: *AA,* October 26, 1953.

294. "Women's essentially": *PI,* January 7, 1955.

294. "They aren't usually": *AA,* July 8, 1957.

295. "I've never encountered": *AA,* July 15, 1968.

295. "because I was working": *AA,* March 29, 1982.

295. "The legends": *AA,* December 17, 1962.

295. "the first god-damned": *AA,* April 2, 1973.

295. "Mother started me": *AA,* April 18, 1966.

295. "I have succeeded": *Newsweek,* October 3, 1966.

295. "a rather remarkable": *AA,* April 5, 1971.

296. "I would buy": *AA,* June 2, 1969.

296. "The idea about": *AA,* April 17, 1967.

296. "I've never been": *AA,* July 27, 1970.

296. "those deceptively": Betty Friedan, *The Feminine Mystique* (Dell edition, 1970), pp. 218–19.

296. "As long as": *AA,* March 18, 1963.

296. "We have thumpingly": *PI,* October 22, 1965.

297. "to grow up to": *PI,* April 22, 1966.

297. "almost a neurotic": *AA,* January 3, 1966.

297. "If you want": *AA,* February 20, 1967.

297. "I'd like to make": Bernice Fitz-Gibbon, *Macy's, Gimbel's, and Me* (1967), p. 269.

297. "I didn't feel": *Marketing/Communications,* September 1968.

297. "Establishment-thinking": *Marketing/Communications,* July 1970.

297. "Advertising has let": *AA,* March 19, 1973.

298. "the perfect example": *AA,* December 7, 1970.

298. "The dilemma": *AA,* January 12, 1970.

298. "a wave of agreement": *AA,* February 23, 1970.

298. "It was very": David Ogilvy to Jane Trahey, February 27, 1964, OP.

298. "Advertising is a very": *AA,* May 22, 1972.

299. "I didn't know": *AA,* January 25, 1971.

299. "You helped": *AA,* July 10, 1972.

299. Women in ads, 1959–1971: M. Venkatesan and Jean Losco in *JAR,* October 1975.

299. Women at JWT: *AA,* September 28, 1970.

299. "Too many": *AA,* May 24, 1971.

300. "We have": *The Promise of Advertising,* ed. C. H. Sandage (1961), p. 20.

300. "a voluntary": *America: Miracle at Work,* ed. William D. Patterson, (1953), p. 22.

300. "Free enterprise": *PI,* January 16, 1953.

301. Brophy told Benson: T. D. Brophy to John Benson, March 2, 1949, Brophy Papers.

Page 301. "What can we": T. D. Brophy to Francis Corkery, September 9, 1957, Brophy Papers.

301. "kicked into": *AA,* May 29, 1961.

302. "Why do you let": David Halberstam, *The Powers That Be* (1979), p. 388.

302. "Is advertising": *AA,* February 12, 1962.

302. "weasel-wording": *AA,* October 14, 1963.

302. "I think that": *AA,* March 22, 1965.

302. "All three": Fairfax Cone to Leo Burnett, August 4, 1961, Cone Papers.

303. "The great mass": Cone to E. William Henry, October 14, 1963, Henry Papers.

303. Cone in *Fortune: Fortune,* July 1965.

303. "When, I wonder": David Ogilvy to Henry, September 30, 1963, OP.

303. "This is a very": *AA,* March 30, 1964.

303. "one of the most": Rosser Reeves to J. T. N. Foley, August 7, 1958, RP.

303. BBDO resignation of *Reader's Digest: PI,* July 26, 1957.

303. Company pressure re Bantron: *AA,* April 6, 1959.

304. "I do not": *AA,* November 29, 1965.

304. "I think a lot": *AA,* June 10, 1968.

304. "During the past": *AA,* March 17, 1969; next quotation from ibid.

304. "If a product": *Newsweek,* August 18, 1969.

305. Baker and Galanoy: Samm Sinclair Baker, *The Permissible Lie* (1968); Terry Galanoy, *Down the Tube* (1970).

305. "The general approach": Baker, op. cit., p. 180.

305. "The industry cannot": *Time,* October 12, 1962.

305. FTC and intent: Richard S. Tedlow in *Business History Review,* spring 1981.

306. "I am, and always": Charlie Brower, *Me, and Other Advertising Geniuses* (1974), p. 124.

306. NARB: *Advertising Self-Regulation,* eds. James P. Neelankavil and Albert B. Stridsberg (1980), p. 135.

306. "Mr. Minow says": *PI,* April 12, 1963.

307. "Print is for": Joe McGinniss, *The Selling of the President 1968* (1969), p. 29: next quotation from ibid., p. 59.

307. "Instead of relying": *PI,* May 25, 1916.

307. "The advertising method": *PI,* November 16, 1916.

308. Lasker paying off Harding's mistress: Francis Russell, *The Shadow of Blooming Grove* (1968), p. 402.

308. Ewald in 1924: *PI,* March 2, 1951.

308. "A political campaign": *AA,* May 3, 1930.

Page 308. "Salesmen should": *AA,* October 11, 1937.

308. "These are the": *AA,* November 4, 1940.

309. "Mr. Bowles is": *AA,* June 17, 1946.

309. Reeves in 1952: Rosser Reeves to Joseph McConnell, January 1954, RP.

310. "The man is": Reeves to William S. Cutchins, September 15, 1952, RP.

310. "Found with this": *AA,* October 6, 1952.

310. "We're a regular": Vance Packard, *The Hidden Persuaders* (1957), p. 188.

310. "The idea that": *AA,* September 3, 1956.

311. "one of the most": *AA,* August 20, 1956.

311. Reeves offer, 1956: Reeves to Thruston B. Morton, April 16, 1956 and Morton to Reeves, June 7, 1956, RP.

311. "a barrage": *AA,* July 18, 1960.

311. "There is just no": *TV Guide,* September 17, 1960; next quotation from ibid.

311. "I think": *Newsweek,* June 8, 1964.

312. "a J. Walter Thompson": *AA,* November 3, 1969.

312. "It seemed to me": Herbert G. Klein, *Making It Perfectly Clear* (1980), pp. 69, 108.

312. "As a professional": William Safire, *Before the Fall* (1975), p. 291.

313. Haldeman "forgetting": H. R. Haldeman with Joseph DiMona, *The Ends of Power* (1978), p. 58; Safire, op. cit., p. 286.

313. "If you want": *NYT,* May 2, 1936.

CHAPTER EIGHT

314. "We will be": *AA,* December 14, 1970.

315. "We've never lost": *AA,* June 4, 1973.

315. "I see my job": *AA,* March 25, 1974.

316. "It now seems": *AA,* September 13, 1971.

316. "When you get": Edward Buxton, *Creative People at Work* (1975), pp. 42-3.

316. "They'll never understand": *AA,* May 17, 1971.

316. "An ad agency": *AA,* June 26, 1978.

317. "In retrospect": *AA,* November 21, 1973.

317. "It hasn't done": *AA,* May 20, 1974.

317. "With change so": *AA,* September 24, 1979.

318. Child psychologists on TV: see Eli A. Rubinstein in *American Scientist,* November 1978.

318. ACT victories: *The Early Window,* eds. Robert M. Liebert et al. (1982), p. 137; *The Commercial Connection,* ed. John W. Wright (1979), p. 242.

Page 319. "in every political": Wilson Bryan Key, *Media Sexploitation* (1976), p. 8.

319. Heinz told FTC: *AA*, December 6, 1976.

319. Campbell told FDA: *AA*, May 29, 1978.

319. "I guess we deserved": *AA*, May 20, 1974.

320. Consumerism in 1970s: Paul N. Bloom and Stephen A. Greyser in *Harvard Business Review*, November–December 1981.

320. Blacks in TV ads 1967–1976: Ronald F. Bush et al. in *JAR*, February 1977.

320. AAAA study 1970–1974: *AA*, October 3, 1977.

320. "a degree of self-deception": *AA*, March 31, 1975.

321. "The ghetto experience": *AA*, November 3, 1969.

321. Sixteen of 110 graduates, Chicago: *AA*, April 7, 1975.

321. "I had trouble": *AA*, November 13, 1980.

321. "Now the black man": *AA*, March 23, 1970.

321. "unable to complete": *AA*, August 2, 1976.

321. Zebra folded: *AA*, June 7, 1976 and November 14, 1977.

321. "It's one thing": *AA*, June 20, 1977.

321. "We have to concentrate": *AA*, May 16, 1977.

321. "Our values": *AA*, March 1, 1982.

322. "In general": *Ms.*, November 1974.

322. "You can sit": *AA*, October 18, 1976.

322. "militant libbers": *AA*, December 10, 1973.

322. "It was more fun": *AA*, May 3, 1976; next quotation from ibid.

322. "I really don't": *Vogue*, February 1978.

322. Wells on women as heads of branch offices: *AA*, December 1, 1980.

323. "It was about time": *AA*, June 4, 1973.

323. Women at O & M: Bernice Kanner in *Working Women*, March 1983.

323. "now you can't": *NYT*, September 9, 1975.

323. "For the first": *AA*, April 7, 1980.

323. Trahey and Wallach novels: Jane Trahey, *Thursdays 'til 9* (1980); Anne Tolstoi Wallach, *Women's Work* (1981).

323. "It took seven": *AA*, July 21, 1980.

324. "Today, thank God": *AA*, May 20, 1974.

324. "The pendulum": David Ogilvy to Maurice Smelt, October 13, 1972, RP.

324. Positioning in late 1950s: *AA*, August 13, 1979.

324. "Positioning is thinking": Al Ries and Jack Trout, *Positioning* (1981), pp. 219–20.

324. "Today, creativity": ibid., p. 228.

325. "If we're so": *NYT*, July 13, 1979.

326. "We remain manic": *AA*, November 21, 1977.

326. "We believe that": *Adweek*, November 9, 1981.

326. "a wide horizontal": *AA*, November 21, 1977.

Page 326.   "The throw-away line": *Adweek,* November 9, 1981.
      326.   "Some CEOs": *AA,* July 28, 1980.
      327.   "They have to be": *NYT,* July 8, 1979.
      327.   "There's a certain malaise": *AA,* October 29, 1979.
      327.   Total spending, 1970–1980: *AA,* September 14, 1981.
      327.   "How puny our": *AA,* March 22, 1976.
      328.   "There were fewer": *AA,* March 21, 1977.-
      328.   "Most advertising these days": *AA,* January 30, 1978.
      328.   "If you believe": *AA,* August 28, 1978.
      328.   "a new creative revolution": *AA,* March 10, 1980.
      328.   Communications research re screening: Raymond A. Bauer and Ste-
             phen A. Greyser, *Advertising in America* (1968), p. 363.
      328.   AAAA study of 1,600 ads: *Commercial Connection,* ed. Wright, p. 35.
      328.   Gallup Poll of ethical standards: *AA,* September 13, 1976.
      329.   "As a practitioner": David Ogilvy to William Shockley, June 22,
             1962, OP.
      329.   "Advertising doesn't": *AA,* June 13, 1977.

INDEX

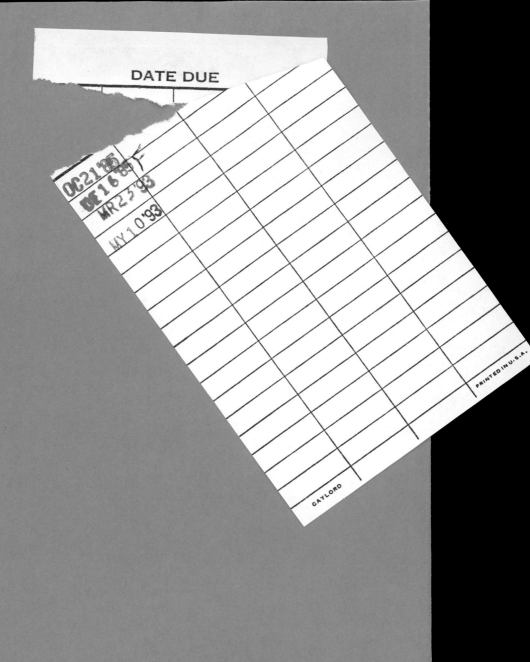